NUMBER TWO HUNDRED AND TWENTY

The Old Farmer's Almanac

CALCULATED ON A NEW AND IMPROVED PLAN FOR THE YEAR OF OUR LORD

2012

BEING LEAP YEAR AND (UNTIL JULY 4) 236TH YEAR OF AMERICAN INDEPENDENCE

Fitted for Boston and the New England states, with special corrections and calculations to answer for all the United States.

Containing, besides the large number of Astronomical Calculations and the Farmer's Calendar for every month in the year, a variety of

NEW, USEFUL, & ENTERTAINING MATTER.

Established in 1792 by Robert B. Thomas (1766–1846)

Nothing is too small to know, and nothing is too big to attempt.

–Sir William C. Van Horne, U.S.-born railroad entrepreneur and Canadian Pacific Railway executive (1843–1915)

ISSN 0078-4516

Library of Congress Card No. 56-29681

Original wood engraving by Randy Miller

THE OLD FARMER'S ALMANAC • DUBLIN, NH 03444 • 603-563-8111 • ALMANAC.COM

Contents

The Old Farmer's Almanac • 2012

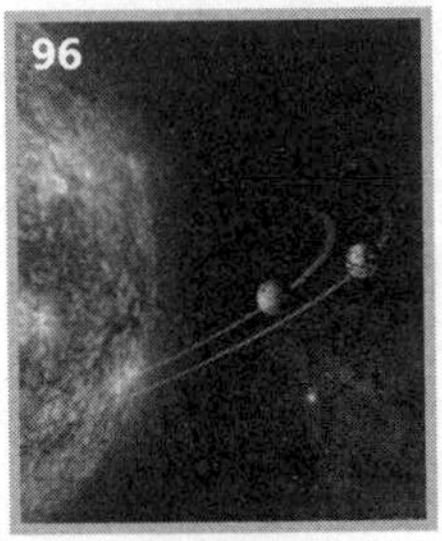

174

About This Almanac

Amusement

Anniversary

Astrology

Astronomy

Calendar

Food

Gardening

Special Report

(continued on page 6)

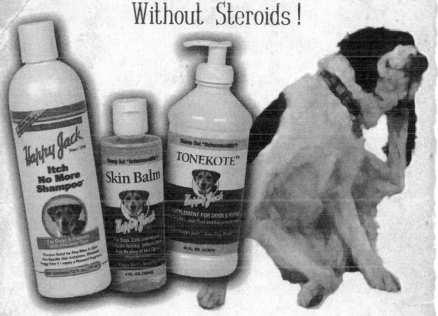

Contents

(continued from page 4)

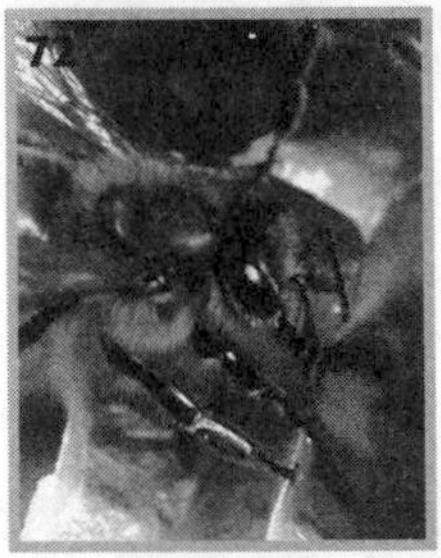

160

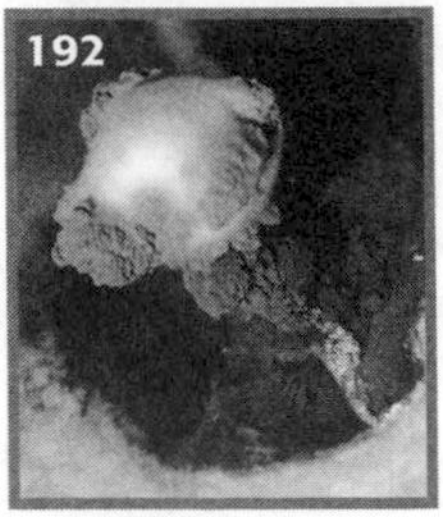

View our List of Advertisers, with Web links, at Almanac.com/Marketplace.

To Patrons

Who Matters Most

This issue marks two milestones for this Almanac: its 220th consecutive U.S. edition and the 30th anniversary of its sister publication, the Canadian Edition. We have faith that its founder, Robert B. Thomas (pictured on the cover), would be proud to see that his *[Old] Farmer's Almanac,* which began as a 48-page pamphlet, has not only endured but thrived.

We suspect, too, that he would be honored to know that we attribute our success, in no small part, to him, and that he would hasten to remind us of our great debt to you, dear readers, and to generations of your ancestors.

Indeed, in 1792, 26-year-old Thomas recognized a timeless and universal characteristic of human nature: People of all ages and walks of life want to be informed and, in that endeavor, to be amused. This tenet defined Thomas's mission for this Almanac: "to be useful, with a pleasant degree of humor."

In the agrarian society of that period, printed matter was scarce yet cherished. Most households possessed two books (only one of which accepted advertising): a Bible and a farmer's almanac.

This is not to say that Thomas had an easy time of it. He set about his chosen task in the face of considerable competition. Numerous regional farmer's almanacs addressed local concerns, giving interest rate tables, court dates and stagecoach schedules, and mileage between places, as well as agricultural information and the calendar.

Determined to distinguish his Almanac, Thomas described his "arrangement" of content in the first edition as "novel"—new, remarkable, and unexpected. He was referring to not only the orderly presentation of astronomical data on the Calendar Pages (so efficient was his design that it has been changed only slightly through the years), but also the voice and variety of the articles.

Today, we as publishers face competitive challenges similar to those that Thomas experienced, albeit on a continental scale and in both print and electronic media. (Even now, look-alike publications attempt to confuse readers who seek our Almanac's promise of "new, useful, and entertaining matter.")

These temptations are why we are eternally grateful for the indulgent preference for *this* Almanac shown by you, our friends and patrons, and why we continue our labors inspired by Thomas's own words in this space in the 1828 edition: "the *Old Farmer's Almanac* yields to none of its predecessors or competitors in the public's estimation . . . or in the quantity of original matter it contains."

–J. S., June 2011

However, it is by our works and not our words that we would be judged. These, we hope, will sustain us in the humble though proud station we have so long held in the name of

Your obedient servant,

2012 AT A GLANCE

Around the House

DIY, THEN SIY

We're making—and selling—canned goods, clothing, and even music. "Folks are grabbing on to the idea that a household doesn't have to be a unit of consumption. It can be a unit of production."

–*Shannon Hayes,*
author of Radical Homemakers: Reclaiming Domesticity From a Consumer Culture

OLD IS NEW

"People are relearning skills that used to be stressed in home economics classes."

–*Jennifer McKnight-Trontz,*
author of Home Economics

We're back to basics . . .

- cooking soups and stews using cheaper cuts of meat
- giving kids more chores to do
- using a broom correctly (short strokes)
- making candy

PEOPLE ARE TALKING ABOUT . . .

- **ladies unwinding in "woman caves"**
- **custom-framed portraits of DNA with bar codes that reveal maternal ancestral origins when scanned**
- **personalized candies with photos**
- **room-size closets with TVs and refrigerators**

PRACTICAL PURSUITS

"It is no longer about having the perfect house and keeping up with the neighbors. . . . Everything we do is so high-tech and refined. People want to have something that unabashedly comes from nature."

–*Candice Olson, HGTV host*

IDEAS THAT MAKE CENTS

- **cooking meats in the fireplace**
- **washers that remove moisture, so that clothes are ready to wear**
- **washers that use stain-absorbing nylon beads and up to 90 percent less water**

compiled by Stacey Kusterbeck

We'll see:

- furniture made from reclaimed wood
- blackboards instead of wallpaper
- stone and wood surfaces
- "glint" fixtures—a less fussy-looking combination of silver and gold

YOUR HOME, YOUR STYLE

"All the rules are broken. You can put colors and patterns together that 10 years ago would have brought you widespread derision."

–James Martin, founder of The Color People, Denver, Colorado

Indoors, we'll see:

- chairs and sofas upholstered in bold patterns (no neutrals)
- **walls that have more than one color in different areas of a room**
- fireplaces that rotate in the middle of the room or hang like a painting on the wall
- **sauna rooms in basements, closets, and backyard sheds**

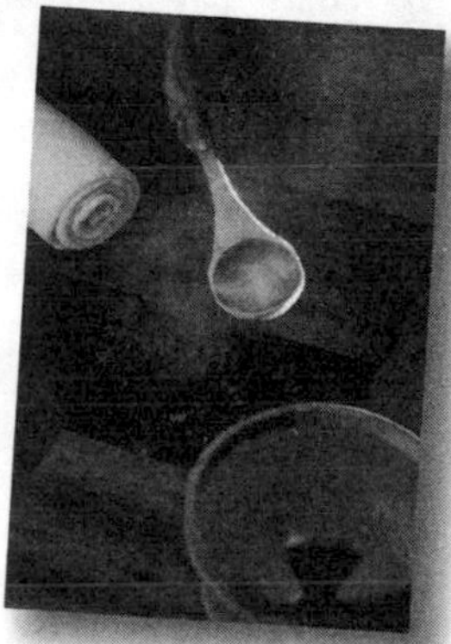

Outdoors, we'll see:

- "dirty" colors with tones of gray and brown (khakis and mustards)
- **front doors in bright tomato reds and palm leaf greens**
- electrically heated mats on front stoops and cables under driveways to melt snow and ice
- **plants climbing up walls to insulate houses**

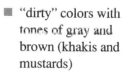

CONTINUED

In the Garden

1

2

–photos, W. Atlee Burpee & Co.

"We are finally beginning to realize that storm water runoff has value as a resource and is not a waste product."

–Ray Mims, sustainability director, U.S. Botanic Garden

PROFESSIONALS' PICKS FOR COLOR AND TASTE

Kitchen Fixin's

- **'Megaton' leek–a uniform variety**
- **'Velour' filet bean–first purple variety**
- **'Pink Lemonade' blueberry–first pink variety [1]**

–Benjamin Hudson, fruit and vegetable specialist, Missouri Botanical Garden

Pot Pleasers

- citrus fruit, blueberries, kiwifruit, water chestnuts, and salad greens: "It's not just tomatoes and peppers anymore."

–Jimmy Turner, senior director of gardens, Dallas Arboretum and Botanical Garden

- sweet potato vine *Lobularia* 'Snow Princess': "the garden equivalent of a slipcover" *–J. T.*
- 'Mara Des Bois' and 'Evie' **[2]** strawberries *–B. H.*

GOLDEN OLDIES

"Gardeners are looking for familiar plants, with improvements . . . still beautiful, but with lower water use, more insect and disease resistance, and better weather tolerance." *–J. T.*

- carefree prairie native *Rudbeckia grandiflora* 'Sundance'—adds height and color
- *Panicum* 'Ruby Ribbons'—for its fiery-tipped fall foliage
- *Penstemon barbatus* 'Red Riding Hood'—a hummingbird's fantasy **[3]**

3

–W. Atlee Burpee & Co.

NEW CLASSICS

"Hellebores are the Beanie Babies of the 2010s." *–J. T.*

- 'Walberton's Rosemary', 'HGC Silvermoon' **[4]**, and 'Cinnamon Snow'

4

–Emily Fraser/Fraser's Thimble Farms

CONTINUED ➡➡➡

HOW WE MEASURE UP

5,000: invasive plant species currently in the United States

PEOPLE ARE TALKING ABOUT . . .

- **weed warriors–groups of volunteers clearing out nonnative plants in and alongside public parks and trails**
- **attacking kudzu by detaching its crown instead of its root system**
- **collecting rain in trenches created by removing pavement edges**

–W. Atlee Burpee & Co.

TOPS IN TOMATOES

- 'Enchantment' *(above)*—stays fresh longer
- 'Mountain Magic'—great flavor
- 'Green Envy'—a sweet green cherry

We're Making the Best Better

Heirloom tomatoes grafted onto hybrid tomato rootstocks give the taste of heirloom varieties, yet with disease resistance and better yield. Future possibilities: a tomato or eggplant top on a potato bottom or a plant using all three. *–B. H.*

CONTINUED

Our Changing Culture

–Exactostock/SuperStock

"We can't prevent the future from arriving, but we can cherry-pick lovelinesses from the past to bring with us as we charge forward."

–Lesley M. M. Blume, author of Let's Bring Back

"NEW" OLD LOVES

- record players, fancy hats, silver tea services, and typewriters
- winter picnics, ice-skating parties, Sunday dinners, parlor games, and reading aloud

CITY SIGHTINGS

- **fast and slow lanes on crowded sidewalks**
- **three-wheel cars in tiny parking spots**
- **private driveways for rent as parking spaces**

PEOPLE ARE TALKING ABOUT . . .

- **technology cleanses: unplugging for a short time**
- **handwriting: it's better for the mind than typing**
- **sharing or renting furniture, clothing, and cars**
- **libraries putting reserved books, tapes, and DVDs in public lockers for checkout after hours**

WORD OF THE YEAR

➡Halfalogue: **half of a cell phone conversation, heard involuntarily**

HOW WE MEASURE UP

4: times per week that people apologize, most often to friends, then strangers, then family or romantic partners

20: percent of people who qualify as "heroes" because they helped a stranger in an emergency or took other selfless action

34: hours, on average, that commuters idle in traffic annually

40: percent of adults who have at least one "step-relative"

71: percent of people who make the bed every day or almost every day

71: percent of people who are "absolutely certain" of God's existence

75: percent of people who plan to cook more meals at home this year

CONTINUED ➡➡➡

HOBBIES FOR HIM

- panning for gold, bullfighting, and learning the cowboy sport of cutting cattle while on horseback
- playing in indoor trampoline parks

NEW PASTIMES

- making personal "life movies," with interviews, photos, and music
- "couch surfing"—looking online for folks who offer a free couch to sleep on
- staging video and photo shoots to prove Santa Claus's existence to skeptical kids
- countering overstimulation by attending dull lectures

CONTINUED

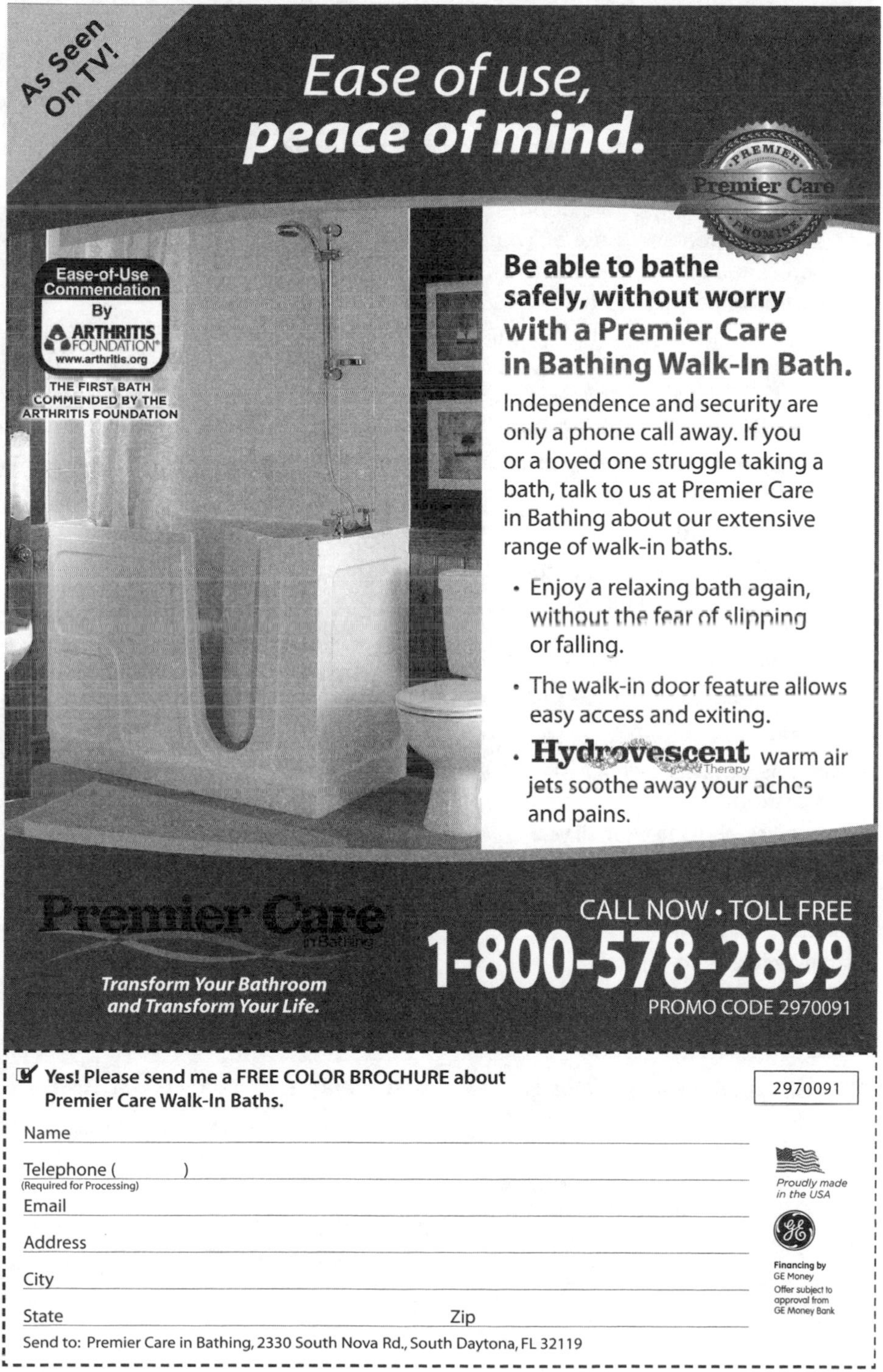
As Seen On TV!
Ease of use,
peace of mind.
PREMIER
Premier Care
PROMISE
Ease-of-Use Commendation
By
ARTHRITIS FOUNDATION®
www.arthritis.org
THE FIRST BATH COMMENDED BY THE ARTHRITIS FOUNDATION
Be able to bathe safely, without worry with a Premier Care in Bathing Walk-In Bath.
Independence and security are only a phone call away. If you or a loved one struggle taking a bath, talk to us at Premier Care in Bathing about our extensive range of walk-in baths.
• Enjoy a relaxing bath again, without the fear of slipping or falling.
• The walk-in door feature allows easy access and exiting.
• Hydrovescent Therapy warm air jets soothe away your aches and pains.
Premier Care in Bathing
Transform Your Bathroom and Transform Your Life.
CALL NOW • TOLL FREE
1-800-578-2899
PROMO CODE 2970091
Yes! Please send me a FREE COLOR BROCHURE about Premier Care Walk-In Baths.
2970091
Name
Telephone ( )
(Required for Processing)
Email
Address
City
State
Zip
Proudly made in the USA
Financing by GE Money
Offer subject to approval from GE Money Bank
Send to: Premier Care in Bathing, 2330 South Nova Rd., South Daytona, FL 32119

The Fashion Forecast

"Even the most improbable adornments from bygone eras are enjoying a limited renaissance, from mutton-chops to bloomers to top hats."

–Lesley M. M. Blume, author of Let's Bring Back

IT'S ALL IN THE DETAILS

Shoppers want to know how garments are designed, produced, and finished.

DOUBLE-DUTY DUDS

"Consumers seek more bang for their buck, and fashion that can do several things."

–Steven Faerm, director of fashion design, Parsons The New School for Design

We'll see:

- **garments that can be worn backward or upside down**
- **seasonless fabrics to wear all year**
- **casual and elegant combinations (fishermen's sweaters with velvet skirts, blazers with opera gloves)**
- **"convertible" shirt collars (they disappear when tucked in)**

CLOSET NO-NO'S

- **Low-cost, throwaway clothing:** "People don't want cheap clothes—they want good value." *–Sally Singer, editor of* T, *the* New York Times *fashion magazine*
- **Bland colors:** "A dire economy is making people seek a 'pick-me-up.'" *–S. F.*

–OJO Images/SuperStock

LADIES ARE KEEPING IT SIMPLE

"All of the flourishes and ruffles and trims of the past decade have been played out to the nth degree. What seems luxurious now is much simpler." *–S. S.*

On women, we'll see:

- tailored trouser suits
- slip dresses and long-sleeve sheath dresses
- jewelry with rivets, nails, nuts, and bolts

GUYS WANT TO TURN BACK TIME

"Men want to look young without looking silly." *–S. S.*

On men, we'll see:

- rumpled-looking casual wear
- worn-out T-shirts
- leggings

CONTINUED ➡➡➡

FADS—OR FAUX PAS?

- **spray-on-the-body fabrics**
- **spray-on liquid makeup (for an airbrushed look)**
- **faux "fur" coats made from plastic price-tag fasteners**
- **rubber boots that use body heat to create current (12 hours of walking will charge a cell phone)**
- **machine-washable tuxedos**

WE'RE PAYING EXTRA FOR . . .

- high-quality tailoring
- wrinkle-free suit jackets made from lotus plant fibers
- elbow gloves
- half-moon manicures

EXTRA! We're wearing fingerless gloves in fancy fabrics, for texting in cold weather.

On the Farm

PEOPLE ARE TALKING ABOUT . . .

- **farmers and ranchers using social media to network about farm life, agriculture, pests, and weather**
- **"crop mobs"—volunteers working for free for small-scale farmers who need extra hands, in return for lessons about farm life**
- **"weed dating"—single ranchers and farmers looking for mates (or friends) amid produce rows, then switching rows to weed alongside other potential partners**

FARMERS ARE US

- Kids love agriculture-related electronic games and "car trip bingo" (spotting farm structures and animals during long car rides).
- Farmers are setting up "geocaches" (hidden objects to be found via GPS through Web clues) to get us onto their farms.
- We're scanning bar codes on produce to learn when and where it was picked.

SWEET!

- **Interest in keeping bees is surging: Profits come from selling honey, queen bees, and beginner hives. (See "The Latest Buzz" on page 72.)**

CONTINUED ➡➡➡

Food News

IDEAS THAT MAKE CENTS

- learning the "lost arts" of food preparation—making sauerkraut, pickles, sausage, and cheese
- seeking "sustainable" seafood—drum, North Carolina rockfish, golden tilefish, tripletail, escolar, sheepshead, cuttlefish, and skate

FOOD FADS

- **chocolate for breakfast–in tea, Belgian waffles, and granola**
- **kale, mung and pinto bean, pea, and wild rice chips**
- **pumpkin salsa, sweet potato butter, and butternut squash pasta sauce**

BY THE NUMBERS

600: number of vintage apple varieties that Renewing America's Food Traditions is bringing back through promotional events and free grafting material

CONTINUED ➡ ➡ ➡

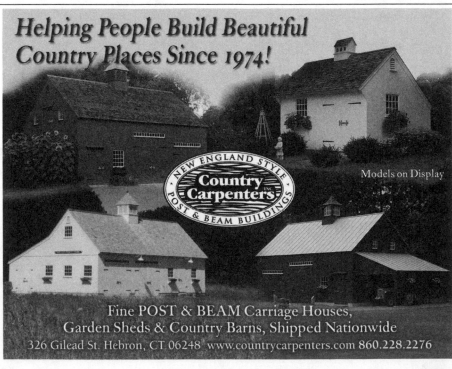

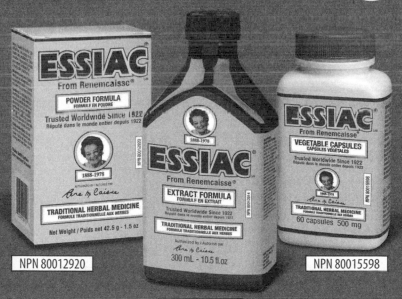

Our Animal Friends

PET-TICULARS

- **pets "sending" greeting cards to their sick or injured canine friends**
- **holiday newsletters written from the family pet's point of view**
- **wheelchairs for injured or ill ferrets, llamas, goats, pigs, and chickens**
- **metal-lined capes that calm dogs during thunderstorms**

Science & Tech

PEOPLE ARE TALKING ABOUT . . .

- **"smart road" surfaces of super-strong glass that melt snow and ice, recharge electric vehicles, and power street-lights**
- **asphalt parking lots embedded with pipes containing hot fluid that also heats adjacent buildings**
- **driverless cars that use mapping technology as a guide**
- **cars powered in part by pedaling passengers**

LEDGER OF LIFE

250,000: sea creatures identified by the first global marine census (750,000 are thought to remain undiscovered)

1,800,000: named species on Earth, as documented by the Encyclopedia of Life project

BY THE NUMBERS

14.4: jobs created for each $1 million spent creating bike lanes (twice the number of jobs created by road repairs)

1,200: passengers in buses that span two traffic lanes and ride high enough to allow cars to travel underneath them

$100,000: price of a jet pack that carries the wearer 8,000 feet into the air

$200,000: price of the Terrafugia Transition, a flying car

CONTINUED

A Picture of Health

"Research is verifying the old adage that 'wanting what you have' is more important to health and well-being than 'getting what you want.'"

–*Robert A. Emmons, Ph.D., editor in chief,* The Journal of Positive Psychology

HOW WE MEASURE UP

$300,000,000,000: value of lost productivity and medical care costs due to overweight Americans and Canadians

HOW TO BE OUR BEST

"The cultivation of compassion will prove to be as important as the exercise movement in improving your health."

–*James R. Doty, M.D., director, Center for the Study of Compassion and Altruism Research, Stanford, California*

EMBODIMENT IS EMPOWERING

- Changing your posture can change your mind. People who sit with slumped shoulders have lower testosterone levels than those who sit in "high-power poses," occupying as much space as possible.

WE'RE RUNNING RAMPANT . . .

- **in indoor marathons, changing directions every 30 minutes to help avoid injury**
- **in 26 marathons (each beginning with a different letter of the alphabet)**
- **with a hotel's "running concierge," who leads running tours of the area**

PEOPLE ARE TALKING ABOUT . . .

- **paralyzed people using brain signals to walk in a full-body device**
- **vending machines with fruit and veggies in special packaging to keep them ripe and firm longer**
- **people who exercise getting fewer colds than sedentary folks**
- **eyeglasses that are manually adjusted for clear vision both close up and far away**

➡ **Be more than a reader: Follow *The Old Farmer's Almanac* on Facebook and Twitter. Get daily fun and folklore, participate in polls, and share your ideas and experiences.**

Stacey Kusterbeck is a frequent contributor to *The Old Farmer's Almanac.*

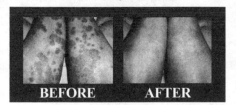

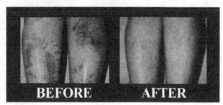

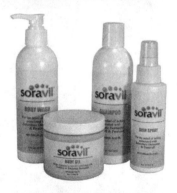

The Shipping News

Any time of year, for any—or even no—occasion, sending a box of home-baked treats spreads love and good cheer.

by Nori Odoi

–photography, Becky Luigart-Stayner; food styling, Ana Kelly; prop styling, Jan Gautro

continued

These baked goods—one savory and several sweet—were developed expressly for special deliveries. To avoid a crumby arrival and make sure that your treats arrive fresh, use our **Ship Tips** on pages 34 and 38.

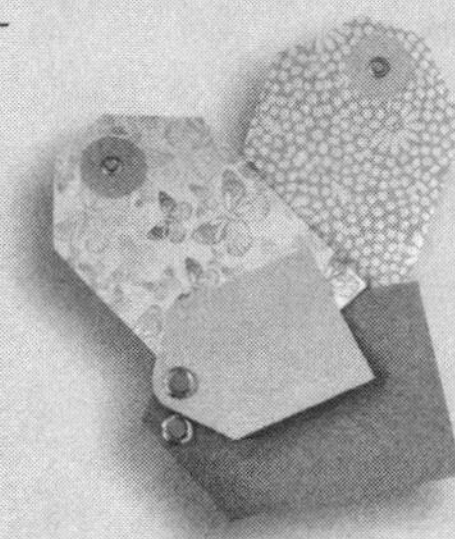

GINGER CRISPS

These spicy wafers have a delightful crunch. You won't be able to eat just one!

1½ cups all-purpose flour
¾ teaspoon cinnamon
¾ teaspoon ground ginger
½ teaspoon ground cloves
½ teaspoon baking soda
¼ teaspoon salt
¾ cup (1½ sticks) unsalted butter, softened
1 cup dark-brown sugar
1 large egg
¼ cup unsulfured molasses

Preheat the oven to 325°F. Line cookie sheets with parchment paper. Mix the flour, cinnamon, ginger, cloves, baking soda, and salt in a bowl. In a separate bowl, cream together the butter and sugar. Add the egg and molasses and beat until combined. Add the flour mixture and mix well. Drop the dough by spoonfuls onto the cookie sheets. Allow 3 inches between each cookie; the dough will spread. Bake for 12 to 15 minutes, or until the cookies darken slightly. Cool the cookies on the cookie sheets for a few minutes before transferring to a rack. They will become quite crisp. Store in an airtight container or a well-sealed plastic bag away from other cookies to ensure that they keep their crispiness. **Makes about 5 dozen cookies.**

continued

PLAN & PREP

ship tips

- Select a variety to send: sweet, savory, crisp, soft, traditional favorites, and unfamiliar flavors.
- Remember to cater to the recipient's needs, food allergies, or dietary requirements.
- Choose treats such as shortbread and drop cookies that will last well at room temperature.
- Prevent a melted mess: Avoid sending cookies with chocolate ingredients during the summer.
- Collect packing materials such as decorator tins, wrapping papers, boxes, and bubble wrap.
- Bake soft bars such as blondies and brownies in disposable aluminum pans and then ship them in the pans.
- Inform the recipient that your package is coming, to make sure that he/she will be home to receive it or available to pick it up, if necessary. (You do not need to reveal the contents.)
- Plan to mail or ship early in the week, so that the package arrives before the weekend.

BLUE CHEESE–WALNUT SHORTBREADS

These dangerously addictive "crackers" melt in your mouth. Freeze extra dough to bake on a moment's notice.

1 cup walnuts, toasted and chopped
4 ounces blue cheese, crumbled
1 cup (2 sticks) unsalted butter, softened and cut into pieces
2 cups all-purpose flour
½ teaspoon black pepper
⅛ teaspoon cayenne pepper
salt*

**Kosher salt works nicely for this recipe because its thin flecks adhere well to each shortbread's surface. For special effect, use finishing salts; they add a distinctive flavor, texture, and/or color. For example, red Hawaiian sea salt adds color and a briny crunch.*

Put all of the ingredients, except the salt, into a food processor and process until dough just forms. Divide the dough in half and place each portion on a sheet of waxed paper. Form each portion into a log that is 2 inches in diameter. Wrap tightly and refrigerate overnight, or until ready to bake.

Preheat the oven to 350°F. Line cookie sheets with parchment paper. Slice the dough into ¼-inch rounds and place them about 1 inch apart on the cookie sheets. Bake for 10 to 13 minutes, or until lightly colored. Sprinkle with salt. Cool the shortbreads on the cookie sheets, then transfer them to a cooling rack. **Makes about 4 dozen shortbreads.**

continued

ULTIMATE RICE KRISPIES TREATS

Have fun: Vary the candy bars to your taste. When shipping, make "sandwiches," as shown; otherwise use the filling as a frosting.

BARS:
2 Snickers bars (1.76 ounces each; almonds optional)
2 Midnight Milky Way bars (1.76 ounces each)
3 Heath Bars (1.4 ounces each)
3 tablespoons unsalted butter
40 large marshmallows (one 10-ounce bag)
7 cups Rice Krispies

FILLING:
1 cup semisweet chocolate chips
1 cup butterscotch chips

Coat a large jelly-roll pan with nonstick spray. Coarsely chop the candy bars.* In a saucepan over low heat, melt the butter, chopped Snickers and Milky Way bars, and marshmallows. Add the Heath Bars and stir well. Add the Rice Krispies and stir until they are covered with the melted candy. Immediately pour the mixture into the prepared pan. Spray your hands with cooking spray, then shape the mixture into a ½-inch-thick rectangle. Shape the ends to be as straight as possible. Set aside to cool.

Remove the rectangle from the pan and cut it in half across its width. Melt the chocolate and butterscotch chips in a pan over low heat. Stir to combine. Spread the melted chips on one half of the bars. Place the other half on top and press lightly. After the chocolate has solidified, cut into 2-inch-square bars. **Makes about 2 dozen bars.**

**To break up the candy bars easily, place them in the freezer for an hour, then pound the wrapped bars several times with a rolling pin or heavy pan.*

continued

PACK & POST

ship tips

- To prevent sogginess, allow baked goods to cool to room temperature before packing them.
- Store sturdy cookies in zipper-lock bags. Stack delicate cookies back-to-back and wrap them with plastic wrap. Pack different types of cookies separately to keep flavors vibrant and prevent moist items from softening crisp ones.
- Cushion your treats well in airtight containers. If you use decorative containers, line the top, bottom, and sides with crumpled paper and separate cookie layers with waxed or parchment paper. Seal with plastic wrap.
- Write a note to the recipient to be packed with the baked goods. Include an appetizing description of each item, a list of special ingredients, and/or the recipes.
- Double-box your baked goods: Put a small, sturdy container inside a large box with 2 to 3 inches of packing material on all sides.
- Before packing it, label the sides of the box "Perishable Foods/Fragile" in large, block letters.
- Ship the package to arrive in a timely manner, such as via 2-day delivery.

LEMON–POPPY SEED–RASPBERRY SANDWICHES

The festive filling brings new life to this classic flavor combination.

1 cup (2 sticks) unsalted butter
½ cup sugar
1 teaspoon vanilla extract
¼ teaspoon salt
zest of 1 lemon, finely grated
2 cups all-purpose flour
⅓ cup poppy seeds
seedless raspberry jam

In an electric mixer set at medium-high speed, cream the butter, sugar, vanilla, salt, and lemon zest until fluffy—about 3 minutes. Add the flour and poppy seeds, mixing on low speed until just combined. Form the dough into two disks and wrap in plastic wrap. Chill for at least 30 minutes.

Preheat the oven to 350°F. On a floured surface, roll out the dough to a ¼-inch thickness. Using a 2-inch cookie cutter (scalloped, if possible, for a pretty edge) cut rounds.

continued

LEMON–POPPY SEED–RASPBERRY SANDWICHES
(continued)

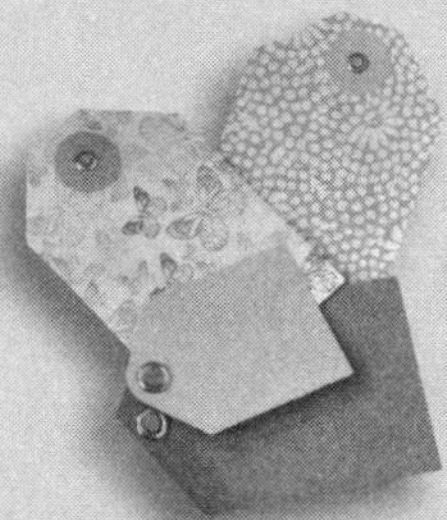

Place the dough rounds on ungreased cookie sheets about ½ inch apart. Bake for 12 to 15 minutes, or until the edges begin to brown. Do not overcook; the cookies will continue to bake after being removed from the oven. Cool on the cookie sheets for several minutes, then transfer to racks when the cookies are firm.

After the cookies have cooled, place 1 tablespoon of raspberry jam on the bottom of one cookie and then gently press the bottom of another cookie into it to spread the jam. Repeat with all of the cookies. **Makes about 2 dozen sandwiches.**

DARK-CHOCOLATE CHILE BALLS

The harmony of chocolate and chile is a Mexican tradition. Surprise chocoholic friends with these rich treats.

6 ounces bittersweet chocolate, chopped
2 ounces unsweetened chocolate, chopped
2 tablespoons unsalted butter
¼ cup all-purpose flour
⅛ teaspoon baking powder
1¼ teaspoons salt
2 teaspoons ground chiles*
2 large eggs
¾ cup sugar
1 tablespoon espresso powder
1 teaspoon vanilla extract
1 cup semisweet chocolate chips
1½ cups chopped walnuts

Preheat the oven to 350°F. Line cookie sheets with parchment paper. In a saucepan over low heat, melt the chocolate with the butter. Set aside to cool. In a bowl, mix the flour, baking powder, salt, and chiles. In a separate bowl, beat the eggs, sugar, espresso powder, and vanilla at high speed for 2 minutes. Add the melted chocolate, beating

**Use ground dried chiles, not chili powder, which is a mixture of spices. Vary to your taste: Ancho chiles have a mild and smoky character; guajillos, more heat; and cayenne, a lot of heat but not much flavor. Chipotles give both heat and a smoky tang.*

DARK-CHOCOLATE CHILE BALLS *(continued)*

to blend. Add the flour mixture and stir until combined. Stir in the chocolate chips and walnuts. The chocolate will begin to solidify, so immediately scoop dough by spoonfuls, shape into balls, and place about 2 inches apart on the cookie sheets. Bake for 10 to 12 minutes, or until the cookies have a shiny skin and are *slightly* firm. Let them cool on the cookie sheets for several minutes, then transfer to a rack. **Makes about 4 dozen cookies.** □□

GRAB A CLAW!

Nori's Almond Claws melt in your mouth, not in the package. Get the recipe at **Almanac.com/Recipes/AlmondClaws.**

Nori Odoi was featured as Best Cook in Town in the 2009 November/December issue of *Yankee.* As a baker and caterer with friends, family, and customers scattered across the nation, she has lots of practice in mailing goodies.

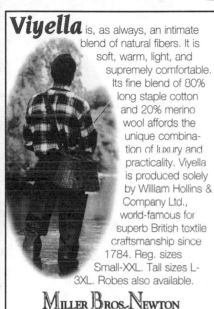

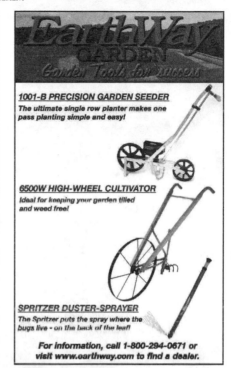

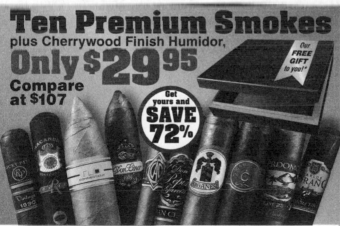

Blue Cheese, Bacon, and
Mushroom Mac and Cheese
(recipe on page 46)

MAC & CHEESE

OUTSIDE THE BOX

by Ken Haedrich

Craving a favorite comfort food? Think outside the box—the macaroni and cheese box, that is. This classic combo is much more versatile than you might imagine. This is not a put-down of packaged versions; it's an invitation to give pasta a few new twists. How? With fresh cheeses like blue, Gouda, or feta. With delectable crab. Or with piquant spices, as in our South Indian version.

Cook the Sauce Through Thick and Thin

In each of these recipes, after adding the milk, heavy cream, or half-and-half, cook and whisk the sauce until it's full-bodied–thicker than milk, thinner than heavy cream, yet not as thick as a white sauce. Then add the cheese, as directed.

CONTINUED

–photography, Becky Luigart-Stayner; food styling, Ana Kelly; prop styling, Jan Gautro

Blue Cheese, Bacon, and Mushroom Mac and Cheese

A surprisingly good combination that is most satisfying to grown-up tastes.

- ½ pound (2 cups) dried corkscrew pasta (cavatappi), cooked
- 4 tablespoons (½ stick) unsalted butter, divided
- 1½ cups sliced mushrooms
- 2 tablespoons all-purpose flour
- 2½ cups half-and-half
- 8 ounces coarsely grated, extra-sharp cheddar cheese
- ½ teaspoon salt
- 1 cup crumbled blue cheese
- 6 strips crisply cooked bacon, crumbled and divided
- 1½ cups Italian-style croutons

(see photo, previous two pages)

Preheat the oven to 350°F. Butter a 13x9-inch baking dish or 2½-quart casserole. Melt 2 tablespoons of butter in a large nonstick saucepan. Add the mushrooms and sauté over medium heat, partially covered, for 4 to 5 minutes, or until softened. Uncover and cook off most of the liquid in the pan. Add the remaining 2 tablespoons of butter to the pan and stir in the flour. Cook for 1 minute over medium-low heat, stirring constantly. Whisk in the half-and-half, in two batches, and cook, whisking often, until it thickens. Add the cheddar, half at a time, whisking and cooking until it melts. Add the salt. Whisk in the blue cheese and half of the crumbled bacon, and remove the pan from the heat. Pour the sauce over the pasta and stir well. Transfer the mixture to the prepared baking dish and smooth the top. Partially crush the croutons in a plastic bag and sprinkle over the dish. Bake for 25 minutes, or until bubbly. Garnish with the remaining crumbled bacon. **Makes 6 servings.**

Macaroni 101

All macaroni and cheese dishes start with pasta. Here's how to prepare it:

Fill a large saucepan with 1 quart of water for each cup of dried pasta. (The pan should be no more than two-thirds full of water.) Bring the water to a boil, then add ½ teaspoon of salt. When the water boils again, add the dried pasta. Stir it with a wooden spoon to keep it from clumping or sticking to the pan and return the water to a boil. Cook for 9 to 10 minutes, until it is barely tender, or according to the package instructions. Drain the pasta, shaking it to remove excess water, and pour the noodles into a large bowl. Add 1 tablespoon of butter or oil, and stir to keep the noodles from clumping. Set aside for use later.

You can also use leftover cooked pasta in these dishes. To shorten the baking time, heat it slightly in the microwave or rinse it under hot water in a colander.

CONTINUED

Greek-Style Mac and Cheese

Traditional Greek ingredients transform the classic American dish. We use spiral noodles, but elbows are fine.

- ½ pound (generous 2 cups) dried spiral noodles (rotini), cooked
- 2 tablespoons olive oil
- 2 cloves garlic
- 8 ounces chopped fresh baby spinach
- 3 tablespoons unsalted butter
- 2 tablespoons all-purpose flour
- 2½ cups light cream or milk
- 6 to 8 ounces coarsely grated Gouda cheese
- 1¼ cups crumbled feta cheese, divided
- ½ teaspoon salt
- large handful cherry tomatoes, quartered
- 1½ cups Italian-style croutons
- ¼ cup chopped fresh Italian parsley, for garnish
- ½ cup chopped pitted olives, for garnish

Preheat the oven to 350°F. Butter a 13x9-inch baking dish or 2½-quart casserole. Heat the olive oil in a large skillet. Add the garlic and sauté gently for several seconds, then stir in the spinach and 2 tablespoons of water. Cover and cook for 3 to 4 minutes, or until tender, stirring occasionally. Remove the pan from the heat. Do not pour off excess liquid. Melt the butter in a large nonstick saucepan. Stir in the flour and cook over medium-low heat for 1 minute, stirring constantly. Whisk in the light cream, in two batches, and cook, whisking often, until it thickens. Add the Gouda cheese, half at a time, whisking until it melts. Remove the pan from the heat and stir in ¾ cup of the feta cheese and the salt. Pour the sauce over the noodles. Stir in the cooked spinach and tomatoes. Transfer the mixture to the prepared baking dish and smooth the top. Partially crush the croutons in a plastic bag and sprinkle over the dish. Bake for 25 minutes, or until bubbly. Serve hot, garnished with the remaining ½ cup of crumbled feta cheese, parsley, and chopped olives. **Makes 6 servings.**

CLASSIC MAC AND CHEESE

Ken's Creamy Classic Mac and Cheese is a little richer and a lot smoother than traditional versions. You'll find it at Almanac.com/MacCheese. Try it and tell us what you think.

CONTINUED

FragranceNet.com
over 13,000 designer brand name fragrances, skincare, makeup, haircare & more…
100% genuine brands • safe & trusted since 1997
DAISY
LOVELY
VERA WANG
princess
OVER 13,000 ITEMS ON SALE THIS WEEK
15% OFF*
enter coupon code: FMRA2
at www.FragranceNet.com
* Designer Exclusions Apply - see website for details
Discounts up to 70% OFF
FREE U.S. Shipping
(min. order required)
redeem coupon at: www.FragranceNet.com
or call us at: 1-800-PARFUMS

Maryland "Crab Cake" Mac and Cheese

Part crab cake, part classic dish, entirely delectable. To serve family-style, use an 8x8-inch baking dish or 2-quart casserole.

- ¼ pound (1 cup) dried elbow macaroni, cooked
- 2 tablespoons unsalted butter
- 1 tablespoon all-purpose flour
- 1⅓ cups half-and-half
- 6 ounces coarsely grated, extra-sharp cheddar cheese
- ⅛ teaspoon salt
- 2½ cups finely cubed fresh white bread, divided
- 1½ teaspoons Old Bay or other seafood seasoning
- 2 tablespoons minced onion
- ⅓ cup ranch salad dressing
- 5 to 6 ounces special or lump crabmeat
- 1 tablespoon unsalted butter, softened

Preheat the oven to 350°F. Butter six 1-cup ramekins and set them aside on a large, heavy baking sheet. Melt the butter over low heat in a large nonstick saucepan. Add the flour and cook over medium-low heat for 1 minute, stirring often. Whisk in the half-and-half, in two batches, and cook, whisking often, until it thickens. Add the cheese, half at a time, and stir until it melts. Add the salt. Remove the pan from the heat. Pour the sauce over the macaroni and stir well. In a medium bowl, combine 1½ cups of the bread cubes, the Old Bay seasoning, and minced onion, then toss to combine. Pour the dressing over the bread cubes and toss gently with a fork. Let this sit for 3 to 4 minutes, then stir it into the macaroni, along with the crab. Divide the mixture evenly among the ramekins and smooth the tops. In a mixing bowl, gently mix the soft butter together with the remaining 1 cup of bread cubes. Divide evenly over the ramekins. Bake for 25 minutes, or until bubbly. **Makes 6 servings.**

CONTINUED

elliott newman
Covered Bridge Charm
Available in sterling silver & 14K gold
3 sizes, from $50.00
Our medium bridge (without loop) fits bead-style bracelets.
For details, visit www.elliottnewman.com
12b Central Street
Woodstock, Vermont 05091
802-457-2344 • 800-619-8757

Downeast Reader's Choice
"Best Chocolate in Maine"
CHOCOLATE COVERED BLUEBERRIES, TURTLES, TRUFFLES & MORE
MAIL ORDER
WEDDINGS
FUNDRAISING
&
CORPORATE GIFTS
Wilbur's of Maine
Chocolate Confections
174 Lower Main St. • Freeport, ME 04032
www.wilburs.com
207-865-4071 • 877-246-2548

The only grill pad compatible with gas and charcoal grills – even fryers!
Will Not Adhere to Composite Decking •
Protects Against Sparks, Spills and Stains •
Naturally Heat and Weather Resistant •
Flexible, Durable and Lightweight •
Available in Various Shapes, Sizes and Colors •
Scan this TAG to view the complete line of grill pads. Don't have a reader? Get the free mobile app for your phone at http://gettag.mobi.
The Original Grill Pad®
What's under your grill?™
MADE IN THE USA
www.grillpad.com | 866.474.5572

South Indian–Style Mac and Cheese

Colorful spices give this dish palate-pleasing warmth and a golden hue. The Almanac's late Group Publisher, John Pierce, won second prize with it in a national ethnic recipe contest.

½ pound (2 cups) dried elbow macaroni, cooked
1 large clove garlic
2 teaspoons minced fresh ginger
½ teaspoon garam masala
½ teaspoon salt
¼ teaspoon turmeric
¼ teaspoon ground cayenne
¼ teaspoon freshly ground black pepper
3 tablespoons unsalted butter
3 tablespoons all-purpose flour
3 cups whole milk, divided
8 ounces coarsely grated sharp cheddar cheese
½ cup fresh bread crumbs
¼ cup freshly grated Asiago cheese
½ teaspoon sweet paprika

Put the garlic and ginger into a food processor. Purée, adding as little water as necessary to make a paste. Preheat the oven to 350°F. Butter a 13x9-inch baking dish or 2½-quart casserole. Combine the garam masala, salt, turmeric, cayenne, and black pepper in a small bowl. Set aside. Melt the butter over low heat in a large nonstick saucepan. Stir in the garlic-ginger paste as the butter is melting and cook for 30 seconds, then stir in the garam masala spices and flour. Cook over medium-low heat for 1 minute, stirring constantly. Add the milk, 1 cup at a time, and cook, whisking often and letting the sauce thicken between each cup. Whisk in the cheddar, half at a time, and cook until it melts. Remove the pan from the heat. Pour the sauce over the macaroni and stir well. Transfer the mixture to the prepared baking dish and smooth the top. In a small bowl, combine the bread crumbs, Asiago cheese, and paprika. Sprinkle evenly over the dish. Bake for 25 minutes, or until bubbly. **Makes 6 servings.** □□

Ken Haedrich is the Julia Child Cookbook Award–winning author of a dozen cookbooks, including *PIE* (Harvard Common Press, 2004), voted best cookbook of 2004 at Amazon.com.

Home Resource
HOME • GARDEN • FOOD
Shop the Online Marketplace at Almanac.com for more unique products and services.

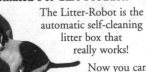

Getting Fresh in the Kitchen

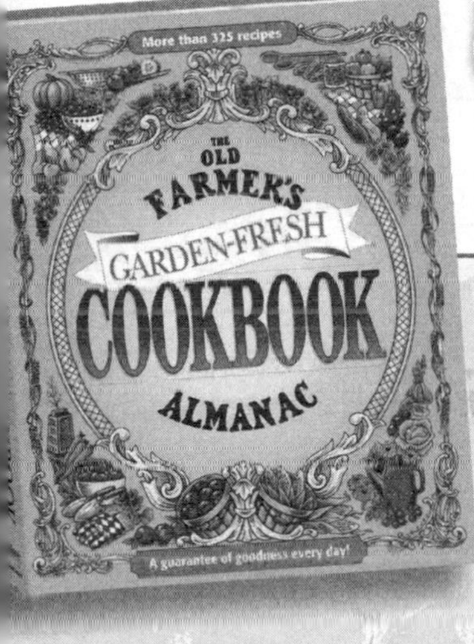

Tiller-to-Table Recipes . . . with Fresh-From-the-Garden Flavor All Year Long!

Fresh ingredients have long been the secret of top chefs. The crunches are crispier . . . the colors are brighter . . . and deep down, you know that fresh fruit and vegetables are better for you!

Whether you grow your own or shop at your local market, you're going to love the great-tasting recipes, timesaving hints, handy charts, and beautiful photography in our just-published *Garden-Fresh Cookbook*. Add a pinch of Almanac wit and wisdom, and eating fresh and nutritious food will never be boring again!

If your idea of "fresh" is opening a can of soggy, salty veggies or a bag of salad, your family and friends are in for a real treat with these delicious recipes. And you can get your own copy of the *Garden-Fresh Cookbook*, with more than 325 recipes, now fresh off the press—see pages 56–57 for details.

We hope that this new collection rekindles your passion for nature, gardening, planting . . . and eating! Growing and sharing the goodness of the farm and garden has been our mission since 1792.

The Editors

TO GET YOUR COPY OF
The Old Farmer's Almanac Garden-Fresh Cookbook,
SEE PAGES 56–57

Enjoy fresh, just-picked produce on even the shortest, darkest, coldest days.

by Robin Sweetser

TAKE A BITE

Rick Faulkner of Durham, Ontario, grows arugula, endive, salad greens, cherry tomatoes, and a variety of herbs year-round in two automated hydroponic garden modules that fit on the kitchen counter. Guy and Barbara Comtois of Sticks and Stones Farm in Barnstead, New Hampshire, grow 10 to 20 acres' worth of food on less than 5 acres of land using hydroponics. Bert Waisanen of Kittredge, Colorado, operates Native Greens, a hydroponic greenhouse in which he produces heirloom tomatoes, cucumbers, greens, and herbs.

What is hydroponics? It's a centuries-old method of growing vegetables, fruit, and flowers in water. One example of this was the Hanging Gardens of Babylon. Today, thanks to innovative technology, it's easier than ever to do at home.

Waisanen began experimenting with hydroponics in 2008. "I quickly

—countertop systems, AeroGrow International, Inc.

OUT OF WINTER

realized that hydroponics can be implemented with off-the-shelf systems or do-it-yourself ingenuity," he says. "The essential components are nutrient-rich water, light, climate control, and crop protection."

Practitioners have found that eliminating soil does away with most disease problems. Plus, the fast growth rate of many crops, especially greens, prevents pests from becoming established.

Of course, there's more to it than plopping a seedling into a pail of water.

–Ildar Sagdejev

The most important ingredient in hydroponics is the water. If you're thinking of trying this, have your water tested. Chlorine and other contaminants can affect plant health. Hard water contains minerals that could upset the balance of nutrients; soft (rain- or distilled) water contains few dissolved minerals.

Although any plant can grow solely in water, some large, heavy plants, such as tomatoes, need root support or a growing medium. Clay pellets, gravel, sand, coconut fiber, perlite, vermiculite, and rock wool are options. High-tech growing media such as polyethylene fibers and cellulose-based substrates are often preferred because they are inert, long-lasting, pH-neutral, and sterile. (Sterility helps to prevent diseases or the growth of unwanted algae.)

(continued)

Top and above: **Clay pellets contain hundreds of tiny pores that retain moisture and allow for maximum oxygen to reach the plants' roots. In a hydroponic tube, lettuce—one of the easiest crops for beginners—is grown in a net pot with a soilless growing medium and nutrient-rich water.**

Left: **A small, countertop hydroponics system can support a variety of plants, from cherry tomatoes and green beans to herbs and salad greens.**

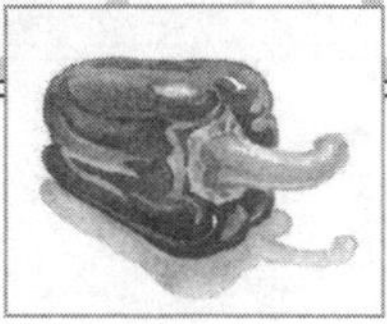

Growers have a choice of water delivery systems. An ebb-and-flow system bathes the roots at regular intervals and then drains it away. A drip system trickles water to plants constantly. These are closed systems, meaning that water is recirculated, not discharged. Plants in these systems can be supported by any medium.

An ebb-and-flow system temporarily floods the grow tray with nutrient solution at regular intervals.

The Comtoises use the drip system. They turned to hydroponics around 2003, devising an array of pipes (patent pending) to make the most of their acreage. "Cukes, bush beans, strawberries, leafy greens, and herbs do the best in it," says Guy. "The plants don't touch anything, the air flow is great—which helps with disease control—and planting and picking are a snap."

—Guy and Barbara Comtois

Another option is a deep-water culture system such as that used by Waisanen. It needs no growing medium. His leafy, green plants thrive in net pots that are set in floating Styrofoam rafts. The plants' roots dangle in an aerated nutrient solution, while the foliage takes the sun.

"Even on the shortest days of winter, we use only natural sunlight and are able to produce heirloom lettuce varieties from seed to table in 55 days," he says. "The addition of high-lumen lighting would boost winter performance."

(continued)

Above: **In this drip system devised by Guy and Barbara Comtois, bok choy, red and green leaf lettuces, and romaine grow almost effortlessly.**

Right: **Pepper plants grown in a drip system can produce an abundunt crop.**

Far right: **Bert Waisanen's deep-water culture system uses net pots and floating Styrofoam.**

—Joseph Kemp

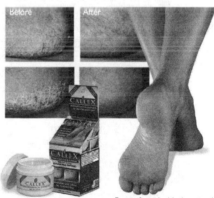

Plants thrive in water when conditions are right. Most vegetable and ornamental plants need a slightly acidic solution (pH 5.5–6.5), which should be tested and adjusted as necessary. Prepared fertilizers are available, or you can mix your own. (Fertilizers not meant for hydroponics can clog pipelines and emitters.)

"Once you get the balance right, a hydroponic garden is easy to maintain," says Waisanen.

For these gardeners, it's not just the growing season that seems endless, but also the possibilities.

It's not just the growing season that seems endless, but also the possibilities.

"I grow basil, hot peppers, tomatoes, tomatillos, parsley, and garlic chives," says Debbie Gile of Hillsborough, New Hampshire. Waisanen has grown small melons. The Comtoises have had pick-your-own strawberries in October.

Here's Where It Gets Fishy

Some enthusiasts, such as Gile, introduce fish to their hydroponics system in a practice called aquaponics. She devised a unique system using a three-shelf rack with fluorescent lights suspended under the top shelf, media-filled growing tubs (with holes in the bottom) on the second shelf, and a 20-gallon aquarium on the bottom level. A pump sends water, which contains ammonia (mostly from the fishes' gills), up from the aquarium to the plants in the tubs. Microbes in the media convert the ammonia to fertilizer that is used by the plants. The cleansed water then rains down into the aquarium through the holes, a process that oxygenates the water for the fish.

This type of three-barrel aquaponics system is used in developing countries. The lowest barrel holds fish, plus water loaded with nutrients from their metabolism. This barrel's water is pumped to the top barrel, redistributed on the grow beds, and then returned to the fish tank.

"It is like a marshland in miniature," says Gile, who is the president of the New Hampshire Aquaculture Association. "This is a tremendously efficient system because you are not throwing out any waste . . . and you can raise fresh fish to eat, such as tilapia, bass, or horned pout, or ornamental fish like koi or goldfish."

(continued)

Waisanen grows tilapia in one of his systems. "It is a great opportunity to produce more than one crop in the same space. Beneficial microbes break down the fish waste into nutrients the plants can use, and the plants filter the water for the fish. The only feed input is fish food. The tilapia act as little farm workers that help to grow the veggies," he says.

Getting Started

Most large and some small seeds can be directly set on the growing medium as long as the watering system doesn't flood to the top and wash them away (most don't). Gile sows greens seeds on perlite. The Comtoises grow corn from seed using coconut coir fiber.

Growers who use a solely liquid-based system must begin with seedlings. Peat pellets or plug trays filled with a soilless mix work well as starter media. For his countertop garden, Faulkner plants seeds in 1-inch cubes of rock wool.

—www.interiorgardens.com

Rock wool *(top)* has hydrophilic qualities that make growing successful. Net pots *(bottom)* are used for transplants and a larger growing medium.

Seedlings are ready when their roots grow through the bottom of the plug, pellet, or other medium. (The roots of any store-bought seedlings should be washed free of soil before using to avoid introducing soilborne diseases to the system.)

Lettuce is an easy crop for beginners, yielding a good-size head in about 1 month. Bok choy and other greens (spinach, Swiss chard), as well as lush herbs such as basil, cilantro, summer savory, and mint, thrive in water and can be directly seeded on the growing medium.

Microgreens (any edible vegetable plant harvested at the seedling stage) suitable for hydroponic gardening include mustards, broccoli, cabbage, radishes, tatsoi, sorrel, purslane, beets, and arugula.

(continued)

For the Windowsill

Learn how to make this small-scale aquaponics unit at www.nativegreens.com. (This system is used for short-term or temporary educational purposes only.)

Cuban sage grows in a homemade hydroponic system using a recycled plastic bottle. Find growing kits at www.popgardens.com.

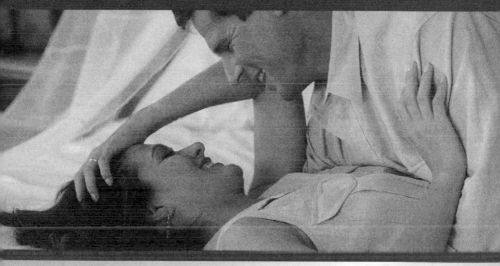

Birds Do It, Bees Do It, Now It's Your Turn

Some plants, such as squashes or cucumbers, need a third party to pollinate them. Indoors, in the absence of birds or bees, that's you. Use an artist's paintbrush to dab pollen from male to female flowers. Once is enough, if it's done at the right time. (Don't know when that is? Do it once a day while the plants are in bloom.)

Indoors, use an artist's paintbrush to dab pollen from male to female flowers.

Outdoors, tomatoes, peppers, and eggplant are among the vegetables that are pollinated by the wind. You can simulate wind indoors with a fan blowing on the plants or you can shake the vines, tap the plants, or vibrate them by touching the stem with the back (not the bristles) of an electric toothbrush.

Plants harvested for their leaves or roots, not fruit, require no pollination.

You can avoid pollinating by planting seedless (parthenocarpic) varieties that bear only female flowers. Greenhouses have used these varieties for years. The seeds (check catalogs) are expensive, but you'll be guaranteed a crop.

(continued)

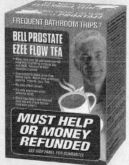

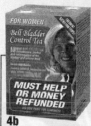

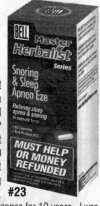

–Exactostock/SuperStock

At Disney's Epcot Center in Florida, hydroponic farming produces over 30 tons of fresh fruit and vegetables yearly, most of which is used in its restaurants.

If You Build It, They Will Grow

Building your own hydroponics system is easy and satisfying. A simple closed-drip system can be constructed by using a plastic storage container as a reservoir, an aquarium pump to circulate the nutrient solution, flexible tubing to channel it, and growing media or net pots to hold the plants.

Be prepared to provide 12 to 14 hours of supplemental light daily. Greens and herbs do best with a simple grow light; flowering and fruiting plants may require the use of high-intensity discharge (HID) lamps.

With a large nutrient reservoir and timers, you can actually go on vacation and (barring a power outage) return home to harvest. □□

Robin Sweetser, garden columnist for the *Concord* (N.H.) *Monitor* and *New Hampshire Home* magazine, lives and gardens in Hillsborough, New Hampshire.

The Latest BUZZ from the beehive

by Ross Conrad

–photo, Éric Tourneret; illustrated border: Bob Dacey/Bandelin-Dacey Studio

For centuries, hive and honeybee products have been used as nutritious foods and natural remedies in the practice known as apitherapy. These traditions continue today.

From Bee-ginning to End

- Greek philosopher Plato (427–347 B.C.) is called the "Athenian Bee." Legend has it that a swarm of bees settled on his mouth when he was lying in his cradle. Consequently, his words flowed with the sweetness of honey.

- St. Ambrose (A.D. 340–397) is often called the "Honey-tongued Doctor" because he is said to have had an experience similar to Plato's. His emblem is the beehive, he is the patron saint of beekeepers, and his feast day is December 7.
- Ancient Greeks observed the sticky substance that guards the gateway to the hive, or "city," of the bees and named it propolis (PROP-uh-lis), after *pro* for "to come before" and *polis* for "city." Today, beekeepers call propolis "bee glue" for its adhesive qualities.

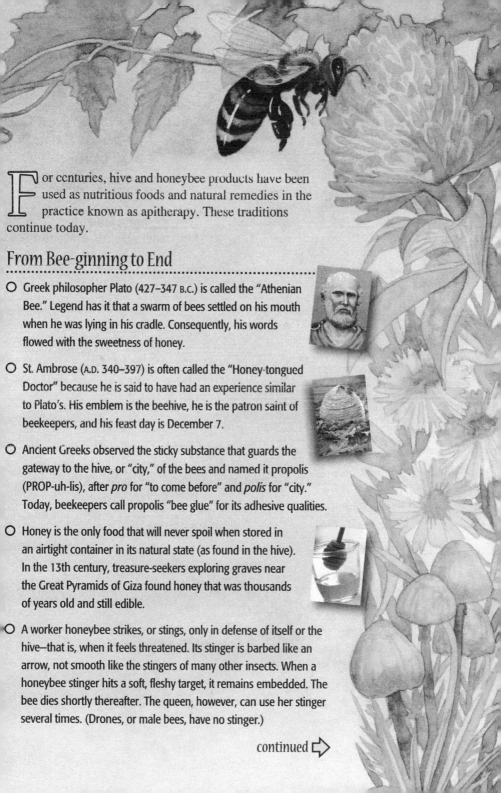

- Honey is the only food that will never spoil when stored in an airtight container in its natural state (as found in the hive). In the 13th century, treasure-seekers exploring graves near the Great Pyramids of Giza found honey that was thousands of years old and still edible.
- A worker honeybee strikes, or stings, only in defense of itself or the hive—that is, when it feels threatened. Its stinger is barbed like an arrow, not smooth like the stingers of many other insects. When a honeybee stinger hits a soft, fleshy target, it remains embedded. The bee dies shortly thereafter. The queen, however, can use her stinger several times. (Drones, or male bees, have no stinger.)

continued ⇨

BEE CAREFUL

For safety, check with your health practitioner and get tested for bee allergies before beginning any apitherapy treatment. Not all remedies are suitable for children. If you are pregnant, nursing, trying to conceive, or have other medical conditions, inform your doctor about any self-treatments. Even natural remedies can interfere with other medicines.

Honey: First Aid in a Jar

Honeybees collect nectar or pollen from flowers, usually one species at a time. In the hive, the bee secretes enzymes into the nectar and then places it into the honeycomb cells. As bees move about the hive, they fan the nectar with their wings, removing moisture, concentrating the sugars, and creating honey. The result—unheated, unfiltered (raw) honey—can be used as a topical wound dressing.

- For a cut or scrape: Apply raw honey and cover with a gauze bandage before bed. All signs of infection and redness are likely to be gone by morning.
- For first- or second-degree burns: Apply raw honey immediately. It reduces the pain and blistering, prevents infection, and helps to speed regeneration of new tissue.
- For sore lips: Coat with raw honey.

Pollen: Pellets With Protein

The process of collecting pollen begins when pollen grains from flowers adhere to honeybees' hair. The bees use stiff hairs on their legs to brush the pollen off their bodies and pack it into pellets, which they carry on their legs to the hive.

At the hive's entrance, the beekeeper places a trap. As the bees pass through its narrow opening, the pellets are knocked off into the collector for later retrieval by the beekeeper.

continued

–photos, Éric Tourneret

ARCTIC FRESH®
Omega 3
ULTRA PURE FISH OIL FORMULA
Proven...
Pure...
Potent !
#1 BRAND RECOMMENDED BY CARDIOLOGISTS
....
KEEPS PURE AND CLEAR IN FREEZER
ARCTIC FRESH HAS EPA 576, DHA 252 PER CAPSULE
....
IS YOURS HIGHER?
Thanks!
37,000 bottles sold!
180 GEL CAPS - $30 - Includes shipping
ARCTICFRESH.COM
941.637.7000

ANTIDOTE FOR POLLEN ALLERGIES

Allergy protocols using pollen are based on oral sensitization: When you consume a small amount of a remedy and gradually increase the portion, tolerance builds up in the body. For example, to reduce symptoms of hay fever, take 1/8 teaspoon of pollen pellets (from the local source plant) on day one. Double that amount daily until a level of 1 teaspoon is reached. Continue taking 1 teaspoon per day, as needed.

Depending on its plant source, pollen is typically 7.5 to 35 percent protein (compare with beef, which is usually 25 to 35 percent protein). It contains all of the amino acids that humans need to live (not always in the exact ratios needed). Orally ingested pollen is rapidly and easily absorbed by the body, where it is believed to . . .

- improve cognitive performance
- boost the immune system
- reduce or eliminate premenstrual and menopausal symptoms
- relieve seasonal pollen allergies

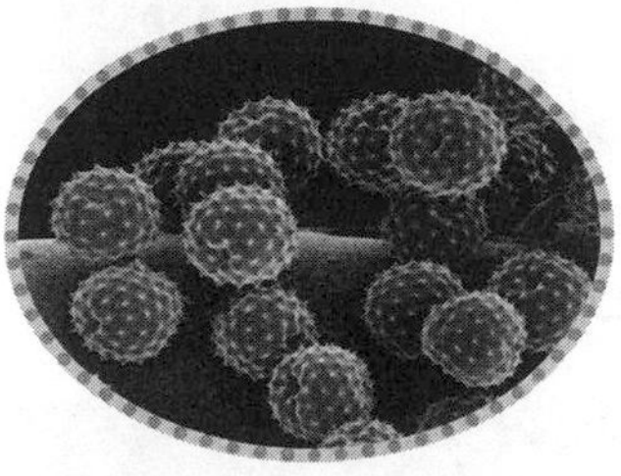

Magnified grains of pollen

–Central Microscopy Research Facilities/University of Iowa, Iowa City, Iowa

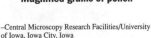

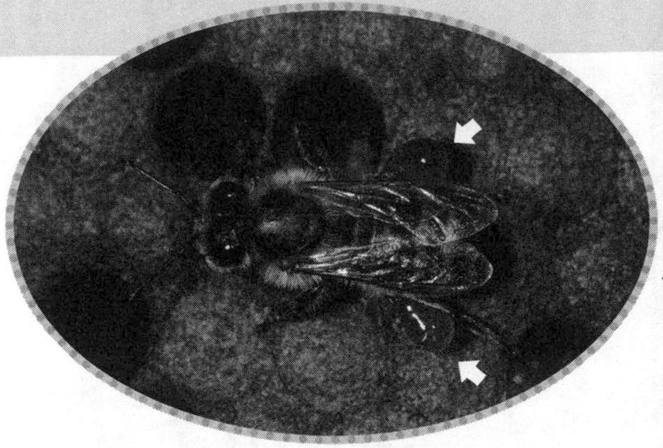

Propolis: "Russian Penicillin"

Honeybees collect waxy, resinous propolis from deciduous trees and transport it to the hive *(above)* in the same way that they carry pollen. They layer it at the hive's entrance and paint a thin coating on the interior of the hive, plugging up any holes. Beekeepers harvest it from both places.

Russian peasants long ago recognized the antibacterial, antifungal, and antiviral properties of propolis—hence the nickname "Russian penicillin," which is still in use today.

Propolis also has powerful antioxidant properties, and it fully metabolizes after 8 hours. One way to consume it is to freeze it, grind it into powder, and add it to honey. Studies have shown it to be good for the liver, the immune system, and the skin.

For a sore throat:

- Drip tincture of propolis down your throat or mix it with water or juice and drink it.
- Place a small chunk of raw propolis between your cheek and gum and suck on it.

continued

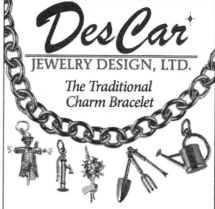

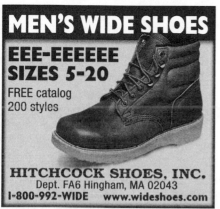

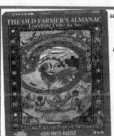

BEE-WARE

- Do not allow children under the age of 1 to consume honey; it may contain bacteria spores.
- When ingested in large quantities, propolis may cause diarrhea or dermatitis, which will go away when use is discontinued.
- Avoid heating raw honey, which destroys the enzyme activity in it and diminishes its healing potential.
- Store fresh pollen in the freezer or refrigerator.
- Suck, do not chew, raw propolis; it will stick to your teeth.

The Stinging Effect

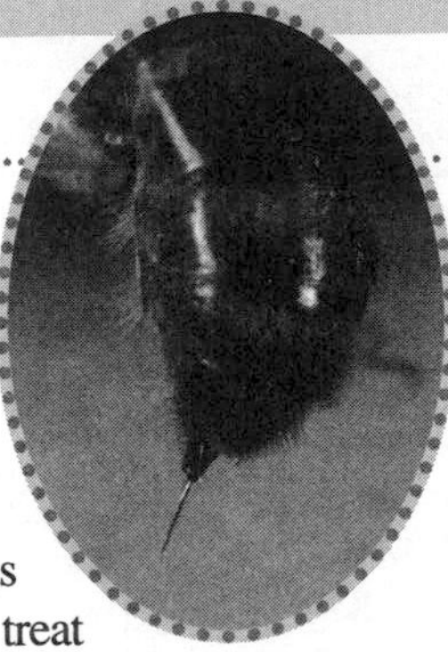

Practitioners of bee venom therapy (BVT) get to the point: They apply worker bees to sore or sensitive "hot spots," areas of the body that correspond to the meridian points recognized by acupuncturists, in such a way as to generate stings. BVT is used to treat the immune, nervous, and endocrine systems; rheumatological diseases, such as arthritis; and multiple sclerosis (MS). The therapy stimulates the body's production of cortisol, the natural version of synthetic cortisone, which is today's conventional treatment for arthritis pain.

Ross Conrad, proprietor of Dancing Bee Gardens in Middlebury, Vermont, maintains about 50 hives. He is the author of *Natural Beekeeping: Organic Approaches to Modern Apiculture* (Chelsea Green, 2007).

–photos, Éric Tourneret

Where the Bees Are

Beekeepers in the United States number about 100,000, including some 1,000 commercial keepers and 5,000 part-timers. The rest are enthusiasts who keep hives in their backyard; about 20 percent of these live in cities and suburbs. Several major cities, including Denver, Detroit, Minneapolis, New York, and Philadelphia, have made beekeeping legal. To see which communities restrict beekeeping, go to www.thedailygreen.com.

–Kim Flottum, editor, Bee Culture *magazine*

Canada has about 7,500 beekeepers operating some 600,000 honeybee colonies. About 80 percent of these are commercial; hobbyists maintain the remainder. The Prairie provinces are home to some 30 percent of Canada's beekeepers, who produce about 80 percent of the nation's honey.

–Canadian Honey Council

For more information about using honeybee hive products for healing and health, contact the American Apitherapy Society at 14942 South Eagle Crest Drive, Draper, UT 84020, or visit www.apitherapy.org.

WEATHERVANES and
CUPOLAS
CAPE COD
CUPOLA
CO., INC.
Visit our Web site at:
www.CapeCodCupola.com
to view quality cupolas in wood and in Azek (PVC) as well as uniquely handcrafted copper weathervanes and finials. Colorful catalog $5.00
78 State Road, Dept. OFA12
North Dartmouth, MA 02747
Phone: 508-994-2119

The Davis Hill Weather Stick®
802-533-2400
davishillco@hotmail.com
P.O. Box 44, Greensboro, VT 05841
Wholesale Inquiries Welcome
$5 Each plus S&H
Min. order 2

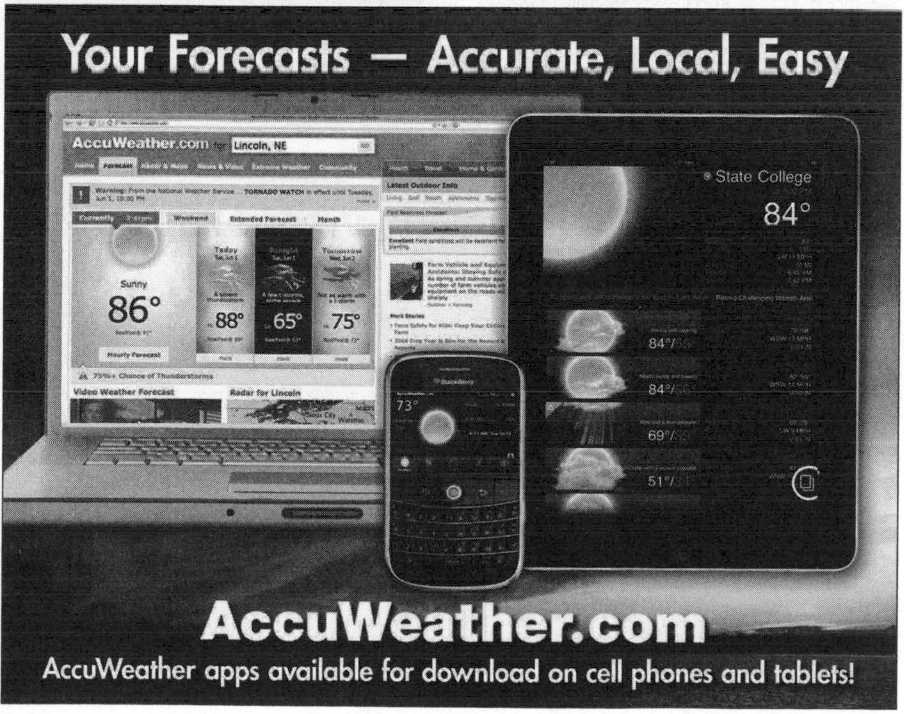
Your Forecasts — Accurate, Local, Easy
AccuWeather.com
Lincoln, NE
Sunny
86°
88°
65°
75°
State College
84°
73°
AccuWeather.com
AccuWeather apps available for download on cell phones and tablets!

WINTER 2011–12

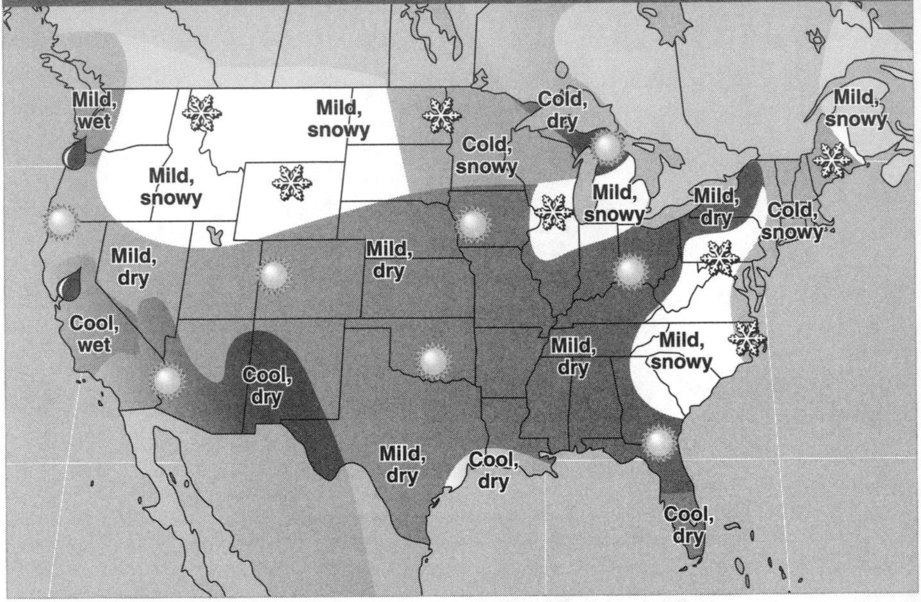

These weather maps correspond to the winter (November through March) and summer (June through August) predictions in the General Weather Forecast (opposite).

SUMMER 2012

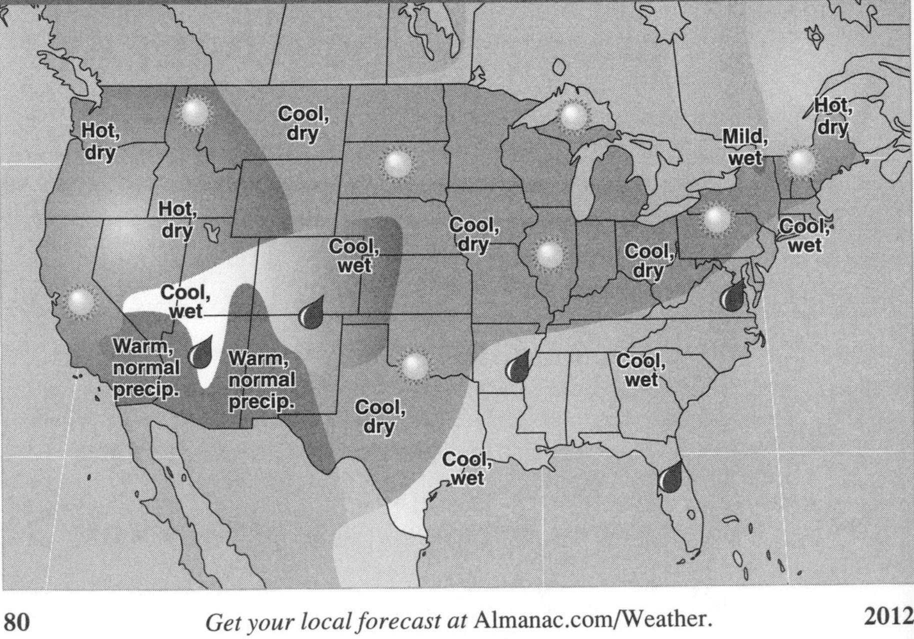

–maps, AccuWeather, Inc.

2011–12 General Weather Forecast

For regional forecasts, see pages 202–217.

The continued low level of sunspot and space weather activity in Solar Cycle 24 reinforces our belief that we are in the midst of a period of significant change. The relatively long length of Solar Cycle 23 (which, at 12.6 years' duration when it ended in December 2008, was the longest cycle in more than 200 years), the change of the PDO (Pacific Decadal Oscillation) to its cold phase in 2010, and the expected change of the AMO (Atlantic Multidecadal Oscillation) to its cold phase in 2012 should combine to bring a gradual cooling of the atmosphere over the coming decade, offset by any warming caused by increased greenhouse gases.

We expect that the winter of 2011–12 will not have a strong El Niño or La Niña. Although temperatures across most of the nation will be above normal, on average, over the November to March winter season, there will be several very cold periods and much of the northern and eastern part of the nation will have above-normal snowfall. While most of the area from Texas and western Louisiana northward to Nebraska and Iowa will have relatively mild temperatures, on average, below-normal precipitation will increase drought concerns.

Spring and summer will be cooler than normal in most of the country, with the chief exception being the West Coast states, where summer will be hotter than normal. The greatest threats in hurricane season will be to North Carolina, Virginia, South Florida, and South Texas.

November through March temperatures will be below normal, on average, in most of New England, the Mid-Atlantic, South Florida, the Upper Midwest, the Desert Southwest, and the Pacific Southwest and above normal elsewhere. Precipitation will be above normal in the eastern Ohio Valley and in northern portions of the Upper Midwest, Pacific Northwest, and Pacific Southwest and below normal elsewhere. Snowfall will be above normal in most locations from New England southward to Georgia and westward across the northern tier of states to the Cascades of Washington and Oregon; it will be below normal in most other areas that typically receive snow.

April and May will be warmer than normal, on average, from Florida to Texas and cooler than normal elsewhere. Rainfall will be above normal from northern New Jersey across southern New England, in most of the Southeast and Deep South, and in the Ohio Valley, Oklahoma, High Plains, Intermountain region, and Pacific Southwest and near or below normal elsewhere.

June through August temperatures will be above normal in northern New England, the northern parts of the Intermountain region, the Pacific Northwest, and the Pacific Southwest and cooler than normal elsewhere. Rainfall will be below normal from central New England through much of Pennsylvania, in the Ohio Valley and Michigan, and west across the northern half of the nation and along the West Coast, with near- or above-normal rainfall in most other areas. Near-normal rainfall in much of Texas will not relieve the drought.

September and October will be warmer than normal in the Northeast and from the High Plains to the West Coast and cooler than normal elsewhere. Rainfall will be above normal in Maine, South Florida, Lower Michigan, the Heartland, South Texas, and Washington State and near or below normal elsewhere.

To learn about how we make our weather predictions and to get the results of our forecast for last winter (hint: we were more than 90 percent accurate), turn to page 200.

The Old Farmer's Almanac

Established in 1792 and published every year thereafter

ROBERT B. THOMAS, *founder* (1766–1846)

YANKEE PUBLISHING INC.

EDITORIAL AND PUBLISHING OFFICES

P.O. Box 520, 1121 Main Street, Dublin, NH 03444
Phone: 603-563-8111 • Fax: 603-563-8252

EDITOR *(13th since 1792)*: Janice Stillman
ART DIRECTOR: Margo Letourneau
COPY EDITOR: Jack Burnett
SENIOR RESEARCH EDITOR: Mare-Anne Jarvela
SENIOR EDITOR: Heidi Stonehill
SENIOR ASSOCIATE EDITOR: Sarah Perreault
ASSOCIATE EDITOR: Amy Nieskens
INTERNS: Molly Buccini, Meredith Shepherd, Jennifer Staltare
WEATHER GRAPHICS AND CONSULTATION: AccuWeather, Inc.

V.P., NEW MEDIA AND PRODUCTION: Paul Belliveau
PRODUCTION DIRECTORS: Susan Gross, David Ziarnowski
SENIOR PRODUCTION ARTISTS: Lucille Rines, Rachel Kipka

WEB SITE: ALMANAC.COM

NEW MEDIA EDITOR: Catherine Boeckmann
WEB DESIGNERS: Lou S. Eastman, Amy O'Brien
ONLINE MARKETING MANAGER: David Weisberg
E-COMMERCE MANAGER: Alan Henning
PROGRAMMING: Reinvented, Inc.

CONTACT US

We welcome your questions and comments about articles in and topics for this Almanac. Mail all editorial correspondence to Editor, The Old Farmer's Almanac, P.O. Box 520, Dublin, NH 03444-0520; fax us at 603-563-8252; or contact us through Almanac.com/Feedback. *The Old Farmer's Almanac* can not accept responsibility for unsolicited manuscripts and will not acknowledge any hard-copy queries or manuscripts that do not include a stamped and addressed return envelope.

All printing inks used in this edition of *The Old Farmer's Almanac* are soy-based. This product is recyclable. Consult local recycling regulations for the right way to do it.

Thank you for buying this Almanac! We hope that you find it "useful, with a pleasant degree of humor." Thanks, too, to everyone who had a hand in it, including advertisers, distributors, printers, and sales and delivery people.

OUR CONTRIBUTORS

Bob Berman, our astronomy editor, is the director of Overlook Observatory in Woodstock and Storm King Observatory in Cornwall, both in New York. In 1976, he founded the Catskill Astronomical Society. Bob has led many aurora and eclipse expeditions, venturing as far as the Arctic and Antarctic.

Tim Clark, a high school English teacher in New Hampshire, has composed the weather doggerel on the Calendar pages since 1980.

Bethany E. Cobb, our astronomer, earned a Ph.D. in astronomy at Yale University and is an Assistant Professor of Honors and Physics at George Washington University. She also conducts research on gamma-ray bursts and follows numerous astronomy pursuits, including teaching astronomy to adults at the Osher Lifelong Learning Institute at UC Berkeley. When she is not scanning the sky, she enjoys playing the violin, figure skating, and reading science fiction.

George Lohmiller, author of the Farmer's Calendar essays, owns Our Town Landscaping in Hancock, New Hampshire. He has been writing for Almanac publications for more than 15 years, including the essays that formerly appeared in our Gardening Calendar and are now available at Almanac.com/GardeningCalEssays.

Celeste Longacre, our astrologer, often refers to astrology as "a study of timing, and timing is everything." A New Hampshire native, she has been a practicing astrologer for more than 25 years. Her book, *Love Signs* (Sweet Fern Publications, 1999), is available for sale on her Web site, www.yourlovesigns.com.

Michael Steinberg, our meteorologist, has been forecasting weather for the Almanac since 1996. In addition to college degrees in atmospheric science and meteorology, he brings a lifetime of experience to the task: He began predicting weather when he attended the only high school in the world with weather Teletypes and radar.

THE 2012 EDITION OF

The Old Farmer's Almanac

Established in 1792 and published every year thereafter

ROBERT B. THOMAS, *founder* (1766–1846)

YANKEE PUBLISHING INC.
P.O. Box 520, 1121 Main Street, Dublin, NH 03444
Phone: 603-563-8111 • Fax: 603-563-8252

PUBLISHER *(23rd since 1792)*: Sherin Pierce
EDITOR IN CHIEF: Judson D. Hale Sr.

FOR DISPLAY ADVERTISING RATES
Call 800-895-9265, ext. 215
Bob Bernbach • 914-769-0051
Steve Hall • 800-736-1100, ext. 320
Go to Almanac.com/Advertising

FOR CLASSIFIED ADVERTISING
Call Gallagher Group • 203-263-7171

AD PRODUCTION COORDINATOR: Janet Grant

PUBLIC RELATIONS
Quinn/Brein • 206-842-8922

TO BUY OR INQUIRE ABOUT ALMANAC PUBLICATIONS
Call 800-ALMANAC (800-256-2622)
or go to Almanac.com/Store

TO SELL ALMANAC PRODUCTS
RETAIL: Cindy Schlosser, 800-895-9265, ext. 126,
or Stacey Korpi, ext. 160

FUND-RAISING WITH ALMANAC PRODUCTS
Sherin Pierce, 800-895-9265, ext. 137

DISTRIBUTORS
NATIONAL: Curtis Circulation Company
New Milford, NJ
BOOKSTORE: Houghton Mifflin Harcourt
Boston, MA

The Old Farmer's Almanac publications are available for sales promotions or premiums. Contact Beacon Promotions, info@beaconpromotions.com.

YANKEE PUBLISHING INCORPORATED

Jamie Trowbridge, *President;* Judson D. Hale Sr., *Senior Vice President;* Paul Belliveau, Jody Bugbee, Judson D. Hale Jr., Brook Holmberg, Sherin Pierce, *Vice Presidents.*

PRINTED IN U.S.A.

Eclipses

■ There will be four eclipses in 2012, two of the Sun and two of the Moon. Solar eclipses are visible only in certain areas and require eye protection to be viewed safely. Lunar eclipses are technically visible from the entire night side of Earth, but during a penumbral eclipse, the dimming of the Moon's illumination is slight.

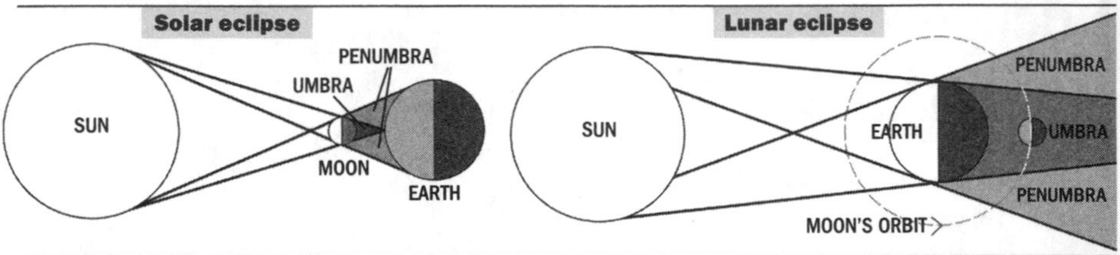

MAY 20: Annular eclipse of the Sun. This rare eclipse will be partially visible from all but eastern North America. For most western locations, the eclipse will begin between 5:00 P.M. and 6:00 P.M. PDT. In Alaska and parts of northern Canada, the eclipse will start an hour earlier and end 2 to 3 hours later (or will be interrupted by sunset). In San Francisco, for example, the eclipse will begin at 5:16 P.M. PDT, reach its maximum at 6:33 P.M., and end at 7:30 P.M., with the Sun very low on the horizon. See page 100 for more.

JUNE 3–4: Partial eclipse of the Moon. In North America, this will be fully visible only from western Alaska; Hawaiians will also have a view. The Moon will enter the penumbra at 10:47 P.M. HAST on June 3, reach a maximum at 1:03 A.M. on June 4, and then leave the penumbra at 3:20 A.M. The eclipse will be partially visible from most of central and western parts of North America; observers will be able to see both a penumbral and umbral eclipse. The Moon will enter the penumbra at 1:47 A.M. PDT on June 4 and then enter the umbra at 2:59 A.M. PDT. However, the Moon will set before completion of the eclipse. Only a penumbral eclipse will be visible from the Northeast, starting at 4:47 A.M. EDT on June 4, before the Moon sets.

NOVEMBER 13–14: Total eclipse of the Sun. This eclipse will not be visible from North America. It will be visible only from Australia, Polynesia, the South Pacific Ocean, southern South America, and Antarctica.

Full-Moon Dates (Eastern Time)

	2012	2013	2014	2015	2016
Jan.	9	26	15	4	23
Feb.	7	25	14	3	22
Mar.	8	27	16	5	23
Apr.	6	25	15	4	22
May	5	25	14	3	21
June	4	23	13	2	20
July	3	22	12	1 & 31	19
Aug.	1 & 31	20	10	29	18
Sept.	29	19	8	27	16
Oct.	29	18	8	27	16
Nov.	28	17	6	25	14
Dec.	28	17	6	25	13

NOVEMBER 28: Penumbral eclipse of the Moon. This eclipse will be fully visible only from Alaska and western parts of Hawaii. The Moon will enter the penumbra at 3:13 A.M. AKST, reach a maximum at 5:33 A.M., and exit the penumbra at 7:53 A.M. In central and western North America, the eclipse will begin at 4:13 A.M. PST, but the Moon will set before the eclipse concludes. No eclipse will be visible from eastern North America.

Transit of Venus

JUNE 5: A rare transit of Venus across the Sun. See "The Sky Is Falling!" on page 96.

Next Total Eclipse of the Sun

March 20, 2015: visible from northern Africa, northern Asia, and Europe.

Bright Stars

Transit Times

■ This table shows the time (EST or EDT) and altitude of a star as it transits the meridian (i.e., reaches its highest elevation while passing over the horizon's south point) at Boston on the dates shown. The transit time on any other date differs from that of the nearest date listed by approximately 4 minutes per day. To find the time of a star's transit for your location, convert its time at Boston using Key Letter C **(see Time Corrections, page 237).**

			Time of Transit (EST/EDT) Bold = P.M. Light = A.M.						
Star	**Constellation**	**Magnitude**	**Jan. 1**	**Mar. 1**	**May 1**	**July 1**	**Sept. 1**	**Nov. 1**	**Altitude (degrees)**
Altair	Aquila	0.8	**12:52**	8:56	5:57	1:57	**9:49**	**5:49**	56.3
Deneb	Cygnus	1.3	**1:43**	9:47	6:47	2:47	**10:39**	**6:40**	92.8
Fomalhaut	Psc. Aus.	1.2	**3:59**	**12:03**	9:03	5:03	1:00	**8:56**	17.8
Algol	Perseus	2.2	**8:09**	**4:13**	**1:13**	9:13	5:09	1:10	88.5
Aldebaran	Taurus	0.9	**9:36**	**5:40**	**2:40**	10:41	6:37	2:37	64.1
Rigel	Orion	0.1	**10:15**	**6:19**	**3:19**	11:19	7:15	3:15	39.4
Capella	Auriga	0.1	**10:17**	**6:21**	**3:21**	11:21	7:18	3:18	93.6
Bellatrix	Orion	1.6	**10:25**	**6:29**	**3:29**	11:30	7:26	3:26	54.0
Betelgeuse	Orion	var. 0.4	**10:55**	**6:59**	**3:59**	**12:00**	7:56	3:56	55.0
Sirius	Can. Maj.	–1.4	**11:45**	**7:49**	**4:49**	**12:49**	8:46	4:46	31.0
Procyon	Can. Min.	0.4	12:43	**8:43**	**5:43**	**1:43**	9:40	5:40	52.9
Pollux	Gemini	1.2	12:49	**8:49**	**5:49**	**1:50**	9:46	5:46	75.7
Regulus	Leo	1.4	3:12	**11:12**	**8:12**	**4:12**	**12:08**	8:09	59.7
Spica	Virgo	var. 1.0	6:28	2:32	**11:28**	**7:28**	**3:25**	11:25	36.6
Arcturus	Boötes	–0.1	7:18	3:22	12:22	**8:19**	**4:15**	**12:15**	66.9
Antares	Scorpius	var. 0.9	9:32	5:36	2:36	**10:32**	**6:28**	**2:29**	21.3
Vega	Lyra	0	11:39	7:43	4:43	12:43	**8:35**	**4:35**	86.4

Rise and Set Times

■ To find the time of a star's rising at Boston on any date, subtract the interval shown at right from the star's transit time on that date; add the interval to find the star's setting time. To find the rising and setting times for your city, convert the Boston transit times above using the Key Letter shown at right before applying the interval **(see Time Corrections, page 237).** The directions in which the stars rise and set, shown for Boston, are generally useful throughout the United States. Deneb, Algol, Capella, and Vega are circumpolar stars—they never set but appear to circle the celestial north pole.

		Rising		Setting	
Star	**Interval (h. m.)**	**Key**	**Dir.***	**Key**	**Dir.***
Altair	6 36	B	EbN	E	WbN
Fomalhaut	3 59	E	SE	D	SW
Aldebaran	7 06	B	ENE	D	WNW
Rigel	5 33	D	EbS	B	WbS
Bellatrix	6 27	B	EbN	D	WbN
Betelgeuse	6 31	B	EbN	D	WbN
Sirius	5 00	D	ESE	B	WSW
Procyon	6 23	B	EbN	D	WbN
Pollux	8 01	A	NE	E	NW
Regulus	6 49	B	EbN	D	WbN
Spica	5 23	D	EbS	B	WbS
Arcturus	7 19	A	ENE	E	WNW
Antares	4 17	E	SEbE	A	SWbW

***b = "by"**

The Twilight Zone

Twilight is the time when the sky is partially illuminated preceding sunrise and again following sunset. The three ranges of twilight are defined according to the Sun's position below the horizon. **Civil twilight** occurs when the Sun is between the horizon and 6 degrees below the horizon (visually, the horizon is clearly defined). **Nautical twilight** occurs when the Sun is between 6 and 12 degrees below the horizon (the horizon is indistinct). **Astronomical twilight** occurs when the Sun is between 12 and 18 degrees below the horizon (sky illumination is imperceptible). When the Sun is at 18 degrees (dawn or dark) or below, there is no illumination.

Length of Astronomical Twilight (hours and minutes)

LATITUDE	Jan. 1 to Apr. 10	Apr. 11 to May 2	May 3 to May 14	May 15 to May 25	May 26 to July 22	July 23 to Aug. 3	Aug. 4 to Aug. 14	Aug. 15 to Sept. 5	Sept. 6 to Dec. 31
25°N to 30°N	1 20	1 23	1 26	1 29	1 32	1 29	1 26	1 23	1 20
31°N to 36°N	1 26	1 28	1 34	1 38	1 43	1 38	1 34	1 28	1 26
37°N to 42°N	1 33	1 39	1 47	1 52	1 59	1 52	1 47	1 39	1 33
43°N to 47°N	1 42	1 51	2 02	2 13	2 27	2 13	2 02	1 51	1 42
48°N to 49°N	1 50	2 04	2 22	2 42	—	2 42	2 22	2 04	1 50

TO DETERMINE THE LENGTH OF TWILIGHT: The length of twilight changes with latitude and the time of year. Use the **Time Corrections** table, **page 237**, to find the latitude of your city or the city nearest you. Use that figure in the chart above with the appropriate date to calculate the length of twilight in your area.

TO DETERMINE WHEN DAWN OR DARK WILL OCCUR: Calculate the sunrise/sunset times for your locality using the instructions in **How to Use This Almanac,** **page 104.** Subtract the length of twilight from the time of sunrise to determine when dawn breaks. Add the length of twilight to the time of sunset to determine when dark descends.

EXAMPLE:

Boston, Mass. (latitude 42°22')

Sunrise, August 1	**5:37 A.M. EDT**
Length of twilight	**– 1 52**
Dawn breaks	**3:45 A.M.**
Sunset, August 1	**8:03 P.M. EDT**
Length of twilight	**+ 1 52**
Dark descends	**9:55 P.M.**

Principal Meteor Showers

SHOWER	BEST VIEWING	POINT OF ORIGIN	DATE OF MAXIMUM*	NO. PER HOUR**	ASSOCIATED COMET
Quadrantid	**Predawn**	**N**	**Jan. 4**	**25**	—
Lyrid	Predawn	S	Apr. 22	10	Thatcher
Eta Aquarid	Predawn	SE	May 4	10	Halley
Delta Aquarid	Predawn	S	July 30	10	—
Perseid	**Predawn**	**NE**	**Aug. 11–13**	**50**	**Swift-Tuttle**
Draconid	Late evening	NW	Oct. 9	6	Giacobini-Zinner
Orionid	Predawn	S	Oct. 21–22	15	Halley
Taurid	Late evening	S	Nov. 9	3	Encke
Leonid	Predawn	S	Nov. 17–18	10	Tempel-Tuttle
Andromedid	Late evening	S	Nov. 25–27	5	Biela
Geminid	**All night**	**NE**	**Dec. 13–14**	**75**	—
Ursid	Predawn	N	Dec. 22	5	Tuttle

May vary by one or two days* ***Moonless, rural sky* **Bold = *most prominent*

The Visible Planets

■ Listed here for Boston are viewing suggestions for and the rise and set times (EST/EDT) of Venus, Mars, Jupiter, and Saturn on specific days each month, as well as when it is best to view Mercury. Approximate rise and set times for other days can be found by interpolation. Use the Key Letters at the right of each listing to convert the times for other localities **(see pages 104 and 237).** *For all planet rise and set times by zip code, visit* **Almanac.com/Astronomy.**

Venus

♀ **During our lifetime, Venus will never again seem as** spectacular as it does this year. Starting as a superb evening star on January 1, it brightens and climbs in the west until reaching maximum elevation in late March and greatest brilliancy in April, at a dazzling –4.7 magnitude. On June 5, its transit of the Sun (see "The Sky Is Falling!," p. 96)—an event that will not recur until 2117—is visible throughout North America. It appears as a striking morning star from July through October. In mid-March and again during the first half of July, it shines near Jupiter, with the Moon joining this resplendent conjunction on July 15.

Jan. 1	**set**	**7:06**	B	Apr. 1	**set**	**11:19**	E	July 1	rise	3:22	B	Oct. 1	rise	3:12	B
Jan. 11	**set**	**7:32**	B	Apr. 11	**set**	**11:29**	E	July 11	rise	2:55	B	Oct. 11	rise	3:33	B
Jan. 21	**set**	**7:56**	B	Apr. 21	**set**	**11:30**	E	July 21	rise	2:36	B	Oct. 21	rise	3:54	C
Feb. 1	**set**	**8:22**	C	May 1	**set**	**11:20**	E	Aug. 1	rise	2:23	A	Nov. 1	rise	4:18	C
Feb. 11	**set**	**8:44**	C	May 11	**set**	**10:53**	E	Aug. 11	rise	2:18	A	Nov. 11	rise	3:41	C
Feb. 21	**set**	**9:05**	D	May 21	**set**	**10:05**	E	Aug. 21	rise	2:19	A	Nov. 21	rise	4:04	D
Mar. 1	**set**	**9:24**	D	June 1	**set**	**8:49**	E	Sept. 1	rise	2:26	B	Dec. 1	rise	4:29	D
Mar. 11	**set**	**10:44**	E	June 11	rise	4:42	A	Sept. 11	rise	2:38	B	Dec. 11	rise	4:53	E
Mar. 21	**set**	**11:02**	E	June 21	rise	3:57	B	Sept. 21	rise	2:54	B	Dec. 21	rise	5:18	E
												Dec. 31	rise	5:40	E

Mars

♂ **Every other year—including 2012—the Red Planet** comes close and seems more intense. Rising in Leo just after 10:00 P.M. on January 1, it brightens steadily until coming closest to Earth on March 5, when it is out all night. This year at its most distant opposition, it looks small through telescopes and does not brighten beyond magnitude –1.2, being bested in brilliance by Venus, Jupiter, and Sirius. Rapidly and then more slowly, it loses its brilliance as it passes through Virgo all summer before dimly accelerating onward through the zodiac during the rest of the year.

Jan. 1	**rise**	**10:02**	C	Apr. 1	set	5:26	D	July 1	set	12:08	C	Oct. 1	**set**	**8:20**	B
Jan. 11	**rise**	**9:31**	C	Apr. 11	set	4:42	D	July 11	**set**	**11:37**	C	Oct. 11	**set**	**8:03**	A
Jan. 21	**rise**	**8:56**	C	Apr. 21	set	4:01	D	July 21	**set**	**11:09**	C	Oct. 21	**set**	**7:49**	A
Feb. 1	**rise**	**8:10**	B	May 1	set	3:23	D	Aug. 1	**set**	**10:40**	C	Nov. 1	**set**	**7:36**	A
Feb. 11	**rise**	**7:20**	B	May 11	set	2:48	D	Aug. 11	**set**	**10:14**	B	Nov. 11	**set**	**6:27**	A
Feb. 21	**rise**	**6:25**	B	May 21	set	2:14	D	Aug. 21	**set**	**9:49**	B	Nov. 21	**set**	**6:20**	A
Mar. 1	**rise**	**5:33**	B	June 1	set	1:38	D	Sept. 1	**set**	**9:23**	B	Dec. 1	**set**	**6:16**	A
Mar. 11	**rise**	**5:33**	B	June 11	set	1:07	D	Sept. 11	**set**	**9:00**	B	Dec. 11	**set**	**6:14**	A
Mar. 21	set	6:18	D	June 21	set	12:37	C	Sept. 21	**set**	**8:39**	B	Dec. 21	**set**	**6:14**	A
												Dec. 31	**set**	**6:15**	A

☞ **Bold = P.M.** ☞ Light = A.M.

–illustrations, Beth Krommes

Jupiter

Brilliant Jove is high in the south at nightfall on January 1. In Aries, it gets lower in February; joins Venus in a prolonged, eye-catching meeting from March 7–18; and then vanishes into the solar glare in April. It returns as a morning star next to Venus in Taurus in late June. The pair ascends higher each day in the predawn east, remaining together during the first week of July; the Moon joins them on July 15 in a spectacular conjunction. Jupiter rises before midnight in September and comes closest to Earth at a brilliant magnitude –2.8 on December 1, when it is out all night.

Jan. 1	set	1:40	D	Apr. 1	**set**	**9:47**	D	July 1	rise	2:53	A	Oct. 1	**rise**	**9:31**	A
Jan. 11	set	1:03	D	Apr. 11	**set**	**9:19**	E	July 11	rise	2:21	A	Oct. 11	**rise**	**8:51**	A
Jan. 21	set	12:27	D	Apr. 21	**set**	**8:52**	E	July 21	rise	1:48	A	Oct. 21	**rise**	**8:10**	A
Feb. 1	**set**	**11:47**	D	May 1	**set**	**8:24**	E	Aug. 1	rise	1:12	A	Nov. 1	**rise**	**7:24**	A
Feb. 11	**set**	**11:14**	D	May 11	**set**	**7:57**	E	Aug. 11	rise	12:39	A	Nov. 11	**rise**	**5:41**	A
Feb. 21	**set**	**10:43**	D	May 21	rise	5:05	B	Aug. 21	rise	12:04	A	Nov. 21	**rise**	**4:57**	A
Mar. 1	**set**	**10:16**	D	June 1	rise	4:29	B	Sept. 1	**rise**	**11:22**	A	Dec. 1	**rise**	**4:13**	A
Mar. 11	**set**	**10:46**	D	June 11	rise	3:57	B	Sept. 11	**rise**	**10:46**	A	Dec. 11	set	6:23	E
Mar. 21	**set**	**10:18**	D	June 21	rise	3:25	A	Sept. 21	**rise**	**10:09**	A	Dec. 21	set	5:38	E
												Dec. 31	set	4:53	E

Saturn

With its shiny rings less edgewise this year, Saturn seems brighter through backyard telescopes, rising well after midnight in January and coming up 2 hours earlier each month thereafter. Near Virgo's blue star, Spica, for most of the year, the Ringed World is closest to Earth at opposition on April 15, when it is out all night at magnitude 0.2. Remaining prominent throughout spring, it becomes solely an evening object in summer and gets low in August while meeting Mars and Spica in the west at nightfall. The Moon joins the trio on August 21. Saturn vanishes in September and emerges as a morning star in November. It forms a tight conjunction with Venus on November 26 and 27.

Jan. 1	rise	1:20	D	Apr. 1	**rise**	**8:12**	D	July 1	set	1:13	C	Oct. 1	**set**	**7:22**	B
Jan. 11	rise	12:44	D	Apr. 11	**rise**	**7:29**	D	July 11	set	12:34	C	Oct. 11	**set**	**6:46**	B
Jan. 21	rise	12:06	D	Apr. 21	**rise**	**6:46**	D	July 21	**set**	**11:51**	C	Oct. 21	**set**	**6:09**	B
Feb. 1	**rise**	**11:20**	D	May 1	set	5:19	C	Aug. 1	**set**	**11:09**	C	Nov. 1	rise	6:42	D
Feb. 11	**rise**	**10:41**	D	May 11	set	4:38	C	Aug. 11	**set**	**10:31**	C	Nov. 11	rise	5:09	D
Feb. 21	**rise**	**10:00**	D	May 21	set	3:57	C	Aug. 21	**set**	**9:54**	B	Nov. 21	rise	4:36	D
Mar. 1	**rise**	**9:23**	D	June 1	set	3:13	C	Sept. 1	**set**	**9:13**	B	Dec. 1	rise	4:02	D
Mar. 11	**rise**	**9:42**	D	June 11	set	2:32	C	Sept. 11	**set**	**8:36**	B	Dec. 11	rise	3:28	D
Mar. 21	**rise**	**8:59**	D	June 21	set	1:52	C	Sept. 21	**set**	**7:59**	B	Dec. 21	rise	2:53	D
												Dec. 31	rise	2:18	D

Mercury

With its brightness and position always changing, orange Mercury is truly mercurial; it alternately darts above the eastern and western skylines roughly every 2 months. It is readily seen only when it is at least 6 degrees above the horizon 40 minutes after sunset or before sunrise and when its brightness exceeds magnitude 0.5. Look in the western sky in late February, early March, and mid-June and in the predawn eastern sky during the first half of December. It will hover to the left of the crescent Moon on February 22.

DO NOT CONFUSE ■ *Saturn with Spica from January through August. Saturn is higher and creamy white.* ■ *Saturn, Spica, and Mars in the west, August 6–21. Spica is blue and Mars is orange.* ■ *Venus with Jupiter in mid-March and early July. Venus is much brighter.* ■ *Mars with Regulus in April. Mars is brighter and orange.*

Astronomical Glossary

Aphelion (Aph.): The point in a planet's orbit that is farthest from the Sun.

Apogee (Apo.): The point in the Moon's orbit that is farthest from Earth.

Celestial Equator (Eq.): The imaginary circle around the celestial sphere that can be thought of as the plane of Earth's equator projected out onto the sphere.

Celestial Sphere: An imaginary sphere projected into space that represents the entire sky, with an observer on Earth at its center. All celestial bodies other than Earth are imagined as being on its inside surface.

Circumpolar: Always visible above the horizon, such as a circumpolar star.

Conjunction: The time at which two or more celestial bodies appear closest in the sky. **Inferior (Inf.):** Mercury or Venus is between the Sun and Earth. **Superior (Sup.):** The Sun is between a planet and Earth. Actual dates for conjunctions are given in the **Right-Hand Calendar Pages, 109–135**; the best times for viewing the closely aligned bodies are given in **Sky Watch** on the **Left-Hand Calendar Pages, 108–134.**

Declination: The celestial latitude of an object in the sky, measured in degrees north or south of the celestial equator; analogous to latitude on Earth. This Almanac gives the Sun's declination at noon.

Eclipse, Lunar: The full Moon enters the shadow of Earth, which cuts off all or part of the sunlight reflected off the Moon. **Total:** The Moon passes completely through the **umbra** (central dark part) of Earth's shadow. **Partial:** Only part of the Moon passes through the umbra. **Penumbral:** The Moon passes through only the **penumbra** (area of partial darkness surrounding the umbra). **See page 86** for more eclipse information.

Eclipse, Solar: Earth enters the shadow of the new Moon, which cuts off all or part of the Sun's light. **Total:** Earth passes through the umbra (central dark part) of the Moon's shadow, resulting in totality for observers within a narrow band on Earth. **Annular:** The Moon appears silhouetted against the Sun, with a ring of sunlight showing around it. **Partial:** The Moon blocks only part of the Sun.

Ecliptic: The apparent annual path of the Sun around the celestial sphere. The plane of the ecliptic is tipped 23½° from the celestial equator.

Elongation: The difference in degrees between the celestial longitudes of a planet and the Sun. **Greatest Elongation (Gr. Elong.):** The greatest apparent distance of a planet from the Sun, as seen from Earth.

Epact: A number from 1 to 30 that indicates the Moon's age on January 1 at Greenwich, England; used for determining the date of Easter.

Equinox: When the Sun crosses the celestial equator. This event occurs two times each year: **Vernal** is around March 20 and **Autumnal** is around September 22.

Evening Star: A planet that is above the western horizon at sunset and less than 180° east of the Sun in right ascension.

Golden Number: A number in the 19-year cycle of the Moon, used for determining the date of Easter. (Approximately every 19 years, the Moon's phases occur on the same dates.) Add 1 to any given year and divide by 19; the remainder is the Golden Number. If there is no remainder, the Golden Number is 19.

Greatest Illuminated Extent (Gr. Illum. Ext.): When the maximum surface area of a planet is illuminated as seen from Earth.

Magnitude: A measure of a celestial object's brightness. **Apparent** magnitude measures the brightness of an object as seen from Earth.

Objects with an apparent magnitude of 6 or less are observable to the naked eye. The lower the magnitude, the greater the brightness. An object with a magnitude of –1, for example, is brighter than an object with a magnitude of +1. **Absolute** magnitude expresses how bright objects would appear if they were all the same distance (about 33 light-years) from Earth.

Midnight: Astronomical midnight is the time when the Sun is opposite its highest point in the sky (local noon). Midnight is neither A.M. nor P.M., although 12-hour digital clocks typically display midnight as 12:00 A.M. On a 24-hour time cycle, 00:00, rather than 24:00, usually indicates midnight.

Moon on Equator: The Moon is on the celestial equator.

Moon Rides High/Runs Low: The Moon is highest above or farthest below the celestial equator.

Moonrise/Moonset: When the Moon rises above or sets below the horizon.

Moon's Phases: The changing appearance of the Moon, caused by the different angles at which it is illuminated by the Sun. **First Quarter:** Right half of the Moon is illuminated. **Full:** The Sun and the Moon are in opposition; the entire disk of the Moon is illuminated. **Last Quarter:** Left half of the Moon is illuminated. **New:** The Sun and the Moon are in conjunction; Moon is darkened because it lines up between Earth and the Sun.

Moon's Place, Astronomical: The actual position of the Moon within the constellations on the celestial sphere. **Astrological:** The astrological position of the Moon within the zodiac, according to calculations made more than 2,000 years ago. Because of precession of the equinoxes and other factors, this is not the Moon's actual position in the sky.

Morning Star: A planet that is above the eastern horizon at sunrise and less than 180° west of the Sun in right ascension.

Node: Either of the two points where a celestial body's orbit intersects the ecliptic. **Ascending:** When the body is moving from south to north of the ecliptic. **Descending:** When the body is moving from north to south of the ecliptic.

Occultation (Occn.): When the Moon or a planet eclipses a star or planet.

Opposition: The Moon or a planet appears on the opposite side of the sky from the Sun (elongation 180°).

Perigee (Perig.): The point in the Moon's orbit that is closest to Earth.

Perihelion (Perih.): The point in a planet's orbit that is closest to the Sun.

Precession: The slowly changing position of the stars and equinoxes in the sky resulting from variations in the orientation of Earth's axis.

Right Ascension (R.A.): The celestial longitude of an object in the sky, measured eastward along the celestial equator in hours of time from the vernal equinox; analogous to longitude on Earth.

Solar Cycle: In the Julian calendar, a period of 28 years, at the end of which the days of the month return to the same days of the week.

Solstice, Summer: When the Sun reaches its greatest declination (23½°) north of the celestial equator, around June 21. **Winter:** When the Sun reaches its greatest declination (23½°) south of the celestial equator, around December 21.

Stationary (Stat.): The brief period of apparent halted movement of a planet against the background of the stars shortly before it appears to move backward/westward (retrograde motion) or forward/eastward (direct motion).

Sun Fast/Slow: When a sundial reading is ahead of (fast) or behind (slow) clock time.

Sunrise/Sunset: The visible rising and setting of the upper edge of the Sun's disk across the unobstructed horizon of an observer whose eyes are 15 feet above ground level.

Twilight: For definitions of civil, nautical, and astronomical twilight, **see page 90.** □□

THE SKY is FALLING!

And this is a good year to catch it.

by Bob Berman

The Mayan calendar changes on December 21, but 2012's truly extraordinary events are all in the sky.

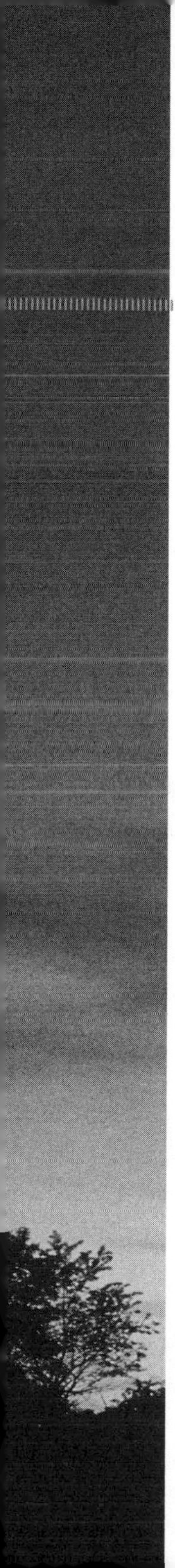

Almost everyone has heard that this is a big year for the Mayan calendar. A film, dozens of books, numerous TV specials, and more than 1.2 million Web pages have been produced as a reminder that one of the three forms of the Mayan calendar (specifically, the "long count" version) turns a page on December 21. That date is the start of the 14th b'ak'tun—a time of celebration, not doom, in Mayan culture. Pop the corks!

Mesoamerican scholars insist that the Maya never regarded calendar year changes as apocalyptic. Nonetheless, the doomsday peddlers claim that a great astronomical event will occur on December 21: The Sun will line up with the center of the galaxy.

Here is where astronomers fall off their chairs laughing. The Sun's path against the background zodiacal stars is precisely the same every year, and the Sun never lines up with the center of the galaxy. Even if it did, so what?

This is an extraordinary year in the sky, however. Rare cycles do come together, and the resulting events are all in-your-face visible. They just don't happen on December 21.

Venus, the Star of the Show

★ The Maya adored this brightest "star" in the heavens. They were aware of its cyclical appearance as an evening and morning star. They knew that it precisely repeats its positions every 8 years and that once every 8 years it is especially prominent. This inspired them to design a calendar to be perfectly synchronized with Venus's motions.

★ **Venus's conspicuous cycle, known as its synodic period, lasts 584 days, or just over 19 months.**

Its evening star phase starts on the first day that it sets after the Sun sets in the west and continues each night for about 9 months.

Then Venus "disappears" in front of the Sun.

The next phase starts on the first day that Venus appears as a morning star (before dawn) in the east and continues daily for about 9 months.

CONTINUED

Then Venus "disappears" behind the Sun before the evening star phase starts again.

Scientifically speaking . . .

- ★ **When Venus is behind the Sun, it is in superior conjunction.**
- ★ **When Venus is in front of the Sun, it is in inferior conjunction.**

Learn more about conjunctions in the Astronomical Glossary, pages 94–95, and How to Use This Almanac, page 107.

This year, Venus, our nearest planetary neighbor, has the best year it will have during our lifetimes. It starts 2012 as a conspicuous evening star and then gets extraordinarily high and bright (magnitude –4.7) from February through early May. It returns as an unusually high morning star from July through October.

That's not all. Roughly twice a century, the planet transits the Sun. A transit is a kind of eclipse; one body blocks the light from a more distant one. However, by tradition, when the foreground body is smaller than the background one, the event is called a transit. This happens on June 5 (June 6 in Asia), starting at 6:04 P.M. EDT (3:06 P.M. PDT), and is visible from all of North America. You don't need a telescope to see it, but eye protection is essential; without it, your retinas could be permanently damaged (see "Get Your Goggles," page 100).

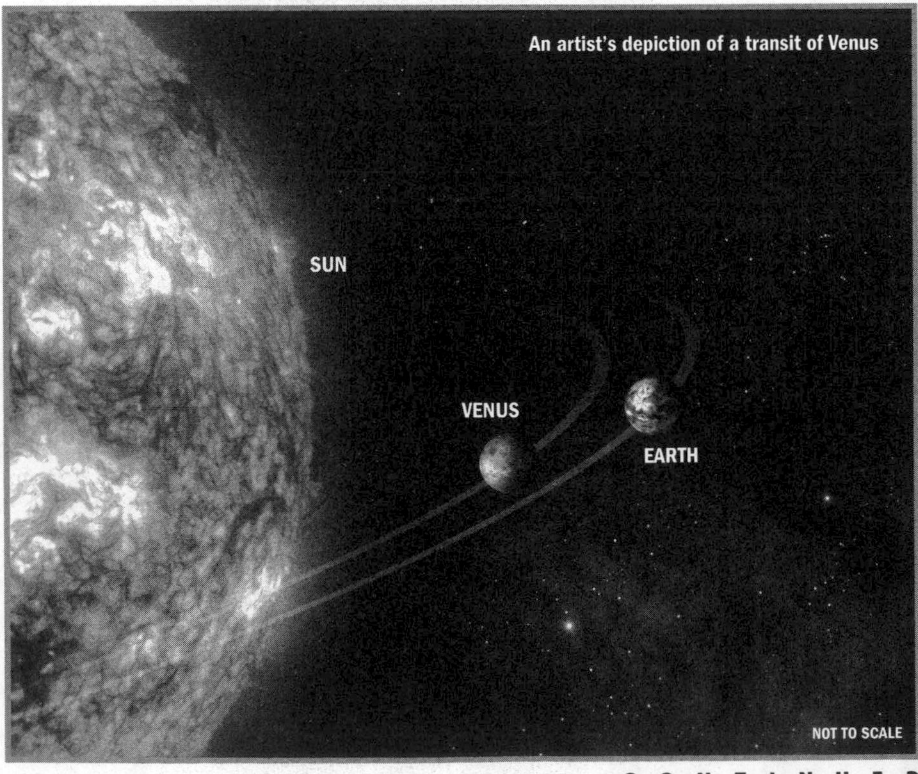

An artist's depiction of a transit of Venus

–Smithsonian Institution Libraries, JPL, Raytheon Corp. Artists: H. Smith, C. Hawley

CONTINUED

Venus transits once made headline news around the world. Costly multinational expeditions were dispatched to observe them in the 18th and 19th centuries. No transits occurred in the 20th century, and 121½ years elapsed prior to the last one, in 2004. Venus's next transit will occur on December 11, 2117.

Venus in Transit

★ **The Venutian transit cycle is complicated. A transit of Venus occurs only in June or December, and in a double cycle, or pair. It repeats in 121 years, then 8 years, then 105½, then 8 years, then 121, and so on. The June 5 transit marks the conclusion of an 8-year cycle that began in June 2004.**

Transit of Venus as seen June 8, 2004

GET YOUR GOGGLES

Be ready to safely view the eclipse and the transit: Go to your nearest welding supply store and get welder's goggles or filters, shade #14 or higher, or search the Internet for "solar eclipse glasses" from a reputable source.

A Solar Eclipse

★ This year brings an annular eclipse, too, and it's a rarity.

On May 20, at about 6:30 P.M. PDT, the Moon centrally eclipses the Sun *(example below)*. It is too far away to completely cover it, but instead, a ring, or annulus, of sunlight shines all around the

lunar orb. A telescope is unnecessary for viewing, but eye protection is essential.

The shadow from this event passes over Reno, Nevada, and Albuquerque, New Mexico, as it sweeps across the western states. From most other regions of the United States and Canada (except for East Coast areas, which are out of range), this appears as a partial solar eclipse; nearly all of the Sun is blocked out.

Mark the date and time (see "Exact Eclipse Times," below). These events happen in North America only every few decades. The last one was in May 1994.

EXACT ECLIPSE TIMES

For the exact time of the eclipse in your town, go to http://eclipse.gsfc.nasa.gov/SEgoogle/SEgoogle2001/SE2012May20Agoogle.html.

A Perseids meteor shower photographed near Boone, North Carolina, on August 12, 2008

Celestial Showers

★ The two major annual meteor showers, the Perseids and the Geminids, occur on August 11–13 and December 13–14, respectively. In most years, one of these events is spoiled by a bright Moon. Both seldom occur in darkness (when the Moon is absent or in a dim crescent phase), but 2012 is not like most years.

For only the fourth time since 2000, meteors will fill the sky undiminished by lunar light. We can only hope that weather conditions don't rain (or snow) on this parade.

Early Seasons

★ In some circles, this cavalcade of celestial events still wouldn't compare to the Mayan mystique unless something unique happened with our Gregorian calendar, too—and it does.

The year 2000 was an "extra" leap year (the first time in four centuries that such a change was made). This tweak in time, combined with 2012 being a routine leap year, jump-starts the seasons. In 2012, the equinoxes and solstices occur earlier than in any year since 1896.

Spring 2012 is particularly notable for its timing. In the Pacific and Mountain time zones, the vernal equinox occurs on March 19—its earliest arrival in any North American time zone in 116 years. Spring has started on this date in the Pacific zone three times in the past and in the Mountain zone, two times—but never at such an early hour as this year. In the Central and Eastern zones, spring began on March 21 during most of the past century. In 2012, it starts on March 20, but soon after midnight and thus almost on the 19th.

With these events and more (see the Astronomy and Calendar pages), 2012 will be brilliant and amazing—all good reasons to gaze up as if there is no tomorrow. □□

Bob Berman is the author of six books, including *The Sun's Heartbeat* (Little, Brown and Company, 2011). He is also the director of astronomy for SLOOH, the global online observatory.

Tidal Glossary

Apogean Tide: A monthly tide of decreased range that occurs when the Moon is at apogee (farthest from Earth).

Diurnal Tide: A tide with one high water and one low water in a tidal day of approximately 24 hours.

Mean Lower Low Water: The arithmetic mean of the lesser of a daily pair of low waters, observed over a specific 19-year cycle called the National Tidal Datum Epoch.

Neap Tide: A tide of decreased range that occurs twice a month, when the Moon is in quadrature (during its first and last quarters, when the Sun and the Moon are at right angles to each other relative to Earth).

Perigean Tide: A monthly tide of increased range that occurs when the Moon is at perigee (closest to Earth).

Semidiurnal Tide: A tide with one high water and one low water every half day. East Coast tides, for example, are semidiurnal, with two highs and two lows during a tidal day of approximately 24 hours.

Spring Tide: A tide of increased range that occurs at times of syzygy each month. Named not for the season of spring but from the German *springen* ("to leap up"), a spring tide also brings a lower low water.

Syzygy: The nearly straight-line configuration that occurs twice a month, when the Sun and the Moon are in conjunction (on the same side of Earth, at the new Moon) and when they are in opposition (on opposite sides of Earth, at the full Moon). In both cases, the gravitational effects of the Sun and the Moon reinforce each other, and tidal range is increased.

Vanishing Tide: A mixed tide of considerable inequality in the two highs and two lows, so that the lower high (or higher low) may appear to vanish. □□

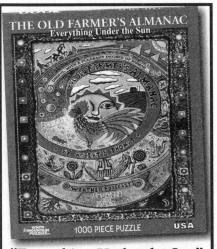

How to Use This Almanac

The Calendar Pages (108–135) are the heart of *The Old Farmer's Almanac*. They present sky sightings and astronomical data for the entire year and are what make this book a true almanac, a "calendar of the heavens." In essence, these pages are unchanged since 1792, when Robert B. Thomas published his first edition. The long columns of numbers and symbols reveal all of nature's precision, rhythm, and glory, providing an astronomical look at the year 2012.

Why We Have Seasons

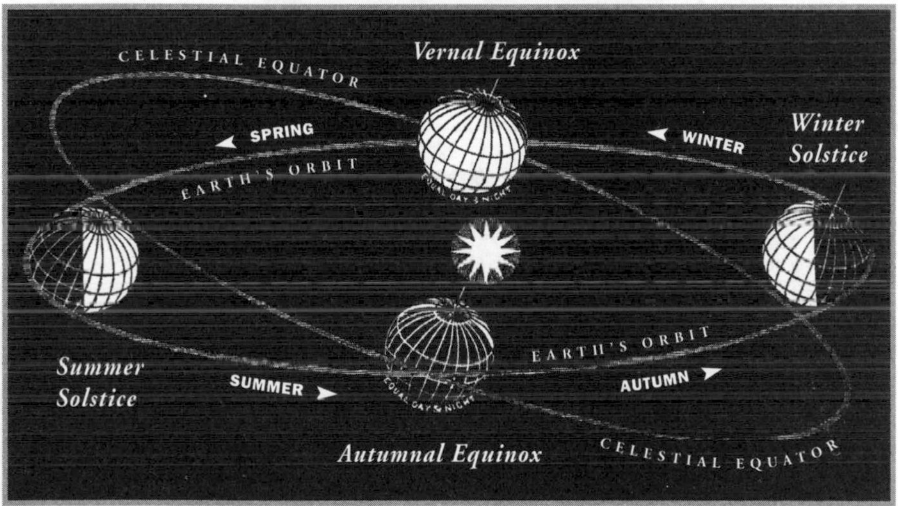

THE SEASONS OF 2012

Spring . . . . March 20, 1:14 A.M. EDT
Summer . . . . June 20, 7:09 P.M. EDT
Autumn . . . . September 22, 10:49 A.M. EDT
Winter . . . . . . December 21, 6:12 A.M. EST

■ The seasons occur because as Earth revolves around the Sun, its axis remains tilted at 23.5 degrees from the perpendicular. This tilt causes different latitudes on Earth to receive varying amounts of sunlight throughout the year.

In the Northern Hemisphere, the summer solstice marks the beginning of summer and occurs when the North Pole is tilted toward the Sun. The winter solstice marks the beginning of winter and occurs when the North Pole is tilted away from the Sun.

The equinoxes occur when the hemispheres equally face the Sun. At this time, the Sun rises due east and sets due west. The vernal equinox marks the beginning of spring; the autumnal equinox marks the beginning of autumn.

In the Southern Hemisphere, the seasons are the reverse of those in the Northern Hemisphere.

(continued)

The Left-Hand Calendar Pages • 108–134

The **Left-Hand Calendar Pages** contain sky highlights, daily Sun and Moon rise and set times, the length of day, high tide times, the Moon's astronomical place and age, and more for Boston. Examples of how to calculate astronomical times for your location follow the sample month.

A SAMPLE MONTH

SKY WATCH ☆ *The box at the top of each Left-Hand Calendar Page describes the best times to view celestial highlights, including conjunctions, meteor showers, and planets. The dates on which select astronomical events occur appear on the Right-Hand Calendar Pages.*

1 2 3 4 5 6 7 8

Purchase these pages with times set to your zip code at MyLocalAlmanac.com.

Day of Year	Day of Month	Day of Week	☼ Rises h. m.	Rise Key	☼ Sets h. m.	Set Key	Length of Day h. m.	Sun Fast m.	Declination of Sun ° '	High Tide Times Boston		☾ Rises h. m.	Rise Key	☾ Sets h. m.	Set Key	☾ Place	☾ Age
1	1	**A**	7:13	E	**4:21**	A	9 08	12	23s.00	4½	**5**	11:13	C	12:00	E	PSC	8
2	2	M.	7:13	E	**4:22**	A	9 09	12	22 55	5½	**6**	11:40	B	12:59	E	PSC	9
3	3	Tu.	7:13	E	**4:23**	A	9 10	12	22 49	6¼	**7**	**12:10**	B	1:58	E	ARI	10

1 To calculate the sunrise/sunset times for your locale: Each sunrise/sunset time is assigned a Key Letter whose value is given in minutes in the **Time Corrections** table on **page 237.** Find your city in the table, or the city nearest you, and add or subtract those minutes to/from Boston's sunrise or sunset time given.

EXAMPLE:

■ To find the time of sunrise in Denver, Colorado, on the first day of the month:

Sunrise, Boston, with Key Letter E (above)	**7:13 A.M. EST**
Value of Key Letter E for Denver (p. 237)	**+ 7 minutes**
Sunrise, Denver	**7:20 A.M. MST**

2 To determine your city's length of day, find the sunrise/sunset Key Letter values for your city on **page 237.** Add or subtract the sunset value to/from Boston's length of day. Then simply *reverse* the sunrise sign (from minus to plus, or plus to minus) and add or subtract this value to/from the result of the first step.

EXAMPLE:

■ To find the length of day in Richmond, Virginia:

Length of day, Boston (above)	**9h. 08m.**
Sunset Key Letter A for Richmond (p. 241)	**+ 41m.**
	9h. 49m.
Reverse sunrise Key Letter E for Richmond (p. 241, +11 to –11)	**– 11m.**
Length of day, Richmond	**9h. 38m.**

3 Use the Sun Fast column to change sundial time to clock time in Boston or another location. A sundial reads natural time, or Sun time, which is neither Standard nor Daylight time. To get Boston clock time, *subtract* the minutes given in the Sun Fast column (except where the number is preceded by an asterisk [*], in which case *add* the minutes) and use Key Letter C in the table on **page 237** to convert the time to your city.

ATTENTION, READERS: *All times given in this edition of the Almanac are for Boston, Massachusetts, and are in Eastern Standard Time (EST), except from 2:00 A.M., March 11, until 2:00 A.M., November 4, when Eastern Daylight Time (EDT) is given. Key Letters (A–E) are provided so that you can calculate times for other localities.*

EXAMPLE:

■ To change sundial time to clock time in Boston, or, for example, in Salem, Oregon:

Sundial reading (Boston or Salem)	**12:00 noon**
Subtract Sun Fast (p. 104)	**– 12 minutes**
Clock time, Boston	**11:48 A.M. EST**
Use Key Letter C for Salem (p. 240)	**+ 27 minutes**
Clock time, Salem	**12:15 P.M. PST**

4 This column gives the degrees and minutes of the Sun from the celestial equator at noon EST or EDT.

5 This column gives the approximate times of high tides in Boston. For example, the first high tide occurs at 4:30 A.M. and the second occurs at 5:00 P.M. the same day. (A dash indicates that high tide occurs on or after midnight and is recorded on the next day.) Figures for calculating high tide times and heights for localities other than Boston are given in the **Tide Corrections** table on **page 235**.

6 To calculate the moonrise/moonset times for localities other than Boston, follow the example in the next column, making a correction for longitude (see table, above right). For the longitude of your city, **see page 237.** (Note: A dash in the moonrise/moonset columns indicates that rise or set times occur on or after midnight and are recorded on the next day.)

Longitude of city	**Correction minutes**
58°–76°	0
77°–89°	+1
90°–102°	+2
103°–115°	+3
116°–127°	+4
128°–141°	+5
142°–155°	+6

EXAMPLE:

■ To determine the time of moonrise in Lansing, Michigan:

Moonrise, Boston, with Key Letter C (p. 104)	**11:13 A.M. EST**
Value of Key Letter C for Lansing (p. 239)	**+ 53 minutes**
Correction for Lansing longitude, 84° 33'	**+ 1 minute**
Moonrise, Lansing	**12:07 P.M. EST**

Use the same procedure to determine the time of moonset.

7 The Moon's Place is its *astronomical* placement in the heavens at midnight. (This should not be confused with the Moon's *astrological* place in the zodiac. All calculations in this Almanac are based on astronomy, not astrology, except for those on **pages 230–232.**)

In addition to the 12 constellations of the zodiac, this column may indicate others: Auriga **(AUR)**, a northern constellation between Perseus and Gemini; Cetus **(CET)**, which lies south of the zodiac, just south of Pisces and Aries; Ophiuchus **(OPH)**, a constellation primarily north of the zodiac but with a small corner between Scorpius and Sagittarius; Orion **(ORI)**, a constellation whose northern limit first reaches the zodiac between Taurus and Gemini; and Sextans **(SEX)**, which lies south of the zodiac except for a corner that just touches it near Leo.

8 The last column gives the Moon's Age, which is the number of days since the previous new Moon. (The average length of the lunar month is 29.53 days.) **(continued)**

The Right-Hand Calendar Pages • 109–135

A SAMPLE MONTH

- Weather prediction rhyme.
- The bold letter is the Dominical Letter (from A to G), a traditional ecclesiastical designation for Sunday determined by the date on which the first Sunday falls. For 2012, a leap year, the Dominical Letter is **A** through February. It then reverts to **G** for the rest of the year.
- Symbols for notable celestial events. (See opposite page for explanations.)
- Sundays and special holy days generally appear in this font.
- Proverbs, poems, and adages generally appear in this font.
- Civil holidays and astronomical events appear in this font.
- Noteworthy historical events, folklore, and legends appear in this font.
- High tide heights, in feet, at Boston.
- Religious feasts generally appear in this font. A^T indicates a major feast that the church has this year temporarily transferred to a date other than its usual one.

Day of Month	Day of Week	Dates, Feasts, Fasts, Aspects, Tide Heights	Weather
1	**A**	New Year's Day • Holy Name • U.S. parcel post service began, 1913 • { 9.1 8.5	*Fields*
2	M.	☾ at apo. • ☌♃☾ • Nor'easter flooded East Coast, 1987 • { 9.0 8.2	*aglitter,*
3	Tu.	*Deep snow in the winter, tall grain in the summer.*	*snowflakes*
4	W.	St. Elizabeth Ann Seton • ⊕ at perihelion • { 9.2 8.1	*flitter,*
5	Th.	Twelfth Night • First divorce granted in American colonies, 1643 • Tides { 9.4 8.2	*neither*
6	Fr.	**Epiphany** • ☾ rides high • ☾ at ☋ • Joan of Arc born, 1412 • { 9.7 8.5	*deep*
7	Sa.	Distaff Day • –40°F, Hawley Lake, Ariz., 1971 • { 10.0 8.8	*nor awfully*
8	**A**	**1st S. af. Ep.** • Andrew Jackson defeated British, Battle of New Orleans, 1815	*bitter.*
9	M.	Plough Monday • **Full Wolf** ○ • 5.7 earthquake, Miramichi, N.B., 1982 • { 10.5 9.3	*Solar*
10	Tu.	Showman "Buffalo Bill" Cody died, 1917 • Tides { 10.7 —	*glare*
11	W.	*Mix work with leisure and you will never go mad.* • { 9.6 10.8	*for*
12	Th.	Declaration of Independence signer John Hancock born, 1737 • Tides { 9.9 10.8	*polar*
13	Fr.	St. Hilary • ☾ on Eq. • ☌☿♇ • ☌♀♆ • Tides { 10.1 10.6	*bears!*
14	Sa.	☌♂☾ • Andean bear Billie Jean gave birth to first of twin cubs, National Zoo, D.C., 2010	*Mind*
15	**A**	**2nd S. af. Ep.** • E. G. Otis received patent for elevator safety brake, 1861	*the*
16	M.	**Martin Luther King Jr.'s Birthday (observed)** • ☌♄☾ • Tides { 10.4 9.5	*rain-snow*
17	Tu.	☾ at perig. • U.S. statesman Benjamin Franklin born, 1706	*line:*
18	W.	*Gorboduc,* first English tragedy, acted before Queen Elizabeth, 1562 • Tides { 10.5 9.0	*It's*
19	Th.	☾ runs low • ☾ at ☊ • FCC OK'd first U.S./Europe space satellite communications link, 1961	*fine!*
20	Fr.	U.S. president Dwight D. Eisenhower lassoed by cowboy at inauguration parade, 1953 • Tides { 10.8 9.3	*A*
21	Sa.	☌♇☾ • Deadly avalanche, Twin Lakes, Colo., 1962 • { 11.0 9.6	*battering,*
22	**A**	**3rd S. af. Ep.** • ☌☿☾ • Tides { 11.1 9.8	*then*
23	M.	**Chinese New Year** • New ● • L. Thompson received world's 1st successful insulin injection, 1922	*just*
24	Tu.	♂ stat. • Former Miss America Pageant host Bob Russell died, 1998 • Tides { 11.0 —	*a*
25	W.	Conversion of Paul • ☌♆☾ • Tides { 10.1 10.8	*smattering.*
26	Th.	Sts. Timothy & Titus • ☾ on Eq. • ☌♀☾ • Tides { 10.0 10.4	*Snow's*

☞ **For explanations of Almanac terms, see the glossaries on pages 94, 102, and 136.**

Predicting Earthquakes

■ Note the dates in the **Right-Hand Calendar Pages** when the Moon rides high or runs low. The date of the high begins the most likely 5-day period of earthquakes in the Northern Hemisphere; the date of the low indicates a similar 5-day period in the Southern Hemisphere. Also noted are the 2 days each month when the Moon is on the celestial equator, indicating the most likely time for earthquakes in either hemisphere.

■ Throughout the **Right-Hand Calendar Pages** are groups of symbols that represent notable celestial events. The symbols and names of the principal planets and aspects are:

☉	**Sun**	♆	**Neptune**
○●☾	**Moon**	♇	**Pluto**
☿	**Mercury**	☌	**Conjunction (on the same celestial longitude)**
♀	**Venus**		
⊕	**Earth**		
♂	**Mars**	☊	**Ascending node**
♃	**Jupiter**	☋	**Descending node**
♄	**Saturn**	☍	**Opposition (180 degrees from Sun)**
⛢	**Uranus**		

E X A M P L E :

☌♃☾ on the 2nd day of the month (see opposite page) means that on that date a conjunction (☌) of Jupiter (♃) and the Moon (☾) occurs: They are aligned along the same celestial longitude and appear to be closest together in the sky.

EARTH AT PERIHELION AND APHELION

■ Perihelion: January 4, 2012. Earth will be 91,402,046 miles from the Sun. Aphelion: July 4, 2012. Earth will be 94,505,932 miles from the Sun.

2012 Calendar Highlights

MOVABLE RELIGIOUS OBSERVANCES

Septuagesima Sunday	**February 5**
Shrove Tuesday	**February 21**
Ash Wednesday	**February 22**
Palm Sunday	**April 1**
Good Friday	**April 6**
First day of Passover	**April 7**
Easter	**April 8**
Orthodox Easter	**April 15**
Rogation Sunday	**May 13**
Ascension Day	**May 17**
Whitsunday–Pentecost	**May 27**
Trinity Sunday	**June 3**
Corpus Christi	**June 10**
First day of Ramadan	**July 20**
Rosh Hashanah	**September 17**
Yom Kippur	**September 26**
First Sunday of Advent	**December 2**
First day of Chanukah	**December 9**

CHRONOLOGICAL CYCLES

Dominical Letter	**A/G**
Epact	**6**
Golden Number (Lunar Cycle)	**18**
Roman Indiction	**5**
Solar Cycle	**5**
Year of Julian Period	**6725**

–Beth Krammes

ERAS

Era	Year	Begins
Byzantine	**7521**	September 14
Jewish (A.M.)*	**5773**	September 17
Chinese (Lunar) [Year of the Dragon]	**4710**	January 23
Roman (A.U.C.)	**2765**	January 14
Nabonassar	**2761**	April 20
Japanese	**2672**	January 1
Grecian (Seleucidae)	**2324**	September 14 (or October 14)
Indian (Saka)	**1934**	March 21
Diocletian	**1729**	September 11
Islamic (Hegira)*	**1434**	November 15

**Year begins at sunset the evening before.*

THE ELEVENTH MONTH • 2011

SKY WATCH ☆ *Venus, at its faintest of the year, slowly emerges from behind the Sun, moving next to and in sync with Mercury from the 1st to the 15th. By midmonth, the duo stands 6 degrees high 35 minutes after sunset. The changing angle of the zodiac to the horizon through the month carries Venus ever higher to meet the crescent Moon in fading twilight 10 degrees up on the 26th. The month's real standout remains Jupiter at brilliant magnitude –2.9, the brightest it ever gets. It's already up in the east at nightfall, then out all night. In most places, nighttime grows by 3 minutes daily at the start of the month but falls to just 1 minute's growth by its end.*

◐	**First Quarter**	2nd day	12th hour	38th minute
○	**Full Moon**	10th day	15th hour	16th minute
◑	**Last Quarter**	18th day	10th hour	9th minute
●	**New Moon**	25th day	1st hour	10th minute

After 2:00 A.M. on November 6, Eastern Standard Time is given.

Purchase these pages with times set to your zip code at MyLocalAlmanac.com.

Day of Year	Day of Month	Day of Week	☼ Rises h. m.	Rise Key	☼ Sets h. m.	Set Key	Length of Day h. m.	Sun Fast m.	Declination of Sun ° '	High Tide Times Boston		☾ Rises h. m.	Rise Key	☾ Sets h. m.	Set Key	☾ Place	☾ Age
305	1	Tu.	7:17	D	**5:38**	B	10 21	32	14 s. 28	4	**4¼**	**1:02**	E	**11:16**	C	SAG	6
306	2	W.	7:18	D	**5:36**	B	10 18	32	14 47	5	**5¼**	**1:35**	E	—	–	CAP	7
307	3	Th.	7:19	D	**5:35**	B	10 16	32	15 06	6	**6¼**	**2:03**	D	12:20	C	AQU	8
308	4	Fr.	7:20	D	**5:34**	B	10 14	32	15 24	7	**7½**	**2:29**	D	1:22	C	AQU	9
309	5	Sa.	7:22	E	**5:33**	B	10 11	32	15 43	8	**8¼**	**2:53**	C	2:23	D	AQU	10
310	6	**B**	6:23	E	**4:31**	B	10 08	32	16 01	7¾	**8¼**	**2:17**	C	2:22	D	PSC	11
311	7	M.	6:24	E	**4:30**	B	10 06	32	16 18	8½	**9**	**2:42**	C	3:21	E	PSC	12
312	8	Tu.	6:25	E	**4:29**	B	10 04	32	16 36	9¼	**9¾**	**3:08**	B	4:20	E	PSC	13
313	9	W.	6:27	E	**4:28**	B	10 01	32	16 53	10	**10½**	**3:38**	B	5:19	E	PSC	14
314	10	Th.	6:28	E	**4:27**	B	9 59	32	17 10	10½	**11**	**4:12**	B	6:18	E	ARI	15
315	11	Fr.	6:29	E	**4:26**	B	9 57	32	17 27	11¼	**11¾**	**4:51**	B	7:17	E	ARI	16
316	12	Sa.	6:30	E	**4:25**	B	9 55	32	17 43	11¾	—	**5:36**	B	8:12	E	TAU	17
317	13	**B**	6:32	E	**4:24**	B	9 52	32	17 59	12¼	**12½**	**6:28**	B	9:04	E	TAU	18
318	14	M.	6:33	E	**4:23**	B	9 50	31	18 15	1	**1**	**7:26**	B	9:51	E	ORI	19
319	15	Tu.	6:34	E	**4:22**	B	9 48	31	18 30	1¾	**1¾**	**8:27**	B	10:33	E	GEM	20
320	16	W.	6:35	E	**4:21**	B	9 46	31	18 45	2½	**2½**	**9:33**	C	11:09	E	GEM	21
321	17	Th.	6:37	E	**4:20**	B	9 43	31	19 00	3¼	**3½**	**10:40**	C	11:42	E	CAN	22
322	18	Fr.	6:38	E	**4:19**	B	9 41	31	19 15	4¼	**4¼**	**11:49**	D	**12:12**	D	LEO	23
323	19	Sa.	6:39	E	**4:19**	B	9 40	30	19 29	5	**5¼**	—	–	**12:41**	D	SEX	24
324	20	**B**	6:40	E	**4:18**	B	9 38	30	19 42	6	**6¼**	12:59	D	**1:10**	C	LEO	25
325	21	M.	6:41	E	**4:17**	B	9 36	30	19 56	7	**7½**	2:12	E	**1:41**	C	VIR	26
326	22	Tu.	6:43	E	**4:17**	B	9 34	30	20 09	7¾	**8¼**	3:27	E	**2:16**	B	VIR	27
327	23	W.	6:44	E	**4:16**	B	9 32	29	20 22	8¾	**9¼**	4:44	E	**2:56**	B	VIR	28
328	24	Th.	6:45	E	**4:15**	A	9 30	29	20 34	9½	**10¼**	6:00	E	**3:43**	B	LIB	29
329	25	Fr.	6:46	E	**4:15**	A	9 29	29	20 46	10½	**11¼**	7:13	E	**4:39**	B	SCO	0
330	26	Sa.	6:47	E	**4:14**	A	9 27	29	20 57	11¼	—	8:17	E	**5:42**	B	OPH	1
331	27	**B**	6:48	E	**4:14**	A	9 26	28	21 08	12	**12¼**	9:11	E	**6:50**	B	SAG	2
332	28	M.	6:50	E	**4:14**	A	9 24	28	21 19	1	**1**	9:56	E	**7:58**	C	SAG	3
333	29	Tu.	6:51	E	**4:13**	A	9 22	27	21 29	1¾	**2**	10:33	E	**9:05**	C	SAG	4
334	30	W.	6:52	E	**4:13**	A	9 21	27	21 s. 39	2¾	**2¾**	11:04	D	**10:10**	C	AQU	5

 To use this page, see p. 104; for Key Letters, see p. 237. ☞ **Bold = P.M.** ☞ Light = A.M.

NOVEMBER HATH 30 DAYS • 2011

Old Frost, the silversmith, has come:
His crisping touch is on the weeds. –Charles Dawson Shanly

Day of Month	Day of Week	Dates, Feasts, Fasts, Aspects, Tide Heights	Weather
1	Tu.	All Saints' • Hurricane battered Union fleet, Cape Hatteras, N.C., 1861	*Remember,*
2	W.	All Souls' • N.Dak. and S.Dak. became 39th and 40th states, 1889 • {9.3 / 9.9	*remember*
3	Th.	*In the eyes of its mother, every turkey is a swan.*	*Gunpowder*
4	Fr.	☌♆☾ • Earthquake rang bells in Notre Dame basilica, Montreal, 1877 • {9.1 / 9.2	*Treason!*
5	Sa.	Sadie Hawkins Day • ☾ on Eq. • Actor Roy Rogers born, 1911 • {9.2 / 9.1	*It's*
6	**B**	**21st S. af. P.** • **Daylight Saving Time ends, 2:00 A.M.** • ☌♅☾	*cool*
7	M.	Magic Johnson announced retirement from basketball, 1991	*for*
8	Tu.	Election Day • ☾ at apo. • Black bears head to winter dens now. • {9.8 / 9.1	*the*
9	W.	☌♃☾ • ♆ stat. • 70°F, Manchester, N.H., 2009	*season.*
10	Th.	**Full Beaver** ○ • National Book Week (U.S.) first observed, 1919 • {10.1 / 9.2	*Snowball*
11	Fr.	St. Martin of Tours • **Veterans Day** • Deadly Armistice Day Storm in central U.S., 1940	*flights*
12	Sa.	Indian Summer • ☾ at ☋ • Lobsters move to offshore waters. • {10.2 / —	*and*
13	**B**	**22nd S. af. P.** • ☾ rides high • Ginger Rogers married Lew Ayres, 1934	*chilly*
14	M.	☿ Gr. Elong. (23° East) • *Ice in November Brings mud in December.* • {8.9 / 10.1	*nights*
15	Tu.	Crab apples are ripe now. • Astronomer Johannes Kepler died, 1630 • {8.8 / 10.0	*give*
16	W.	Radio commentator Mary Margaret McBride born, 1899 • UNESCO established, 1945	*way*
17	Th.	St. Hugh of Lincoln • Turkey plucked in 1 minute 30 seconds, setting world record, 1980	*to*
18	Fr.	Composer Carl Maria von Weber born, 1786 • {9.1 / 9.7	*rising*
19	Sa.	☾ on Eq. • ☌♂☾ • Skunks hibernate now.	*temperature;*
20	**B**	**23rd S. af. P.** • Alcan Highway dedicated, Soldier's Summit, Y.T., 1942	*snow*
21	M.	Verrazano-Narrows Bridge opened, N.Y.C., 1964	*whitens,*
22	Tu.	☌♄☾ • Storm caused deadly mudslide, Prince Rupert, B.C., 1957 • Tides {11.1 / 10.2	*sun*
23	W.	St. Clement • ☾ at perig. • Intercollegiate Football Association formed, 1876	*brightens*
24	Th.	**Thanksgiving Day** • ☿ stat. • Transit of Venus first observed, 1639 • {12.0 / 10.5	*for*
25	Fr.	**Eclipse** ⊙ • **New** ● • ☾ at ☊ • 1st door to Tut's tomb opened, 1922	*Turkey*
26	Sa.	**Islamic New Year** • ☾ runs low • ☌☿☾ • ☌♀☾ • Tides {12.2 / —	*Day,*
27	**B**	**1st S. of Advent** • ☌♇☾ • Tides {10.5 / 11.9	*we're*
28	M.	*Plenty sits still; Hunger is a wanderer.* • Tides {10.3 / 11.5	*sure.*
29	Tu.	Enos became first chimp to orbit Earth, 1961 • {10.0 / 10.9	*Pelting,*
30	W.	St. Andrew • British prime minister Sir Winston Churchill born, 1874	*then melting!*

He who slings mud generally loses ground. –Adlai Stevenson

Farmer's Calendar

■ The psychrometer is a scientific instrument for the exact measurement of relative humidity. It's a clever little rig, invented around 1890 by a German physician and meteorologist, which works because of the different rates at which wet and dry objects cool. Two thermometers are mounted in a tube, protected against outside heat and cold. The bulb of one thermometer is dry; the other, wet. Because the moisture on the wet bulb evaporates and cools the bulb more quickly than the dry bulb cools, a comparison of their readings indicates the water content of the ambient air.

Today's humidity meters rely on electronics to measure the air's moisture. Those who prefer their psychrometry low-tech, however, need not despond, at least not in this house. We measure humidity by a device so simple it has only one moving part—the old plank door leading to the cellar. Each year, on a day in November, this door, which has been stuck tight since late spring, suddenly opens easily. All summer, the damp air has been swelling the door's pine planks, causing it to expand into its frame and jam. Now, with cooler, drier air outdoors and heating indoors, the boards give up their moisture and shrink. In June the door will jam up again, but for now it's back in business and furnishes as good a humidity gauge as we will ever need.

DECEMBER

THE TWELFTH MONTH • 2011

SKY WATCH ☆ *Earth's two nearest neighbors finally show dramatic improvement. In fading evening twilight, Venus stands 10 degrees up on the 1st and incrementally doubles that height by the 31st. It's to the left of the Moon on the 26th, beginning a glorious apparition that will peak in late winter and spring. Mars rises before midnight and gains a half magnitude from 0.7 to a conspicuous 0.2, in Leo. Jupiter fades a bit but still dominates the night on the Aries–Pisces border. The moments just before dawn on the 10th bring a total lunar eclipse visible from everywhere in North America except the East. A nearly full Moon washes out the Geminid meteor shower on the 13th–14th. Winter begins with the solstice at 12:30* A.M. *on the 22nd.*

◐ **First Quarter**	2nd day	4th hour	52nd minute
○ **Full Moon**	10th day	9th hour	36th minute
◑ **Last Quarter**	17th day	19th hour	48th minute
● **New Moon**	24th day	13th hour	6th minute

All times are given in Eastern Standard Time.

Purchase these pages with times set to your zip code at MyLocalAlmanac.com.

Day of Year	Day of Month	Day of Week	☼ Rises h. m.	Rise Key	☼ Sets h. m.	Set Key	Length of Day h. m.	Sun Fast m.	Declination of Sun ° '	High Tide Times Boston		☾ Rises h. m.	Rise Key	☾ Sets h. m.	Set Key	☾ Place	☾ Age
335	1	Th.	6:53	E	**4:12**	A	9 19	27	21 s. 49	3½	**3¾**	11:31	D	**11:13**	D	CAP	6
336	2	Fr.	6:54	E	**4:12**	A	9 18	26	21 58	4½	**4¾**	11:56	D	—	–	AQU	7
337	3	Sa.	6:55	E	**4:12**	A	9 17	26	22 06	5½	**5¾**	**12:20**	C	12:13	D	PSC	8
338	4	**B**	6:56	E	**4:11**	A	9 15	26	22 15	6¼	**6¾**	**12:45**	C	1:12	E	PSC	9
339	5	M.	6:57	E	**4:11**	A	9 14	25	22 22	7	**7½**	**1:11**	C	2:11	E	PSC	10
340	6	Tu.	6:58	E	**4:11**	A	9 13	25	22 30	8	**8½**	**1:39**	B	3:11	E	PSC	11
341	7	W.	6:59	E	**4:11**	A	9 12	24	22 37	8¾	**9¼**	**2:11**	B	4:10	E	ARI	12
342	8	Th.	7:00	E	**4:11**	A	9 11	24	22 43	9¼	**10**	**2:49**	B	5:09	E	ARI	13
343	9	Fr.	7:01	E	**4:11**	A	9 10	23	22 49	10	**10¾**	**3:32**	B	6:06	E	TAU	14
344	10	Sa.	7:02	E	**4:11**	A	9 09	23	22 55	10¾	**11¼**	**4:22**	B	7:00	E	TAU	15
345	11	**B**	7:02	E	**4:11**	A	9 09	23	23 00	11¼	—	**5:19**	B	7:49	E	TAU	16
346	12	M.	7:03	E	**4:11**	A	9 08	22	23 04	12	**12**	**6:20**	B	8:33	E	GEM	17
347	13	Tu.	7:04	E	**4:11**	A	9 07	22	23 09	12¾	**12¾**	**7:25**	C	9:11	E	GEM	18
348	14	W.	7:05	E	**4:12**	A	9 07	21	23 12	1¼	**1½**	**8:32**	C	9:45	E	CAN	19
349	15	Th.	7:06	E	**4:12**	A	9 06	21	23 16	2	**2¼**	**9:40**	D	10:16	D	CAN	20
350	16	Fr.	7:06	E	**4:12**	A	9 06	20	23 19	2¾	**3**	**10:48**	D	10:44	D	LEO	21
351	17	Sa.	7:07	E	**4:13**	A	9 06	20	23 21	3¾	**4**	**11:58**	E	11:13	C	LEO	22
352	18	**B**	7:08	E	**4:14**	A	9 06	19	23 23	4½	**5**	—	–	11:42	C	VIR	23
353	19	M.	7:08	E	**4:14**	A	9 06	19	23 24	5½	**6**	1:10	E	**12:13**	C	VIR	24
354	20	Tu.	7:09	E	**4:14**	A	9 05	18	23 25	6½	**7**	2:23	E	**12:49**	B	VIR	25
355	21	W.	7:09	E	**4:14**	A	9 05	18	23 26	7½	**8**	3:37	E	**1:32**	B	LIB	26
356	22	Th.	7:10	E	**4:15**	A	9 05	17	23 26	8½	**9**	4:50	E	**2:22**	B	LIB	27
357	23	Fr.	7:10	E	**4:16**	A	9 06	17	23 25	9¼	**10**	5:57	E	**3:20**	B	OPH	28
358	24	Sa.	7:11	E	**4:17**	A	9 06	16	23 24	10¼	**11**	6:56	E	**4:26**	B	OPH	0
359	25	**B**	7:11	E	**4:17**	A	9 06	16	23 23	11	**11¾**	7:46	E	**5:35**	B	SAG	1
360	26	M.	7:12	E	**4:18**	A	9 06	15	23 21	**12**	—	8:27	E	**6:44**	C	SAG	2
361	27	Tu.	7:12	E	**4:19**	A	9 07	15	23 19	12½	**12¾**	9:02	E	**7:52**	C	CAP	3
362	28	W.	7:12	E	**4:19**	A	9 07	14	23 16	1¼	**1½**	9:31	D	**8:57**	D	AQU	4
363	29	Th.	7:13	E	**4:20**	A	9 07	14	23 13	2¼	**2¼**	9:58	D	**10:00**	D	AQU	5
364	30	Fr.	7:13	E	**4:21**	A	9 08	13	23 09	3	**3¼**	10:23	C	**11:00**	D	PSC	6
365	31	Sa.	7:13	E	**4:22**	A	9 09	13	23 s. 05	3¾	**4**	10:47	C	—	–	PSC	7

DECEMBER HATH 31 DAYS • 2011

The quiet day in winter beauty closes,
And sunset clouds are tinged with crimson dye. –Sarah Doudney

Day of Month	Day of Week	Dates, Feasts, Fasts, Aspects, Tide Heights	Weather
1	Th.	☌♀♇ • ☌♆☾ • New York's Eric Canal closed due to weather, 1831 • {9.4 / 9.7}	*It's*
2	Fr.	St. Viviana • ☾ on Eq. • Ambrose Small sold Canadian theater chain and disappeared, 1919	*sopping*
3	Sa.	Johann Ludwig Krapf and Johannes Rebmann first Europeans to see Mt. Kenya, 1849 • {9.1 / 8.8}	*for*
4	**B**	**2nd S. of Advent** • ☌♅☾ • ☿ in inf. ☌	*shopping.*
5	M.	☾ at apo. • *When snow falls dry, / It means to lie; / But flakes light and soft / Bring rain oft.* • {9.2 / 8.5}	*Snow*
6	Tu.	St. Nicholas • ☌♃☾ • Wind toppled national Christmas tree, White House, D.C., 1970	*spits*
7	W.	St. Ambrose • **Nat'l Pearl Harbor Remembrance Day** • Tides {9.6 / 8.6}	*give*
8	Th.	First concert by San Francisco Symphony, 1911 • Musician John Lennon died, 1980	*us*
9	Fr.	Frozen-food tycoon Clarence Birdseye born, 1886 • {10.0 / 8.8}	*fits,*
10	Sa.	St. Eulalia • **Full Cold** ○ • **Eclipse** ☾ • ☾ rides high • ☾ at ☋ • ♅ stat.	*then*
11	**B**	**3rd S. of Advent** • Winterberry fruit especially showy now. • {10.3 / —}	*mix*
12	M.	**Our Lady of Guadalupe** • Joseph Hayne Rainey first African-American to serve as a U.S. rep., 1870	*with*
13	Tu.	St. Lucia • ☿ stat. • *The fuel in the lamp consumes itself but lights others.*	*rain—*
14	W.	Ember Day • Prince Albert, Prince Consort of Queen Victoria, died, 1861 • Tides {9.2 / 10.3}	*what a*
15	Th.	Halcyon Days begin. • Fire at the U.S. Patent Office, 1836 • Tides {9.3 / 10.2}	*pain.*
16	Fr.	Ember Day • 8.1 earthquake, northeast Ark., 1811 • {9.5 / 10.0}	*Snowmageddon!*
17	Sa.	Ember Day • ☾ on Eq. • ☌♂☾ • {9.7 / 9.8}	*Skies*
18	**B**	**4th S. of Advent** • Beware the Pogonip. • {10.0 / 9.6}	*are*
19	M.	First conversation between Britain and Canada over CANTAT-1 transatlantic cable, 1961 • {10.3 / 9.4}	*leaden,*
20	Tu.	☌♄☾ • First successful water-powered cotton-spinning mill in U.S., Pawtucket, R.I., 1790	*each*
21	W.	St. Thomas • First day of Chanukah • ☾ at perig. • {11.0 / 9.5}	*road's*
22	Th.	**Winter Solstice** • ☌☿☾ • ☿ gr. elong. (22° west) • Tides {11.3 / 9.7}	*a rink!*
23	Fr.	☾ runs low • ☾ at ☊ • –50°F, Williston, N.Dak., 1983 • {11.6 / 9.9}	*Santa's*
24	Sa.	**New** ● • ☌♇☾ • Jason Varitek named captain of Boston Red Sox, 2004 • {11.7 / 10.1}	*team*
25	**B**	**Christmas** • *Words that come from the heart stay warm three winters long.* • {11.7 / 10.1}	*needs*
26	M.	St. Stephen • **Boxing Day (Canada)** • **First day of Kwanzaa** • ♃ stat.	*skates,*
27	Tu.	St. John • ☌♀☾ • Canadian prime minister Lester Pearson died, 1972 • {10.1 / 11.2}	*we think!*
28	W.	Holy Innocents • ☌♆☾ • U.S. patent #4,000,000 issued, 1976	*We're*
29	Th.	☌♇☉ • Actress Mary Tyler Moore born, 1936 • {9.7 / 10.1}	*overdue*
30	Fr.	☾ on Eq. • *Many drops will fill the pot.* • Tides {9.5 / 9.5}	*for*
31	Sa.	St. Sylvester • ☌♅☾ • 15" snow, Meridian, Miss., 1963	*two-oh-one-two!*

Farmer's Calendar

■ *December 22.* First day of winter. Feels like the hundredth. Snow came early, and now the roads are covered with semi-frozen slush, the Sun is hardly to be seen, and a keen little north wind cuts down out of a sky the color of a prison wall.

Despite the chill, I decide to take the dogs down the road. They need the outing. So do I. The difference is, they don't believe it. They're dachshunds, which is to say, independent thinkers. They're also old. Time was, they couldn't wait for their walk. They surged ahead, quartering avidly back and forth across the road. Today, however, they plod gloomily along, dragging their feet, pulling up lame, feeling sorry for themselves. You can't blame them, they're 15. By one formula, this makes them 90 in human years; by another, 105.

Now, the fact is, I'm no longer young in human years myself, and so, short of our normal halfway point, I stop and prepare to turn back. And here, a miraculous rejuvenation is seen to bless the dogs. Human years, dog years, years in general fall away. They perk right up. Their lameness vanishes. They commence trotting briskly on the return leg of our walk. I follow. Perhaps I, too, feel a certain lightening. For all of us, however we count our years, when they begin to accumulate, the shortest way is the way home.

JANUARY

THE FIRST MONTH • 2012

SKY WATCH ☆ *An eventful sky year begins with brilliant Jupiter high up on the Aries–Pisces border at nightfall. Earth arrives at perihelion on the evening of the 4th. Dazzling Venus opens its amazing year already conspicuously 20 degrees high in the west at nightfall. It sits next to faint-blue Neptune on the 11th–12th. Mars, in Leo and rapidly brightening (it will double in the course of the month), rises just after 10:00 P.M. and is nicely high at midnight. Saturn, in Virgo, rises at 1:30 A.M. The Moon hovers above Jupiter on the 2nd and is then near Saturn on the 16th, to the right of Venus on the 25th, above Venus on the 26th, and to the right of Jupiter on the 29th.*

◐	**First Quarter**	1st day	1st hour	15th minute
○	**Full Moon**	9th day	2nd hour	30th minute
◑	**Last Quarter**	16th day	4th hour	8th minute
●	**New Moon**	23rd day	2nd hour	39th minute
◐	**First Quarter**	30th day	23rd hour	10th minute

All times are given in Eastern Standard Time.

Purchase these pages with times set to your zip code at MyLocalAlmanac.com.

Day of Year	Day of Month	Day of Week	☼ Rises h. m.	Rise Key	☼ Sets h. m.	Set Key	Length of Day h. m.	Sun Fast m.	Declination of Sun ° '	High Tide Times Boston		☾ Rises h. m.	Rise Key	☾ Sets h. m.	Set Key	☾ Place	☾ Age
1	1	**A**	7:13	E	**4:21**	A	9 08	12	23s.00	4½	**5**	11:13	C	12:00	E	PSC	8
2	2	M.	7:13	E	**4:22**	A	9 09	12	22 55	5½	**6**	11:40	B	12:59	E	PSC	9
3	3	Tu.	7:13	E	**4:23**	A	9 10	12	22 49	6¼	**7**	**12:10**	B	1:58	E	ARI	10
4	4	W.	7:13	E	**4:24**	A	9 11	11	22 43	7¼	**7¾**	**12:45**	B	2:57	E	ARI	11
5	5	Th.	7:13	E	**4:25**	A	9 12	11	22 37	8	**8¾**	**1:26**	B	3:55	E	TAU	12
6	6	Fr.	7:13	E	**4:26**	A	9 13	10	22 30	8¾	**9½**	**2:14**	B	4:51	E	TAU	13
7	7	Sa.	7:13	E	**4:27**	A	9 14	10	22 22	9½	**10¼**	**3:08**	B	5:42	E	TAU	14
8	8	**A**	7:13	E	**4:28**	A	9 15	9	22 15	10¼	**11**	**4:09**	B	6:29	E	GEM	15
9	9	M.	7:12	E	**4:29**	A	9 17	9	22 06	11	**11½**	**5:14**	C	7:10	E	GEM	16
10	10	Tu.	7:12	E	**4:30**	A	9 18	8	21 58	11¾	—	**6:21**	C	7:46	E	CAN	17
11	11	W.	7:12	E	**4:31**	A	9 19	8	21 49	12¼	**12¼**	**7:30**	C	8:19	E	CAN	18
12	12	Th.	7:12	E	**4:32**	A	9 20	8	21 39	1	**1**	**8:40**	D	8:49	D	LEO	19
13	13	Fr.	7:11	E	**4:34**	A	9 23	7	21 29	1¾	**2**	**9:50**	E	9:17	D	SEX	20
14	14	Sa.	7:11	E	**4:35**	A	9 24	7	21 19	2½	**2¾**	**11:00**	E	9:46	C	LEO	21
15	15	**A**	7:10	E	**4:36**	A	9 26	7	21 08	3¼	**3¾**	—	–	10:17	C	VIR	22
16	16	M.	7:10	E	**4:37**	A	9 27	6	20 57	4	**4½**	12:12	E	10:50	B	VIR	23
17	17	Tu.	7:09	E	**4:38**	A	9 29	6	20 45	5	**5¾**	1:24	E	11:29	B	VIR	24
18	18	W.	7:09	E	**4:39**	A	9 30	6	20 33	6	**6¾**	2:35	E	**12:15**	B	LIB	25
19	19	Th.	7:08	E	**4:41**	B	9 33	5	20 21	7¼	**7¾**	3:43	E	**1:08**	B	SCO	26
20	20	Fr.	7:08	E	**4:42**	B	9 34	5	20 08	8¼	**9**	4:44	E	**2:09**	B	OPH	27
21	21	Sa.	7:07	E	**4:43**	B	9 36	5	19 55	9¼	**9¾**	5:36	E	**3:15**	B	SAG	28
22	22	**A**	7:06	E	**4:44**	B	9 38	4	19 41	10	**10¾**	6:21	E	**4:23**	C	SAG	29
23	23	M.	7:06	E	**4:46**	B	9 40	4	19 27	11	**11½**	6:58	E	**5:32**	C	CAP	0
24	24	Tu.	7:05	E	**4:47**	B	9 42	4	19 13	11¾	—	7:30	D	**6:38**	C	AQU	1
25	25	W.	7:04	E	**4:48**	B	9 44	4	18 59	12¼	**12½**	7:58	D	**7:43**	D	AQU	2
26	26	Th.	7:03	E	**4:49**	B	9 46	3	18 44	1	**1¼**	8:24	D	**8:45**	D	AQU	3
27	27	Fr.	7:03	E	**4:51**	B	9 48	3	18 28	1¾	**2**	8:50	C	**9:46**	E	PSC	4
28	28	Sa.	7:02	E	**4:52**	B	9 50	3	18 13	2¼	**2¾**	9:15	C	**10:46**	E	PSC	5
29	29	**A**	7:01	E	**4:53**	B	9 52	3	17 57	3	**3½**	9:41	B	**11:46**	E	PSC	6
30	30	M.	7:00	E	**4:55**	B	9 55	3	17 41	3¾	**4¼**	10:10	B	—	–	PSC	7
31	31	Tu.	6:59	E	**4:56**	B	9 57	3	17s.24	4¾	**5¼**	10:43	B	12:44	E	ARI	8

 To use this page, see p. 104; for Key Letters, see p. 237. ☞ **Bold = P.M.** ☞ Light = A.M.

January hath 31 days • 2012

Hark! The Old Year is gone!
And the young New Year is coming! –Bryan Waller Procter

Day of Month	Day of Week	Dates, Feasts, Fasts, Aspects, Tide Heights	Weather
1	**A**	**New Year's Day** • **Holy Name** • U.S. parcel post service begun, 1913 • {9.1 8.5	*Fields*
2	M.	☾ at apo. • ☌♃☾ • Nor'easter flooded East Coast, 1987 • {9.0 8.2	*aglitter,*
3	Tu.	*Deep snow in the winter, tall grain in the summer.*	*snowflakes*
4	W.	**St. Elizabeth Ann Seton** • ⊕ at perihelion • {9.2 8.1	*flitter,*
5	Th.	Twelfth Night • First divorce granted in American colonies, 1643 • Tides {9.4 8.2	*neither*
6	Fr.	**Epiphany** • ☾ rides high • ☾ at ☋ • Joan of Arc born, 1412 • {9.7 8.5	*deep*
7	Sa.	Distaff Day • –40°F, Hawley Lake, Ariz., 1971 • {10.0 8.8	*nor awfully*
8	**A**	**1st S. af. Ep.** • Andrew Jackson defeated British, Battle of New Orleans, 1815	*bitter.*
9	M.	Plough Monday • **Full Wolf** ○ • 5.7 earthquake, Miramichi, N.B., 1982 • {10.5 9.3	*Solar*
10	Tu.	Showman "Buffalo Bill" Cody died, 1917 • Tides {10.7 —	*glare*
11	W.	*Mix work with leisure and you will never go mad.* • {9.6 10.8	*for*
12	Th.	Declaration of Independence signer John Hancock born, 1737 • Tides {9.9 10.8	*polar*
13	Fr.	**St. Hilary** • ☾ on eq. • ☌☿♇ • ☌♀♆ • Tides {10.1 10.6	*bears!*
14	Sa.	☌♂☾ • Andean bear Billie Jean gave birth to first of twin cubs, National Zoo, D.C., 2010	*Mind*
15	**A**	**2nd S. af. Ep.** • E. G. Otis received patent for elevator safety brake, 1861	*the*
16	M.	**Martin Luther King Jr.'s Birthday (observed)** • ☌♄☾ • Tides {10.4 9.5	*rain-snow*
17	Tu.	☾ at perig. • U.S. statesman Benjamin Franklin born, 1706	*line:*
18	W.	*Gorboduc,* first English tragedy, acted before Queen Elizabeth, 1562 • Tides {10.5 9.0	*It's*
19	Th.	☾ runs low • ☾ at ☊ • FCC OK'd first U.S./Europe space satellite communications link, 1961	*fine!*
20	Fr.	U.S. president Dwight D. Eisenhower lassoed by cowboy at inauguration parade, 1953 • Tides {10.8 9.3	*A*
21	Sa.	☌♇☾ • Deadly avalanche, Twin Lakes, Colo., 1962 • {11.0 9.6	*battering,*
22	**A**	**3rd S. af. Ep.** • ☌☿☾ • Tides {11.1 9.8	*then*
23	M.	**Chinese New Year** • **New** ● • L. Thompson received world's 1st successful insulin injection, 1922	*just*
24	Tu.	♂ stat. • Former Miss America Pageant host Bob Russell died, 1998 • Tides {11.0 —	*a*
25	W.	**Conversion of Paul** • ☌♆☾ • Tides {10.1 10.8	*smattering.*
26	Th.	**Sts. Timothy & Titus** • ☾ on eq. • ☌♀☾ • Tides {10.0 10.4	*Snow's*
27	Fr.	☌⛢☾ • Raccoons mate now. • Western Union sent its last telegram, 2006	*abating;*
28	Sa.	**St. Thomas Aquinas** • Pianist Arthur Rubinstein born, 1887 • Tides {9.7 9.4	*it's*
29	**A**	**4th S. af. Ep.** • 21-lb. 8-oz. bowfin caught in Forest Lake, S.C., 1980 • {9.4 8.8	*safe*
30	M.	☾ at apo. • ☌♃☾ • Chess grandmaster Boris Spassky born, 1937 • {9.2 8.4	*for*
31	Tu.	*The man who rolls up his sleeves seldom loses his shirt.*	*skating.*

Farmer's Calendar

■ The mouse darted across the snow, desperately seeking shelter—to no avail. An owl swooped down through the darkness, swiftly snatching its victim with its talons. I didn't see it happen, but yesterday's fresh coating of snow recorded every detail of last night's event. I observed the mouse's tracks that abruptly ended under the imprints of the great bird's body and wings.

Even though I feel peacefully alone snowshoeing silently through the winter woods, the many animal tracks and signs tell me otherwise. Large deer tracks and steaming scat tell me that a huge buck was in this spot minutes before I arrived. Squirrels high in the treetops sit idly chattering as I approach, but their telltale tracks and holes in the snow say that earlier they had been scurrying about retrieving acorns stored in hidden caches.

Wild animals are secretive, and many are nocturnal. This is why the sightings of some creatures, such as bobcats and fishers, are rare. Their tracks, rubs, gnawings, droppings, and other autographs, however, reveal their existence.

My vintage wooden snowshoes with rawhide webbings also leave quite an impression on the snowy forest floor. I wonder if the animals enjoy studying my tracks as much as I enjoy interpreting theirs.

FEBRUARY

THE SECOND MONTH • 2012

SKY WATCH ☆ *Venus floats higher each day as evening twilight ends. Use binoculars to find it to the right of green Uranus on the 9th. (It's a close conjunction.) Jupiter, in Aries, is halfway up the southwestern sky at nightfall and remains visible for a few hours. Mars, brightening explosively, retrogrades through Leo. At midmonth, the Red Planet rises at around 8:00 P.M., while Saturn rises at around 11:00 P.M. Mercury, very low in the evening twilight, is to the left of the crescent Moon on the 22nd. The Moon passes closely above Venus on the 25th and to the right of Jupiter on the 26th. Leap Day, the 29th, shifts the calendar so that 2012's equinoxes and solstices occur earlier than in any year since 1896.*

○	**Full Moon**	7th day	16th hour	54th minute
◑	**Last Quarter**	14th day	12th hour	4th minute
●	**New Moon**	21st day	17th hour	35th minute
◐	**First Quarter**	29th day	20th hour	21st minute

All times are given in Eastern Standard Time.

Purchase these pages with times set to your zip code at MyLocalAlmanac.com.

Day of Year	Day of Month	Day of Week	☼ Rises h. m.	Rise Key	☼ Sets h. m.	Set Key	Length of Day h. m.	Sun Fast m.	Declination of Sun ° '	High Tide Times Boston		☾ Rises h. m.	Rise Key	☾ Sets h. m.	Set Key	☾ Place	☾ Age
32	1	W.	6:58	E	**4:57**	B	9 59	2	17s.07	5½	**6**	11:21	B	1:42	E	ARI	9
33	2	Th.	6:57	E	**4:58**	B	10 01	2	16 50	6½	**7**	**12:05**	B	2:38	E	TAU	10
34	3	Fr.	6:56	E	**5:00**	B	10 04	2	16 32	7¼	**8**	**12:56**	B	3:31	E	TAU	11
35	4	Sa.	6:55	E	**5:01**	B	10 06	2	16 15	8¼	**8¾**	**1:53**	B	4:20	E	ORI	12
36	5	**A**	6:53	D	**5:02**	B	10 09	2	15 57	9	**9¾**	**2:56**	B	5:04	E	GEM	13
37	6	M.	6:52	D	**5:04**	B	10 12	2	15 38	9¾	**10¼**	**4:04**	C	5:43	E	GEM	14
38	7	Tu.	6:51	D	**5:05**	B	10 14	2	15 20	10½	**11**	**5:13**	C	6:18	E	CAN	15
39	8	W.	6:50	D	**5:06**	B	10 16	2	15 01	11¼	**11¾**	**6:24**	D	6:49	D	LEO	16
40	9	Th.	6:49	D	**5:08**	B	10 19	2	14 42	**12**	—	**7:36**	D	7:20	D	SEX	17
41	10	Fr.	6:47	D	**5:09**	B	10 22	2	14 22	12½	**12¾**	**8:49**	E	7:49	C	LEO	18
42	11	Sa.	6:46	D	**5:10**	B	10 24	2	14 03	1¼	**1½**	**10:02**	E	8:20	C	VIR	19
43	12	**A**	6:45	D	**5:12**	B	10 27	2	13 43	2	**2½**	**11:15**	E	8:53	B	VIR	20
44	13	M.	6:44	D	**5:13**	B	10 29	2	13 23	2¾	**3¼**	—	–	9:31	B	VIR	21
45	14	Tu.	6:42	D	**5:14**	B	10 32	2	13 03	3¾	**4¼**	12:26	E	10:14	B	LIB	22
46	15	W.	6:41	D	**5:15**	B	10 34	2	12 42	4¾	**5½**	1:34	E	11:04	B	SCO	23
47	16	Th.	6:39	D	**5:17**	B	10 38	2	12 21	5¾	**6½**	2:36	E	**12:01**	B	OPH	24
48	17	Fr.	6:38	D	**5:18**	B	10 40	2	12 01	7	**7¾**	3:31	E	**1:04**	B	SAG	25
49	18	Sa.	6:37	D	**5:19**	B	10 42	2	11 40	8	**8¾**	4:17	E	**2:10**	C	SAG	26
50	19	**A**	6:35	D	**5:20**	B	10 45	2	11 18	9	**9¾**	4:56	E	**3:17**	C	SAG	27
51	20	M.	6:34	D	**5:22**	B	10 48	2	10 57	10	**10½**	5:30	E	**4:23**	C	AQU	28
52	21	Tu.	6:32	D	**5:23**	B	10 51	2	10 35	10¾	**11¼**	5:59	D	**5:28**	D	CAP	0
53	22	W.	6:31	D	**5:24**	B	10 53	2	10 13	11½	**11¾**	6:26	D	**6:31**	D	AQU	1
54	23	Th.	6:29	D	**5:26**	B	10 57	3	9 51	**12**	—	6:52	C	**7:32**	D	PSC	2
55	24	Fr.	6:28	D	**5:27**	B	10 59	3	9 29	12½	**12¾**	7:17	C	**8:33**	E	PSC	3
56	25	Sa.	6:26	D	**5:28**	B	11 02	3	9 07	1	**1½**	7:43	C	**9:33**	E	PSC	4
57	26	**A**	6:25	D	**5:29**	B	11 04	3	8 45	1¾	**2**	8:12	B	**10:32**	E	PSC	5
58	27	M.	6:23	D	**5:31**	C	11 08	3	8 22	2½	**2¾**	8:43	B	**11:30**	E	ARI	6
59	28	Tu.	6:21	D	**5:32**	C	11 11	3	8 00	3	**3½**	9:18	B	—	–	ARI	7
60	29	W.	6:20	D	**5:33**	C	11 13	4	7 s.37	4	**4½**	9:59	B	12:27	E	TAU	8

 To use this page, see p. 104; for Key Letters, see p. 237. ☞ **Bold = P.M.** ☞ Light = A.M.

FEBRUARY HATH 29 DAYS • 2012

Bright Sirius! that when Orion pales
To dotlings under moonlight still art keen. –George Meredith

Day of Month	Day of Week	Dates, Feasts, Fasts, Aspects, Tide Heights	Weather
1	W.	**St. Brigid** • *Fogs in February mean frosts in May.*	*Groundhogs*
2	Th.	**Candlemas** • Groundhog Day • ☾ AT ☋ • Tides {8.9/7.8}	*need*
3	Fr.	☾ RIDES HIGH • XI Winter Olympics began, Sapporo, Japan, 1972 • Tides {9.1/8.0}	*sunblock.*
4	Sa.	Shays' rebellion failed, Petersham, Mass., 1787 • {9.5/8.4}	*Winter*
5	**A**	**Septuagesima** • 3.7" snow, San Francisco, Calif., 1887 • {9.9/8.8}	*won't*
6	M.	*The calf* [parchment], *the goose* [quill], *the bee* [sealing wax]: *The world is ruled by these three.* • {10.3/9.3}	*unlock*
7	Tu.	**Full Snow** ○ • ☿ IN SUP. ☌ • Writer Charles Dickens born, 1812 • {10.7/9.8}	*for*
8	W.	♄ STAT. • Simon Willard granted patent for the banjo clock, 1802 • Tides {11.0/10.3}	*a*
9	Th.	☾ ON EQ. • Jefferson Davis named president of the Confederate States of America, 1861 • {11.1/—}	*while*
10	Fr.	☌♂☾ • ☌♀⛢ • Ontario's first free public library opened, Guelph, 1883 • {10.7/11.1}	*yet,*
11	Sa.	☾ AT PERIG. • Glowing oval object reported hovering in Milford, Ohio, 1967 • Tides {10.9/10.8}	*I'll*
12	**A**	**Sexagesima** • ☌♄☾ • U.S. president Abe Lincoln born, 1809 • {11.0/10.4}	*bet.*
13	M.	☌☿♆ • The last original *Peanuts* comic strip ran in newspapers, 2000 • {10.9/9.9}	*Love's*
14	Tu.	**Sts. Cyril & Methodius** • **Valentine's Day** • 1-hour tour of White House on TV, 1962	*the*
15	W.	☾ AT ☊ • Susan B. Anthony born, 1820 • Tides {10.5/9.0}	*best*
16	Th.	☾ RUNS LOW • Massive ice storm in Ky., Va., W.Va., N.C., S.C., 1987 • Tides {10.3/8.8}	*remedy*
17	Fr.	☌♇☾ • Winter's back breaks. • *Faults are thick where love is thin.* • {10.2/8.9}	*for*
18	Sa.	First unmanned test flight of space shuttle *Enterprise* mounted on another aircraft, 1977 • {10.3/9.1}	*frozen*
19	**A**	**Quinquagesima** • ☌♆☉ • {10.5/9.5}	*extremities!*
20	M.	**Washington's Birthday (observed)** • Deadly tornado, Shreveport to Abner, La., 1912	*White:*
21	Tu.	**Shrove Tuesday** • **New** ● • ☌♆☾ • Tides {10.6/10.0}	*No*
22	W.	**Ash Wednesday** • ☾ ON EQ. • Explorer Amerigo Vespucci died, 1512	*relief*
23	Th.	☌☿☾ • Federal Radio Commission established, 1927	*in*
24	Fr.	**St. Matthias** • ☌⛢☾ • *Every flow has its ebb.* • {10.1/10.1}	*sight.*
25	Sa.	☌♀☾ • 92°F, San Antonio, Tex., 2008 • Tides {10.0/9.7}	*Drifts*
26	**A**	**1st S. in Lent** • Composer Hagood Hardy born, 1937 • Tides {9.8/9.3}	*too*
27	M.	**Pure Monday** • ☾ AT APO. • ☌♃☾ • Poet Henry Wadsworth Longfellow born, 1807	*steep*
28	Tu.	**St. Romanus** • Baltimore and Ohio railroad incorporated, 1827 • Tides {9.3/8.4}	*to*
29	W.	Ember Day • Leap Day • ☾ AT ☋ • Tides {9.1/8.1}	*leap!*

We can complain because rosebushes have thorns, or rejoice because thornbushes have roses. –Abraham Lincoln

Farmer's Calendar

■ I am passionate about cooking on an outdoor grill: ribs slathered with zesty barbecue sauce; thick, juicy steaks seasoned with spicy rubs; marinated salmon fillets; and, of course, the traditional hot dogs and hamburgers. I even have a basket for grilling vegetables.

As much as I enjoy cooking outside in every season, I am one of those hearty souls who likes winter grilling the best. I love the contrast between the heat of the glowing fire and the crisp winter air, the way the smoke hangs low to the ground, and the lack of mosquitoes. While I'm bundled up and sitting in a lawn chair close to my fire pit grill, my imagination goes to primitive times when using fire was the only way that people cooked. Sometimes a whiff of smoke brings me back to my Scouting days and campfire songs.

Yet, I do have my moments of weakness. Once, in the height of winter, I threw a cookout for a few friends. While they prepared salads and side dishes, I went out to the patio to grill the steaks. The temperature was in the teens and a brisk wind made it feel subzero. The cold and wind cooled the fire and slowed the cooking, but eventually the steaks were done to perfection. As I entered the warm house shivering, holding a platter of sizzling T-bones, I thought to myself: Maybe a few mosquitoes aren't all that bad.

The Third Month • 2012

SKY WATCH ☆ *Mercury is brightly visible low in the west 40 minutes after the sunset in the first week. Mars, out all night, reaches opposition on the 3rd and, at magnitude –1.2, comes closest to Earth on the 5th. At 60 million miles distant, this poor opposition makes Martian details telescopically challenging. Dazzling Venus meets brilliant Jupiter above the sunset point between the 7th and the 18th. Venus's greatest separation from the Sun is on the 27th. The Moon hovers below Saturn and the blue star Spica on the 10th, before sitting spectacularly to the right of Jupiter on the 25th and to the left of Venus on the 26th. The equinox will arrive at 1:14 A.M. on the 20th, marking the earliest start of spring in 116 years.*

○	**Full Moon**	8th day	4th hour	39th minute
◑	**Last Quarter**	14th day	21st hour	25th minute
●	**New Moon**	22nd day	10th hour	37th minute
◐	**First Quarter**	30th day	15th hour	41st minute

After 2:00 A.M. on March 11, Eastern Daylight Time is given.

Day of Year	Day of Month	Day of Week	☼ Rises h. m.	Rise Key	☼ Sets h. m.	Set Key	Length of Day h. m.	Sun Fast m.	Declination of Sun ° '	High Tide Times Boston		☾ Rises h. m.	Rise Key	☾ Sets h. m.	Set Key	☾ Place	☾ Age
61	1	Th.	6:18	D	**5:34**	C	11 16	4	7 s. 14	4¾	**5½**	10:46	B	1:20	E	TAU	9
62	2	Fr.	6:17	D	**5:35**	C	11 18	4	6 51	5¾	**6¼**	11:40	B	2:10	E	TAU	10
63	3	Sa.	6:15	D	**5:37**	C	11 22	4	6 28	6¾	**7¼**	**12:39**	B	2:55	E	GEM	11
64	4	**G**	6:13	D	**5:38**	C	11 25	4	6 05	7½	**8¼**	**1:43**	C	3:36	E	GEM	12
65	5	M.	6:12	D	**5:39**	C	11 27	5	5 42	8½	**9**	**2:51**	C	4:12	E	CAN	13
66	6	Tu.	6:10	C	**5:40**	C	11 30	5	5 18	9¼	**9¾**	**4:01**	D	4:46	E	CAN	14
67	7	W.	6:08	C	**5:41**	C	11 33	5	4 55	10	**10½**	**5:14**	D	5:17	D	LEO	15
68	8	Th.	6:07	C	**5:43**	C	11 36	5	4 32	10¾	**11¼**	**6:28**	E	5:48	D	LEO	16
69	9	Fr.	6:05	C	**5:44**	C	11 39	6	4 08	11¾	—	**7:43**	E	6:19	C	VIR	17
70	10	Sa.	6:03	C	**5:45**	C	11 42	6	3 45	12	**12½**	**8:59**	E	6:53	C	VIR	18
71	11	**G**	7:02	C	**6:46**	C	11 44	6	3 21	12¾	**2¼**	**11:13**	E	8:30	B	VIR	19
72	12	M.	7:00	C	**6:47**	C	11 47	6	2 58	2½	**3¼**	—	–	9:13	B	LIB	20
73	13	Tu.	6:58	C	**6:48**	C	11 50	7	2 34	3½	**4**	12:25	E	10:02	B	SCO	21
74	14	W.	6:57	C	**6:50**	C	11 53	7	2 10	4½	**5**	1:30	E	10:57	B	OPH	22
75	15	Th.	6:55	C	**6:51**	C	11 56	7	1 46	5½	**6¼**	2:27	E	11:59	B	SAG	23
76	16	Fr.	6:53	C	**6:52**	C	11 59	7	1 23	6½	**7¼**	3:16	E	**1:03**	B	SAG	24
77	17	Sa.	6:51	C	**6:53**	C	12 02	8	0 59	7¾	**8½**	3:56	E	**2:09**	C	SAG	25
78	18	**G**	6:50	C	**6:54**	C	12 04	8	0 35	8¾	**9½**	4:31	E	**3:14**	C	CAP	26
79	19	M.	6:48	C	**6:55**	C	12 07	8	0 s. 12	9¾	**10¼**	5:02	D	**4:18**	C	AQU	27
80	20	Tu.	6:46	C	**6:57**	C	12 11	9	0 N. 11	10¾	**11**	5:29	D	**5:21**	D	AQU	28
81	21	W.	6:44	C	**6:58**	C	12 14	9	0 35	11½	**11¾**	5:55	D	**6:22**	D	PSC	29
82	22	Th.	6:43	C	**6:59**	C	12 16	9	0 59	**12**	—	6:20	C	**7:23**	E	PSC	0
83	23	Fr.	6:41	C	**7:00**	C	12 19	9	1 22	12¼	**12¾**	6:46	C	**8:23**	E	PSC	1
84	24	Sa.	6:39	C	**7:01**	C	12 22	10	1 46	1	**1¼**	7:14	C	**9:22**	E	PSC	2
85	25	**G**	6:37	C	**7:02**	C	12 25	10	2 09	1½	**2**	7:44	B	**10:20**	E	ARI	3
86	26	M.	6:36	C	**7:03**	C	12 27	10	2 33	2¼	**2¾**	8:18	B	**11:17**	E	ARI	4
87	27	Tu.	6:34	C	**7:04**	C	12 30	11	2 56	2¾	**3¼**	8:57	B	—	–	TAU	5
88	28	W.	6:32	C	**7:06**	D	12 34	11	3 20	3½	**4**	9:41	B	12:11	E	TAU	6
89	29	Th.	6:31	C	**7:07**	D	12 36	11	3 43	4¼	**5**	10:31	B	1:02	E	TAU	7
90	30	Fr.	6:29	C	**7:08**	D	12 39	12	4 06	5	**5¾**	11:26	B	1:48	E	ORI	8
91	31	Sa.	6:27	C	**7:09**	D	12 42	12	4 N. 30	6	**6¾**	**12:27**	B	2:29	E	GEM	9

 To use this page, see p. 104; for Key Letters, see p. 237. ☞ **Bold = P.M.** ☞ Light = A.M.

March hath 31 days • 2012

The Earth awakes: Already her deep heart
Begins to stir, and send its life abroad. –Thomas Buchanan Read

Day of Month	Day of Week	Dates, Feasts, Fasts, Aspects, Tide Heights	Weather
1	Th.	St. David • ☾ rides high • *Sts. David and Chad, Sow peas good or bad.* • {8.9 / 7.9	*Sunny*
2	Fr.	St. Chad • Ember Day • Microsoft's Bill Gates became honorary knight, 2005 • {8.9 / 7.9	*but*
3	Sa.	Ember Day • ♂ at ☍ • Anne Sullivan began teaching deaf/blind Helen Keller, 1887 • {9.0 / 8.1	*raw—*
4	G	**2nd S. in Lent** • **Sunday of Orthodoxy** • {9.4 / 8.6	*signs*
5	M.	St. Piran • ☿ gr. elong. (18° east) • ♂ at closest approach • Tides {9.8 / 9.2	*of a*
6	Tu.	☌☿♅ • The Alamo fell, 1836 • Writer Louisa May Alcott died, 1888 • {10.3 / 9.8	*thaw?*
7	W.	St. Perpetua • Astronomer Henry Draper born, 1837	*Naw!*
8	Th.	**Full Worm** ○ • ☾ on Eq. • ☌♂☾ • Tides {11.1 / 11.1	*Frost*
9	Fr.	Napoléon Bonaparte married Joséphine de Beauharnais, Paris, 1796 • Tides {11.3 / —	*heaves*
10	Sa.	☾ at perig. • U.S. national paper currency first issued, 1862 • Tides {11.5 / 11.3	*make*
11	G	**3rd S. in Lent** • **Daylight Saving Time begins, 2:00 A.M.** • ☌♄☾ • ☿ stat.	*for*
12	M.	Juliette Low founded Girl Scouts, Ga., 1912 • {11.6 / 10.5	*bumpy*
13	Tu.	☾ at ☊ • 13" snow fell, Birmingham, Ala., 1993	*rides,*
14	W.	☾ runs low • Women granted right to vote in Saskatchewan, 1916 • Tides {10.9 / 9.5	*jumpy*
15	Th.	Beware the ides of March. • ☌☿♅ • ☌♀♃ • ☌♇☾ • {10.5 / 9.1	*insides.*
16	Fr.	Physicist Georg Ohm born, 1789 • Tides {10.1 / 8.9	*Irish*
17	Sa.	St. Patrick • *Lucky men need no counsel.* • Tides {9.9 / 9.0	*eyes*
18	G	**4th S. in Lent** • Sumatran tiger born, Sacramento Zoo, Calif., 2010 • {9.9 / 9.3	*are*
19	M.	St. Joseph • $245,000 stolen from bank in N.Y.C., 1831	*smiling;*
20	Tu.	**Vernal Equinox** • ☌♆☾ • Communications satellite *NATO 1* launched, 1970 • {10.1 / 9.8	*it's*
21	W.	☾ on Eq. • ☿ in inf. ☌ • Debi Thomas won ladies' World Figure Skating Championship, 1986	*damp,*
22	Th.	**New** ● • ☌☿☾ • ☌♅☾ • Tides {10.1 / —	*but*
23	Fr.	SS *Yongala* sank in a cyclone, near Townsville, Australia, 1911 • Tides {10.1 / 10.0	*beguiling.*
24	Sa.	☌♅☉ • Chipmunks emerge from hibernation now. • {10.2 / 9.8	*Temperature's*
25	G	**5th S. in Lent** • ☌♃☾ • Musician Elton John born, 1947	*soaring!*
26	M.	Annunciation[T] • ☾ at apo. • ☌♀☾ • Tides {10.0 / 9.2	*March*
27	Tu.	☾ at ☋ • ♀ gr. elong. (46° east) • 9.2 earthquake, Prince William Sound, Alaska, 1964	*goes*
28	W.	☾ rides high • 22 tornados churned through the Carolinas, 1984 • Tides {9.5 / 8.6	*out*
29	Th.	Sunbeam 1000 HP first car to exceed 200 mph, 1927	*like a*
30	Fr.	Vincent van Gogh's *Sunflowers* painting sold for more than $39 million, 1987 • Tides {9.1 / 8.2	*lion,*
31	Sa.	*Who sows wind will harvest storm.* • Tides {9.1 / 8.3	*roaring.*

Farmer's Calendar

■ From my kitchen window, I watch as three crows peck at the cracked corn that I had scattered underneath my bird feeders. A fourth crow stands high atop a nearby pine, ready to alert the others if danger approaches.

Crows aren't welcome at all feeders. Many folks consider them to be nuisance birds that steal seeds from gardens and ruin crops. While it is true that crows raid a garden on occasion, they also help it by eating insect pests and rodents that damage crops.

Crows are among the most admirable of birds and display many qualities that people would do well to emulate. They live in tight-knit communities and are swift to come to each other's aid when threatened by predators. Adult crows mate for life and are completely devoted to their partner. They take turns at sitting on the nest and bringing food. Young crows stay with their parents for a year or more and help them to gather nesting materials and protect the new brood.

Known to be good judges of character, crows can remember a hazardous location or the face of a dangerous human for up to 2 years. They pass the information to other crows through a series of caws.

I love to watch crows and learn from them. These remarkable creatures will always be welcome at my feeders.

APRIL

THE FOURTH MONTH • 2012

SKY WATCH ☆ *Use binoculars to see dazzling Venus visit the Pleiades star cluster on the 2nd and 3rd. Jupiter is visible in the evening twilight early in the month, then sinks and vanishes into the Sun's glare. Saturn comes closest to Earth on the 15th and is out all night. Its rings have now opened up to our view to create its brightest opposition since 2008—a stunning sight through backyard telescopes. Venus reaches greatest brilliancy (magnitude –4.7) late in the month; it floats spectacularly near the Moon on the 24th. Orange Mars continues retrograding through Leo. It loses half of its light by month's end yet creates a nice color contrast with blue Regulus to its right. The Moon stands below them both on the 30th.*

○	**Full Moon**	6th day	15th hour	19th minute
◑	**Last Quarter**	13th day	6th hour	50th minute
●	**New Moon**	21st day	3rd hour	18th minute
◐	**First Quarter**	29th day	5th hour	57th minute

All times are given in Eastern Daylight Time.

Purchase these pages with times set to your zip code at MyLocalAlmanac.com.

Day of Year	Day of Month	Day of Week	☼ Rises h. m.	Rise Key	☼ Sets h. m.	Set Key	Length of Day h. m.	Sun Fast m.	Declination of Sun ° '	High Tide Times Boston		☾ Rises h. m.	Rise Key	☾ Sets h. m.	Set Key	☾ Place	☾ Age
92	1	**G**	6:25	C	**7:10**	D	12 45	12	4 N. 53	7	**7¾**	**1:31**	C	3:07	E	CAN	10
93	2	M.	6:24	C	**7:11**	D	12 47	12	5 16	8	**8½**	**2:39**	C	3:41	E	CAN	11
94	3	Tu.	6:22	C	**7:12**	D	12 50	13	5 39	8¾	**9½**	**3:48**	D	4:12	D	LEO	12
95	4	W.	6:20	C	**7:14**	D	12 54	13	6 02	9¾	**10¼**	**5:01**	D	4:43	D	SEX	13
96	5	Th.	6:19	C	**7:15**	D	12 56	13	6 24	10½	**11**	**6:16**	E	5:14	C	LEO	14
97	6	Fr.	6:17	C	**7:16**	D	12 59	14	6 47	11½	**11¾**	**7:32**	E	5:47	C	VIR	15
98	7	Sa.	6:15	B	**7:17**	D	13 02	14	7 09	**12¼**	—	**8:50**	E	6:23	B	VIR	16
99	8	**G**	6:13	B	**7:18**	D	13 05	14	7 32	12½	**1¼**	**10:05**	E	7:05	B	LIB	17
100	9	M.	6:12	B	**7:19**	D	13 07	14	7 54	1½	**2**	**11:16**	E	7:53	B	LIB	18
101	10	Tu.	6:10	B	**7:20**	D	13 10	15	8 16	2¼	**3**	—	–	8:48	B	OPH	19
102	11	W.	6:09	B	**7:21**	D	13 12	15	8 38	3¼	**3¾**	12:18	E	9:50	B	OPH	20
103	12	Th.	6:07	B	**7:23**	D	13 16	15	9 00	4¼	**5**	1:12	E	10:55	B	SAG	21
104	13	Fr.	6:05	B	**7:24**	D	13 19	15	9 22	5¼	**6**	1:56	E	**12:02**	C	SAG	22
105	14	Sa.	6:04	B	**7:25**	D	13 21	16	9 43	6¼	**7**	2:33	E	**1:08**	C	CAP	23
106	15	**G**	6:02	B	**7:26**	D	13 24	16	10 05	7½	**8**	3:05	E	**2:12**	C	AQU	24
107	16	M.	6:00	B	**7:27**	D	13 27	16	10 26	8½	**9**	3:33	D	**3:14**	D	AQU	25
108	17	Tu.	5:59	B	**7:28**	D	13 29	16	10 47	9½	**9¾**	3:59	D	**4:15**	D	AQU	26
109	18	W.	5:57	B	**7:29**	D	13 32	17	11 08	10¼	**10½**	4:24	C	**5:16**	E	PSC	27
110	19	Th.	5:56	B	**7:30**	D	13 34	17	11 28	11	**11¼**	4:50	C	**6:15**	E	PSC	28
111	20	Fr.	5:54	B	**7:32**	D	13 38	17	11 49	11¾	**11¾**	5:17	C	**7:14**	E	PSC	29
112	21	Sa.	5:53	B	**7:33**	D	13 40	17	12 09	**12¼**	—	5:46	B	**8:13**	E	ARI	0
113	22	**G**	5:51	B	**7:34**	D	13 43	17	12 29	12½	**1**	6:19	B	**9:10**	E	ARI	1
114	23	M.	5:50	B	**7:35**	D	13 45	18	12 49	1	**1½**	6:56	B	**10:05**	E	ARI	2
115	24	Tu.	5:48	B	**7:36**	D	13 48	18	13 09	1¾	**2¼**	7:38	B	**10:57**	E	TAU	3
116	25	W.	5:47	B	**7:37**	D	13 50	18	13 28	2¼	**3**	8:26	B	**11:44**	E	TAU	4
117	26	Th.	5:45	B	**7:38**	D	13 53	18	13 48	3	**3¾**	9:19	B	—	–	ORI	5
118	27	Fr.	5:44	B	**7:39**	D	13 55	18	14 07	3¾	**4½**	10:17	B	12:27	E	GEM	6
119	28	Sa.	5:42	B	**7:41**	E	13 59	18	14 25	4½	**5¼**	11:18	C	1:05	E	GEM	7
120	29	**G**	5:41	B	**7:42**	E	14 01	18	14 44	5½	**6**	**12:23**	C	1:39	E	CAN	8
121	30	M.	5:40	B	**7:43**	E	14 03	19	15 N. 02	6¼	**7**	**1:29**	C	2:10	D	LEO	9

 To use this page, see p. 104; for Key Letters, see p. 237. ☞ **Bold = P.M.** ☞ Light = A.M.

April hath 30 days • 2012

April cold with dripping rain
Willows and lilacs brings again. –Ralph Waldo Emerson

Day of Month	Day of Week	Dates, Feasts, Fasts, Aspects, Tide Heights	Weather
1	G	**Palm Sunday** • All Fools' • Tides {9.2, 8.6}	*Smart*
2	M.	Wind gusted to at least 199.5 mph, Cannon Mtn., N.H., 1973	*fellas*
3	Tu.	☌♂☾ • ☿ STAT. • Naturalist John Burroughs born, 1837 • {9.9, 9.8}	*carry*
4	W.	☾ ON EQ. • Susanna Medora Salter became first U.S. woman mayor, Argonia, Kans., 1887	*umbrellas.*
5	Th.	**Maundy Thursday** • Physicist J. R. Oppenheimer won Enrico Fermi award, 1963	*This is*
6	Fr.	**Good Friday** • Full Pink ○ • Tides {11.1, 11.7}	*criminal:*
7	Sa.	**First day of Passover** • ☾ AT PERIG. • ☌♄☾	*Sunshine's*
8	G	**Easter** • U.S. president FDR signed "hold-the-line" order to combat inflation, 1943	*minimal.*
9	M.	**Easter Monday** • ☾ AT ☊ • Britain's Prince Charles wed Camilla P. Bowles, 2005	*It's*
10	Tu.	☾ RUNS LOW • ♇ STAT. • Trans-Canada Air Lines created by Parliament, 1937 • {12.0, 10.6}	*moister*
11	W.	*Folly and learning often dwell together.* • Tides {11.6, 10.1}	*in*
12	Th.	☌♇☾ • Texaco filed for Chapter 11, largest bankruptcy to that date, 1987 • {11.0, 9.7}	*the*
13	Fr.	U.S. president Thomas Jefferson born, 1743 • Tornado tore through Iowa City, Iowa, 2006 • {10.5, 9.4}	*cloister;*
14	Sa.	11:40 P.M., RMS *Titanic* struck iceberg during maiden voyage, 1912 • Tides {10.0, 9.2}	*dank*
15	G	**2nd S. of Easter** • **Orthodox Easter** • ♂ STAT. • ♄ AT ☍ • {9.7, 9.3}	*in the*
16	M.	☌♆☾ • Walter Cronkite started as *CBS Evening News* anchorman, 1962 • Tides {9.6, 9.5}	*bank.*
17	Tu.	☾ ON EQ. • 6-lb. 10-oz. goldfish caught in Lake Hodges, Calif., 1996 • Tides {9.6, 9.7}	*Thanks!*
18	W.	☌☿☾ • ☿ GR. ELONG. (27° WEST) • *Cloudy April, dewy May.* • {9.6, 9.9}	*At*
19	Th.	☌⛢☾ • Leslie Irvin made the first free-fall parachute jump, Dayton, Ohio, 1919 • Tides {9.6, 10.1}	*last*
20	Fr.	George Clinton became first U.S. vice president to die in office, 1812 • Tides {9.6, 10.2}	*it's*
21	Sa.	New ● • ☌☿⛢ • 13-yr.-old Morgan Pozgar became U.S. nat'l texting champion, 2007	*spring,*
22	G	**3rd S. of Easter** • ☾ AT APO. • ☌♃☾ • {10.2, 9.5}	*at*
23	M.	**St. George** • ☾ AT ☋ • Hank Aaron hit his first major league home run, 1954	*last*
24	Tu.	☌♀☾ • *Old Farmer's Almanac* founder Robert B. Thomas born, 1766 • Tides {10.1, 9.1}	*it's*
25	W.	**St. Mark** • ☾ RIDES HIGH • "Purple People Bridge" reopened, Cincinnati, 2003 • {10.0, 8.9}	*fine!*
26	Th.	"Mother of the blues" singer Ma Rainey born, 1886 • {9.8, 8.8}	*Fling*
27	Fr.	*The sleepy fox has seldom feathered breakfast.* • {9.6, 8.7}	*your*
28	Sa.	35" snow fell in Bayard, W.Va., 1928 • Tides {9.5, 8.7}	*laundry*
29	G	**4th S. of Easter** • Poplars leaf out about now. • Tides {9.4, 8.9}	*on a*
30	M.	♀ GR. ILLUM. EXT. • U.S. patent #2,000,000 issued, 1935	*line!*

A word before is worth two behind. –English proverb

Farmer's Calendar

■ In late April, the wispy white clouds of shad flowers decorate streambeds and roadsides—a sure sign that winter has passed and spring has truly arrived. Belonging to the genus *Amelanchier,* most shads are native small trees or shrubs that have been used as "indicator plants" for centuries, reminding folks of naturally occurring events, often with more accuracy than a calendar.

The plants were named shad because they bloom when shad (a fish related to the herring) begin to spawn in rivers and estuaries. Another name, serviceberry, may have come about because the plants flower when the ground begins to thaw. In the past, this meant that graves could once again be dug, funeral services could be conducted, and traveling preachers could begin to make their rounds.

Shads have become popular choices for the landscape because of their four-season appeal. The blueberry-like fruit mature in early summer (hence another name: Juneberry) and are excellent for making pies, jellies, and preserves. The rich-green summer foliage turns to autumn tones of apricot yellow, fiery orange, and deep red that rival even maple hues for attention. In winter, the smooth, gray-streaked bark and interesting branching patterns provide a pleasing effect. All in all, shads are beautiful plants by any name.

The Fifth Month • 2012

SKY WATCH ☆ *The Moon, gloriously full, reaches perigee (its closest point to Earth) at midnight on the 5th–6th. Saturn, at bright magnitude 0.4, is out all night above the blue star Spica in Virgo. Venus, now a striking crescent through binoculars, moves rapidly lower toward the twilight glare with each passing day but might be glimpsed to the right of the crescent Moon on the 22nd. Mars, its retrograde finished, pulls away from Regulus and sits above the Moon on the 28th. An annular solar eclipse, visible with eye protection as a partial solar eclipse over most of North America, occurs in the early evening on the 20th (see "The Sky Is Falling!," p. 96).*

○	**Full Moon**	5th day	23rd hour	35th minute
◑	**Last Quarter**	12th day	17th hour	47th minute
●	**New Moon**	20th day	19th hour	47th minute
◐	**First Quarter**	28th day	16th hour	16th minute

All times are given in Eastern Daylight Time.

Purchase these pages with times set to your zip code at MyLocalAlmanac.com.

Day of Year	Day of Month	Day of Week	☼ Rises h. m.	Rise Key	☼ Sets h. m.	Set Key	Length of Day h. m.	Sun Fast m.	Declination of Sun ° '	High Tide Times Boston		☾ Rises h. m.	Rise Key	☾ Sets h. m.	Set Key	☾ Place	☾ Age
122	1	Tu.	5:38	B	**7:44**	E	14 06	19	15 N. 20	7¼	**8**	**2:38**	D	2:40	D	SEX	10
123	2	W.	5:37	B	**7:45**	E	14 08	19	15 38	8¼	**8¾**	**3:49**	E	3:10	D	LEO	11
124	3	Th.	5:36	B	**7:46**	E	14 10	19	15 56	9¼	**9¾**	**5:03**	E	3:41	C	VIR	12
125	4	Fr.	5:34	B	**7:47**	E	14 13	19	16 13	10¼	**10½**	**6:20**	E	4:15	C	VIR	13
126	5	Sa.	5:33	B	**7:48**	E	14 15	19	16 30	11	**11¼**	**7:37**	E	4:54	B	VIR	14
127	6	**G**	5:32	B	**7:49**	E	14 17	19	16 47	**12**	—	**8:52**	E	5:39	B	LIB	15
128	7	M.	5:31	B	**7:50**	E	14 19	19	17 03	12¼	**12¾**	**10:01**	E	6:32	B	SCO	16
129	8	Tu.	5:29	B	**7:52**	E	14 23	19	17 19	1	**1¾**	**11:01**	E	7:33	B	OPH	17
130	9	W.	5:28	B	**7:53**	E	14 25	19	17 35	2	**2¾**	**11:50**	E	8:39	B	SAG	18
131	10	Th.	5:27	B	**7:54**	E	14 27	19	17 51	3	**3½**	—	–	9:48	B	SAG	19
132	11	Fr.	5:26	B	**7:55**	E	14 29	19	18 06	3¾	**4½**	12:31	E	10:57	C	CAP	20
133	12	Sa.	5:25	B	**7:56**	E	14 31	19	18 21	4¾	**5½**	1:06	E	**12:03**	C	AQU	21
134	13	**G**	5:24	B	**7:57**	E	14 33	19	18 36	6	**6½**	1:36	D	**1:07**	D	AQU	22
135	14	M.	5:23	B	**7:58**	E	14 35	19	18 50	7	**7½**	2:03	D	**2:09**	D	AQU	23
136	15	Tu.	5:22	B	**7:59**	E	14 37	19	19 04	8	**8½**	2:28	C	**3:09**	D	PSC	24
137	16	W.	5:21	B	**8:00**	E	14 39	19	19 18	9	**9¼**	2:54	C	**4:09**	E	PSC	25
138	17	Th.	5:20	B	**8:01**	E	14 41	19	19 31	9¾	**10**	3:20	C	**5:08**	E	PSC	26
139	18	Fr.	5:19	B	**8:02**	E	14 43	19	19 44	10½	**10¾**	3:49	B	**6:07**	E	PSC	27
140	19	Sa.	5:18	A	**8:03**	E	14 45	19	19 57	11¼	**11¼**	4:20	B	**7:04**	E	ARI	28
141	20	**G**	5:17	A	**8:04**	E	14 47	19	20 09	**12**	12	4:56	B	**8:00**	E	ARI	0
142	21	M.	5:16	A	**8:05**	E	14 49	19	20 21	**12½**	—	5:37	B	**8:53**	E	TAU	1
143	22	Tu.	5:15	A	**8:06**	E	14 51	19	20 33	12½	**1¼**	6:23	B	**9:42**	E	TAU	2
144	23	W.	5:15	A	**8:07**	E	14 52	19	20 44	1¼	**1¾**	7:15	B	**10:26**	E	TAU	3
145	24	Th.	5:14	A	**8:08**	E	14 54	19	20 55	2	**2½**	8:11	B	**11:05**	E	GEM	4
146	25	Fr.	5:13	A	**8:09**	E	14 56	19	21 06	2½	**3¼**	9:11	B	**11:40**	E	GEM	5
147	26	Sa.	5:13	A	**8:10**	E	14 57	19	21 16	3¼	**4**	10:14	C	—	–	CAN	6
148	27	**G**	5:12	A	**8:10**	E	14 58	18	21 26	4	**4¾**	11:18	C	12:12	E	CAN	7
149	28	M.	5:11	A	**8:11**	E	15 00	18	21 36	5	**5½**	**12:24**	D	12:41	D	LEO	8
150	29	Tu.	5:11	A	**8:12**	E	15 01	18	21 45	5¾	**6½**	**1:32**	D	1:10	D	LEO	9
151	30	W.	5:10	A	**8:13**	E	15 03	18	21 53	6¾	**7¼**	**2:42**	E	1:39	C	VIR	10
152	31	Th.	5:10	A	**8:14**	E	15 04	18	22 N. 02	7¾	**8¼**	**3:55**	E	2:11	C	VIR	11

 To use this page, see p. 104; for Key Letters, see p. 237. ☞ **Bold = P.M.** ☞ Light = A.M.

MAY HATH 31 DAYS • 2012

Among the changing months, May stands confessed
The sweetest, and in fairest colors dressed! –James Thomson

Day of Month	Day of Week	Dates, Feasts, Fasts, Aspects, Tide Heights	Weather
1	Tu.	Sts. Phillip & James • May Day • ☌♂☾	*Deplorable:*
2	W.	St. Athanasius • ☾ on Eq. • Tornado struck Port Royal Island, S.C., 1762	*This*
3	Th.	*Cut thistles in May, / They grow in a day.* • {10.2 / 11.1	*weather's*
4	Fr.	☌♄☾ • Actress Julia Louis-Dreyfus received misspelled Hollywood Walk of Fame star, 2010	*horrible!*
5	Sa.	Cinco de Mayo • Full Flower ○ • ☾ at perig. • {10.9 / 12.1	*Don't*
6	G	5th S. of Easter • "Chunnel" between England and France opened, 1994 • {11.0 / —	*get*
7	M.	☾ at ☊ • Poet Robert Browning born, 1812 • Tides {12.4 / 11.0	*your*
8	Tu.	St. Julian of Norwich • ☾ runs low • Coca-Cola went on sale, 1886 • {12.3 / 10.8	*truck*
9	W.	St. Gregory of Nazianzus • ☌♇☾ • Tides {12.1 / 10.6	*stuck*
10	Th.	Cranberries in bud now. • Patriot Paul Revere died, 1818 • {11.6 / 10.2	*in the*
11	Fr.	First heart-lung transplant took place, Baltimore, Md., 1987 • Three • Tides {11.0 / 9.9	*muck,*
12	Sa.	*Never let your feet run faster than your shoes.* • Chilly	*Buck!*
13	G	Rogation S. • ☌♃☉ • ☌♆☾ • Saints	*Beamish*
14	M.	☾ on Eq. • Copyright registered for J. Phillip Sousa's "Stars and Stripes Forever," 1897 • {9.5 / 9.5	*noon,*
15	Tu.	♀ stat. • 94°F, Theilman, Minn., 2007 • Tides {9.2 / 9.6	*frosty*
16	W.	☌♅☾ • Grackles attacked pedestrians in Houston, Tex., to protect fallen offspring, 2005	*morn:*
17	Th.	Ascension • Fire began that destroyed part of St. Louis, Mo., 1849 • {9.1 / 9.9	*still*
18	Fr.	*A trout in the pot is better than a salmon in the sea.* • {9.1 / 10.0	*too*
19	Sa.	St. Dunstan • ☾ at apo. • 99°F, Central Park, N.Y.C., 1962 • {9.1 / 10.1	*cool*
20	G	1st S. af. Asc. • New ● • Eclipse ☉ • ☌☿☾ • ☌♃☾	*to*
21	M.	Victoria Day (Canada) • ☾ at ☋ • First Canadian aboriginal senator, James Gladstone, born, 1887	*plant*
22	Tu.	☾ rides high • ☌☿♃ • ☌♀☾ • Tides {10.2 / 9.1	*your*
23	W.	Business tycoon John D. Rockefeller died, 1937 • {10.2 / 9.1	*corn.*
24	Th.	Orthodox Ascension • United States and USSR agreed to cooperate in space exploration, 1972 • {10.1 / 9.1	*Pinch*
25	Fr.	St. Bede • First meeting to create U.S. constitution, Philadelphia, 1787 • {10.0 / 9.1	*yourself;*
26	Sa.	*Life is short but a smile takes barely a second.* • {9.9 / 9.1	*rub*
27	G	Whit S. • Pentecost • Shavuot • ☿ in sup. ☌	*your*
28	M.	Memorial Day (observed) • Sierra Club founded, 1892 • {9.7 / 9.5	*eyes.*
29	Tu.	☾ on Eq. • ☌♂☾ • Hailstorm caused $6 million of crop damage, Kans., 1951	*Summer's*
30	W.	Ember Day • Aviator Wilbur Wright died, 1912 • {9.7 / 10.4	*here:*
31	Th.	Visit. of Mary • *May showers bring milk and meal.*	*Surprise!*

Farmer's Calendar

■ I belong to the best "club" in town, and it doesn't require dues. As a matter of fact, its members are paid to participate. The club is the Hancock Fire Department. Although the men and women of small-town fire departments are often referred to as volunteers, in some localities they may be reimbursed for responding to emergency calls and for training. But no one is in it for the money. Firefighting is about dedication, pride, and—most of all—helping people.

Members have a lot of fun going to musters, where local fire departments gather to compete in friendly games of skill. They also enjoy driving the trucks in parades, hosting chicken barbecues, and just joking around at meetings. But when it comes to training and calls, they are all business.

Small-town volunteers have challenges that city firefighters seldom face. When they respond to an accident or structure fire, there is a good chance that they will know the people involved. Giving continued support after the call is another rewarding part of the job.

In the Hancock Fire Department, we now have several capable and dedicated young people. After 36 years of service, I felt comfortable in stepping aside as a volunteer. The chief said that he was sorry to see me go, but that I would always be welcome at the "clubhouse."

THE SIXTH MONTH • 2012

SKY WATCH ☆ *A skimpy partial lunar eclipse, visible from western North America, occurs just before dawn on the 4th. The year's celestial highlight, visible in the afternoon in the United States and Canada, is the transit of Venus across the Sun on the 5th. This rare event will not recur until 2117 (see "The Sky Is Falling!," p. 96). Observing this transit requires eye protection but no other equipment. Meanwhile, Mercury is a low evening star, at its brightest and most easily seen from the 12th to the 20th. Mars crosses into Virgo and hovers above the Moon on the 25th. Saturn, high in the south at nightfall, sits to the left of the Moon on the 27th. The solstice brings summer at 7:09 P.M. on the 20th.*

○	**Full Moon**	4th day	7th hour	12th minute
◑	**Last Quarter**	11th day	6th hour	41st minute
●	**New Moon**	19th day	11th hour	2nd minute
◐	**First Quarter**	26th day	23rd hour	30th minute

All times are given in Eastern Daylight Time.

Purchase these pages with times set to your zip code at MyLocalAlmanac.com.

Day of Year	Day of Month	Day of Week	☼ Rises h. m.	Rise Key	☼ Sets h. m.	Set Key	Length of Day h.	m.	Sun Fast m.	Declination of Sun °	'	High Tide Times Boston		☾ Rises h. m.	Rise Key	☾ Sets h. m.	Set Key	☾ Place	☾ Age
153	1	Fr.	5:09	A	**8:14**	E	15	05	18	22	N. 10	8¾	**9¼**	**5:10**	E	2:46	C	VIR	12
154	2	Sa.	5:09	A	**8:15**	E	15	06	18	22	17	9¾	**10**	**6:25**	E	3:26	B	LIB	13
155	3	**G**	5:08	A	**8:16**	E	15	08	17	22	25	10¾	**11**	**7:37**	E	4:15	B	LIB	14
156	4	M.	5:08	A	**8:17**	E	15	09	17	22	31	11¾	**12**	**8:43**	E	5:12	B	OPH	15
157	5	Tu.	5:08	A	**8:17**	E	15	09	17	22	38	**12½**	—	**9:38**	E	6:16	B	OPH	16
158	6	W.	5:07	A	**8:18**	E	15	11	17	22	44	12¾	**1½**	**10:25**	E	7:26	B	SAG	17
159	7	Th.	5:07	A	**8:19**	E	15	12	17	22	50	1¾	**2½**	**11:03**	E	8:37	C	SAG	18
160	8	Fr.	5:07	A	**8:19**	E	15	12	16	22	55	2½	**3¼**	**11:36**	D	9:47	C	AQU	19
161	9	Sa.	5:07	A	**8:20**	E	15	13	16	23	00	3½	**4¼**	—	–	10:54	C	CAP	20
162	10	**G**	5:06	A	**8:20**	E	15	14	16	23	04	4½	**5**	12:05	D	11:58	D	AQU	21
163	11	M.	5:06	A	**8:21**	E	15	15	16	23	08	5½	**6**	12:32	D	**1:00**	D	PSC	22
164	12	Tu.	5:06	A	**8:21**	E	15	15	16	23	12	6¼	**7**	12:58	C	**2:01**	E	PSC	23
165	13	W.	5:06	A	**8:22**	E	15	16	15	23	15	7¼	**7¾**	1:24	C	**3:00**	E	PSC	24
166	14	Th.	5:06	A	**8:22**	E	15	16	15	23	18	8¼	**8½**	1:51	B	**3:59**	E	PSC	25
167	15	Fr.	5:06	A	**8:23**	E	15	17	15	23	20	9¼	**9¼**	2:22	B	**4:57**	E	ARI	26
168	16	Sa.	5:06	A	**8:23**	E	15	17	15	23	22	10	**10**	2:56	B	**5:54**	E	ARI	27
169	17	**G**	5:06	A	**8:23**	E	15	17	15	23	23	10¾	**10¾**	3:35	B	**6:48**	E	TAU	28
170	18	M.	5:07	A	**8:24**	E	15	17	14	23	25	11½	**11½**	4:20	B	**7:39**	E	TAU	29
171	19	Tu.	5:07	A	**8:24**	E	15	17	14	23	25	**12¼**	—	5:10	B	**8:25**	E	TAU	0
172	20	W.	5:07	A	**8:25**	E	15	18	14	23	26	12¼	**12¾**	6:05	B	**9:06**	E	GEM	1
173	21	Th.	5:07	A	**8:25**	E	15	18	14	23	26	12¾	**1½**	7:05	B	**9:43**	E	GEM	2
174	22	Fr.	5:07	A	**8:25**	E	15	18	14	23	25	1½	**2**	8:07	C	**10:15**	E	CAN	3
175	23	Sa.	5:08	A	**8:25**	E	15	17	13	23	24	2¼	**2¾**	9:11	C	**10:46**	D	CAN	4
176	24	**G**	5:08	A	**8:25**	E	15	17	13	23	23	3	**3½**	10:16	D	**11:14**	D	LEO	5
177	25	M.	5:08	A	**8:25**	E	15	17	13	23	21	3¾	**4¼**	11:22	D	**11:43**	C	SEX	6
178	26	Tu.	5:09	A	**8:25**	E	15	16	13	23	19	4½	**5**	**12:30**	E	—	–	LEO	7
179	27	W.	5:09	A	**8:25**	E	15	16	13	23	16	5½	**6**	**1:40**	E	12:12	C	VIR	8
180	28	Th.	5:09	A	**8:25**	E	15	16	12	23	13	6½	**6¾**	**2:51**	E	12:44	C	VIR	9
181	29	Fr.	5:10	A	**8:25**	E	15	15	12	23	10	7½	**7¾**	**4:04**	E	1:21	B	VIR	10
182	30	Sa.	5:10	A	**8:24**	E	15	14	12	23	N. 06	8½	**8¾**	**5:16**	E	2:04	B	LIB	11

 To use this page, see p. 104; for Key Letters, see p. 237. ☞ **Bold = P.M.** ☞ Light = A.M.

JUNE HATH 30 DAYS • 2012

O wondrous June! Our lives should be like thee
With such calm grace fulfilling destiny. –Susan Louisa Higginson

Day of Month	Day of Week	Dates, Feasts, Fasts, Aspects, Tide Heights	Weather
1	Fr.	Ember Day • ☌☿♀ • ☌♄☾ • *It is better to be born lucky than rich.* • {10.0 11.4	*Much*
2	Sa.	Ember Day • 13-yr.-old Anurag Kashyap spelled "appoggiatura" to win National Scripps Spelling Bee, 2005	*too*
3	G	**Trinity • Orthodox Pentecost** • ☾ at ☊ • ☾ at perig.	*damp*
4	M.	**Full Strawberry** ○ • **Eclipse** ☾ • ☾ runs low • Tides {10.6 12.3	*for*
5	Tu.	**St. Boniface** • ♀ in inf. ☌ • ♀ transit over ☉ • ☌♇☾ • ♆ stat.	*Gramps:*
6	W.	D-Day, 1944 • Henry Seely granted patent for the first electric flatiron, 1882 • Tides {12.2 10.6	*We're*
7	Th.	42-tornado outbreak began in Upper Midwest, 1984	*under*
8	Fr.	Astronaut Bruce McCandless II born, 1937 • {11.5 10.3	*sunlamps!*
9	Sa.	Deanna Brasseur and Jane Foster became Canada's first female CF-18 jet fighter pilots, 1989	*Cooler*
10	G	**Corpus Christi • Orthodox All Saints'** • ☌♆☾ • {10.3 9.9	*and*
11	M.	**St. Barnabas** • ☾ on Eq. • Broad Street Riot, Boston, Mass., 1837 • {9.7 9.7	*wetter,*
12	Tu.	☌♅☾ • *Where there is love, there is no darkness.* • {9.2 9.6	*then*
13	W.	First Hall of Fame Game (Chicago Cubs beat Boston Red Sox, 10–9), Doubleday Field, Cooperstown, N.Y., 1940	*much*
14	Th.	**St. Basil** • Flash flood devastated Heppner, Oreg., 1903 • Tides {8.7 9.6	*better.*
15	Fr.	☾ at apo. • Singer Judy Garland married Vincente Minnelli, 1945 • {8.6 9.7	*Memorize*
16	Sa.	Geneticist Barbara McClintock born, 1902 • Tides {8.6 9.9	*your*
17	G	**3rd S. af. P.** • ☾ at ☋ • ☌♀☾ • ☌♃☾	Alma
18	M.	☾ rides high • United States declared war on Great Britain, 1812 • Tides {8.8 10.2	Mater;
19	Tu.	**New** ● • Law adopted limiting U.S. workers with federal contracts to 8-hour day, 1912	*sing*
20	W.	**Summer Solstice** • Britain's Queen Victoria's 2-day Golden Jubilee celebration began, 1887 • {10.3 9.1	*it*
21	Th.	☌☿☾ • *SpaceShipOne* attained spaceflight, 2004 • {10.3 9.2	*loud!*
22	Fr.	**St. Alban** • Columnist Ann Landers died, 2002 • Tides {10.3 9.3	*It's*
23	Sa.	*When [pigs] lie in the mud, / No fears of a flood.* • {10.3 9.5	*getting*
24	G	**4th S. af. P.** • Midsummer Day • 6.54" rain, Brooklyn, N.Y.C., 1962	*hotter,*
25	M.	**Nativ. John the Baptist**[T] • ☾ on Eq. • Tides {10.1 9.9	*almost*
26	Tu.	☌♂☾ • ♄ stat. • Opening ceremonies for St. Lawrence Seaway, 1959	*frying:*
27	W.	♀ stat. • Balloonists Maxie Anderson and Don Ida died, 1983 • Tides {9.8 10.4	*Send*
28	Th.	**St. Irenaeus** • ☌♄☾ • Philosopher Jean-Jacques Rousseau born, 1712 • {9.6 10.7	*those*
29	Fr.	**Sts. Peter & Paul** • ♇ at ☍ • Tides {9.6 11.0	*mortarboards*
30	Sa.	☿ Gr. Elong. (26° East) • Canada's "loonie" coin in circulation, 1987	*a-flying!*

There is no greater fan of fly-fishing than the worm. –Patrick F. McManus

Farmer's Calendar

■ There was a time when a meticulously maintained lawn was a sign of affluence. If that were still the case, I would be considered impoverished. I love my lawn as it is: a colorful patchwork quilt of sunny yellow dandelions, white and purple violets, and fiery red hawkweed.

While having a "perfect" lawn can be a source of pride, many of us take pleasure in knowing that our weedy lawns are helping the environment. They thrive on neglect, which means little, if any, watering and no fertilizer or chemicals. Weeds invite bees, butterflies, and other pollinating insects, as well as predatory insects that protect plants from insect pests.

Several lawn weeds are edible, if untreated. In fact, settlers grew dandelions, purslane, and other "weedy" plants for food. Over the years, these have crept into lawns, and now *we* can enjoy them. I look forward to a spring salad of dandelion greens from my yard as much as I do the first fresh-picked lettuce from my vegetable plot. As an added bonus, there are enough tiny wild strawberries so that I can usually harvest a cup or two in early June.

A weed can be defined as a plant growing where it isn't wanted. If this is correct, then there is not a single weed in my "imperfect" lawn—and at least I *feel* as though I am a wealthy man.

THE SEVENTH MONTH • 2012

SKY WATCH ☆ *Earth reaches aphelion on the night of the 4th. Mercury is dim, but technically visible, low in the west during the first few days of the month. Mars, at magnitude 1, approaches Saturn, which hovers above Virgo's blue star, Spica. This trio, with similar brightnesses but contrasting colors, stands 20 degrees high in the southwest as twilight fades. The Moon hovers below them on the 24th. Meanwhile, in the predawn east, bright returning Jupiter meets dazzling Venus, now at its greatest morning star brilliancy, during the first half of the month. In one of the year's best conjunctions, the crescent Moon floats between them on the 15th.*

○	**Full Moon**	3rd day	14th hour	52nd minute
◑	**Last Quarter**	10th day	21st hour	48th minute
●	**New Moon**	19th day	0 hour	24th minute
◐	**First Quarter**	26th day	4th hour	56th minute

All times are given in Eastern Daylight Time.

Purchase these pages with times set to your zip code at MyLocalAlmanac.com.

Day of Year	Day of Month	Day of Week	☼ Rises h. m.	Rise Key	☼ Sets h. m.	Set Key	Length of Day h. m.	Sun Fast m.	Declination of Sun ° '	High Tide Times Boston		☾ Rises h. m.	Rise Key	☾ Sets h. m.	Set Key	☾ Place	☾ Age
183	1	**G**	5:11	A	**8:24**	E	15 13	12	23 N. 02	9½	**9¾**	**6:23**	E	2:55	B	SCO	12
184	2	M.	5:11	A	**8:24**	E	15 13	12	22 57	10½	**10¾**	**7:23**	E	3:55	B	OPH	13
185	3	Tu.	5:12	A	**8:24**	E	15 12	11	22 52	11½	**11¾**	**8:14**	E	5:02	B	SAG	14
186	4	W.	5:13	A	**8:24**	E	15 11	11	22 47	**12¼**	—	**8:57**	E	6:13	B	SAG	15
187	5	Th.	5:13	A	**8:23**	E	15 10	11	22 41	12½	**1¼**	**9:33**	E	7:25	C	CAP	16
188	6	Fr.	5:14	A	**8:23**	E	15 09	11	22 35	1½	**2**	**10:05**	D	8:35	C	AQU	17
189	7	Sa.	5:14	A	**8:23**	E	15 09	11	22 28	2¼	**2¾**	**10:33**	D	9:42	D	AQU	18
190	8	**G**	5:15	A	**8:22**	E	15 07	11	22 21	3	**3¾**	**11:00**	C	10:46	D	PSC	19
191	9	M.	5:16	A	**8:22**	E	15 06	10	22 14	4	**4½**	**11:26**	C	11:49	E	PSC	20
192	10	Tu.	5:17	A	**8:21**	E	15 04	10	22 06	4¾	**5¼**	**11:54**	C	**12:50**	E	PSC	21
193	11	W.	5:17	A	**8:21**	E	15 04	10	21 58	5¾	**6¼**	—	–	**1:49**	E	PSC	22
194	12	Th.	5:18	A	**8:20**	E	15 02	10	21 50	6¾	**7**	12:23	B	**2:48**	E	ARI	23
195	13	Fr.	5:19	A	**8:20**	E	15 01	10	21 41	7½	**7¾**	12:56	B	**3:46**	E	ARI	24
196	14	Sa.	5:20	A	**8:19**	E	14 59	10	21 32	8½	**8¾**	1:33	B	**4:41**	E	TAU	25
197	15	**G**	5:21	A	**8:18**	E	14 57	10	21 22	9¼	**9½**	2:15	B	**5:33**	E	TAU	26
198	16	M.	5:21	A	**8:18**	E	14 57	10	21 12	10¼	**10¼**	3:03	B	**6:21**	E	TAU	27
199	17	Tu.	5:22	A	**8:17**	E	14 55	10	21 02	11	**11**	3:57	B	**7:04**	E	ORI	28
200	18	W.	5:23	A	**8:16**	E	14 53	9	20 51	11¾	**11¾**	4:56	B	**7:43**	E	GEM	29
201	19	Th.	5:24	A	**8:16**	E	14 52	9	20 40	12¼	—	5:58	C	**8:18**	E	CAN	0
202	20	Fr.	5:25	A	**8:15**	E	14 50	9	20 29	**12½**	**1**	7:02	C	**8:49**	D	CAN	1
203	21	Sa.	5:26	A	**8:14**	E	14 48	9	20 17	1	**1¾**	8:07	D	**9:19**	D	LEO	2
204	22	**G**	5:27	A	**8:13**	E	14 46	9	20 05	1¾	**2¼**	9:14	D	**9:47**	D	SEX	3
205	23	M.	5:28	A	**8:12**	E	14 44	9	19 52	2½	**3**	10:22	D	**10:17**	C	LEO	4
206	24	Tu.	5:29	B	**8:11**	E	14 42	9	19 40	3¼	**3¾**	11:31	E	**10:48**	C	VIR	5
207	25	W.	5:30	B	**8:10**	E	14 40	9	19 27	4¼	**4¾**	**12:41**	E	**11:22**	B	VIR	6
208	26	Th.	5:31	B	**8:09**	E	14 38	9	19 13	5	**5½**	**1:52**	E	—	–	VIR	7
209	27	Fr.	5:32	B	**8:08**	E	14 36	9	19 00	6	**6½**	**3:02**	E	12:02	B	LIB	8
210	28	Sa.	5:33	B	**8:07**	E	14 34	9	18 46	7¼	**7½**	**4:09**	E	12:48	B	LIB	9
211	29	**G**	5:34	B	**8:06**	E	14 32	9	18 31	8¼	**8½**	**5:11**	E	1:43	B	OPH	10
212	30	M.	5:35	B	**8:05**	E	14 30	9	18 17	9¼	**9½**	**6:04**	E	2:45	B	SAG	11
213	31	Tu.	5:36	B	**8:04**	E	14 28	9	18 N. 02	10¼	**10½**	**6:50**	E	3:53	B	SAG	12

 To use this page, see p. 104; for Key Letters, see p. 237. ☞ **Bold** = P.M. ☞ Light = A.M.

JULY HATH 31 DAYS • 2012

On the warm and perfumed dark
Glows the firefly's tender spark. –Horatio Nelson Powers

Day of Month	Day of Week	Dates, Feasts, Fasts, Aspects, Tide Heights	Weather
1	G	**Canada Day (traditional)** • ☾ RUNS LOW • ☾ AT ☊ • ☾ AT PERIG. • {9.8 11.6	*Lightning*
2	M.	Alligator fell from sky during thunderstorm, Charleston, S.C., 1843 • Tides {10.0 11.9	*flashes*
3	Tu.	Dog Days begin. • **Full Buck** ○ • ☌♇☾ • {10.2 11.9	*south*
4	W.	**Independence Day** • ⊕ AT APHELION • *The ground of liberty is to be gained by inches.*	*and*
5	Th.	William Booth established Christian Mission (now Salvation Army), 1865 • Tides {11.9 10.5	*north,*
6	Fr.	Pianist Vladimir Ashkenazy born, 1937 • {11.6 10.5	*pyrotechnics*
7	Sa.	☌♆☾ • Mother Frances Xavier Cabrini became 1st American saint to be canonized, 1946 • {11.2 10.4	*for*
8	G	**6th S. af. P.** • ☾ ON EQ. • Paris celebrated its 2,000th birthday, 1951	*the*
9	M.	*Grumbling makes the loaf no larger.* • Tides {10.1 9.9	*Fourth!*
10	Tu.	☌♅☾ • Armadillos mate now. • Tides {9.5 9.7	*This*
11	W.	35-lb. chum salmon caught, Edye Pass, B.C., 1995 • {9.0 9.5	*heat*
12	Th.	♀ GR. ILLUM. EXT. • *Queen Elizabeth* first feature length film shown in United States, 1912	*can't*
13	Fr.	☾ AT APO. • ♅ STAT. • Northwest Ordinance adopted by U.S. Congress, 1787 • {8.3 9.4	*be*
14	Sa.	Bastille Day • ☾ AT ☋ • ☌♃☾ • ☿ STAT. • {8.3 9.5	*beat.*
15	G	**7th S. af. P.** • ☾ RIDES HIGH • ☌♀☾ • Tides {8.3 9.7	*Steamy*
16	M.	Cornscateous air is everywhere. • *Apollo 11* launched, Cape Kennedy, Fla., 1969	*but*
17	Tu.	U.S. National Cemetery Act passed, 1862 • {8.7 10.1	*dreamy.*
18	W.	*Forked lightning at night, / The next day clear and bright.*	*Thunder*
19	Th.	**New** ● • Fiberglass sutures first used, by Dr. Roy Scholz, St. Louis, Mo., 1939	*grumbles,*
20	Fr.	**First day of Ramadan** • ☌☿☾ • Martial artist Bruce Lee died, 1973 • {10.5 9.5	*owls*
21	Sa.	Severe flooding occurred in Mercer County, N.J., 1975	*too-hoo,*
22	G	**8th S. af. P.** • ☾ ON EQ. • Black-eyed Susans in bloom now. • {10.6 10.1	*at*
23	M.	**St. Mary Magdalene**[T] • Rain delayed Giants/Mets game 3 hrs. 39 min., 1994 • Tides {10.5 10.3	*our*
24	Tu.	☌♂☾ • Cyclist Lance Armstrong set record by winning his 7th consecutive Tour de France race, 2005	*evening*
25	W.	**St. James** • ☌♄☾ • Adult gypsy moths emerge.	*barbecue.*
26	Th.	**St. Anne** • 96°F, Eastport, Maine, 1963 • {9.7 10.7	*Freedom's*
27	Fr.	*He who does most at once, does least.* • Tides {9.5 10.8	*nice;*
28	Sa.	☾ AT ☊ • ☿ IN INF. ☌ • 1st oil reached Valdez Marine Terminal from Alaskan Pipeline, 1977	*don't*
29	G	**9th S. af. P.** • ☾ RUNS LOW • ☾ AT PERIG. • Tides {9.3 11.1	*forget*
30	M.	☌♇☾ • 107°F, Portland, Oreg., 1965 • Tides {9.5 11.2	*the*
31	Tu.	**St. Ignatius of Loyola** • French became the official language of Quebec, 1974 • {9.8 11.4	*price.*

Farmer's Calendar

■ The Fourth of July is upon us. Tomorrow night, there will be a spectacular display of fireworks set off from across the pond in the center of town. The beach parking lot will be filled with cars, and spectators will line the beach shoulder to shoulder, anticipating the first volley of rockets. The fun starts with a loud "whoosh" of the launch. Then, a colorful display of light disrupts the night sky, followed by the predictable boom and cheers of the crowd.

But I prefer quieter evenings, sitting at home in my lawn chair and watching the silent light show put on by dozens of fireflies in my field. As a boy, I took great joy in seeing how many of these insects I could catch. I would put them into an empty jar, punch breathing holes in the lid, and place the jar on my bedroom bookshelf. Soon after I fell asleep to the hypnotic flashes, my mother would release the fireflies back outside. I didn't mind—catching them was half the fun.

Last Fourth of July, I was invited to watch the fireworks from a friend's home on the side of Mt. Monadnock. They were launched from a town several miles away, so we had the tranquil pleasure of seeing the light show without the accompanying sound. I admit that I did enjoy them, but I think that I paid more attention to the fireflies flashing back in response.

THE EIGHTH MONTH • 2012

SKY WATCH ☆ *Venus reaches its greatest Sun separation on the 15th and rises 4 hours before sunrise. Jupiter gets ever higher before dawn, while Venus, below it, remains seven times brighter. Mercury joins the predawn action from the 7th to the 27th. Excellent conditions prevail for the Perseid meteor shower on the night of the 11th–12th; expect one per minute after midnight. The Moon hovers above Jupiter on the 11th, above Venus on the 13th, and below Venus on the 14th. In the evening sky, Mars, Saturn, and Spica meet from the 6th to the 21st. The crescent Moon joins them, 10 degrees above the western horizon, 45 minutes after sunset on the 21st.*

○	**Full Moon**	1st day	23rd hour	27th minute
◑	**Last Quarter**	9th day	14th hour	55th minute
●	**New Moon**	17th day	11th hour	54th minute
◐	**First Quarter**	24th day	9th hour	54th minute
○	**Full Moon**	31st day	9th hour	58th minute

All times are given in Eastern Daylight Time.

Purchase these pages with times set to your zip code at MyLocalAlmanac.com.

Day of Year	Day of Month	Day of Week	☼ Rises h. m.	Rise Key	☼ Sets h. m.	Set Key	Length of Day h. m.	Sun Fast m.	Declination of Sun ° ′	High Tide Times Boston		☾ Rises h. m.	Rise Key	☾ Sets h. m.	Set Key	☾ Place	☾ Age
214	1	W.	5:37	B	**8:03**	E	14 26	10	17 N.46	11¼	**11½**	**7:29**	E	5:03	C	SAG	13
215	2	Th.	5:38	B	**8:02**	E	14 24	10	17 31	**12**	—	**8:03**	D	6:14	C	AQU	14
216	3	Fr.	5:39	B	**8:00**	E	14 21	10	17 15	12¼	**12¾**	**8:33**	D	7:22	D	CAP	15
217	4	Sa.	5:40	B	**7:59**	E	14 19	10	16 59	1	**1½**	**9:01**	D	8:29	D	AQU	16
218	5	**G**	5:41	B	**7:58**	E	14 17	10	16 43	1¾	**2¼**	**9:28**	C	9:33	D	PSC	17
219	6	M.	5:42	B	**7:57**	E	14 15	10	16 26	2¾	**3**	**9:55**	C	10:36	E	PSC	18
220	7	Tu.	5:43	B	**7:55**	E	14 12	10	16 09	3½	**3¾**	**10:24**	B	11:37	E	PSC	19
221	8	W.	5:44	B	**7:54**	E	14 10	10	15 52	4¼	**4½**	**10:56**	B	**12:36**	E	PSC	20
222	9	Th.	5:45	B	**7:53**	E	14 08	10	15 35	5	**5½**	**11:31**	B	**1:35**	E	ARI	21
223	10	Fr.	5:46	B	**7:51**	E	14 05	11	15 17	6	**6¼**	—	–	**2:31**	E	ARI	22
224	11	Sa.	5:47	B	**7:50**	E	14 03	11	14 59	6¾	**7¼**	12:11	B	**3:24**	E	TAU	23
225	12	**G**	5:48	B	**7:48**	D	14 00	11	14 41	7¾	**8**	12:56	B	**4:14**	E	TAU	24
226	13	M.	5:49	B	**7:47**	D	13 58	11	14 23	8¾	**9**	1:48	B	**4:59**	E	ORI	25
227	14	Tu.	5:50	B	**7:46**	D	13 56	11	14 04	9½	**9¾**	2:44	B	**5:40**	E	GEM	26
228	15	W.	5:51	B	**7:44**	D	13 53	11	13 45	10¼	**10½**	3:45	C	**6:16**	E	GEM	27
229	16	Th.	5:52	B	**7:43**	D	13 51	12	13 26	11	**11¼**	4:48	C	**6:50**	E	CAN	28
230	17	Fr.	5:53	B	**7:41**	D	13 48	12	13 07	11¾	12	5:54	C	**7:21**	D	LEO	0
231	18	Sa.	5:54	B	**7:40**	D	13 46	12	12 48	**12½**	—	7:02	D	**7:50**	D	SEX	1
232	19	**G**	5:56	B	**7:38**	D	13 42	12	12 28	12¾	**1**	8:11	D	**8:20**	C	LEO	2
233	20	M.	5:57	B	**7:37**	D	13 40	13	12 08	1½	**1¾**	9:20	E	**8:51**	C	VIR	3
234	21	Tu.	5:58	B	**7:35**	D	13 37	13	11 48	2¼	**2½**	10:31	E	**9:25**	B	VIR	4
235	22	W.	5:59	B	**7:33**	D	13 34	13	11 28	3	**3½**	11:43	E	**10:03**	B	VIR	5
236	23	Th.	6:00	B	**7:32**	D	13 32	13	11 07	4	**4¼**	**12:53**	E	**10:47**	B	LIB	6
237	24	Fr.	6:01	B	**7:30**	D	13 29	14	10 47	4¾	**5¼**	**2:01**	E	**11:39**	B	LIB	7
238	25	Sa.	6:02	B	**7:29**	D	13 27	14	10 26	5¾	**6¼**	**3:03**	E	—	–	OPH	8
239	26	**G**	6:03	B	**7:27**	D	13 24	14	10 05	7	**7¼**	**3:58**	E	12:37	B	OPH	9
240	27	M.	6:04	B	**7:25**	D	13 21	15	9 44	8	**8¼**	**4:46**	E	1:41	B	SAG	10
241	28	Tu.	6:05	B	**7:24**	D	13 19	15	9 23	9	**9½**	**5:26**	E	2:49	C	SAG	11
242	29	W.	6:06	B	**7:22**	D	13 16	15	9 01	10	**10¼**	**6:01**	E	3:57	C	CAP	12
243	30	Th.	6:07	B	**7:20**	D	13 13	15	8 40	11	**11¼**	**6:32**	D	5:06	C	CAP	13
244	31	Fr.	6:08	B	**7:19**	D	13 11	16	8 N.18	11¾	—	**7:01**	D	6:12	D	AQU	14

 To use this page, see p. 104; for Key Letters, see p. 237. ☞ **Bold = P.M.** ☞ Light = A.M.

AUGUST HATH 31 DAYS • 2012

A sylphid fleet of the thistle's light and feathery seeds,
And August passeth by. –Edith Matilda Thomas

Day of Month	Day of Week	Dates, Feasts, Fasts, Aspects, Tide Heights	Weather
1	W.	Lammas Day • Full Sturgeon ○ • Roman emperor Claudius born, 10 B.C.	*Nightly*
2	Th.	Frontiersman "Wild Bill" Hickok died, 1876 • {10.3 —	*barrages*
3	Fr.	☌♆☾ • *When it rains in August, it rains honey and wine.* • Tides {11.4 10.4	*shake*
4	Sa.	☾ ON EQ. • Thomas Stevens first to bicycle across the United States, 1884 • Tides {11.1 10.5	*our*
5	G	**10th S. af. P.** • Actress Marilyn Monroe died, 1962 • {10.8 10.3	*garages,*
6	M.	**Transfiguration** • ☌♅☾ • *Old habits are iron shirts.*	*producing*
7	Tu.	☿ STAT. • 106°F, Philadelphia, Pa., 1918 • Tides {9.8 9.9	*jolts*
8	W	**St. Dominic** • Gray squirrels have second litters now. • Tides {9.3 9.6	*from*
9	Th.	Fatal missile silo explosion, Searcy, Ark., 1965 • {8.8 9.4	*fiery*
10	Fr.	**St. Lawrence** • ☾ AT ☋ • ☾ AT APO. • Tides {8.4 9.2	*bolts.*
11	Sa.	**St. Clare** • Dog Days end. • ☌♃☾ • Tides {8.2 9.2	*Hit*
12	G	**11th S. af. P.** • ☾ RIDES HIGH • Frisbee designer Ed Headrick died, 2002 • {8.1 9.3	*the*
13	M.	☌♀☾ • Last spike driven for first stage of Esquimalt-Nanaimo Railway, Cliffside, B.C., 1886	*beaches,*
14	Tu.	*Money is like manure: Unless you spread it around, it doesn't do much good.* • Tides {8.5 9.8	*head*
15	W.	**Assumption** • ♀ GR. ELONG. (46° WEST) • Culinary expert Julia Child born, 1912 • {8.8 10.1	*for*
16	Th.	☌☿☾ • ☿ GR. ELONG. (19° WEST) • U.S./Canadian Migratory Bird Treaty signed, 1916 • {9.3 10.4	*the*
17	Fr.	Cat Nights commence. • New ● • ☌♂♄ • {9.7 10.7	*hills,*
18	Sa.	Lucy became first partially paralyzed dog to walk 7.6-mile Auto Road up Mt. Washington, N.H., 2010 • {10.1 —	*seek*
19	G	**12th S. af. P.** • ☾ ON EQ. • Tides {10.8 10.5	*out*
20	M.	Deadly tornado hit Sudbury, Ont., 1970 • Ragweed in bloom. • Tides {10.9 10.8	*roller coaster*
21	Tu.	☌♄☾ • Basketball player Wilt Chamberlain born, 1936 • Tides {10.7 11.0	*thrills.*
22	W.	☌♂☾ • Theodore Roosevelt first U.S. president to ride in an automobile, 1902 • {10.5 11.0	*Rainy*
23	Th.	☾ AT PERIG. • *One generation builds the street on which the next will walk.* • Tides {10.1 11.0	*days,*
24	Fr.	**St. Bartholomew** • ☾ AT ☊ • ♆ AT ☍ • Tides {9.7 10.8	*cool*
25	Sa.	☾ RUNS LOW • Closest approach to Saturn by *Voyager 2*, 1981 • Tides {9.4 10.7	*relief,*
26	G	**13th S. af. P.** • ☌♇☾ • Hummingbirds migrate south. • {9.2 10.6	*remind*
27	M.	Charles Gerard Conn received patent for all-metal clarinet, 1889	*us*
28	Tu.	**St. Augustine of Hippo** • Hurricane struck New England (Julian calendar date), 1675	*summer's*
29	W.	**St. John the Baptist** • The Beatles' last tour concert, San Francisco, 1966 • {9.8 10.9	*all*
30	Th.	First night launch of a space shuttle *(Challenger)*, Kennedy Space Center, Fla., 1983 • {10.1 10.9	*too*
31	Fr.	**Full Red** ○ • ☌♆☾ • *An enemy will agree, but a friend will argue.* • {10.3 —	*brief.*

Farmer's Calendar

■ Old Home Day in my small New Hampshire town is always celebrated on the third Saturday in August, with a parade, games, and chicken barbecue on the common. For many, this marks the end of summer. In a couple of weeks, the kids will be back in school. Several vacationers have already put their summer homes to bed, and the campground is thinning out.

Even though August has some of the hottest days of the summer, the nights are often chilly here. The days have also become cruelly shorter. In response, my summer squashes have stopped producing and their vines are withering. Already, a number of birds have started their journeys south and a few maples in the swamps are showing a hint of color—clues that autumn isn't far away. With the shorter days comes an urgency to complete the tasks so easily put off in June and July. Painting the barn must be postponed in favor of filling the woodshed.

But it is still summer after all, and we shouldn't let the last precious days slip away. August offers a plethora of fun activities: farmers' markets, county fairs, town celebrations, and firemen's musters. These are part of the season's last hurrah, a time to be spent with family and friends before the busy autumn begins. Old Home Day has come—a reminder that summer isn't over yet.

SEPTEMBER

The Ninth Month • 2012

SKY WATCH ☆ *Jupiter brightens by 50 percent and rises at around midnight this month. The Giant World hovers near the Moon on the 7th. Venus continues to rise 4 hours before sunrise, becoming nicely high by dawn, but less bright. It stands to the left of the Moon on the 12th. Mars and Saturn grow dimmer and lower, although the Red Planet can be readily found near the crescent Moon on the 19th. Uranus reaches its year's closest point to Earth on the 28th and is at opposition the next night (binoculars are required to see it). The Green World passes the month in the constellation Cetus, the whale. The earliest autumn since 1896 arrives at 10:49* A.M. *on the 22nd.*

◑	**Last Quarter**	8th day	9th hour	15th minute
●	**New Moon**	15th day	22nd hour	11th minute
◐	**First Quarter**	22nd day	15th hour	41st minute
○	**Full Moon**	29th day	23rd hour	19th minute

All times are given in Eastern Daylight Time.

Purchase these pages with times set to your zip code at MyLocalAlmanac.com.

Day of Year	Day of Month	Day of Week	☼ Rises h. m.	Rise Key	☼ Sets h. m.	Set Key	Length of Day h. m.	Sun Fast m.	Declination of Sun ° ′	High Tide Times Boston		☾ Rises h. m.	Rise Key	☾ Sets h. m.	Set Key	☾ Place	☾ Age
245	1	Sa.	6:09	B	**7:17**	D	13 08	16	7 N. 56	12	**12½**	**7:29**	C	7:17	D	PSC	15
246	2	**G**	6:10	B	**7:15**	D	13 05	16	7 35	12¾	**1**	**7:56**	C	8:21	E	PSC	16
247	3	M.	6:11	B	**7:14**	D	13 03	17	7 13	1½	**1¾**	**8:25**	B	9:23	E	PSC	17
248	4	Tu.	6:12	C	**7:12**	D	13 00	17	6 50	2¼	**2½**	**8:56**	B	10:23	E	PSC	18
249	5	W.	6:13	C	**7:10**	D	12 57	17	6 28	3	**3¼**	**9:30**	B	11:22	E	ARI	19
250	6	Th.	6:15	C	**7:08**	D	12 53	18	6 06	3¾	**4**	**10:08**	B	**12:20**	E	ARI	20
251	7	Fr.	6:16	C	**7:07**	D	12 51	18	5 43	4½	**4¾**	**10:51**	B	**1:14**	E	TAU	21
252	8	Sa.	6:17	C	**7:05**	D	12 48	18	5 21	5¼	**5½**	**11:39**	B	**2:05**	E	TAU	22
253	9	**G**	6:18	C	**7:03**	D	12 45	19	4 58	6¼	**6½**	—	–	**2:51**	E	TAU	23
254	10	M.	6:19	C	**7:01**	D	12 42	19	4 35	7¼	**7½**	12:32	B	**3:34**	E	GEM	24
255	11	Tu.	6:20	C	**7:00**	D	12 40	19	4 12	8	**8¼**	1:30	B	**4:12**	E	GEM	25
256	12	W.	6:21	C	**6:58**	D	12 37	20	3 49	9	**9¼**	2:32	C	**4:46**	E	CAN	26
257	13	Th.	6:22	C	**6:56**	C	12 34	20	3 26	9¾	**10**	3:37	C	**5:19**	D	CAN	27
258	14	Fr.	6:23	C	**6:54**	C	12 31	20	3 03	10½	**10¾**	4:44	D	**5:49**	D	LEO	28
259	15	Sa.	6:24	C	**6:53**	C	12 29	21	2 40	11¼	**11½**	5:53	D	**6:20**	D	SEX	0
260	16	**G**	6:25	C	**6:51**	C	12 26	21	2 17	**12**	—	7:03	E	**6:51**	C	VIR	1
261	17	M.	6:26	C	**6:49**	C	12 23	22	1 54	12¼	**12½**	8:16	E	**7:25**	C	VIR	2
262	18	Tu.	6:27	C	**6:47**	C	12 20	22	1 31	1	**1¼**	9:29	E	**8:03**	B	VIR	3
263	19	W.	6:28	C	**6:45**	C	12 17	22	1 07	1¾	**2¼**	10:42	E	**8:46**	B	LIB	4
264	20	Th.	6:29	C	**6:44**	C	12 15	23	0 44	2¾	**3**	11:52	E	**9:36**	B	LIB	5
265	21	Fr.	6:30	C	**6:42**	C	12 12	23	0 N. 21	3½	**4**	**12:56**	E	**10:33**	B	OPH	6
266	22	Sa.	6:31	C	**6:40**	C	12 09	23	0 S. 02	4½	**5**	**1:54**	E	**11:35**	B	OPH	7
267	23	**G**	6:33	C	**6:38**	C	12 05	24	0 25	5¾	**6**	**2:43**	E	—	–	SAG	8
268	24	M.	6:34	C	**6:37**	C	12 03	24	0 48	6¾	**7**	**3:26**	E	12:41	C	SAG	9
269	25	Tu.	6:35	C	**6:35**	C	12 00	24	1 12	7¾	**8¼**	**4:02**	E	1:48	C	CAP	10
270	26	W.	6:36	C	**6:33**	C	11 57	25	1 35	8¾	**9¼**	**4:34**	D	2:55	C	AQU	11
271	27	Th.	6:37	C	**6:31**	C	11 54	25	1 58	9¾	**10¼**	**5:03**	D	4:01	D	AQU	12
272	28	Fr.	6:38	C	**6:30**	C	11 52	25	2 22	10½	**11**	**5:31**	C	5:05	D	PSC	13
273	29	Sa.	6:39	C	**6:28**	C	11 49	26	2 45	11¼	**11¾**	**5:58**	C	6:08	D	PSC	14
274	30	**G**	6:40	C	**6:26**	C	11 46	26	3 S. 08	**12**	—	**6:26**	C	7:10	E	PSC	15

 To use this page, see p. 104; for Key Letters, see p. 237. ☞ **Bold** = P.M. ☞ Light = A.M.

SEPTEMBER HATH 30 DAYS • 2012

Over! The sweet summer closes,
The reign of the roses is done. –Alfred, Lord Tennyson

Day of Month	Day of Week	Dates, Feasts, Fasts, Aspects, Tide Heights	Weather
1	Sa.	☾ ON EQ. • Alberta became a province of Canada, 1905	*Thunder*
2	G	14th S. af. P. • ☌♅☾ • Businessman Peter Ueberroth born, 1937	*is*
3	M.	Labor Day • Poet e. e. cummings died, 1962 • Tides {10.3 10.3	*tolling,*
4	Tu.	*When the stars begin to huddle, The earth will soon become a puddle.* • Tides {9.9 10.1	*buses*
5	W.	After 30 years, ABC canceled TV show *American Bandstand,* 1987 • Tides {9.5 9.9	*are*
6	Th.	☾ AT ☋ • *Hardy Boys* writer Leslie McFarlane died, 1977 • Tides {9.1 9.6	*rolling,*
7	Fr.	☾ AT APO. • First international lifeboat race took place, N.Y.C., 1927 • Tides {8.7 9.3	*sunshine*
8	Sa.	☾ RIDES HIGH • ☌♃☾ • Cranberry bog harvest begins, Cape Cod, Mass. • {8.3 9.1	*spilling*
9	G	15th S. af. P. • Arthur Ashe won U.S. Open tennis title, 1968 • {8.1 9.1	*on*
10	M.	☿ IN SUP. ☌ • Hurricane Dora made landfall, St. Augustine, Fla., 1964 • {8.1 9.2	*scholars*
11	Tu.	**Patriot Day** • Ford introduced the Pinto, 1970 • Tides {8.3 9.4	*unwilling.*
12	W.	☌♀☾ • *Luna 2* spacecraft launched, 1959 • {8.7 9.7	*Lads*
13	Th.	Astronomer Horace Babcock born, 1912 • {9.2 10.1	*and*
14	Fr.	**Holy Cross** • Typewriter ribbon patented, 1886 • {9.8 10.5	*lasses*
15	Sa.	**New** ● • ☾ ON EQ. • *One hour's sleep before midnight is worth two after.* • {10.3 10.8	*wear*
16	G	16th S. af. P. • ☌☿☾ • Physicist Gabriel Daniel Fahrenheit died, 1736	*sweaters*
17	M.	**Rosh Hashanah** • ♇ STAT. • U.S. Constitution signed, 1787	*to*
18	Tu.	☾ AT PERIG. • ☌♄☾ • Columbus landed in what is now Costa Rica, 1502 • {11.0 11.5	*classes.*
19	W.	Ember Day • ☌♂☾ • Betty and Barney Hill allegedly abducted by aliens, N.H., 1961	*Afternoons*
20	Th.	**St. Eustace** • ☾ AT ☊ • Giant anteater Harley born, Caldwell Zoo, Tex., 2010	*burning,*
21	Fr.	**St. Matthew** • Ember Day • ☾ RUNS LOW • {10.1 11.2	*leaves*
22	Sa.	Ember Day • Harvest Home • **Autumnal Equinox** • Tides {9.7 10.8	*turning.*
23	G	17th S. af. P. • ☌♇☾ • Manon Rhéaume first woman player in an NHL game, 1992	*Showers:*
24	M.	*An inch of gold will not buy an inch of time.* • Tides {9.3 10.3	*The*
25	Tu.	Early snow flurries, Fort Wayne, Ind., 1942 • {9.4 10.3	*night's*
26	W.	**Yom Kippur** • Parthenon partially destroyed by Venetians, Athens, Greece, 1687 • {9.6 10.3	*12*
27	Th.	**St. Vincent de Paul** • ☌♆☾ • Woodchucks hibernate now. • {9.9 10.3	*hours!*
28	Fr.	☾ ON EQ. • Grand jury indicted eight White Sox players for fixing 1919 World Series, Chicago, 1920 • {10.2 10.3	*No*
29	Sa.	**St. Michael** • **Full Harvest** ○ • ♅ AT ☍ • Tides {10.4 10.3	*more*
30	G	18th S. af. P. • ☌♅☾ • *Anger has no eyes.*	*flowers.*

A good teacher is better than a barrelful of books. –Chinese proverb

Farmer's Calendar

■ My grandfather took pride in his long, straight rows of firewood, which evoked compliments from passersby. Grampy knew that the purpose of a properly built woodpile, however aesthetically pleasing, was to dry or "season" the wood. Leaving wood in a heap doesn't allow for good air circulation, and it absorbs moisture from the ground. When stacked in a single row up off the ground, each log is exposed to the sun and wind and will dry quickly.

I remember as a boy watching him expertly stack his woodpile from beginning to end. He would start by placing two long wooden poles about 20 inches apart on level ground. Then he would run his first course of logs across the poles and check it for straightness. Each piece had been cut exactly 24 inches long and split to a uniform size. Next, he boxed the ends of the pile by crisscrossing the wood in alternating layers to form two 4-foot-high towers. The rest of the wood was stacked tightly between the stable ends, but leaving enough space between each piece for air circulation.

I keep most of my firewood stacked haphazardly in my woodshed. But, once in a while, I have extra that I stack neatly outside where it can be seen. So far, no one has complimented me on my wood stacks, but I can't help thinking that my grandfather would be proud.

THE TENTH MONTH • 2012

SKY WATCH ☆ *Jupiter, in Taurus since its late June reappearance, steadily brightens as it approaches Earth. The Giant World rises by 9:30 P.M. at midmonth and dominates the sky thereafter. Fading Venus now rises 3 hours before sunrise. Mars reaches its dimmest magnitude and smallest size and hangs low in the southwest at nightfall, attracting little attention. Saturn goes behind the Sun in a conjunction on the 25th. Theoretically, Mercury is an evening star all month; in reality, it's too low to be seen from anywhere except the tropics or Southern Hemisphere. The crescent Moon hovers to the right of Venus on the 12th. Then, in its spooky, football-shape gibbous phase, it floats above Jupiter on Halloween.*

◑	**Last Quarter**	8th day	3rd hour	33rd minute
●	**New Moon**	15th day	8th hour	3rd minute
◐	**First Quarter**	21st day	23rd hour	32nd minute
○	**Full Moon**	29th day	15th hour	49th minute

All times are given in Eastern Daylight Time.

Purchase these pages with times set to your zip code at MyLocalAlmanac.com.

Day of Year	Day of Month	Day of Week	☼ Rises h. m.	Rise Key	☼ Sets h. m.	Set Key	Length of Day h.	m.	Sun Fast m.	Declination of Sun °	'	High Tide Times Boston		☾ Rises h. m.	Rise Key	☾ Sets h. m.	Set Key	☾ Place	☾ Age
275	1	M.	6:41	C	**6:24**	C	11	43	26	3 s.	32	12½	**12½**	**6:56**	B	8:11	E	PSC	16
276	2	Tu.	6:42	C	**6:23**	C	11	41	27	3	55	1	**1¼**	**7:29**	B	9:11	E	ARI	17
277	3	W.	6:43	C	**6:21**	C	11	38	27	4	18	1¾	**2**	**8:06**	B	10:09	E	ARI	18
278	4	Th.	6:45	D	**6:19**	C	11	34	27	4	41	2½	**2½**	**8:47**	B	11:05	E	TAU	19
279	5	Fr.	6:46	D	**6:18**	C	11	32	28	5	04	3	**3¼**	**9:33**	B	11:57	E	TAU	20
280	6	Sa.	6:47	D	**6:16**	C	11	29	28	5	27	4	**4**	**10:23**	B	**12:45**	E	TAU	21
281	7	**G**	6:48	D	**6:14**	C	11	26	28	5	50	4¾	**5**	**11:18**	B	**1:28**	E	ORI	22
282	8	M.	6:49	D	**6:12**	C	11	23	28	6	13	5½	**5¾**	—	–	**2:07**	E	GEM	23
283	9	Tu.	6:50	D	**6:11**	C	11	21	29	6	36	6½	**6¾**	12:17	C	**2:42**	E	GEM	24
284	10	W.	6:51	D	**6:09**	C	11	18	29	6	58	7¼	**7¾**	1:19	C	**3:15**	E	CAN	25
285	11	Th.	6:52	D	**6:07**	C	11	15	29	7	21	8¼	**8½**	2:24	C	**3:46**	D	LEO	26
286	12	Fr.	6:54	D	**6:06**	C	11	12	29	7	43	9	**9½**	3:31	D	**4:16**	D	SEX	27
287	13	Sa.	6:55	D	**6:04**	B	11	09	30	8	06	9¾	**10¼**	4:40	D	**4:47**	C	LEO	28
288	14	**G**	6:56	D	**6:03**	B	11	07	30	8	28	10½	**11**	5:52	E	**5:20**	C	VIR	29
289	15	M.	6:57	D	**6:01**	B	11	04	30	8	50	11¼	**11¾**	7:06	E	**5:57**	C	VIR	0
290	16	Tu.	6:58	D	**5:59**	B	11	01	30	9	12	**12¼**	—	8:21	E	**6:39**	B	VIR	1
291	17	W.	6:59	D	**5:58**	B	10	59	31	9	34	12¾	**1**	9:35	E	**7:28**	B	LIB	2
292	18	Th.	7:01	D	**5:56**	B	10	55	31	9	56	1½	**1¾**	10:44	E	**8:24**	B	SCO	3
293	19	Fr.	7:02	D	**5:55**	B	10	53	31	10	18	2½	**2¾**	11:46	E	**9:27**	B	OPH	4
294	20	Sa.	7:03	D	**5:53**	B	10	50	31	10	39	3½	**3¾**	**12:40**	E	**10:33**	B	SAG	5
295	21	**G**	7:04	D	**5:52**	B	10	48	31	11	00	4¼	**4¾**	**1:25**	E	**11:41**	C	SAG	6
296	22	M.	7:05	D	**5:50**	B	10	45	31	11	21	5½	**5¾**	**2:03**	E	—	–	CAP	7
297	23	Tu.	7:07	D	**5:49**	B	10	42	32	11	42	6½	**6¾**	**2:36**	D	12:48	C	AQU	8
298	24	W.	7:08	D	**5:47**	B	10	39	32	12	03	7½	**8**	**3:06**	D	1:54	D	AQU	9
299	25	Th.	7:09	D	**5:46**	B	10	37	32	12	24	8½	**9**	**3:34**	D	2:58	D	AQU	10
300	26	Fr.	7:10	D	**5:44**	B	10	34	32	12	44	9½	**9¾**	**4:01**	C	4:00	D	PSC	11
301	27	Sa.	7:11	D	**5:43**	B	10	32	32	13	04	10¼	**10¾**	**4:29**	C	5:02	E	PSC	12
302	28	**G**	7:13	D	**5:42**	B	10	29	32	13	24	11	**11¼**	**4:58**	C	6:02	E	PSC	13
303	29	M.	7:14	D	**5:40**	B	10	26	32	13	44	11½	—	**5:29**	B	7:02	E	ARI	14
304	30	Tu.	7:15	D	**5:39**	B	10	24	32	14	04	12	**12¼**	**6:05**	B	8:01	E	ARI	15
305	31	W.	7:16	D	**5:38**	B	10	22	32	14 s.	23	12¾	**12¾**	**6:44**	B	8:57	E	TAU	16

 To use this page, see p. 104; for Key Letters, see p. 237. ☞ **Bold = P.M.** ☞ Light = A.M.

OCTOBER HATH 31 DAYS • 2012

Among dead fern
The sumacs burn. –Eben Eugene Rexford

Day of Month	Day of Week	Dates, Feasts, Fasts, Aspects, Tide Heights	Weather
1	M.	**St. Gregory** • **Sukkoth** • Actor Rudy Bond born, 1912 • Tides {10.1 / 10.4}	*Mild*
2	Tu.	Racer's Storm made landfall near Matamoros, Mexico, 1837	*and*
3	W.	Cartoonist William Steig died, 2003 • Tides {9.6 / 10.1}	*drizzly,*
4	Th.	**St. Francis of Assisi** • ☾ AT ☋ • ☾ AT APO. • ♃ STAT. • {9.3 / 9.9}	*hair*
5	Fr.	☾ RIDES HIGH • ☌♃☾ • 116°F, Sentinel, Ariz., 1917 • Tides {8.9 / 9.6}	*gets*
6	Sa.	☌☿♄ • Engineer George Westinghouse born, 1846 • Actress Bette Davis died, 1989	*frizzly.*
7	**G**	**19th S. af. P.** • *A bold heart is half the battle.* • Tides {8.4 / 9.2}	*Bright*
8	M.	**Columbus Day (observed)** • **Thanksgiving Day (Canada)** • Deadly forest fire, Peshtigo, Wisc., 1871	*spot!*
9	Tu.	**Leif Eriksson Day** • Meteorite struck car in Peekskill, N.Y., 1992 • Tides {8.4 / 9.1}	*Now*
10	W.	U.S. president Woodrow Wilson sent signal to blast Gamboa Dike, completing construction of Panama Canal, 1913	*it's*
11	Th.	Michael Gallen ate 63 bananas in 10 minutes, 1972 • {9.1 / 9.7}	*not.*
12	Fr.	☌♀☾ • Opera singer Luciano Pavarotti born, 1935 • {9.7 / 10.1}	*Rain*
13	Sa.	☾ ON EQ. • U.S. Navy Memorial dedicated, D.C., 1987 • {10.3 / 10.4}	*spills*
14	**G**	**20th S. af. P.** • *Speech is silver; silence is golden.*	*on*
15	M.	**New ●** • Poet Virgil born, 70 B.C. • Tides {11.5 / 11.0}	*quilted*
16	Tu.	☾ AT PERIG. • ☌☿☾ • ☌♄☾ • Giant "discovered," Cardiff, N.Y., 1869 • {11.9 / —}	*hills.*
17	W.	**St. Ignatius of Antioch** • ☾ AT ☊ • Tides {11.0 / 12.1}	*Maples*
18	Th.	**St. Luke** • ☌♂☾ • St. Luke's little summer. • Tides {10.9 / 12.0}	*mustard,*
19	Fr.	☾ RUNS LOW • British general Cornwallis surrendered to French and American forces, Yorktown, Va., 1781	*scarlet,*
20	Sa.	☌♇☾ • 49th parallel determined as western U.S./Canadian border, 1818 • {10.2 / 11.3}	*ochre;*
21	**G**	**21st S. af. P.** • First successful test of T. Edison's carbon-filament incandescent light bulb, 1879	*birches*
22	M.	Timber rattlesnakes move to winter dens. • Tides {9.6 / 10.3}	*custard;*
23	Tu.	**St. James of Jerusalem** • Football player Doug Flutie born, 1962 • {9.5 / 10.0}	*oaks*
24	W.	**United Nations Day** • ☌♆☾ • A. Phillips's phosphorus friction matches patented, 1836	*are*
25	Th.	☾ ON EQ. • ☌♄☉ • Little brown bats hibernate now. • Tides {9.8 / 9.8}	*mocha.*
26	Fr.	☿ GR. ELONG. (24° EAST) • –10°F, Bismarck, N.Dak., 1919 • Tides {10.0 / 9.7}	*Mist*
27	Sa.	☌♅☾ • *A good October and a good blast, To blow the hog acorn and mast.* • Tides {10.2 / 9.7}	*gives*
28	**G**	**22nd S. af. P.** • Harvard College founded, Mass., 1636 • Tides {10.3 / 9.7}	*way*
29	M.	**Sts. Simon & Jude**[T] • **Full Hunter's ○** • Tides {10.4 / —}	*to*
30	Tu.	First Toronto street vacuum, 1947 • Tides {9.6 / 10.4}	*sapphire*
31	W.	**All Hallows' Eve** • **Reformation Day** • ☾ AT ☋ • Tides {9.4 / 10.3}	*days.*

Farmer's Calendar

■ My *Scrabble* buddy, Peggy, invited me to go to the Brattleboro Farmers' Market in Vermont. I had never been to one before. My reasoning was, Since I grow just about all of the fruit and vegetables that I need, why waste the time?

It was a crisp October morning with the foliage near peak, so I decided to go along for the scenery. From the packed parking lot, we walked down the narrow path into the heart of the market, which was nestled under tall pines and blazing maples. Vendors' stands circled the grassy common, where shoppers were enjoying lunch, sampling a variety of local and ethnic fare. Peggy devoured a cheesecake brownie, and I had a hot dog, made of grass-fed beef, on a freshly baked sourdough bun.

The variety of produce offered was amazing: strings of colorful peppers; bags of succulent baby greens; tiny, purple, salad turnips; and even fresh ginger. There were organic meats from humanely cared-for animals, baked goods, and crafts. I tasted samples from a Vermont winery and purchased a bottle of rhubarb wine for a friend's birthday.

Peggy and I left the market with the makings for dinner and plans to share a meal and a game of *Scrabble*. Since then, I've become a regular shopper at farmers' markets, and it has never been a waste of time.

THE ELEVENTH MONTH • 2012

SKY WATCH ☆ *Jupiter stands above the Moon on the 1st, rises soon after nightfall, remains out all night, and reaches its maximum brightness for the year by month's end. This year's total solar eclipse on the 13th is visible from only northern Australia and the South Pacific Ocean. The Moon hovers above low, dim Mars on the 16th and is very close to Jupiter in a beautiful conjunction on the 28th. Meanwhile, in the east before dawn, Venus rises 2 hours before sunrise, hovers to the left of the crescent Moon on the 11th, and diminishes in brightness to its minimum by month's end. Venus and returning Saturn form a close predawn conjunction on the mornings of the 26th and 27th.*

◑	**Last Quarter**	6th day	19th hour	36th minute
●	**New Moon**	13th day	17th hour	8th minute
◐	**First Quarter**	20th day	9th hour	31st minute
○	**Full Moon**	28th day	9th hour	46th minute

After 2:00 A.M. on November 4, Eastern Standard Time is given.

Purchase these pages with times set to your zip code at MyLocalAlmanac.com.

Day of Year	Day of Month	Day of Week	☼ Rises h. m.	Rise Key	☼ Sets h. m.	Set Key	Length of Day h. m.	Sun Fast m.	Declination of Sun ° '	High Tide Times Boston		☾ Rises h. m.	Rise Key	☾ Sets h. m.	Set Key	☾ Place	☾ Age
306	1	Th.	7:18	D	**5:36**	B	10 18	32	14 s. 42	1¼	**1½**	**7:28**	B	9:50	E	TAU	17
307	2	Fr.	7:19	D	**5:35**	B	10 16	32	15 01	2	**2**	**8:17**	B	10:40	E	TAU	18
308	3	Sa.	7:20	D	**5:34**	B	10 14	32	15 20	2¾	**2¾**	**9:10**	B	11:24	E	ORI	19
309	4	**G**	6:21	D	**4:33**	B	10 12	32	15 38	2½	**2½**	**9:07**	B	11:04	E	GEM	20
310	5	M.	6:23	E	**4:32**	B	10 09	32	15 56	3¼	**3¼**	**10:06**	C	11:40	E	GEM	21
311	6	Tu.	6:24	E	**4:30**	B	10 06	32	16 14	4	**4¼**	**11:08**	C	**12:13**	E	CAN	22
312	7	W.	6:25	E	**4:29**	B	10 04	32	16 32	4¾	**5**	—	–	**12:44**	D	CAN	23
313	8	Th.	6:26	E	**4:28**	B	10 02	32	16 49	5¾	**6**	12:12	D	**1:13**	D	LEO	24
314	9	Fr.	6:28	E	**4:27**	B	9 59	32	17 06	6½	**7**	1:18	D	**1:43**	D	LEO	25
315	10	Sa.	6:29	E	**4:26**	B	9 57	32	17 23	7½	**7¾**	2:26	E	**2:14**	C	VIR	26
316	11	**G**	6:30	E	**4:25**	B	9 55	32	17 39	8¼	**8¾**	3:38	E	**2:48**	C	VIR	27
317	12	M.	6:31	E	**4:24**	B	9 53	32	17 55	9	**9¾**	4:52	E	**3:27**	B	VIR	28
318	13	Tu.	6:33	E	**4:23**	B	9 50	31	18 11	10	**10½**	6:08	E	**4:13**	B	LIB	0
319	14	W.	6:34	E	**4:22**	B	9 48	31	18 27	10¾	**11½**	7:21	E	**5:07**	B	LIB	1
320	15	Th.	6:35	E	**4:21**	B	9 46	31	18 42	11½	—	8:30	E	**6:09**	B	OPH	2
321	16	Fr.	6:36	E	**4:20**	B	9 44	31	18 57	12¼	**12½**	9:29	E	**7:17**	B	SAG	3
322	17	Sa.	6:38	E	**4:20**	B	9 42	31	19 11	1¼	**1½**	10:20	E	**8:27**	C	SAG	4
323	18	**G**	6:39	E	**4:19**	B	9 40	30	19 25	2	**2¼**	11:02	E	**9:37**	C	SAG	5
324	19	M.	6:40	E	**4:18**	B	9 38	30	19 39	3	**3¼**	11:38	E	**10:45**	C	AQU	6
325	20	Tu.	6:41	E	**4:17**	B	9 36	30	19 53	4	**4½**	**12:09**	D	**11:50**	D	CAP	7
326	21	W.	6:42	E	**4:17**	B	9 35	30	20 06	5	**5½**	**12:38**	D	—	–	AQU	8
327	22	Th.	6:44	E	**4:16**	A	9 32	29	20 18	6	**6½**	**1:05**	C	12:54	D	PSC	9
328	23	Fr.	6:45	E	**4:15**	A	9 30	29	20 31	7	**7½**	**1:32**	C	1:55	D	PSC	10
329	24	Sa.	6:46	E	**4:15**	A	9 29	29	20 43	8	**8½**	**2:01**	C	2:56	E	PSC	11
330	25	**G**	6:47	E	**4:14**	A	9 27	29	20 54	8¾	**9¼**	**2:31**	B	3:55	E	PSC	12
331	26	M.	6:48	E	**4:14**	A	9 26	28	21 06	9½	**10**	**3:05**	B	4:54	E	ARI	13
332	27	Tu.	6:49	E	**4:13**	A	9 24	28	21 16	10	**10¾**	**3:43**	B	5:51	E	ARI	14
333	28	W.	6:50	E	**4:13**	A	9 23	28	21 27	10¾	**11¼**	**4:25**	B	6:45	E	TAU	15
334	29	Th.	6:52	E	**4:13**	A	9 21	27	21 37	11¼	12	**5:13**	B	7:36	E	TAU	16
335	30	Fr.	6:53	E	**4:12**	A	9 19	27	21 s. 46	**12**	—	**6:05**	B	8:23	E	TAU	17

NOVEMBER HATH 30 DAYS • 2012

E'en in these bleak November days
There's gladness for the heart that heeds. –Charles Dawson Shanly

Day of Month	Day of Week	Dates, Feasts, Fasts, Aspects, Tide Heights	Weather
1	Th.	All Saints' • ☾ AT APO. • ☌♃☾ • Tides { 9.3 10.2	*Flurries*
2	Fr.	All Souls' • ☾ RIDES HIGH • Record-breaking piñata measured 60' long and 23'10.5" wide, 2008	*early,*
3	Sa.	Sadie Hawkins Day • *A good wife makes a good husband.*	*pristine*
4	G	23rd S. af. P. • Daylight Saving Time ends, 2:00 A.M. • { 8.7 9.5	*and*
5	M.	Dominion Observatory time signal first broadcast by CBC Radio, 1939 • Tides { 8.6 9.3	*pearly.*
6	Tu.	Election Day • ☿ STAT. • Composer Peter Ilyich Tchaikovsky died, 1893	*Winter's*
7	W.	In a cartoon by Thomas Nast, the elephant was first used to represent the Republican party, 1874 • { 8.7 9.2	*come*
8	Th.	Black bears head to winter dens now. • Tides { 9.0 9.3	*calling!*
9	Fr.	☾ ON EQ. • Jim Thorpe's Carlisle Indians beat Dwight Eisenhower's Army Cadets in football, 27–6, 1912	*Can*
10	Sa.	*Turkeys perched on trees and refusing to descend indicates snow.* • Tides { 10.1 9.8	*we endure*
11	G	24th S. af. P. • Veterans Day • ☌♀☾ • ♆ STAT.	*so*
12	M.	Indian Summer • ☌♄☾ • Lobsters move to offshore waters. • Tides { 11.4 10.5	*premature*
13	Tu.	New ● • Eclipse ☉ • ☾ AT ☊ • Tides { 11.9 10.7	*a*
14	W.	☾ AT PERIG. • ☌☿☾ • Eugene Ely piloted first airplane take-off from a ship, 1910	*falling?*
15	Th.	Islamic New Year • ☾ RUNS LOW • Artist Georgia O'Keeffe born, 1887 • { 12.4 —	*Some*
16	Fr.	☌♂☾ • ☌♇☾ • Crab apples are ripe now. • { 10.8 12.2	*may*
17	Sa.	St. Hugh of Lincoln • ☿ IN INF. ☌ • Tides { 10.6 11.9	*find*
18	G	25th S. af. P. • Physicist Niels Bohr died, 1962 • Tides { 10.3 11.3	*this*
19	M.	Skunks hibernate now. • "Boss" Tweed sentenced to 12 years in prison, N.Y.C., 1873 • { 10.1 10.7	*trend*
20	Tu.	☌♆☾ • 18" snow, Paradise, Mich., 1987	*distressing—*
21	W.	☾ ON EQ. • First circumnavigation of N. America in single voyage, by HMCS *Labrador,* 1954	*others*
22	Th.	Thanksgiving Day • *Feather by feather, the goose is plucked.* • Tides { 9.7 9.3	*bend*
23	Fr.	St. Clement • ☌♅☾ • Jukebox debuted, San Francisco, 1889 • { 9.7 9.1	*to*
24	Sa.	Joseph Glidden granted patent for barbed wire fencing, 1874	*say a*
25	G	26th S. af. P. • René Lévesque became premier of Quebec, 1976 • { 10.0 9.1	*blessing*
26	M.	☿ STAT. • Kappa Alpha Society founded, Union College, Schenectady, N.Y., 1825 • { 10.1 9.1	*over*
27	Tu.	☾ AT ☋ • ☌♂♇ • ☌♀♄ • Snowstorm with lightning, eastern S.Dak., 1983	*sage*
28	W.	Full Beaver ○ • Eclipse ☾ • ☾ AT APO. • ☌♃☾ • { 10.2 9.1	*and*
29	Th.	☾ RIDES HIGH • Megamouth shark caught, Catalina Island, Calif., 1984 • Tides { 10.2 9.0	*onion*
30	Fr.	St. Andrew • *The earth does not shake when the flea coughs.* • Tides { 10.2 —	*dressing.*

He that is of a merry heart hath a continual feast. –Proverbs 15:15

Farmer's Calendar

■ With my garden harvested and much of the crop squirreled away in the root cellar, I feel a deep sense of satisfaction knowing that I will have a safe and healthy supply of vegetables and fruit throughout most of the winter. These days, with fresh produce available year-round at the supermarket, root cellars are not usually a necessity, but in years past, they were as essential to a home as a refrigerator is today.

A typical root cellar was a room in the north corner of the basement that was vented to the outside to keep the cellar air cool and circulating. Fruit, vegetables, and other foods that needed chilly temperatures were stored inside. Shelves were often stocked with milk, butter, jars of preserves, and crocks of salt pork, while smoked meat hung from hooks in the ceiling. Barrels of homemade beer, cider, and wine were frequently kept there, too. Gardeners used the area to rest potted plants, such as geraniums, over the winter, and to force spring bulbs into early bloom.

My storage is limited to mostly root crops and a bushel or two of 'Baldwin' apples. Vines of green tomatoes hang from the ceiling to ripen over several weeks. My produce usually lasts into early spring, but if it falls a little short, I can take another route—the one to the supermarket, 15 minutes away.

DECEMBER

THE TWELFTH MONTH • 2012

SKY WATCH ☆ *Venus continues to drop ever closer to the sunrise glare; by year's end, it is very low and completes its magnificent apparition. Mercury dangles below Venus in the month's first half. Jupiter reaches its closest point to Earth on the 1st and then its opposition, in Taurus, on the 2nd, dominating the sky all night with a blazing magnitude –2.8. The Moon is absent on the 13th; it will not interfere with the intense Geminid meteor shower beginning at 8:00* P.M. *that night. The Moon and Jupiter form a strikingly close holiday conjunction on the 25th, with the orange star Aldebaran dangling below them. The earliest winter since 1896 arrives with the solstice at 6:12* A.M. *on the 21st.*

◑	**Last Quarter**	6th day	10th hour	31st minute
●	**New Moon**	13th day	3rd hour	42nd minute
◐	**First Quarter**	20th day	0 hour	19th minute
○	**Full Moon**	28th day	5th hour	21st minute

All times are given in Eastern Standard Time.

Purchase these pages with times set to your zip code at MyLocalAlmanac.com.

Day of Year	Day of Month	Day of Week	☼ Rises h. m.	Rise Key	☼ Sets h. m.	Set Key	Length of Day h. m.	Sun Fast m.	Declination of Sun ° '	High Tide Times Boston		☾ Rises h. m.	Rise Key	☾ Sets h. m.	Set Key	☾ Place	☾ Age
336	1	Sa.	6:54	E	**4:12**	A	9 18	26	21 s. 56	12½	**12¾**	**7:00**	B	9:04	E	GEM	18
337	2	**G**	6:55	E	**4:12**	A	9 17	26	22 04	1¼	**1¼**	**7:59**	C	9:41	E	GEM	19
338	3	M.	6:56	E	**4:12**	A	9 16	26	22 13	2	**2**	**8:59**	C	10:15	E	CAN	20
339	4	Tu.	6:57	E	**4:11**	A	9 14	25	22 20	2¾	**2¾**	**10:00**	C	10:46	D	CAN	21
340	5	W.	6:58	E	**4:11**	A	9 13	25	22 28	3½	**3½**	**11:03**	D	11:14	D	LEO	22
341	6	Th.	6:59	E	**4:11**	A	9 12	24	22 35	4¼	**4½**	—	–	11:43	D	SEX	23
342	7	Fr.	7:00	E	**4:11**	A	9 11	24	22 42	5	**5½**	12:09	D	**12:12**	C	LEO	24
343	8	Sa.	7:01	E	**4:11**	A	9 10	24	22 48	6	**6¼**	1:16	E	**12:43**	C	VIR	25
344	9	**G**	7:01	E	**4:11**	A	9 10	23	22 53	6¾	**7¼**	2:26	E	**1:18**	B	VIR	26
345	10	M.	7:02	E	**4:11**	A	9 09	23	22 59	7¾	**8¼**	3:39	E	**1:59**	B	VIR	27
346	11	Tu.	7:03	E	**4:11**	A	9 08	22	23 03	8½	**9¼**	4:53	E	**2:48**	B	LIB	28
347	12	W.	7:04	E	**4:11**	A	9 07	22	23 08	9½	**10¼**	6:04	E	**3:46**	B	SCO	29
348	13	Th.	7:05	E	**4:12**	A	9 07	21	23 12	10½	**11**	7:10	E	**4:51**	B	OPH	0
349	14	Fr.	7:05	E	**4:12**	A	9 07	21	23 15	11¼	—	8:07	E	**6:03**	C	SAG	1
350	15	Sa.	7:06	E	**4:12**	A	9 06	20	23 18	12	**12¼**	8:54	E	**7:16**	C	SAG	2
351	16	**G**	7:07	E	**4:12**	A	9 05	20	23 20	1	**1**	9:35	E	**8:27**	C	CAP	3
352	17	M.	7:08	E	**4:13**	A	9 05	19	23 22	1¾	**2**	10:09	D	**9:37**	D	AQU	4
353	18	Tu.	7:08	E	**4:13**	A	9 05	19	23 24	2¾	**3**	10:40	D	**10:43**	D	AQU	5
354	19	W.	7:09	E	**4:14**	A	9 05	18	23 25	3½	**4**	11:08	C	**11:46**	D	PSC	6
355	20	Th.	7:09	E	**4:14**	A	9 05	18	23 26	4½	**5**	11:36	C	—	–	PSC	7
356	21	Fr.	7:10	E	**4:14**	A	9 04	17	23 26	5½	**6**	**12:04**	C	12:48	E	PSC	8
357	22	Sa.	7:10	E	**4:15**	A	9 05	17	23 25	6½	**7**	**12:34**	B	1:48	E	PSC	9
358	23	**G**	7:11	E	**4:16**	A	9 05	16	23 24	7¼	**8**	**1:06**	B	2:47	E	ARI	10
359	24	M.	7:11	E	**4:16**	A	9 05	16	23 23	8¼	**8¾**	**1:42**	B	3:45	E	ARI	11
360	25	Tu.	7:11	E	**4:17**	A	9 06	15	23 21	9	**9½**	**2:23**	B	4:40	E	TAU	12
361	26	W.	7:12	E	**4:18**	A	9 06	15	23 19	9¾	**10¼**	**3:09**	B	5:32	E	TAU	13
362	27	Th.	7:12	E	**4:18**	A	9 06	14	23 16	10¼	**11**	**3:59**	B	6:20	E	TAU	14
363	28	Fr.	7:12	E	**4:19**	A	9 07	14	23 13	11	**11½**	**4:54**	B	7:04	E	GEM	15
364	29	Sa.	7:13	E	**4:20**	A	9 07	13	23 10	11¾	—	**5:52**	B	7:43	E	GEM	16
365	30	**G**	7:13	E	**4:20**	A	9 07	13	23 06	12¼	**12¼**	**6:52**	C	8:18	E	CAN	17
366	31	M.	7:13	E	**4:21**	A	9 08	13	23 s. 01	12¾	**1**	**7:53**	C	8:49	E	CAN	18

 To use this page, see p. 104; for Key Letters, see p. 237. ☞ **Bold = P.M.** ☞ Light = A.M.

DECEMBER HATH 31 DAYS • 2012

Like mimic meteors the snow
In silence out of heaven sifts. –Frank Dempster Sherman

Day of Month	Day of Week	Dates, Feasts, Fasts, Aspects, Tide Heights	Weather
1	Sa.	First drive-in gasoline service station opened, Pittsburgh, Pa. 1913 • Tides {9.0 10.1	*Roads*
2	G	**1st S. of Advent** • ♃ at ☍ • Tides {8.9 9.9	*are*
3	M.	Race car driver Bobby Allison born, 1937 • Polar bear cub born, Toledo Zoo, Ohio, 2009 • {8.9 9.7	*icy,*
4	Tu.	☿ Gr. Elong. (21° West) • 20" snow, New Haven, Conn., 1786 • Tides {8.9 9.5	*driving*
5	W.	*Thunder in December presages fine weather.* • Tides {9.0 9.4	*dicey.*
6	Th.	**St. Nicholas** • ☾ on Eq. • Ship explosion devastated Halifax, N.S., 1917 • {9.2 9.2	*Mild*
7	Fr.	**St. Ambrose** • **National Pearl Harbor Remembrance Day** • "Blue Marble" Earth photo taken, 1972	*but*
8	Sa.	92°F, Ojai, Calif., 1938 • Element 111, roentgenium, first created, 1994 • {9.9 9.3	*sopping;*
9	G	**First day of Chanukah** • Marguerite d'Youville became first Canadian-born saint, 1990	*better*
10	M.	**St. Eulalia** • ☌♄☾ • Winterberry fruit especially showy now. • {10.9 9.8	*do*
11	Tu.	☾ at ☊ • ☌☿☾ • ☌♀☾ • Boll weevil monument up, Enterprise, Ala., 1919	*your*
12	W.	**Our Lady of Guadalupe** • ☾ runs low • ☾ at perig. • Tides {11.9 10.4	*holiday*
13	Th.	**St. Lucia** • **New ●** • ♅ stat. • Tides {12.2 10.6	*shopping.*
14	Fr.	Halcyon Days begin. • ☌♇☾ • Millau Viaduct, highest bridge, officially opened, France, 2004	*Rainy,*
15	Sa.	☌♂☾ • *Put up with small annoyances to gain great results.* • Tides {10.7 12.2	*snowy,*
16	G	**3rd S. of Advent** • Students' satellite *STARSHINE-2* deployed, 2001	*cold*
17	M.	*The Nutcracker* ballet premiered, St. Petersburg, Russia, 1892	*and*
18	Tu.	☌♆☾ • N.J. became third state to ratify the U.S. Constitution, 1787 • Tides {10.2 10.5	*blowy;*
19	W.	Ember Day • ☾ on Eq. • Beware the Pogonip. • Writer Emily Brontë died, 1848	*look*
20	Th.	☌♅☾ • 24-lb. 8-oz. horse-eye jack caught, Miami, Fla., 1982 • Tides {9.7 9.2	*out,*
21	Fr.	**St. Thomas** • Ember Day • **Winter Solstice** • Tides {9.6 8.8	*belowy!*
22	Sa.	Ember Day • First Lady Claudia "Lady Bird" Johnson born, 1912 • {9.5 8.5	*Yow!*
23	G	**4th S. of Advent** • *A lucky dog is rarer than a white crow.* • {9.5 8.4	*Santa's*
24	M.	☾ at ☋ • 63° to –21°F in 12 hours, Fairfield, Mont., 1924 • Tides {9.6 8.4	*driving*
25	Tu.	**Christmas** • ☾ at apo. • ☌♃☾ • Tides {9.7 8.6	*a plow!*
26	W.	**St. Stephen** • **Boxing Day (Canada)** • **First day of Kwanzaa** • ☾ rides high	*Feeling*
27	Th.	**St. John** • "Father of Aviation" Sir George Cayley born, 1773 • Tides {10.0 8.8	*yuckier?*
28	Fr.	**Holy Innocents** • **Full Cold ○** • Snowstorm caused 1,000 traffic accidents, Mich., 1987	*Hope*
29	Sa.	Ashrita Furman stood on a Swiss exercise ball for 3 hours, 38 minutes, 30 seconds, 2003 • Tides {10.2 —	*'13*
30	G	**1st S. af. Ch.** • ☌♇☉ • U.S. pres. Rutherford B. Hayes married Lucy Webb, 1852	*is*
31	M.	**St. Sylvester** • *All happiness is in the mind.* • {9.2 10.1	*luckier!*

Farmer's Calendar

■ Turning the calendar to December evokes cherished childhood memories of cutting the yearly Christmas tree from the woodlot behind our farmhouse. Sometimes, we spooked a deer on our way into the woods, adding to the excitement. I remember how proud I was on the day when my dad let me cut the tree for the first time. He pulled back hard on the branches so that the blade wouldn't bind, while I worked the bow saw back and forth with all the strength that a 6-year-old could muster.

The balsams and spruces that we harvested back then hardly resembled the well-shaped, plantation-grown trees that are commonplace today. Most of our trees had a sparse side that we hid against the wall. To fill a gap, we often had to drill a hole in the trunk and insert a branch into it. The huge spaces between the whorls of limbs were ideal for displaying the pinecones that we had gathered from the yard, the garlands of hand-strung popcorn and cranberries, and the dozens of fragile ornaments that had been passed down from one generation to the next.

My family still harvests Christmas trees from the same woodlot. It's a bit shadier now, so the trees grow with even bigger spaces between the branches. But that's okay—our collection of decorations has increased over the years as well.

Glossary of Almanac Oddities

■ Many readers have expressed puzzlement over the rather obscure notations that appear on our **Right-Hand Calendar Pages, 109–135.** These "oddities" have long been fixtures in the Almanac, and we are pleased to provide some definitions. (Once explained, they may not seem so odd after all!)

–Beth Krommes

Ember Days: The four periods observed by the Anglican church (and formerly by Roman Catholics) for prayer, fasting, and the ordination of clergy are called Ember Days. Specifically, these are the Wednesdays, Fridays, and Saturdays that occur in succession following (1) the First Sunday in Lent; (2) Whitsunday–Pentecost; (3) the Feast of the Holy Cross, September 14; and (4) the Feast of St. Lucia, December 13. The word *ember* is perhaps a corruption of the Latin *quatuor tempora,* "four times."

Folklore has it that the weather on each of the 3 days foretells the weather for the next 3 months; that is, for September's Ember Days, Wednesday forecasts the weather for October, Friday for November, and Saturday for December.

Distaff Day (January 7): This was the first day after Epiphany (January 6), when women were expected to return to their spinning following the Christmas holiday. A distaff is the staff that women used for holding the flax or wool in spinning. (Hence the term "distaff" refers to women's work or the maternal side of the family.)

Plough Monday (January): Traditionally, the first Monday after Epiphany was called Plough Monday because it was the day when men returned to their plough, or daily work, following the Christmas holiday. (Every few years, Plough Monday and Distaff Day fall on the same day.) It was customary at this time for farm laborers to draw a plough through the village, soliciting money for a "plough light," which was kept burning in the parish church all year. One proverb notes that

"Yule is come and Yule is gone,
and we have feasted well;
so Jack must to his flail again
and Jenny to her wheel."

Three Chilly Saints (May): Mamertus, Pancras, and Gervais were three early Christian saints. Because their feast days, on May 11, 12, and 13, respectively, are traditionally cold, they have come to be known as the Three Chilly Saints. An old French saying translates to: "St. Mamertus, St. Pancras, and St. Gervais do not pass without a frost."

Midsummer Day (June 24): To the farmer, this day is the midpoint of the growing season, halfway between planting and harvest. (Midsummer Eve is an occasion for festivity and celebrates fertility.) The Anglican church considered it a "Quarter Day," one of the four major divisions of the liturgical year. It also marks the feast day of St. John the Baptist.

Cornscateous Air (July): First used by early almanac makers, this term signifies warm, damp air. Though it signals ideal climatic conditions for growing corn, it poses a danger to those affected by asthma and other respiratory problems.

Dog Days (July 3–August 11): These are the hottest and most unhealthy days of the year. Also known as Canicular Days, their name derives from the Dog Star, Sirius. The traditional 40-day period of Dog Days once coincided with the heliacal (at sunrise) rising of Sirius.

Lammas Day (August 1): Derived from the Old English *hlaf maesse,* meaning "loaf mass," Lammas Day marked the beginning of the harvest. Traditionally, loaves of bread were baked from the first-ripened grain and brought to the churches to be consecrated. Eventually, "loaf mass" became "Lammas." In Scotland, Lammastide fairs became famous as the time when trial marriages could be made. These marriages could end after a year with no strings attached.

Cat Nights Begin (August 17): This term harks back to the days when people believed in witches. An Irish legend says that a witch could turn into a cat and regain herself eight times, but on the ninth time (August 17), she couldn't change back, hence the saying: "A cat has nine lives." Because August is a "yowly" time for cats, this may have initially prompted the speculation about witches on the prowl.

Harvest Home (September): In Europe and Britain, the conclusion of the harvest each autumn was once marked by festivals of fun, feasting, and thanksgiving known as "Harvest Home." It was also a time to hold elections, pay workers, and collect rents. These festivals usually took place around the autumnal equinox. Certain groups in this country, particularly the Pennsylvania Dutch, have kept the tradition alive.

St. Luke's Little Summer (October): This is a spell of warm weather that occurs on or near St. Luke's feast day (October 18) and is sometimes called Indian summer.

Indian Summer (November): A period of warm weather following a cold spell or a hard frost, Indian summer can occur between St. Martin's Day (November 11) and November 20. Although there are differing dates for its occurrence, for more than 200 years the Almanac has adhered to the saying "If All Saints' (November 1) brings out winter, St. Martin's brings out Indian summer." Some say that the term comes from early Native Americans, some of whom believed that the condition was caused by a warm wind sent from the court of their southwestern god, Cautantowwit.

Halcyon Days (December): This refers to about 2 weeks of calm weather that often follow the blustery winds of autumn's end. Ancient Greeks and Romans experienced this weather around the time of the winter solstice, when the halcyon, or kingfisher, was brooding. In a nest floating on the sea, the bird was said to have charmed the wind and waves so that the waters were especially calm during this period.

Beware the Pogonip (December): The word *pogonip* is a term used to describe an uncommon occurrence—frozen fog. The word was coined by Native Americans to describe the frozen fogs of fine ice needles that occur in the mountain valleys of the western United States and Canada. According to their tradition, breathing the fog is injurious to the lungs. □□

Holidays and Observances

For Movable Religious Observances, see page 107. **Federal holidays listed in bold.**

Jan. 1	**New Year's Day**
Jan. 16	**Martin Luther King Jr.'s Birthday** ***(observed)***
Jan. 19	Robert E. Lee Day *(Fla., Ky., La., S.C.)*
Feb. 2	Groundhog Day
Feb. 12	Abraham Lincoln's Birthday
Feb. 14	Valentine's Day
Feb. 15	Susan B. Anthony's Birthday *(Fla., Wis.)* National Flag of Canada Day
Feb. 20	**Washington's Birthday** ***(observed)***
Feb. 21	Mardi Gras *(Baldwin & Mobile counties, Ala.; La.)*
Feb. 29	Leap Day
Mar. 2	Texas Independence Day
Mar. 6	Town Meeting Day *(Vt.)*
Mar. 15	Andrew Jackson Day *(Tenn.)*
Mar. 17	St. Patrick's Day Evacuation Day *(Suffolk Co., Mass.)*
Mar. 26	Seward's Day *(Alaska)*
Apr. 2	Pascua Florida Day
Apr. 16	Patriots Day *(Maine, Mass.)*
Apr. 21	San Jacinto Day *(Tex.)*
Apr. 22	Earth Day
Apr. 27	National Arbor Day
May 5	Cinco de Mayo
May 8	Truman Day *(Mo.)*
May 13	Mother's Day
May 19	Armed Forces Day
May 21	Victoria Day *(Canada)*
May 22	National Maritime Day
May 28	**Memorial Day** ***(observed)***
June 5	World Environment Day
June 11	King Kamehameha I Day *(Hawaii)*
June 14	Flag Day
June 17	Father's Day Bunker Hill Day *(Suffolk Co., Mass.)*
June 19	Emancipation Day *(Tex.)*
June 20	West Virginia Day
July 1	Canada Day (traditional)
July 4	**Independence Day**
July 24	Pioneer Day *(Utah)*
Aug. 1	Colorado Day
Aug. 6	Civic Holiday *(Canada)*
Aug. 16	Bennington Battle Day *(Vt.)*
Aug. 19	National Aviation Day
Aug. 26	Women's Equality Day
Sept. 3	**Labor Day**
Sept. 9	Grandparents Day Admission Day *(Calif.)*
Sept. 11	Patriot Day
Sept. 17	Constitution Day
Sept. 21	International Day of Peace
Oct. 1	Child Health Day
Oct. 8	**Columbus Day** ***(observed)*** Native Americans' Day *(S.Dak.)* Thanksgiving Day *(Canada)*
Oct. 9	Leif Eriksson Day
Oct. 18	Alaska Day
Oct. 24	United Nations Day
Oct. 26	Nevada Day
Oct. 31	Halloween
Nov. 4	Will Rogers Day *(Okla.)*
Nov. 6	Election Day
Nov. 11	**Veterans Day** Remembrance Day *(Canada)*
Nov. 19	Discovery Day *(Puerto Rico)*
Nov. 22	**Thanksgiving Day**
Nov. 23	Acadian Day *(La.)*
Dec. 7	National Pearl Harbor Remembrance Day
Dec. 15	Bill of Rights Day
Dec. 17	Wright Brothers Day
Dec. 25	**Christmas Day**
Dec. 26	Boxing Day *(Canada)* First day of Kwanzaa

CALENDAR

2011

January
S	M	T	W	T	F	S
						1
2	3	4	5	6	7	8
9	10	11	12	13	14	15
16	17	18	19	20	21	22
23	24	25	26	27	28	29
30	31					

February
S	M	T	W	T	F	S
		1	2	3	4	5
6	7	8	9	10	11	12
13	14	15	16	17	18	19
20	21	22	23	24	25	26
27	28					

March
S	M	T	W	T	F	S
		1	2	3	4	5
6	7	8	9	10	11	12
13	14	15	16	17	18	19
20	21	22	23	24	25	26
27	28	29	30	31		

April
S	M	T	W	T	F	S
					1	2
3	4	5	6	7	8	9
10	11	12	13	14	15	16
17	18	19	20	21	22	23
24	25	26	27	28	29	30

May
S	M	T	W	T	F	S
1	2	3	4	5	6	7
8	9	10	11	12	13	14
15	16	17	18	19	20	21
22	23	24	25	26	27	28
29	30	31				

June
S	M	T	W	T	F	S
			1	2	3	4
5	6	7	8	9	10	11
12	13	14	15	16	17	18
19	20	21	22	23	24	25
26	27	28	29	30		

July
S	M	T	W	T	F	S
					1	2
3	4	5	6	7	8	9
10	11	12	13	14	15	16
17	18	19	20	21	22	23
24	25	26	27	28	29	30
31						

August
S	M	T	W	T	F	S
	1	2	3	4	5	6
7	8	9	10	11	12	13
14	15	16	17	18	19	20
21	22	23	24	25	26	27
28	29	30	31			

September
S	M	T	W	T	F	S
				1	2	3
4	5	6	7	8	9	10
11	12	13	14	15	16	17
18	19	20	21	22	23	24
25	26	27	28	29	30	

October
S	M	T	W	T	F	S
						1
2	3	4	5	6	7	8
9	10	11	12	13	14	15
16	17	18	19	20	21	22
23	24	25	26	27	28	29
30	31					

November
S	M	T	W	T	F	S
		1	2	3	4	5
6	7	8	9	10	11	12
13	14	15	16	17	18	19
20	21	22	23	24	25	26
27	28	29	30			

December
S	M	T	W	T	F	S
				1	2	3
4	5	6	7	8	9	10
11	12	13	14	15	16	17
18	19	20	21	22	23	24
25	26	27	28	29	30	31

2012

January
S	M	T	W	T	F	S
1	2	3	4	5	6	7
8	9	10	11	12	13	14
15	16	17	18	19	20	21
22	23	24	25	26	27	28
29	30	31				

February
S	M	T	W	T	F	S
			1	2	3	4
5	6	7	8	9	10	11
12	13	14	15	16	17	18
19	20	21	22	23	24	25
26	27	28	29			

March
S	M	T	W	T	F	S
				1	2	3
4	5	6	7	8	9	10
11	12	13	14	15	16	17
18	19	20	21	22	23	24
25	26	27	28	29	30	31

April
S	M	T	W	T	F	S
1	2	3	4	5	6	7
8	9	10	11	12	13	14
15	16	17	18	19	20	21
22	23	24	25	26	27	28
29	30					

May
S	M	T	W	T	F	S
		1	2	3	4	5
6	7	8	9	10	11	12
13	14	15	16	17	18	19
20	21	22	23	24	25	26
27	28	29	30	31		

June
S	M	T	W	T	F	S
					1	2
3	4	5	6	7	8	9
10	11	12	13	14	15	16
17	18	19	20	21	22	23
24	25	26	27	28	29	30

July
S	M	T	W	T	F	S
1	2	3	4	5	6	7
8	9	10	11	12	13	14
15	16	17	18	19	20	21
22	23	24	25	26	27	28
29	30	31				

August
S	M	T	W	T	F	S
			1	2	3	4
5	6	7	8	9	10	11
12	13	14	15	16	17	18
19	20	21	22	23	24	25
26	27	28	29	30	31	

September
S	M	T	W	T	F	S
						1
2	3	4	5	6	7	8
9	10	11	12	13	14	15
16	17	18	19	20	21	22
23	24	25	26	27	28	29
30						

October
S	M	T	W	T	F	S
	1	2	3	4	5	6
7	8	9	10	11	12	13
14	15	16	17	18	19	20
21	22	23	24	25	26	27
28	29	30	31			

November
S	M	T	W	T	F	S
				1	2	3
4	5	6	7	8	9	10
11	12	13	14	15	16	17
18	19	20	21	22	23	24
25	26	27	28	29	30	

December
S	M	T	W	T	F	S
						1
2	3	4	5	6	7	8
9	10	11	12	13	14	15
16	17	18	19	20	21	22
23	24	25	26	27	28	29
30	31					

2013

January
S	M	T	W	T	F	S
		1	2	3	4	5
6	7	8	9	10	11	12
13	14	15	16	17	18	19
20	21	22	23	24	25	26
27	28	29	30	31		

February
S	M	T	W	T	F	S
					1	2
3	4	5	6	7	8	9
10	11	12	13	14	15	16
17	18	19	20	21	22	23
24	25	26	27	28		

March
S	M	T	W	T	F	S
					1	2
3	4	5	6	7	8	9
10	11	12	13	14	15	16
17	18	19	20	21	22	23
24	25	26	27	28	29	30
31						

April
S	M	T	W	T	F	S
	1	2	3	4	5	6
7	8	9	10	11	12	13
14	15	16	17	18	19	20
21	22	23	24	25	26	27
28	29	30				

May
S	M	T	W	T	F	S
			1	2	3	4
5	6	7	8	9	10	11
12	13	14	15	16	17	18
19	20	21	22	23	24	25
26	27	28	29	30	31	

June
S	M	T	W	T	F	S
						1
2	3	4	5	6	7	8
9	10	11	12	13	14	15
16	17	18	19	20	21	22
23	24	25	26	27	28	29
30						

July
S	M	T	W	T	F	S
	1	2	3	4	5	6
7	8	9	10	11	12	13
14	15	16	17	18	19	20
21	22	23	24	25	26	27
28	29	30	31			

August
S	M	T	W	T	F	S
				1	2	3
4	5	6	7	8	9	10
11	12	13	14	15	16	17
18	19	20	21	22	23	24
25	26	27	28	29	30	31

September
S	M	T	W	T	F	S
1	2	3	4	5	6	7
8	9	10	11	12	13	14
15	16	17	18	19	20	21
22	23	24	25	26	27	28
29	30					

October
S	M	T	W	T	F	S
		1	2	3	4	5
6	7	8	9	10	11	12
13	14	15	16	17	18	19
20	21	22	23	24	25	26
27	28	29	30	31		

November
S	M	T	W	T	F	S
					1	2
3	4	5	6	7	8	9
10	11	12	13	14	15	16
17	18	19	20	21	22	23
24	25	26	27	28	29	30

December
S	M	T	W	T	F	S
1	2	3	4	5	6	7
8	9	10	11	12	13	14
15	16	17	18	19	20	21
22	23	24	25	26	27	28
29	30	31				

Joseph Justus Scaliger

THE JULIAN PERIOD:

Time to Get Organized

French astronomer Joseph Justus Scaliger (1540–1609) was fascinated by universal history, the notion that different ways of keeping track of time across the centuries could be combined into a coherent whole. His goal was to standardize calendar years so that all historical eras would fall on a single time line and all years would be consecutive and positive. As a result, he developed

by Heidi Stonehill

–calendar art, The Granger Collection, New York

the Julian Period in the 16th century.

To create his time line, Scaliger merged three calendar-related cycles already in use: the Solar, Golden Number, and Indiction cycles.

- **The Solar cycle is a 28-year cycle after which the dates of the Julian calendar again fall on the same days of the week. (The Julian calendar was commonly used in Scaliger's time.)**
- **The Golden Number cycle is the 19-year Metonic cycle, used in ancient times, after which the Moon phases fall (approximately) on the same calendar dates; each year of the cycle is given a Golden Number.**
- **The Indiction is a 15-year ancient Roman tax cycle that was used as late as the Middle Ages to date legal documents.**

Then Scaliger did the math: 28 x 19 x 15 = 7,980. He found that every 7,980 years, the starting dates of these three cycles would coincide. Scaliger called this time span the "Julian Period" because of its relationship with the Julian calendar.

Scaliger now needed to choose a date on the historical time line when the first Julian Period would start (all cycles would begin at year 1). He wanted it to be a year for which no historical record existed, in order to prevent confusion in record-keeping. Following calendar tradition, he based his calculations on an epoch—the year of Christ's birth as determined by Dionysius Exiguus, a 6th-century scholar. Scaliger knew that in that year, the Solar, Golden Number, and Indiction cycles were at 9, 1, and 3, respectively. He used this information to determine that the year of Christ's birth corresponded to year 4713 of his newly devised Julian Period. Working backward, he found that year 1 of this Julian Period began on January 1, 4713 B.C. (Julian calendar date).

In 2012, we are in year 6725 (4713 + 2012) of the current Julian Period. The next Julian Period will start in A.D. 3268 (for both the Julian calendar and the Gregorian calendar, which is commonly used today). The current Solar, Golden Number, and Indiction cycles, as well as the Year of the Julian Period, are cited in "How to Use This Almanac" on page 107.

It's a New Day (at Noon)

Astronomers use the Julian Period to determine the Julian Date, whose number represents the total of full days and fraction of a day since the start of the current Julian Period. Julian Date 0 occurred on January 1, 4713 B.C.

A Julian day starts at noon Universal Time (Greenwich Mean Time) so that one night's astronomical events all occur on the same Julian Date. For example, on February 14, 2012, at noon, the Julian Date is 2,455,972.0. On February 15, 2012, at midnight (12:00 A.M., the start of the day on a common calendar), the Julian Date is 2,455,972.5. □□

Heidi Stonehill, a calendar editor at *The Old Farmer's Almanac,* was born in year 6677 of the current Julian Period.

Create an Astronomical Garden

Any garden can include a sundial; an astronomical garden can be a sundial.

by Judith Young

–illustrations, Renée Quintal Daily

We've all heard of botanical, vegetable, and zoological gardens, but an astronomical garden?

For over 25 years, I have been an avid gardener and professor of astronomy. Inspired in 1992 by an astronomically aligned stone circle, or Sunwheel, that I saw on former Blackfeet Indian territory in Montana, I decided to blend my interests by creating one to use in teaching astronomy at the University of Massachusetts at Amherst. In so doing, I began my adventure in astronomical gardening.

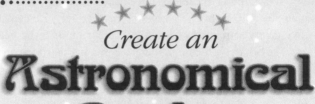

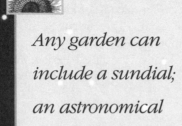

An astronomical garden should contain elements that have a direct connection to astronomy or the sky. The connections can be simple:

- **plants with appropriate names, such as sunflower, moonflower, 'Summer Sky' coneflower, and 'New Moon' iris**
- **a plot in the shape of a heavenly body, such as the Sun, with its rays; a crescent Moon; a planet (e.g., Saturn, with its rings); a constellation; or a spiral galaxy.**

- **flowers of a single color—red for Mars or white for the Moon, for example**

However, an astronomical garden of the most elegant kind is one with celestial alignments that connect you to the universe and remind you of your place in it—or simply make you look up.

The best-known and oldest example of an astronomical garden is probably Stonehenge in England. With its 25-foot-tall stones and alignments with the rising and setting Sun on the solstices, it is a landscaped locale, a calendar, and an observatory.

In a home garden, Stonehenge-scale stones are not practical, but alignments must be true to the sky. Because of this, it is necessary to observe each alignment.

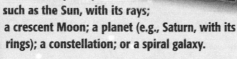

CONTINUED

Details of the local horizon—hills, buildings, trees, atmospheric refraction, altitude, and other factors—will influence where you see the Sun rise.

First, choose what to mark or include in your garden. If you choose to include alignments with celestial events, your interests and available space will determine these:

- **Are you an early riser? Set sunrise alignments.**
- **Do you have a favorable westerly view? Mark the sunsets.**
- **Is your view of the Sun's rise and set impeded? Mark noontime shadows.**
- **Or, hitch your wagon to a star: Choose Polaris, the North Star, and mark the cardinal directions.**

Next, identify a viewing spot or garden center. For example, if you include sunrise and/or sunset alignments, delineate the area from which the sightings will be made. This could be . . .

- **a spot marked with plantings**
- **an area outlined with stones**
- **a rock that you stand on**
- **a bench on which you sit**

From this spot, you will observe and mark the direction to the solar risings and/or settings, the solstices and equinoxes, your birthday, and any other special days of the year.

Based on your astronomical interests and available space, you may want to choose a plot plan from among the three suggestions on the following pages.

1

Sunrise/Sunset GARDEN

If you have good views of the sky to both the east and west and adequate space, mark the Sun risings and settings throughout the year. (Many ancient stone circles were made in this pattern.) Mark the alignments with stones, paths, or garden beds.

The solstice sunrise and sunset alignments are ideal to include because these are the most northerly (in June) and most southerly (in December) of the year. (See the Calendar Pages, 108–134, or Almanac.com/Astronomy, for times.)

If you have only a small amount of space and nearby buildings and trees partially or completely block the view of sunrise and/or sunset, see the next plot plan.

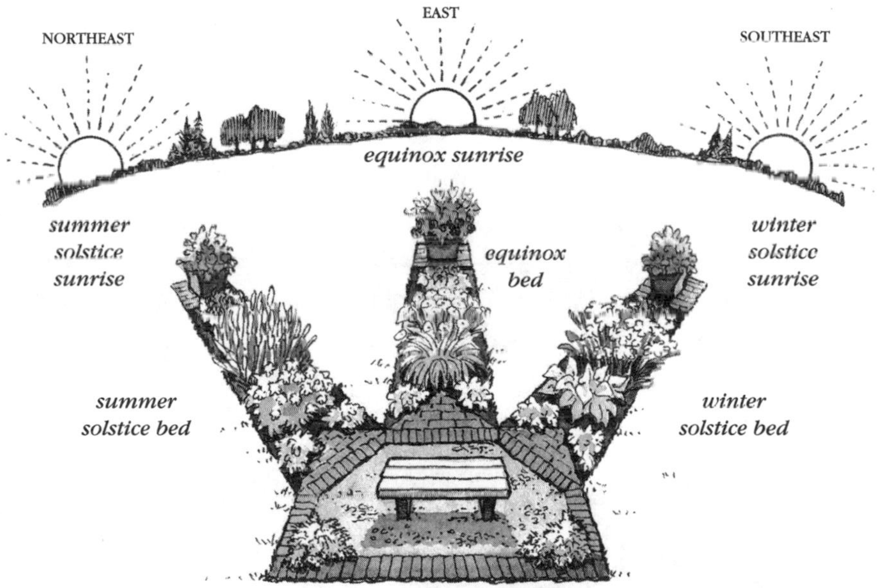

2

Noontime Shadows GARDEN

This arrangement uses the noontime Sun and noontime shadow lengths throughout the year. In marking the "noontime" shadow, use 12:00 P.M. when on Standard Time and 1:00 P.M. while on Daylight Saving Time.

Locate the garden so that the noontime Sun is visible for as much of the year as possible. You will need a gnomon—a fixed object such as a standing stone or garden sculpture—to cast the noontime shadows. Ideally, the gnomon should be at least 5 feet tall so that its noontime shadow on the summer solstice, the day of shortest noontime shadows, will be at least 1½ feet long (the length at midnorthern or midsouthern latitudes).

Consider including a pond or garden bed that runs north–south at the base of the gnomon. You can then mark the length of the gnomon's noontime shadow along the pond or garden bed every 2 to 4 weeks. You're making a calendar of the Sun! Personalize this garden throughout the year by placing a stone or planting at the end of the shadow at the precise moment of any memorable event, such as a birthday.

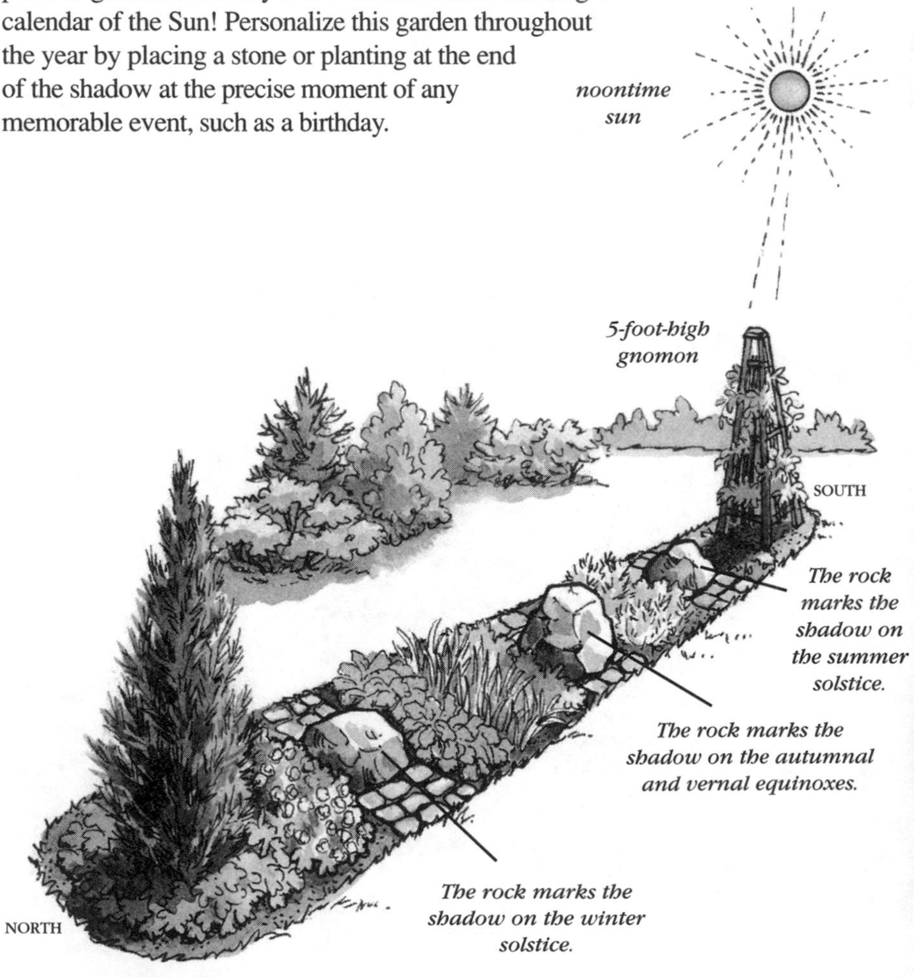
noontime sun
5-foot-high gnomon
SOUTH
The rock marks the shadow on the summer solstice.
The rock marks the shadow on the autumnal and vernal equinoxes.
The rock marks the shadow on the winter solstice.
NORTH

This garden bed is three times the height of the gnomon and is designed for full sun. (See page 103 for solstice and equinox dates.)

3

Cardinal Directions GARDEN

The cardinal directions come from astronomy:

- **True north comes from the direction to the North Star, Polaris.**
- **For those of us at midnorthern latitudes, south comes from the direction of the "noontime" Sun as it transits on its daily arc across the sky.**
- **Due east and west come from the sunrise and sunset on the equinoxes.**

This garden has the most flexible design in terms of size and layout.

Locate and mark the center of the garden. Then decide on the overall size and shape, including how far from the center you will mark the cardinal directions. The markers can be incorporated into the garden bed, at the perimeter, or beyond the confines of the plantings. Use a compass to determine N, S, E, and W (for true astronomical directions, see "Find True North," page 150) and mark these directions by placing markers—large rocks or stone cairns—at a chosen distance away. (These markers should be of sufficient size that they can not be kicked out of place accidentally.)

You can connect the cardinal directions in several ways:

- **Make garden beds that run north–south and east–west (shown below).**
- **Create a circle with garden beds, plantings, or smaller stones.**
- **Set garden rocks in rows or make paths in N–S and E–W directions to connect the center of the garden to the four directions.**

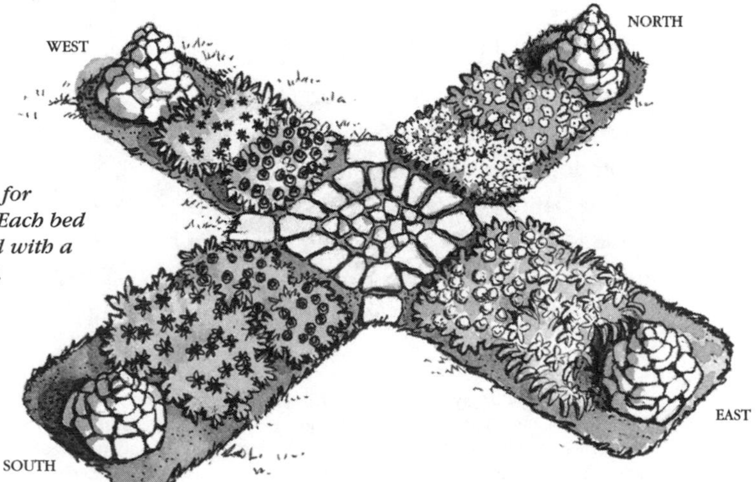

This garden is for shade or sun. Each bed can be planted with a different color.

CONTINUED

Ground Rules

There is only one rule in creating the garden: Anything is acceptable as long as it is true to the sky. Your astronomical garden can be in the sun or shade, on flat ground or sloping terrain. You can make it any size and mark the alignments in whatever way you wish. For example, you can allow flower beds or pruned hedges to guide the eye from your observation spot toward selected alignments. Or, use paths and open space to indicate the alignments, with garden beds adjacent. You can plant it with astronomically named specimens, plants themed by color, or plantings that bloom at a given time of year. The possibilities are endless. In whatever way you choose to create your astronomical garden, you will be embarking on a lifelong adventure connecting Earth and sky, matter and energy, you and the universe. Not only will you enrich your own life, but also you will open up a sky full of possibilities for all who experience your astronomical garden.

Find True North

A compass will give you magnetic (not astronomical) directions; the magnetic North Pole does not coincide with the north end of the Earth's rotation axis. You can determine true astronomical north by making the magnetic declination correction, which depends on your location. Find that correction here: www.ngdc.noaa.gov/geomagmodels/Declination.jsp.

Judith Young, Ph.D., is a professor of astronomy at the University of Massachusetts at Amherst, an award-winning astrophysicist, and the author of over 120 scientific publications on star formation in galaxies. She built the Sunwheel, the first astronomically aligned stone circle on a university campus in the world. For more information, visit www.astronomyandspirituality.com.

VEGETABLE RIFFS

Elvin Bishop *(right)* turned a raggedy lawn into a garden filled with fruit, vegetables, and flowers.

–photos, Bob Hakins

Harmony yields a hefty harvest.

by Kirk Longpré

Blues guitarist Elvin Bishop grew up in the 1940s on a farm without electricity or running water in an extremely rural part of Iowa. "What we ate," he says, "was what we grew. There was always a cellar full of canned goods, and my dad had a smokehouse. I just remembered the food—how good it was."

These days, 36 years after his group's pop single "Fooled Around and Fell in Love" reached #3 on the *Billboard* Hot 100 chart, Bishop "fools around" in a ¾-acre organic garden in Marin County, north of San Francisco. Every inch of it flourishes with domestic fruit and vegetables, Asian specialties, exotic rarities such as pineapple guava from Paraguay, and flowers.

The property wasn't always so lush.

When he moved there in 1974, he tore down the dilapidated deck on the house, used the lumber to build a greenhouse, and then dug up the raggedy lawn. The soil was hard clay, acidified from the conifers nearby. Six inches to a foot down, he found "fractured granite" and bedrock. He sifted the earth, one shovelful at a time, through a 1-inch wire mesh frame and then discarded the rocks.

To plant fruit trees, he pounded out holes with an iron bar. At times, his progress was measured at 1 inch per hour.

His first successful crop was potatoes grown in a mixture of soil and wood chips. His harvest increased dramatically once he located a source of manure. "For the kind of soil we've got here, you can till in 6 inches of manure and put on another 6 inches and till that in, and it won't be too much," he says. Every year, he digs in 30 pickup-truck loads.

Bishop prefers not to give exact gardening directions because everybody's place is different, but he is happy to share a few of the techniques that work for him.

(continued)

Corn Circles

Corn is usually planted in square or oblong patches, and the stalks at the edges don't get pollinated. In his 10x10-foot plot, Bishop lays down a water drip line in a spiral of ever-increasing circles spaced 1 foot apart. Then he plants the seeds at each emitter. The circular planting pattern allows for more even pollination.

Carrot Tricks

He grows carrots in a raised bed that he fertilized a year before, to allow the nitrogen level to diminish. Hairy roots can result from too much nitrogen. Before seeding in April, he digs in a couple of bags of sand, combined with buckets of potting soil (used as well as new), to give the roots something to grow through easily. Because he hates thinning, he uses pellet carrot seeds. Each one is coated with white clay, making it easy to see and space. To retain moisture, he spreads a sheet of shade cloth over the bed. "Never fails," he says.

Bean Poles

Every year, Bishop grows pole beans in the same raised beds in lots of manure.

For the beans, he built a wooden trellis running east to west and consisting of two 8-foot-high, 20-foot-long, parallel rectangular frames mounted vertically 4 feet apart and connected for stability (see photo, p. 152). Along the center of the bed between the frames, he placed a line of 2x6-inch planks with nails evenly spaced along the length of both sides. He ran strings from the nails on the 2x6s to the top rails of the frames, creating 70 to 80 "Vs."

At planting time, he puts one bean next to each nail on the north side. About 2 weeks later, he plants more beans on the south side. In this way, the plants on the north side aren't in the shade. Eventually, the vines reach the top of the frame and the beans hang down outside the strings, where they are easy to see and pick.

Gobo Gobs

One of Bishop's favorite plants is Japanese gobo (a cousin to wild American burdock).

Japanese farmers, whose plants produce long, straight roots, dig a ditch about 1½ feet wide, line it with a viscous liner, and fill it with sandy soil.

Bishop has modified this method. He uses 4-foot-high hog wire to form a circular frame. He lines this with black plastic, which he then fills with soil from old flower pots and baskets. This plant bed produces beautiful, straight, gobo roots.

Crop Cover

Bishop's harvest continues through the winter. Several years ago, he obtained a metal-frame car cover kit, dispensed with the canvas, and placed the frame in his garden. In July, he plants his seeds under it. Around November 1, he covers the frame with 4-mil plastic. From this "greenhouse," he reaps Asian mustard greens, bok choy, Chinese cabbage, daikon radishes, green onions, lettuce, mizuna, and spinach from winter through spring.

This is also when he preserves 300 to 400 jars of fruit and vegetables and makes hot sauce and jams.

"If it tastes good, it's worth growing," he says. □□

Kirk Longpré writes, teaches, and gardens in Victoria, British Columbia.

Green Thumbs' Tell

Almanac readers share time- and money-saving methods.

For Quick Compost . . .

■ Put fruit and vegetable peels into the blender, add water, and process. Spread around fruit trees, in pots, and in the herb garden.

When Starting Seeds, Use . . .

■ **old ice cube trays, plastic trays from microwavable dinners, and empty plastic pudding cups**

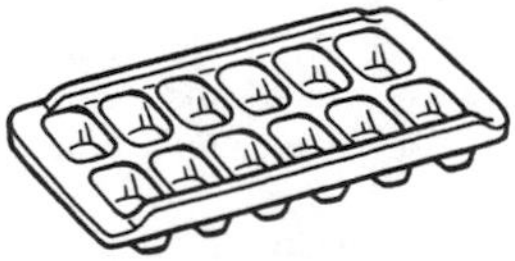

■ peat pellets set in the plastic trays from cookie packages

■ **eggshell halves–once the seeds sprout, plant the whole thing**

–illustrations, Kim Kurki

■ grocery store containers for cooked whole chickens as mini-greenhouses

■ **old plastic venetian blind slats, cut to size with scissors, as seedling markers and plant identifiers**

Contain Yourself

■ Use an antique porcelain bedpan for an indoor plant, old shoes for flowers, and hollowed-out tree stumps for pansies or marigolds.

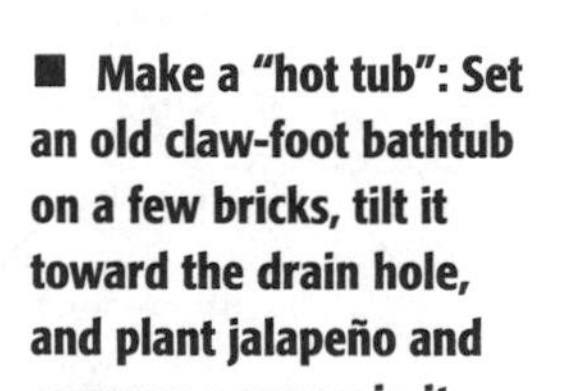

■ **Make a "hot tub": Set an old claw-foot bathtub on a few bricks, tilt it toward the drain hole, and plant jalapeño and cayenne peppers in it.**

■ Use wine-barrel halves as raised beds.

■ **Grow lettuce and radishes in a section of old roof gutter.**

For Luscious Tomatoes,

■ **plant five seedlings in a circle, then . . .**

Punch holes in the side of a bucket, with two rows in the middle, two rows near the bottom, and a few single holes scattered elsewhere in it. Sink the bucket into the soil in the center of the tomatoes, such that their roots almost touch it. Put a lump of fertilizer into the bucket and fill it with water. The water will drain out slowly, fertilizing the plants.

■ **In the center of the tomato circle, make a low, circular fence of chicken wire. Wrap it with black plastic, then fill it with aged horse manure. When watering, soak the manure.**

All Tales

The liquid running out will fertilize the plants. (Instead of a wire enclosure, you can use a laundry basket with the bottom removed.)

■ Set a few stakes around each tomato plant, then wrap clear plastic around them to encircle the plant. Secure the wrap to the stakes with clothespins or wire. Cover half of the top with plastic, leaving a vent hole. The wrap acts like a greenhouse, keeping in warmth and moisture. Remove the wrap when nights are above 50°F.

Get a Toehold

■ **Use panty hose to support melons growing on an arbor. The nylon stretches as the melons grow and keeps them off the ground.**

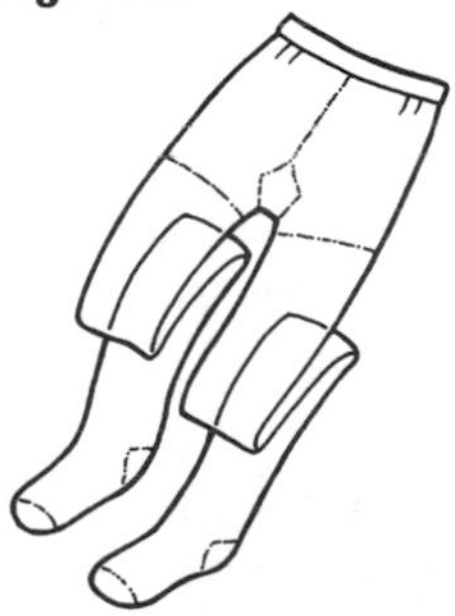

It's Wacky, but It Works

■ A friend filled a couple of old tires with dirt and mulch, and planted several seed potatoes in each tire. When the potatoes started to grow over the top of the tires, he added another tire and more mulch. He kept doing this and ended up with several bushels of potatoes that were very easy to harvest.

(Editor's note: Line the tires with plastic if you are concerned about toxins possibly leaching into the soil.)

■ **From a restaurant, my husband got a discarded salad station with the sneeze guard and a drain hole. I put gravel and soil where the salad once went and planted herbs. They grew all summer and winter on the back porch. I store all my tools underneath, behind the sliding doors.**

To Eliminate or Deter . . .

■ BLIGHT ON TOMATOES: **Sprinkle a little sulfur at the base of the plants.**

■ WHITEFLIES ON TOMATOES: Spray plants with a solution made from 1 cup of rubbing alcohol, 1 tablespoon of dish detergent, and 1 quart of water.

■ RABBITS: **Install a fence that is 4 feet high and bury it 6 inches deep. Bend the top foot of the fence away from the garden like a security fence, so that they can't climb or jump over it.**

continued ☞

■ **DEER:** Combine 1 raw egg, ½ cup of milk, 1 tablespoon of cooking oil, 1 tablespoon of dish detergent, and 1 gallon of water. Lightly spray the mixture over plants. Respray after rain.

■ **CHIPMUNKS, MOLES, AND SQUIRRELS FROM TUNNELING: Sprinkle coffee grounds on the soil.**

■ **SQUASH VINE BORERS:** Sprinkle diatomaceous earth around the stalks when the squash vines are small. Reapply after rain. Also, build up the soil around the vines.

■ **ANTS: Sprinkle cornmeal wherever they appear.**

Yet Another Tactic Against Slugs

■ Cut the spout end off a plastic beverage bottle just where it reaches the fattest diameter. Now, turn the pour-spout around so that it's pointing inside the bottle and fasten it with staples or duct tape. Pour a little beer into the bottle (add extra yeast, if desired) and lay it on its side in the garden. Slugs will be drawn to the beer and they won't be able to get out of the bottle. □□

GOT A GOOD IDEA?
Share it at **Almanac.com/Feedback** or on **Facebook.com/TheOldFarmersAlmanac.**

When it's time to teach your youngster how to fish, do what dads (and moms) have done for decades: Set a hook for bluegills.

by Lee Tolliver

The omnipresent bluegill has introduced more people to fishing than any other fish. Its abundance and willingness to participate in this right of passage make it the perfect catch. Maybe that's why it often is referred to as America's fish.

Lepomis macrochirus, aka the bluegill, bream, or brim, is native to about a third of the United States and a small portion of Mexico. It's been introduced to the rest of North America and thrives in freshwater lakes and rivers as well as in brackish tidal waters.

You can find bluegill action year-round in every state, but catching is better in the South, where fish have longer growing seasons and are typically bigger. The best time to catch them is during the late spring, when

CATCH

waters approach 70°F. In the dog days of July and August, look for them along shallow shorelines; they go deeper when the water gets really cold.

Anglers in northern states and Canada can extend their season with ice fishing. Even down deep under the ice, the fish have got to eat.

continued

FOR the RECORD

Bluegills at least 10 inches long are keepers. In most states that have angler recognition programs, one that is above-average in weight (a half pound is average) is large enough to earn a citation—a plaque or certificate for the bragging wall. It does happen: Records show that this little fish has big aspirations. Many often reach between 2 and 4 pounds.

The International Game Fish Association world record bluegill for anglers using any kind of hook and line is a 4-pound 12-ouncer caught in Alabama's Ketona Lake in 1950. Rumors of fish heavier than 5 pounds are common but unofficial.

—fish illustrat.or, www.usbr.gov; photo, RubberBall/SuperStock

pumpkinseed

green sunfish

longear

redbreast

redear

Speaking of eating, bluegills are delicious and often become the centerpiece of a fish fry menu. And whether you've got a youngster who's eager to get fishing or you want to try your own luck, learning how is easy.

Set the Bait

When bluegills are hungry, they'll eat almost anything. Live bait reigns supreme with diehard bluegillers. Red wigglers, night crawlers, crickets, grubs, and grass shrimp will attract hungry 'gills. When that's not handy, pieces of hot dog, corn, dough balls, and a variety of manmade baits, such as "Fishbites," will do.

SHADES of BLUE

Bluegills have several cousins in the sunfish world, all equally fun to catch. These include the pumpkinseed, green sunfish, longear, redbreast, and redear or shellcracker (considered by many to be the most aggressive; it strikes with ferocity when it takes a bait). Most of these fish are found throughout the United States and in parts of southern Canada. Some are region-specific.

In the past few decades, fish farms have been producing fast-growing hybrid bluegills, a cross between a male bluegill and female green sunfish that can grow at a rate of a half to three-quarters of a pound every year. The fish are used for stocking ponds and small lakes.

–fish illustrations: top, third, and fourth, New York State Department of Environmental Conservation; second and bottom, Arizona Game and Fish Department

Serious anglers go after them with small spinner baits like Beetle Spins (lead-head jigs tipped with curly-tailed rubber grubs), plastic swimming baits, or popping bugs for flycasting.

Work the Tackle

Many anglers use rods and line that overpower these little fish. The most sporting way calls for an ultralight spinning rod and a reel spooled with 2-, 4-, or 6-pound test line. A simple cane pole, line, hook, and bobber will work, too.

Find the Fish

One old-timer's technique involves tossing a handful of crickets into the water several feet from the shoreline. If bluegills are present, the crickets usually disappear with a resounding "pop" when a fish rises to the surface and sucks one in. If the crickets return safely to land, try another waterfront.

You can visually determine whether fish are around, too. During the early spring prespawn, average-size males will use their tails to fan out small, bowl-like depressions along shoreline mud in waters less than 5 feet deep and sometimes as shallow as a foot. Bigger bluegills have a tendency to spawn in deeper waters (up to 10 feet deep), making the beds more difficult to find.

When the females are ready, they lay their eggs in the bowls. The males then fertilize them and usually hang around for a few days to protect the fingerlings from predators.

After the spawn, smaller parent fish usually stay in shallow waters, while most of the trophy-size specimens go deeper.

Get Hooked

You'll know that you've hooked a bluegill when it starts to swim in circles as much as 5 feet in diameter. Keep your line tight and don't try to "horse" the fish in (pull too hard and maybe break the line), especially if you're using light line. Be ready for some resistance. This fish's round, flat shape helps to make it one of the toughest bantam fighters in the water. It swims sideways to the angler, and reeling one in is akin to pulling a dinner plate, edge up, through the water. When your bluegill surges, hold on. Even experienced anglers can be surprised by how it pulls line off the reel.

In deeper waters, anglers often take large bluegills by a technique called "split-shotting": A hook is tied to the end of the line and a split-shot sinker is attached about a foot above the hook. The baited rig is tossed out and allowed to sink to the bottom. Then it's worked along the bottom. Try it: You'll know pretty quick if Mr. Gill is around.

Whether you're using a cane pole or a spinning rod, releasing your fish or keeping a mess to eat, once you hook a bluegill, you're hooked on fishing. □□

Lee Tolliver is the outdoors writer for *The Virginian-Pilot,* a daily newspaper that covers southeastern Virginia and northeastern North Carolina. His first angling experience came early, when his dad and grandpa took him fishing for—what else?—bluegills.

Best Fishing Days and Times

The best times to fish are when the fish are naturally most active. The Sun, Moon, tides, and weather all influence fish activity. For example, fish tend to feed more at sunrise and sunset. During a full Moon, tides are higher than average and fish tend to feed more. However, most of us go fishing when we can get the time off, not because it is the best time. But there *are* best times, according to fishing lore:

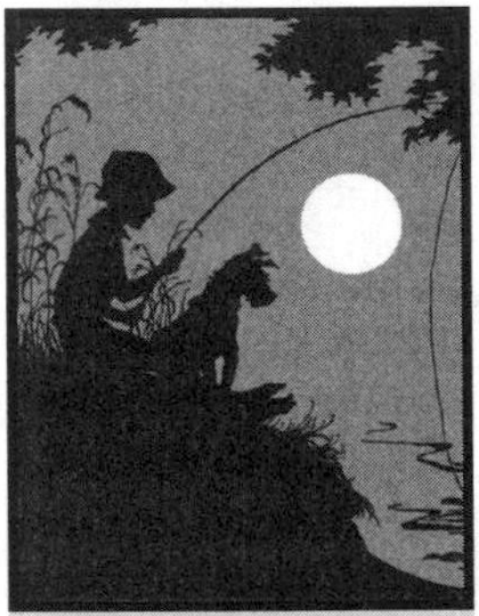

The Best Fishing Days for 2012, when the Moon is between new and full:

- January 1–9
- January 23–February 7
- February 21–March 8
- March 22–April 6
- April 21–May 5
- May 20–June 4
- June 19–July 3
- July 19–August 1
- August 17–31
- September 15–29
- October 15–29
- November 13–28
- December 13–28

- **One hour before and one hour after high tides, and one hour before and one hour after low tides. (The times of high tides for Boston are given on pages 108–134; also see pages 235–236. Inland, the times for high tides correspond with the times when the Moon is due south. Low tides are halfway between high tides.)**
- During the "morning rise" (after sunup for a spell) and the "evening rise" (just before sundown and the hour or so after).
- **During the rise and set of the Moon.**
- When the barometer is steady or on the rise. (But even during stormy periods, the fish aren't going to give up feeding. The smart fisherman will find just the right bait.)
- **When there is a hatch of flies—caddis flies or mayflies, commonly.**
- When the breeze is from a westerly quarter, rather than from the north or east.
- **When the water is still or rippled, rather than during a wind.**

How to Estimate the Weight of a Fish

Measure the fish from the tip of its nose to the tip of its tail. Then measure its girth at the thickest portion of its midsection.

The weight of a fat-bodied fish (bass, salmon) = (length x girth x girth)/800

The weight of a slender fish (trout, northern pike) = (length x girth x girth)/900

Example: If a fish is 20 inches long and has a 12-inch girth, its estimated weight is (20 x 12 x 12)/900 = 2,880/900 = 3.2 pounds

salmon

trout

catfis

WACKY WISDOM FROM THE TIP OF THE TONGUE

BY ALICE CARY

Spit can be a **CARD GAME,** a **STRIP OF LAND JUTTING OUT INTO THE SEA,** a **POINTED ROD THRUST THROUGH MEAT,** or, of course, **SALIVA.** Now, with your mouth watering, sit back and ponder the **CUSTOMS, CONCERNS,** and **CURIOSITIES** of this ever-present and essential fluid.

What's in It for YOU?

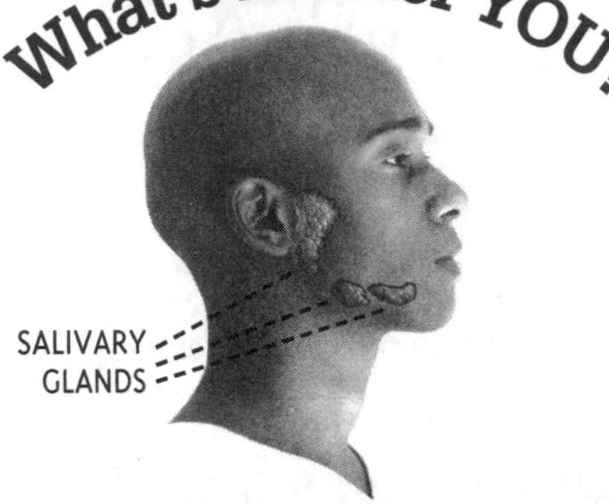

Two percent of spit consists of electrolytes, enzymes, mucus, and antibacterial compounds; the rest is water. Spit helps with digestion, swallowing, and keeping teeth clean and mouths moist. Three pairs of major salivary glands and many minor ones constantly make about 2 quarts, on average, each day. Production slows during sleep.

People once thought that spit (salivary) glands helped to filter blood like kidneys do. The idea that these glands secreted something was first mentioned in a London scientific publication in 1656. Today, spit tells all: Scientists can identify the person who licked an envelope by testing the saliva's DNA.

IN OTHER WORDS

Synonyms for "spit," as a noun, include **saliva, spittle, slobber, drool,** and **expectorate.**

The word "spit" or a form of it appears often in our vernacular.

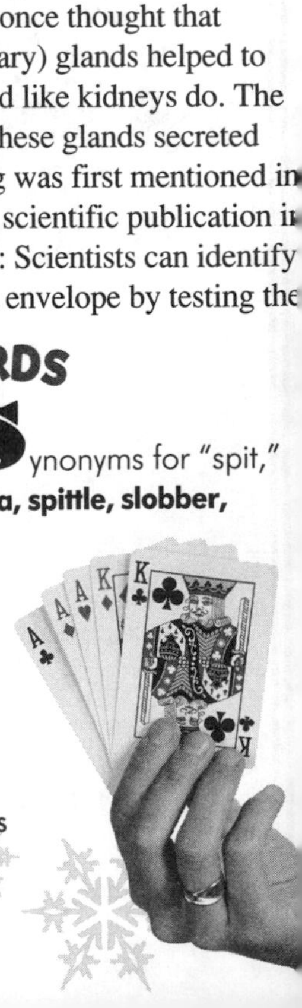

- "Spit in the Ocean" is a draw poker game.
- A spitting rain or snow is light precipitation.

- A spitting image is a perfect likeness.
- The term "spit and polish," meaning extreme attention to cleanliness, originated from the practice of polishing objects such as shoes by spitting on them and then rubbing them with a cloth.

- A frying pan is said to be spitting when grease splatters.
- To be within spitting distance is to be in close proximity.

AT the Table

Spitting at meals was allowed in the Middle Ages, but diners were encouraged to spit under the table. Hunters often spat on or across the table, a custom that polite society frowned upon.

Today, spitting out anything at the table, even onto a plate or into a napkin, is taboo. If you must remove a pit or piece of bone from your mouth, etiquette maven "Emily Post" advises using your thumb and first finger to place it in your napkin.

ON the Table

The swiftlet is a bird that builds its nest from its own saliva. This nest is considered **precious** and is used to make bird's nest soup, a Chinese delicacy.

–Minden Pictures/SuperStock

SALIVA IN SCIENCE

ON CUE

Russian scientist Ivan Petrovich Pavlov made **drooling dogs** famous with his landmark studies of digestion and canines. He noticed that dogs in his lab drooled at the sight of white lab coats because they thought that food was on the way. Pavlov began ringing a bell when feeding the dogs, and soon the ringing also made the dogs drool.

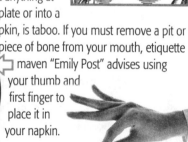

"Conditioned reflex," as he called this learning process, is the basis for much of learned human behavior.

CONTINUED

SALIVA IN SCIENCE
(continued)

IN YOU

The idea of **licking your wounds** sounds disgusting, but the concept is so old that the phrase has its own meaning: to recuperate after a defeat. Animals often lick their wounds, and now we know why. In 2008, scientists in the Netherlands published a report identifying a protein in saliva called histatin that greatly speeds up the healing process. Researchers hope to find ways to use it in drugs.

A SYNDROME, TOO

A Swedish eye doctor named Henrik Sjögren discovered a strange disease whereby patients don't have enough spit. This autoimmune disease, in which white blood cells attack salivary and other moisture-producing glands, now bears his name: **Sjögren's syndrome.**

FROM Public Nuisance . . .

➡ **Kansas Secretary of Health Dr. Samuel J. Crumbine** became famous for his crusades, including the promotion of fly swatter use. He hated spit as much as he despised flies. During his lifetime (1862–1954), Crumbine led campaigns against a number of germ-spreading practices and even had **"Don't Spit on Sidewalk"** stamped onto paving bricks in Kansas.

Spitting in public is now illegal in many places, including New York; Washington, D.C.; and Vancouver, B.C. However, these laws can be difficult to enforce.

. . . TO Public Enemy . . .

➡ In 1917, **Houston, Texas's health officer, Dr. P. H. Scardino,** who was concerned about spreading tuberculosis, proclaimed: "It would be far better for the police officers to prevent people from spitting on sidewalks, [in]

COOL DROOL

When spit freezes before it hits the ground, the air temperature is at –50°F or lower.

streetcars, and in other public places than to catch a . . . common criminal, for the man who spits . . . eventually kills more people by the transmission of disease than all the criminals of the world combined."

Fast-forward to 2007: A U.S. appeals court ruled that a person who intentionally spits at another can be charged with criminal assault.

. . . TO Public Display

➡ **Spitting from the Old Iron Bridge** that spans the Colorado River in Bastrop, Texas, is encouraged. The tradition dates from 1961, when a citizen decided to emulate a bridge-spitting incident in *The Andy Griffith Show.* Evidently, the custom doesn't detract from the town's charm. The National Trust for Historic Preservation named Bastrop as one of its "Dozen Distinctive Destinations" in 2010.

Containing It

Spittoons, or cuspidors—receptacles for expectorants,

—The Granger Collection, New York

especially tobacco juices—were once common in 19th- and early 20th-century homes and public places. The containers came in many sizes and shapes, even decorative ones such as fish and turtles.

Many U.S. spittoons were made of brass, but these were later melted for scrap during World War II. Today, each of the nine justices at the U.S. Supreme Court has a green ceramic spittoon (used for trash).

SPORTING SPIT SPATS

THE SPLENDID SPITTER

On August 7, 1956, **Red Sox star Ted Williams** (aka "The Splendid Splinter") was fined $5,000 for spitting at Boston fans who booed his performance against the New York Yankees.

—Transcendental Graphics/Getty Images

CONTINUED . . .

SPORTING SPIT SPATS

The incident started when Williams dropped a fly ball by Mickey Mantle for a two-base error. Afterward, Williams told reporters: "I'm not a bit sorry for what I did. I was right, and I'd spit again at the same fans who booed me today. . . . Nobody's going to stop me from spitting."

WHEN YOU SPIT UPON A STAR . . .

Makes no difference who you are. In 2010, a Philadelphia Eagles employee filmed himself spitting on the Dallas star emblem inside the Cowboys Stadium before an NFL matchup of the two teams, prompting fury and a name for the incident: Spitgate. (The Eagles lost, 24–0.)

DEADLY DISCHARGES

- **Spitting cobras defend themselves by expectorating venom into the eyes of their enemy.**
- **Spitting spiders discharge a poisonous, silky, sticky substance on their prey.**

- **The saliva of Indonesia's Komodo dragons contains no less than 50 strains of bacteria that poison the animal's prey, killing it within 24 hours.**

Expectorant Lore

Through the years, people have traditionally thought of spit as lucky. In search of luck, people spit on found money, on the first fish caught on a given day, on tools, and on boxing gloves.

In many cultures, spitting on someone, especially in the face, is an insult, but spitting on yourself could bring good news. According to an African custom, spitting on the first stone seen when starting a journey ensures a safe return. □□

Alice Cary is a regular contributor to the Almanac. Her favorite form of spit is the card game.

WINNERS
in the 2011 Essay Contest

My Best Original Money-Saving Habit

FIRST PRIZE

Mother always scolded us for paying too much for greeting cards. After she had admired the card and read the verse as well as the personal message we had added, she would flip it over to see the price. So my father, brother, and I began to ink out the price, much to Mother's chagrin. Later, after my father's death and my brother's marriage and departure—and when my mother was in the beginning stages of Alzheimer's—money was becoming tight. One day, I was putting a card into our greeting card box, a collection marking numerous holidays and events over 50 years, now neatly sorted, with those for each occasion bound together by ribbon. An idea came to my frugal mind: Mother and I could recycle these oldies! These 5- to 25-cent cards are actually far lovelier than those you can buy today. All we had to do was add a new date and message—and reading the old messages was a joyful trip down memory lane.

–Elizabeth J. Gortemoller, Elkhorn, Wisconsin

SECOND PRIZE

An employee at work gave me a red Christmas cactus for the holiday, explaining that a leaf would grow a new plant. Each formation had a minimum of six formed leaves. I gently tore leaves off at the joint, planting each upright in an old soup can. That night, I started 24 plants, placed them on trays, and carried them into the garage, where the cool air and low light were ideal for growing them. Eleven months later, I had 24 lush plants. My grandson and I decorated the cans with wrapping paper and green ribbons. Eight cans became gifts to various family members. We donated ten to the church benefit sale, gave his homeroom teacher and bus driver one each, and gave one to the mailman. We took the last three to patients in intensive care at our local hospital. All of the plants had tags explaining how to multiply them. We not only saved money but also saw the gratitude from all who received one.

–Eileen Spears, Rogerville, Tennessee

THIRD PRIZE

I worked in an office that had a pretty stringent dress code. If you wore a dress, you could not have bare legs. One day, while getting ready for work, I discovered that I did not have a good pair of panty hose. They all had a run or hole in them. I did, however, have several pairs that had one good leg. Since I always bought the same brand and color, I cut the bad leg off of each pair and slipped both of the good pairs on. The bonus was extra control.

–Regi Johnson, Manhattan, Montana

HONORABLE MENTIONS

I invented this in the mid-1980s, when I was in my 20s: When you get home from work, look around the kitchen and make note of any dinner-worthy ingredients. Put on walking shoes and leave the house with only $1 in your pocket. Walk to a grocery store that is at least 1½ miles away. On the way, think about what you can make with the stuff that's in your pantry, plus one dollar's worth of new ingredients. On the way home, congratulate yourself on your frugality and for having tricked yourself into at least a 3-mile walk. Over the years, I've saved money and kept my weight under control, too.

–Robert Frohoff, Prairie Village, Kansas

I have been doing this since I was 8 years old. In my bedroom, I have two separate folders. One is labeled "money-spending folder" and the other is blank. When I receive cash, I put a quarter of it into my spending folder and the rest goes into the blank one. At the end of the month, I deposit the money from the blank folder in the bank. I am now 17 years old, and I have $8,000 in that account.

–Zachary Sciuto, Somerville, Massachusetts

I use a solar/wind-powered clothes dryer—a clothesline, the type that folds like an umbrella. I made a fabric canopy to put on top of it when I am not drying clothes. It makes a nice shady spot where I can sit on hot days.

–Nancy Riggs, New Cumberland, Pennsylvania

I bought a large dry-erase board and hung it on the wall. I made it family policy to enter every purchase on the board to keep a running total of our balance. All purchases were rounded up to the nearest dollar, labeled as to where the purchase was made, and dated. I learned that I prefer not to make a wasteful purchase, knowing that I'll have to publish it on the board. Rounding up adds a cash cushion to my statement balance. Last year it was almost $500.

–Amy Bailey, Perry, New York

□□

Thank you to everyone who sent us a money-saving practice. We received many on similar themes, such as saving coins in jars, growing your own food, making soap, buying socks of one color, frequenting thrift stores, and writing lists (and contest entries) on scrap paper. Then there were these tips: Add water to almost-empty salad dressing bottles, then use the liquid in soups and pasta; hang drapes over doorways to contain heat; use a heater or furnace as a stove top; buy meat in bulk; and make napkins from flour sacks.

ANNOUNCING THE 2012 ESSAY CONTEST TOPIC:

How the Almanac Has Influenced My Life

In 200 words or less, please tell us how *The Old Farmer's Almanac* **has influenced your life. See page 179 for contest rules.**

The Patron Saint *of* PEPPERS

One hundred years ago, Wilbur Scoville revolutionized the way we eat hot peppers.

by Jeff Baker

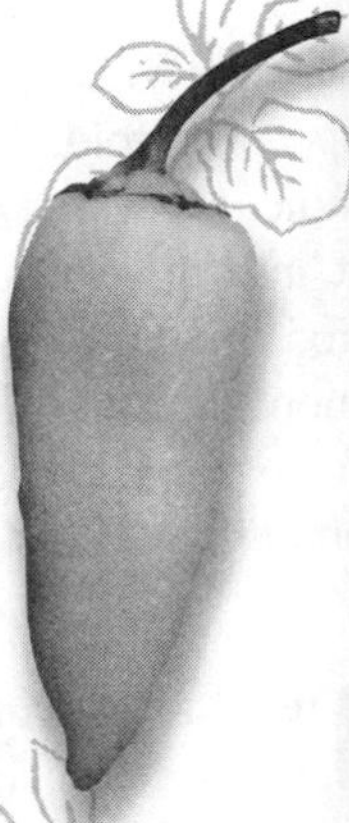

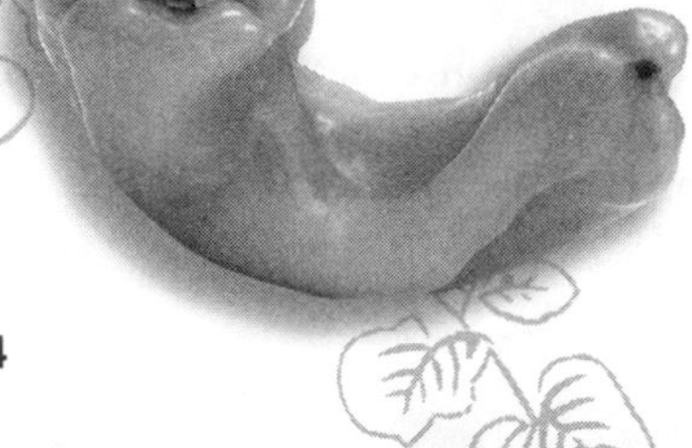

–Scoville portrait, Sunbelt Archives

Some people labor for years in hope that their name will appear in the history books, while others achieve renown by accident. Wilbur L. Scoville (1865–1942) was just doing his job.

In 1912, Scoville, a chemist employed by Detroit's Parke Davis Pharmaceutical Company, was tasked with developing a method to gauge the piquancy ("heat") of various chile peppers. The results would aid the company in using capsaicin, the compound that makes hot peppers hot, in salves for sore muscles. Scoville brought a depth of knowledge to the assignment, having published *The Art of Compounding,* a well-regarded textbook, in 1895.

After considering an array of technical apparatuses, Scoville realized that the most sensitive gauge was right under his nose—his mouth. His goal was to compare several varieties of pepper, so he devised the Scoville Organoleptic Test, which measured the amount of dilution required for each pepper to lose its hot taste; this he expressed in Scoville Heat Units (SHU).

Scoville first ground the peppers and soaked the powder in alcohol overnight; this extracted the capsaicin. He then added sugar water to the capsaicin-infused alcohol in increments and tasted each blend until he could no longer detect any heat. For example, a sweet bell pepper, which has no heat, was ranked at zero SHU (no capsaicin could be detected even when undiluted). By contrast, the extract of cayenne peppers had to be diluted 30,000 to 50,000 times before the

Scoville Chile Heat Chart

TYPE OF PEPPER	SCOVILLE HEAT UNITS
Pure capsaicin	*15,000,000*
Pepper spray	*2,000,000–5,300,000*
Naga Viper	*1,359,000*
Bhut Jolokia	*1,000,000*
Red Savina	*577,000*
Habanero	*200,000–350,000*
Chiltepin	*100,000–250,000*
Cayenne	*30,000–50,000*
Arbol	*15,000–30,000*
Manzano	*12,000–30,000*
Serrano	*8,000–23,000*
Yellow Hot	*5,000–8,000*
Jalepeño	*3,500–8,000*
Guajillo	*2,500–4,000*
Chilaca	*1,500–2,500*
Pasilla	*1,000–2,500*
Pablano	*1,000–2,000*
Anaheim	*500–2,000*
Chile Verde	*500–1,500*
Yellow Genetics	*500–1,000*
Red Chile	*500–750*
Sweet Bell	*0*

capsaicin was no longer discernible by Scoville's taste buds, thus earning it a rating of 30,000 to 50,000 SHU.

Scoville found that he could detect pure capsaicin even after it was diluted by a million drops of water, yet no laboratory test could detect such low amounts.

Other scientists questioned his method, but Scoville remained convinced that he'd found the best tool in the lab. "Physiological tests are tabooed in some quarters," he said, "yet when the tongue is sensitive to less than a millionth of a grain, it certainly has an advantage."

Once Scoville had established the process, he enlisted a panel of five tasters. There were limitations to his organic method, however.

- **The tasters didn't always agree on the dilution point at which a particular pepper's heat ceased to be detectable or even how hot it felt, and Scoville had to calculate their measurements as averages to minimize the discrepancies.**
- **The human tongue becomes sensitized to the effects of capsaicin (this is why the last jalapeño slice on nachos seems bland compared to the first one).**
- **The tasters had to take a break between each tasting session to "reset" their palates and could test only six samples in an 8-hour period.**

As laboratory technology progressed, Scoville's team of tasters went out of fashion. His original assignment, to help his employer formulate a salve, was successful, and several pepper-powered products are still available on drugstore shelves today (the aptly named Capzasin™ among them).

Scoville went on to be a celebrated chemist, winning several industry awards and receiving an honorary doctorate of science from Columbia University. Yet it is his scale that has made his name recognizable today among cooks, gardeners, food scientists, and self-described "chileheads" (those for whom too much capsaicin is never enough) everywhere.

Jeff Baker, a native of Alabama and frequent contributor to this Almanac, is occasionally challenged to jalapeño-eating contests by his father—and most often loses.

If the SHU Fits . . .

Today, the heat of peppers is measured by a computerized high-pressure liquid chromatograph that can test up to 30 samples in an 8-hour period. The machine's data are objective, so there are no differences among measurements.

The American Spice Trade Association (ASTA) strongly favors the modern method. For a time, its members lobbied for pepper heat to be universally expressed in ASTA units, but the Scoville name was so inextricably linked to ranking hot peppers that they ultimately dropped the idea and developed a formula to convert their measurements into SHUs. □□

Table of Measures

APOTHECARIES'
1 scruple = 20 grains
1 dram = 3 scruples
1 ounce = 8 drams
1 pound = 12 ounces

AVOIRDUPOIS
1 ounce = 16 drams
1 pound = 16 ounces
1 hundredweight = 100 pounds
1 ton = 2,000 pounds
1 long ton = 2,240 pounds

LIQUID
4 gills = 1 pint
63 gallons = 1 hogshead
2 hogsheads = 1 pipe or butt
2 pipes = 1 tun

DRY
2 pints = 1 quart
4 quarts = 1 gallon
2 gallons = 1 peck
4 pecks = 1 bushel

LINEAR
1 hand = 4 inches
1 link = 7.92 inches
1 span = 9 inches
1 foot = 12 inches
1 yard = 3 feet
1 rod = 5½ yards
1 mile = 320 rods = 1,760 yards = 5,280 feet
1 international nautical mile = 6,076.1155 feet
1 knot = 1 nautical mile per hour
1 fathom = 2 yards = 6 feet
1 furlong = ⅛ mile = 660 feet = 220 yards
1 league = 3 miles = 24 furlongs
1 chain = 100 links = 22 yards

SQUARE
1 square foot = 144 square inches
1 square yard = 9 square feet
1 square rod = 30¼ square yards = 272¼ square feet
1 acre = 160 square rods = 43,560 square feet
1 square mile = 640 acres = 102,400 square rods
1 square rod = 625 square links
1 square chain = 16 square rods
1 acre = 10 square chains

CUBIC
1 cubic foot = 1,728 cubic inches
1 cubic yard = 27 cubic feet
1 cord = 128 cubic feet
1 U.S. liquid gallon = 4 quarts = 231 cubic inches
1 imperial gallon = 1.20 U.S. gallons = 0.16 cubic foot
1 board foot = 144 cubic inches

KITCHEN
3 teaspoons = 1 tablespoon
16 tablespoons = 1 cup
1 cup = 8 ounces
2 cups = 1 pint
2 pints = 1 quart
4 quarts = 1 gallon

TO CONVERT CELSIUS AND FAHRENHEIT:

°C = (°F − 32)/1.8
°F = (°C × 1.8) + 32

Metric Conversions

LINEAR
1 inch = 2.54 centimeters
1 centimeter = 0.39 inch
1 meter = 39.37 inches
1 yard = 0.914 meter
1 mile = 1.61 kilometers
1 kilometer = 0.62 mile

SQUARE
1 square inch = 6.45 square centimeters
1 square yard = 0.84 square meter
1 square mile = 2.59 square kilometers
1 square kilometer = 0.386 square mile
1 acre = 0.40 hectare
1 hectare = 2.47 acres

CUBIC
1 cubic yard = 0.76 cubic meter
1 cubic meter = 1.31 cubic yards

HOUSEHOLD
½ teaspoon = 2 mL
1 teaspoon = 5 mL
1 tablespoon = 15 mL
¼ cup = 60 mL
⅓ cup = 75 mL
½ cup = 125 mL
⅔ cup = 150 mL
¾ cup = 175 mL
1 cup = 250 mL
1 liter = 1.057 U.S. liquid quarts
1 U.S. liquid quart = 0.946 liter
1 U.S. liquid gallon = 3.78 liters
1 gram = 0.035 ounce
1 ounce = 28.349 grams
1 kilogram = 2.2 pounds
1 pound = 0.45 kilogram

WINNERS
in the 2011 Coffee Recipe Contest

FIRST PRIZE

Mocha Truffle Loaf

2 cups heavy cream, divided
3 egg yolks, beaten
12 ounces semisweet chocolate chips
½ cup light corn syrup
½ cup (1 stick) unsalted butter
2 teaspoons instant espresso powder
2 ounces cream cheese, at room temperature, cut into chunks
¼ cup sifted confectioners' sugar
1 teaspoon vanilla extract
2 tablespoons coffee nib bits, optional

Line a 9x5x2½-inch loaf pan with plastic wrap. In a small bowl, whisk ½ cup of cream and the yolks. Set aside. In a saucepan over medium heat, warm the chocolate, corn syrup, butter, and espresso powder, stirring until the chocolate is melted. Reduce the heat to low, then slowly whisk in the egg yolk mixture. Whisk for 3 minutes. Remove from the heat and set aside to cool to room temperature. In a large bowl, beat the remaining cream, cream cheese, sugar, and vanilla until soft peaks form. Fold in the chocolate mixture just until blended. Pour into the loaf pan, then sprinkle the top with coffee nib bits, if desired. Refrigerate overnight or chill in the freezer until firm, about 3 hours. To serve, remove the chocolate loaf from pan. Peal off the plastic wrap. Rest the loaf at room temperature for 10 minutes, then slice with a sharp knife. **Makes 10 to 12 servings.**

–Margee Berry, White Salmon, Washington

SECOND PRIZE

Chocolate Coffee Oatmeal Sugar Cookies

½ cup granulated sugar
¼ cup cocoa powder
¼ cup instant coffee
2 cups whole wheat flour
1¾ cups rolled oats
1 teaspoon baking soda
1 teaspoon baking powder
1 cup (2 sticks) butter, softened
2 cups brown sugar
2 eggs, beaten

Heat the oven to 350°F. In a small bowl, combine the granulated sugar, cocoa powder, and coffee. In a medium bowl, combine the flour, oats, baking soda, and baking powder. In a large bowl, cream the butter and brown sugar. Add the coffee mixture and mix until it becomes mealy. Add the eggs and blend well. Add the flour mixture and stir until combined. Form 1-inch balls and arrange them on ungreased cookie sheets. Press each ball lightly with a fork. Bake for 8 to 12 minutes, or until the cookies are firm enough to lift off the cookie sheets. Cool. **Makes about 3 dozen cookies.**

–Julie-Ann Buchowski, Goderich, Ontario

THIRD PRIZE

Slow-Cooker Smoky Chili

1 pound stew meat
salt and pepper, to taste
2 tablespoons olive oil
3 slices bacon, chopped
1 onion, chopped
1 red bell pepper, chopped
1 yellow bell pepper, chopped
1 medium clove garlic, minced
2 cans (14.5 ounces each) fire-roasted tomatoes
2 tablespoons ground ancho chiles
1 tablespoon chili powder
1½ teaspoons cumin
1½ teaspoons paprika
1 teaspoon salt
½ cup red wine
1 cup brewed coffee
1 can (4 ounces) diced green chiles
1 can (15 ounces) red kidney beans
1 can (15 ounces) cannellini beans
1 avocado, peeled and sliced, for garnish
shredded cheddar cheese, for garnish
chopped green onions, for garnish

Pat the meat dry and sprinkle with salt and pepper. In a large skillet over medium heat, warm the oil. Add the meat, bacon, and onion and brown. Add the remaining ingredients, except the beans and garnishes. Stir well, then transfer to a slow cooker and cook on high for 5 hours. About 15 minutes before serving, add the beans. Ladle into serving bowls and top with garnishes. **Makes 6 servings.**

–Terri Crandall, Gardnerville, Nevada

HONORABLE MENTION

Rich and Spicy Beef Stew

1 cup strong brewed coffee, cooled
1½ pounds beef tips
1 yellow onion, chopped
1 green bell pepper, chopped
½ cup peeled and chopped carrots
3 large potatoes, peeled and chopped
2 cups salsa
2 tablespoons garlic salt
1 tablespoon black pepper, or to taste
½ cup green peas

Place all of the ingredients, except the peas, into a slow cooker and stir. Cook on low for 6 to 8 hours. About 15 minutes before serving, add the peas. **Makes 6 servings.**

–Denise Montgomery, Irondale, Alabama

ENTER THE 2012 RECIPE CONTEST: BACON

To participate, send us your favorite recipe using bacon (not other cuts or styles of pork). It must be yours, original, and unpublished. Amateur cooks only, please. See contest rules below.

RECIPE AND ESSAY CONTEST RULES

Cash prizes (first, $250; second, $150; third, $100) will be awarded for the best recipe using bacon and the best essay on the subject "How the Almanac Has Influenced My Life" (see page 173). All entries become the property of Yankee Publishing, which reserves all rights to the material. The deadline for entries is Friday, January 27, 2012. Label "Recipe Contest" or "Essay Contest" and mail to The Old Farmer's Almanac, P.O. Box 520, Dublin, NH 03444. You can also enter at Almanac.com/RecipeContest or Almanac.com/EssayContest. Include your name, mailing address, and email address. Winners will appear in *The 2013 Old Farmer's Almanac* and on our Web site, Almanac.com.

HAM on the LAM!

by Andrea Curry

Guard the garden, protect the pets: Feral hogs are up to NO GOOD!

If you want to make a park service employee flinch, say *Sus scrofa.* That's the scientific name for the wild boar, aka wild pig, wild hog, feral hog, or razorback, an animal that now thrives in the wild across much of the continent. Wild pigs have been reported in at least 43 states and four Canadian provinces, and experts say that they cause more than $1.5 billion in damage and crop loss every year.

Early European settlers brought boars

to North America. Over the years, those released for hunting bred like rabbits, farm-raised swine went feral, and the two groups continually interbred. Today's wild hog is the result, and it has farmers, legislators, and conservationists tearing out their hair.

Experts believe that wild pigs are more prolific than any other large mammal. Females can begin breeding at just 6 months of age and can have two litters per year of 4 to 12 piglets each. At that rate, a healthy herd often quadruples its numbers annually.

All of these pigs leave unmistakable signs of their presence. They root up soil like so many snorting power tillers, marring the landscape and killing seedlings. They eat almost everything in sight: acorns and berries; most plants; earthworms; baby lambs and goats; reptiles and amphibians; turtle, turkey, and quail eggs; and carrion. Such a diet enables them to achieve a normal weight of between 75 and 250 pounds; if they have unlimited access to food, they can grow much larger.

–Fred Hazelhoff/Foto Natura/Minden Pictures/National Geographic Stock

Farmers in many regions, especially Texas, home to about half the U.S. population of wild pigs, have known the nuisance of these creatures for years. The beasts often carry *Escherichia coli* and may have been partly responsible for the *E. coli* outbreak in bagged spinach in 2006.

continued

Pigs in a Poke

- **In 2010, a wild pig went—well—wild in Melbourne, Florida. Police tried to stun it with a Taser, but the animal's tough hide left the Taser damaged and the pig unfazed. A trapper was eventually able to lasso the pig inside a house.**
- **Another Florida pig, this one in the Cove area of Panama City, garnered almost 1,300 Facebook friends and the nickname "Freedom Pig" after evading wildlife officials for over 5 months. Neither Tasing nor tranquilizer darts (four at a time) could keep this pig down.**
- **In Germany, two teenage car thieves ran into the woods to evade police. One of the teens came upon a herd of wild pigs protecting their young and called out for the police to rescue him.**

Because swine are the most disease-susceptible of any farm animal, farmers worry that the pigs they raise for pork will catch diseases like leptospirosis, trichinosis, and swine brucellosis (pseudo-rabies) from wild pigs. Researchers at Purdue University have calculated that if foot-and-mouth disease broke out among wild pigs in the United States, it would be impossible to eradicate and would cost American agriculture $14 billion to $21 billion.

Now, these wild pigs are poking their snouts into suburban and even urban areas, and some experts hold little hope of getting control of the situation. According to Dr. Ben West, an expert in wildlife management (especially wild pigs) with the University of Tennessee Extension, the future of pig management is "bleak."

"While eradication on any large scale is nearly impossible, we do know that we can greatly reduce their numbers with aggressive control programs"—a combination of hunting, trapping, and aerial shooting. "These efforts, however, are costly and have to go on essentially forever," he says.

Hunters and trappers, who describe the pigs as "smart," "spooky," "scary," "fearless," "crafty," even "hate-filled," are more than willing to do their part. Boar hunting is a popular pastime, especially in the South.

Once hunters show up, wild pigs become twice as guarded and four times as wily. They become trap-wary, feeding only at night, and will move 10 or more miles from the scene of the hunt in 24 hours.

In response, many hunters now make nighttime expeditions with thermal imaging technology and sound-suppressed weapons. "Hog doggin'" (hunting with dogs) is also popular.

Currently, only professional hunters on contract with states are allowed to hunt wild pigs from the air, but this may change. In general, laws governing the hunting of wild pigs are becoming more permissive—and generous. The Canadian province

Pigmentations

- A PIG'S WHISPER: **a short period of time (the duration of a grunt)**
- TO THROW A LEG ACROSS A PIGSKIN (A SADDLE): **to mount a horse**
- PIGS AND WHISTLES: **trifles**
- TO GO TO PIGS AND WHISTLES: **to be ruined**
- PIGS IN CLOVER: **rich but impolite people**
- TO DRIVE PIGS: **to snore**
- TO DRIVE YOUR PIGS TO MARKET: **to snore very loudly**

of Alberta's government, for example, offered a $50 bounty to anyone who killed a pig (and proved it by turning in a pair of ears). Authorities in the municipal district of Big Lakes are prepared to double that, if certain conditions are met.

Wild pigs have natural enemies. Bobcats, coyotes, wolves, mountain lions, black bears, and even owls will prey on the piglets. But boars so far outnumber their predators in the wild that predation can't keep populations down. At the wild pig's rate of reproduction, 75 percent of the population in a given year must be killed just to keep the snout count stable.

North America isn't the only continent that wild pigs have taken by storm. Australia is leading the way in testing the use of toxic baits, and patented poisons (known by trade names PIGOUT and HOG-GONE) have helped to reduce boar populations there.

Here, we have a wider variety of midsize mammals (black bears, for example) that could accidentally consume poisoned bait intended for wild pigs. If scientists and trappers can devise a bait delivery system that will target only pigs, then, says Dr. West, toxic bait could come to play an important role in *Sus scrofa* management on this continent.

A Pigheaded Custom

● In old England, it was customary at Christmas to serve boar's head and announce it with trumpets and a carol sung by a choir. The custom is thought to derive from a Norse myth about Freyr, the god of peace and plenty, who rode on his boar to a Yuletide festival during which a boar was sacrificed in his honor.

Hog-Wild for Wild Hogs

● The biannual Wild Pig Conference, sponsored by The Berryman Institute, will be held in April 2012 in San Antonio and cover wild pig topics from behavior and genetics to damage assessment and control measures, including trapping techniques. Attendees in 2010 came from 29 states and 7 nations and included representatives from private industry as well as from wildlife management and other scientific disciplines. For more information, see www.wildpigconference.com.

□□

Andrea Curry, a frequent contributor to this Almanac, lives and writes in North Carolina, where boar imported for a game preserve in 1912 escaped into the wild in the 1920s.

Gestation and Mating Tables

	Proper Age for First Mating	Period of Fertility (yrs.)	Number of Females for One Male	Period of Gestation (days) AVERAGE	RANGE
Ewe	1 yr. or 90 lbs.	6		147 / 151[1]	142–154
Ram	12–14 mos., well matured	7	50–75[2] / 35–40[3]		
Mare	3 yrs.	10–12		336	310–370
Stallion	3 yrs.	12–15	40–45[4] / record 252[5]		
Cow	15–18 mos.[6]	10–14		283	279–290[7] 262–300[8]
Bull	1 yr., well matured	10–12	50[4] / thousands[5]		
Sow	5–6 mos. or 250 lbs.	6		115	110–120
Boar	250–300 lbs.	6	50[2] / 35–40[3]		
Doe goat	10 mos. or 85–90 lbs.	6		150	145–155
Buck goat	well matured	5	30		
Bitch	16–18 mos.	8		63	58–67
Male dog	12–16 mos.	8	8–10		
Queen cat	12 mos.	6		63	60–68
Tom cat	12 mos.	6	6–8		
Doe rabbit	6 mos.	5–6		31	30–32
Buck rabbit	6 mos.	5–6	30		

[1]For fine wool breeds. [2]Hand-mated. [3]Pasture. [4]Natural. [5]Artificial. [6]Holstein and beef: 750 lbs.; Jersey: 500 lbs. [7]Beef; 8–10 days shorter for Angus. [8]Dairy.

Incubation Period of Poultry (days)

Chicken	21
Duck	26–32
Goose	30–34
Guinea	26–28

Average Life Span of Animals in Captivity (years)

Cat (domestic)	14
Chicken (domestic)	8
Dog (domestic)	13
Duck (domestic)	10
Goat (domestic)	14
Goose (domestic)	20
Horse	22
Rabbit (domestic)	6

	Estral/Estrous Cycle (including heat period) AVERAGE	RANGE	Length of Estrus (heat) AVERAGE	RANGE	Usual Time of Ovulation	When Cycle Recurs If Not Bred
Mare	21 days	10–37 days	5–6 days	2–11 days	24–48 hours before end of estrus	21 days
Sow	21 days	18–24 days	2–3 days	1–5 days	30–36 hours after start of estrus	21 days
Ewe	16½ days	14–19 days	30 hours	24–32 hours	12–24 hours before end of estrus	16½ days
Doe goat	21 days	18–24 days	2–3 days	1–4 days	Near end of estrus	21 days
Cow	21 days	18–24 days	18 hours	10–24 hours	10–12 hours after end of estrus	21 days
Bitch	24 days	16–30 days	7 days	5–9 days	1–3 days after first acceptance	Pseudo-pregnancy
Queen cat		15–21 days	3–4 days, if mated	9–10 days, in absence of male	24–56 hours after coitus	Pseudo-pregnancy

WHAT WOULD YOU

To mark the centennial of the founding of the Girl Scouts of the USA, as well as the awarding of the first Eagle Scout badge by the Boy Scouts of America, take a survival quiz.

by Heidi Stonehill

You forget to bring matches or a lighter on a camping trip. You can produce flame by using . . .

a. a magnifying glass

b. a flat piece of softwood and a straight piece of hardwood

c. a battery and fine steel wool

d. a steel knife and a rock such as flint or quartzite

e. any of the above

Answer: e.

a. Use a magnifying glass to focus sunlight on tinder until a flame starts.

b. Make a hand drill: Put one end of the hardwood (spindle) into a depressed area of the softwood (fireboard). Spin the spindle between your palms, moving them up and down the spindle to impart downward force and create friction in the depression. When an ember is produced, move it to the tinder. To learn more about it, go to Almanac .com/HandDrill.

c. Use batteries from a flashlight, headlamp, etc. (e.g., 9-volt, C, D, or AA; if you use AA, you will need to hold two of them together end to end). The steel wool must touch both the positive (+) and the negative (–) terminals of the battery at the same time. Hold—do not rub—the steel wool on the terminals. Very quickly, the steel wool will become hot and glow. Transfer it to the tinder carefully, blowing on the wool to keep the flame going, if necessary. Note: Holding the steel wool on the terminals too long will quickly drain the battery.

d. Place the rock near tinder. Scrape the knife's sharp edge across the rock to produce sparks that land on the tinder. Blow gently whenever a spark is transferred to the tinder.

While hiking, you startle a grizzly bear. It huffs, stands on its hind legs, and seems to look at and smell you. You should . . .

a. run at a right angle to the bear, while moving your arms up and down rapidly and screaming.

b. drop an inedible item, such as a hat; move away slowly, diagonally, unless it starts to follow, in which case, stop (it might charge if it thinks that you are fleeing); avoid eye contact; speak in a low monotone; and move your arms up and down slowly.

c. climb a tree, while avoiding eye contact; make loud, bearlike huffing noises.

Answer: b.

The dropped item might distract the bear, while food might encourage it. Talking helps the bear to identify you as human, as does arm movement, which also makes you appear a little larger than you are. The bear might run after you if you flee; bears can run faster than humans. Climbing a tree is seldom recommended; many bears can climb, too. If the bear attacks because it has been surprised or feels threatened, drop to the ground and play dead, while protecting your neck and face. If it appears to be attacking as a predator, fight aggressively with whatever you have at hand. In bear country, it's recommended that you carry bear pepper spray. Using firearms can make a bear even more dangerous.

The best prevention is to make lots of noise before you ever see a bear. Most times, it will avoid you.

continued ➡

While doing strenuous exercise on a hot day, you feel nauseous and dizzy and experience muscle cramps, a headache, and general weakness. Your skin becomes clammy and you begin sweating heavily. You get thirsty and notice a rapid, weak pulse. You likely have . . .

a. heat stroke

b. heat exhaustion

c. heat cramps

Answer: b.

To alleviate heat exhaustion, cool down immediately (get into air-conditioning or shade, direct a fan at yourself, and/or apply cool water to the skin) and rest. Drink cold, nonalcoholic, noncaffeinated beverages.

Heat exhaustion can lead to heat stroke, which can result in high body temperature (above 103°F); rapid, strong pulse; flushed, nonsweating skin; confusion; and possible seizures. Call 911, if necessary.

A snake that might be venomous bites your friend on the leg. You can't transport your buddy to the hospital and a medical crew is on the way, but it will not arrive for 20 to 30 minutes. You should keep the affected area below the heart and . . .

a. Immobilize the leg; use a splint if needed, but do not wrap the leg tightly.

b. Put a tourniquet above the bite mark to restrict the flow of venom to the rest of the body. Make a crosslike incision near the bite, put your open mouth on it, and suck out the venom. Spit out—do not swallow—the venom.

c. Apply an ice pack to the wound and keep the leg still.

Answer: a.

Also, remove any constricting clothing and, if possible, gently wash the bite with soap and water.

Except in special cases, tourniquets may contribute to loss of limb or life.

Removing venom by suction is ineffective, especially if help comes within 30 minutes.

Applying ice may lead to localized limb damage.

You are stranded on an island and want to signal a boat or plane with fire at night. To send an international distress signal, you could build fires in the shape of . . .

a. a triangle

b. an arrow

c. an X

d. an H

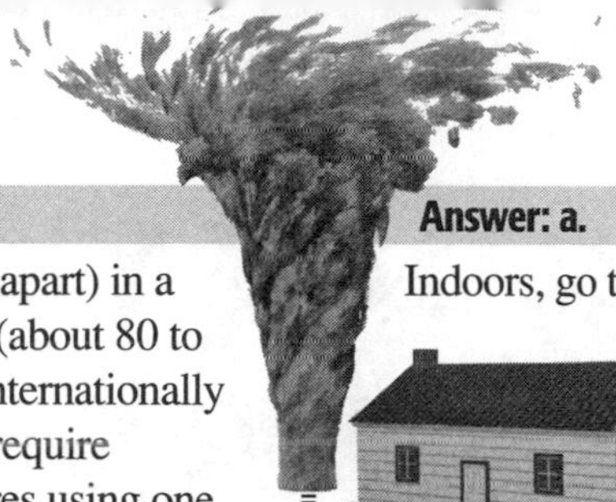

Answer: a.

Three fires (30 to 50 feet apart) in a triangle or a straight line (about 80 to 100 feet apart) are both internationally recognized as meaning “require assistance.” (Ignite the fires using one of the techniques in question 2.)

A hurricane has struck, and your water supply is contaminated with bacteria. To purify drinking water, you should keep it at a rolling boil for at least . . .

a. 30 seconds

b. 1 minute

c. 5 minutes

d. 10 minutes

Answer: b.

Boiling water will kill microorganisms, such as most bacteria, viruses, and parasites. (Let the water cool before drinking it.)

Boiling water for any amount of time will not purify water containing other contaminants, such as chemicals, oil, or sewage.

A tornado warning has been issued in your area.

At home, you should . . .

a. Take shelter under something sturdy in the basement.

b. Open the windows to equalize the pressure between the house and outdoors so that the building doesn’t explode.

Answer: a.

Indoors, go to an interior room on the lowest level available (basement or ground floor). Because tornadoes in the United States often (but not always!) approach from the southwest, that side of a basement can be the most dangerous when the house shifts.

Opening windows causes more harm than good, since wind speed is the destructive factor during a tornado, not pressure.

In a car, you should . . .

a. Get out and take shelter under an overpass.

b. Get out, find a ditch or low-lying area, and lie flat, face down, with your hands protecting your head and neck.

Answer: b.

When you are outdoors during a tornado, it is best to be as low to the ground as possible, on the lowest ground.

The area under an overpass acts as a wind tunnel, causing even higher winds that can hurl debris—and you. □□

FRONTIER FIXES

Red ants, black thread, manure, and spunk water. You be the judge.

by Martha Deeringer

North America's pioneers were a hardy lot. A testimony to their resilience can be found in how many of them survived. Pioneer families seldom saw a doctor. Most doctors lived many miles away and would expect payment in cash—not a ready commodity for those stalwart folks. What's more, prior to 1874, anyone claiming to be a physician could practice medicine, whether he had studied for the profession or not.

Taking a chance with elixirs, brews, and rituals seemed the best course of action for frontiersmen and -women. They believed that these curatives were magic, not medicine, which explained why many could be helpful to humans yet detrimental to bugs and other critters.

–The Granger Collection, New York

Pioneers also thought that they could rid themselves of disease by transferring the illness to another person, animal, plant, or object. As difficult to fathom as this may seem today, faith in these formulas gave settlers hope and helped them to find relief.

By the way, we don't recommend that you try these at home, but you might have some fun talking about them. (For real relief, go to Almanac.com/NaturalRemedies.)

• • • • •

Arthritis: Find a tree stump that has "spunk" water (rainwater) collected in it. Put the water on an arthritic joint.

Baldness: Smear the head with fresh cow manure to "fertilize" the growth of new hair.

Boils: Eat roadrunner soup.

Chicken pox: Remove your clothing and run around the chicken house three times.

Chills: Go to a dogwood tree before dawn and stand behind it until sunrise.

Colds: Pound dried frog skins into a fine powder. Mix the powder with fruit juice and drink.

Cuts: Apply a large red ant so that its jaws grip each side of the wound. Pinch off the ant's body right behind the head. The jaws will keep the edges of the wound clamped together while it heals.

Fever blisters: Coat the blister with earwax.

Headache: Lean your head against a tree. Have someone on the opposite side of the tree drive a nail into the trunk.

Hiccups: Lay a broom on the floor and jump over it three times.

Lockjaw: Steep cockroaches in hot water. Drink several cups of the resulting tea.

Lice: Undress and put your clothing on an anthill. The ants will devour the lice.

Pinkeye: Catch and kill a chicken snake. Fry it until some grease collects in the pan. Rub the grease on the sore eye.

Rheumatism: Fry pill bugs (aka sow bugs or rollie-pollies) and eat them.

Sore throat: Tie nine knots in a piece of black thread, soak the thread in turpentine, and wear it around your neck.

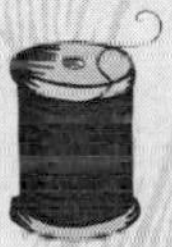

Sty: Stand at a crossroads and repeat these words: "Sty, sty, leave my eye. Catch the next one passing by." When someone passes the crossroads, your sty will be gone.

Toothache: Spit into a frog's mouth and ask it to leave with the toothache.

Warts: Dip the eye of a dead cat in spunk water and place it on the wart.

Martha Deeringer, of McGregor, Texas, is thankful that she's never needed a cup of cockroach tea.

Weather

ASH, and You Shall Receive

–Dr. Robert F. Griggs/National Geographic Stock

On June 6, 1912, citizens of the lively fishing village of Kodiak, Alaska, were bustling about, hauling in and canning their salmon catch, when they heard a distant boom.

In that moment, the world changed.

Novarupta, a volcano located 100 miles to the northwest on the Alaskan Peninsula, had exploded. (Residents of Juneau, 750 miles away, heard the boom a full hour later.) Ash and gases spewed from the earth, forming a huge cloud that surged toward Kodiak within 4 hours. It ultimately engulfed the area in a hot, suffocating haze of sulfur and jagged pumice.

Volcanic eruptions can mean weather disruptions.

by Evelyn Browning Garriss

Left: **For 4 hours on June 6, 1912, thick plumes of smoke spewed violently from the Novarupta volcano, rising 20 miles into the atmosphere and eventually engulfing the Alaskan Peninsula in hot, suffocating gases and debris.**

Below: **Katmai National Park and Preserve, overlooking The Valley of Ten Thousand Smokes, which the Novarupta eruption filled with up to 660 feet of ash-flow deposits**

–R. McGimsey/USGS

Below: **Novarupta's lava dome–a 300-foot-high pile of rock–is all that remains of the 1912 volcanic explosion that devastated the region.**

–G. Iwatsubo/USGS

For 3 days, an impenetrable, dark, ash fog hung over the region, cutting off radio communication and obliterating even the light of a lantern held at arm's length. Lightning knifed through the acidic fog, setting buildings and woodlands on fire. As ash accumulated like snow up to a foot deep, roofs collapsed. The corpses of millions of birds and animals that had been blinded and choked by the soot littered the wilderness. Water in streams became undrinkable and thousands of fish died. (Seven years passed before the salmon industry recovered.)

By June 9, acid rain had disintegrated garments hanging on clotheslines in Vancouver and sulfurous ash had fallen on Seattle. By June 10, the ash had passed over Virginia. On June 17, it reached Algeria in North Africa.

The eruption finally ended after 3 days, but its ash lingered in the atmosphere for years. Some scientists now believe that Novarupta's ash contributed to the cold, dreary rains that filled soldiers' trenches during World War I as well as to chilly temperatures in 1912 and 1917—the two coldest years in official U.S. records. Recent models also indicate that the cool land temperatures, another outcome of ash in the atmosphere, disrupted global monsoons, killing crops as far away as Egypt and India.

continued

All that remains of Novarupta's mighty blast is the eerie, ash-covered Valley of Ten Thousand Smokes and a 300-foot-high pile of lava rock.

Why did Novarupta impact weather across the globe?

Because of the altitude that the ash reached. The higher a column of volcanic debris (rock, chemicals, and volcanic glass) rises, the longer it lingers in the atmosphere and the longer it affects Earth's weather and climate. Novarupta's ash plume rose 20 miles into the atmosphere.

Altitude Matters

Fifty to 70 volcanic eruptions occur on Earth each year, on average. Despite more than 200 years of study, we know neither how to predict volcano eruptions accurately nor how to model a specific one's effect on weather. We do know, however, that each eruption is different in size, location, and chemical composition and that each one affects weather differently. Even moderate explosions with ash clouds that rise 3 miles have four effects on climate, three of which are considered undesirable:

Volcanic ash reflects incoming sunlight and absorbs infrared radiation (heat). As a result, less sunlight reaches Earth's surface. When land and ocean surfaces receive less solar warming, they cool.

The chemicals in volcanic ash, particularly sulfur and hydrogen chloride, combine with moisture in the atmosphere to create aerosols. These form clouds that block incoming sunlight, resulting in cooling on Earth. This cooling effect is particularly strong if the clouds have a high sulfur content, which will make them shiny enough to reflect the sunlight back into space.

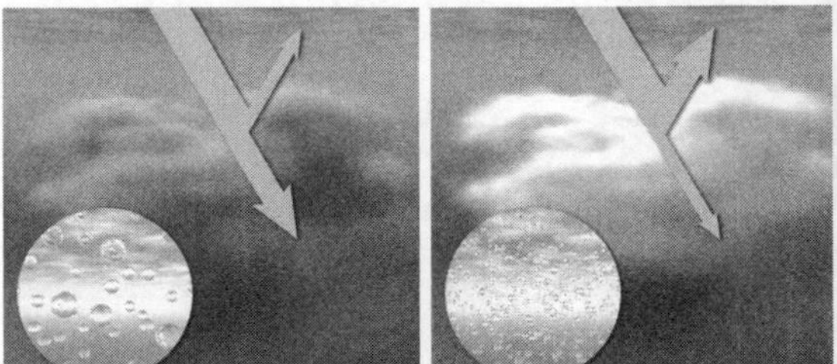

Low concentrations of volcanic aerosols form translucent clouds *(left)*. High concentrations *(right)* form dense clouds that reflect light back up into space, lingering for

HOW TO MEASURE VOLCANIC ERUPTIONS

The Volcanic Explosivity Index (VEI)

VEI/Description	Plume Height	Volume of Debris
0/Nonexplosive	<330 ft.	3.53×10^4 ft.^{3}
1/Gentle	330–3,300 ft.	3.53×10^5 ft.^{3}
2/Explosive	.5–3 mi.	3.53×10^7 ft.^{3}
3/Severe	2–9 mi.	3.53×10^8 ft.^{3}
4/Cataclysmic	6–15.5 mi.	3.53×10^9 ft.^{3}
5/Paroxysmal	>15.5 mi.	1.31×10^9 yds.^{3}
6/Colossal	>15.5 mi.	1.31×10^{10} yds.^{3}
7/Supercolossal	>15.5 mi.	1.31×10^{11} yds.^{3}
8/Megacolossal	>15.5 mi.	1.31×10^{12} yds.^{3}

years before gathering enough moisture to precipitate out into the atmosphere, usually as heavy rain or snowfall.

➡ **Volcanic aerosols filter sunlight and create spectacularly colorful sunsets.** The 1883 eruption of Krakatau in what is now Indonesia affected global sunsets for years, turning skies so vividly red that fire engines were called out to qucnch apparent conflagrations in New York City; Poughkeepsie, New York; and New Haven, Connecticut.

Recently, scientists have discovered that when volcanic ash enters the stratosphere, it has a fifth effect on climate:

➡ **As volcanic ash warms (see first effect), it heats the stratosphere below it, causing that air layer to expand and changing its pressure.** These changes alter air pressure in the troposphere, which is beneath the stratosphere. Global wind patterns are shaped by air pressure, so the changes imposed by large eruptions and widespread aerosols can result in enormous changes in weather for months—even years. (For example: Circumpolar winds blow around the Arctic and can trap the cold polar air mass in the north. If these winds weaken, frigid air surges south.)

How Big = How Bad

- **SMALL ERUPTIONS, with a Volcanic Explosivity Index (VEI) of 2 or a plume less than 3 miles high, affect local areas for only hours or days.**
- **MODERATE ERUPTIONS, with a VEI of 3 or a plume 3 to 6 miles high, can last for a few weeks and affect areas hundreds, even thousands, of miles away.**
- **LARGE ERUPTIONS, with a VEI of 4+ or a plume 6 to 10 miles high, depending on location, send ash and chemicals into and through the troposphere to the stratosphere, where it orbits Earth and can influence the weather for years.**

continued

Latitude Matters

Following World War I, many experts focused more on the impact of *tropical* volcanoes (those located between the latitudinal tropics of Cancer and Capricorn). One of the most profound facts that these studies revealed is that a drop of only fractions of a degree Fahrenheit can create major changes in global precipitation patterns.

Then, on April 14, 2010, Iceland's Eyjafjallajökull erupted; its ash plume disrupted air travel in Europe for almost 6 weeks. Scientists began to focus on the impact of northern volcanoes, and what they discovered was startling.

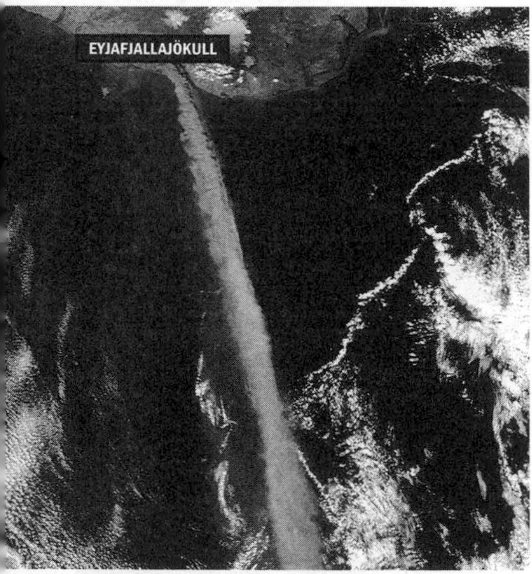

–NASA

Iceland's Eyjafjallajökull volcanic ash plume as seen from space on May 11, 2010.

The impact of a *polar* volcano (between 60° and 90° latitude) is very different from that of a tropical one. While global winds spread the debris from tropical volcanoes worldwide, the debris from polar volcanoes tends to be trapped by Arctic winds. Depending on the size of the eruption, this debris seldom travels farther south than the United States, China, and the Mediterranean. The aerosols of polar volcanoes are concentrated, and they have significant local impact.

Most surprisingly, studies since the recent Icelandic blast have revealed that 2009 was a "year of the volcano." Two cataclysmic eruptions occurred in the northwest Pacific that year: those of Alaska's Mount Redoubt, with an 11-mile-high plume in March, and Russia's Sarychev Peak, with a 13-mile-high plume in June. Neither came close to the size of Novarupta's, but the combined debris from these eruptions created weather havoc. It blocked solar radiation, causing the Arctic air mass to remain frigid and the jet stream (and stormy cold fronts) to veer southward. As a result:

- **Summer 2009 was one of the coolest in recent U.S. history, with some 300 low-temperature records, despite the presence of an El Niño that warmed the tropical Pacific.**
- **The eastern half of the United States endured almost endless rainfall.**
- **From the Canadian prairies to the U.S. Midwest, farmers struggled with a cool, delayed planting season and sluggish crop development.**
- **In September, the El Niño blessed Canada with warm temperatures, while the United**

On June 12, 2009, Russia's Sarychev Peak erupted. The 13-mile-high column of volcanic ash and debris that it produced contributed to many disruptive weather patterns that year.

–Astronaut team, International Space Station/NASA/JSC

States suffered through the slowest harvest in 35 years, with farmers gathering waterlogged crops well into December.

➡ In winter 2009–10, the plunging jet stream caused unusually warm and dry conditions in Canada, while record-breaking blizzards slammed the mid-Atlantic states and bitterly cold Arctic air engulfed the U.S. plains, the East, and the Deep South.

➡ Europe shivered through its coldest winter in decades, and hundreds died.

➡ Beijing suffered its coldest winter in 40 years, and numerous snowfalls crushed thousands of buildings in northern China and East Asia.

➡ The Indian subcontinent endured a 25 percent drop in average precipitation, causing a drought that affected 700 million people—primarily due to the northern volcanoes and the El Niño that disrupted the South Asian monsoon.

A volcano on the scale of Novarupta could happen again. According to the U.S. Geological Service: "Of the numerous volcanoes scattered across southern Alaska, at least ten are capable of exploding in a 1912-scale eruption."

–Alaska Volcano Observatory

The active lava dome of Alaska's Mount Redoubt spews a plume of smoke on May 8, 2009, several weeks after its March eruption.

continued

A Few Historic Blowouts

–National Geographic

NOVARUPTA, ALASKA, 1912

With a Volcanic Explosivity Index (VEI) of 6 and a 20-mile-high plume, this eruption was 30 times more forceful than that of Mount St. Helens and three times more powerful than that of Mount Pinatubo.

–Alaska Volcano Observatory

MOUNT REDOUBT, ALASKA, 2009

VEI: 4

–Max Haase

EYJAFJALLAJÖKULL, ICELAND, 2010

VEI: 4

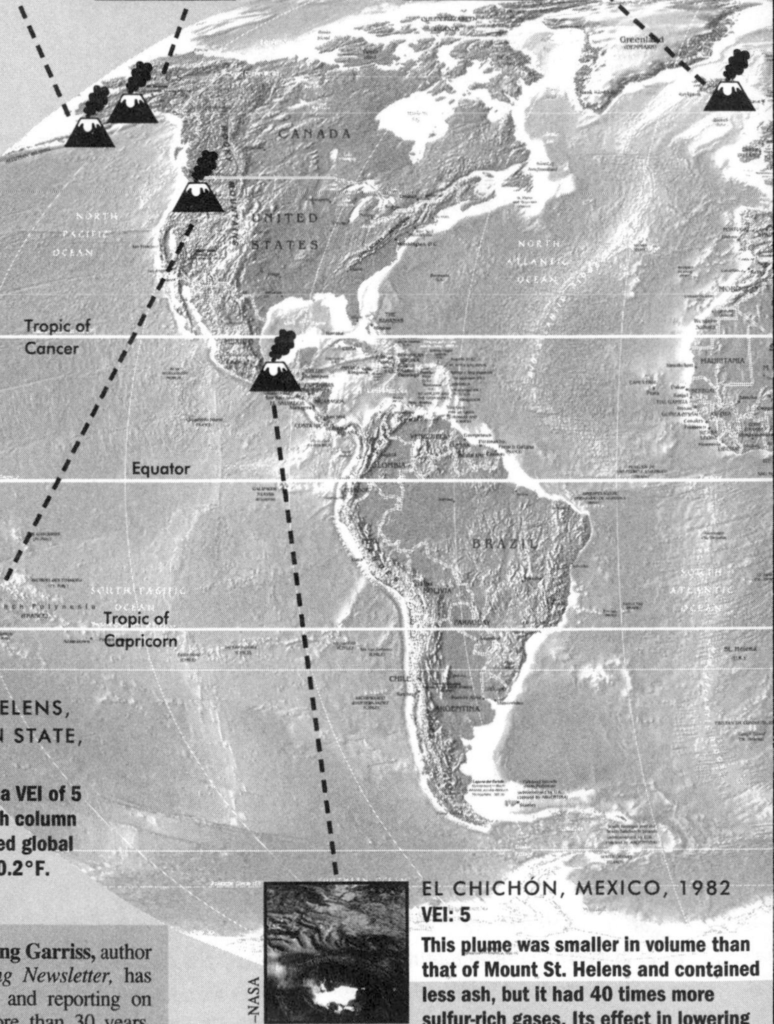

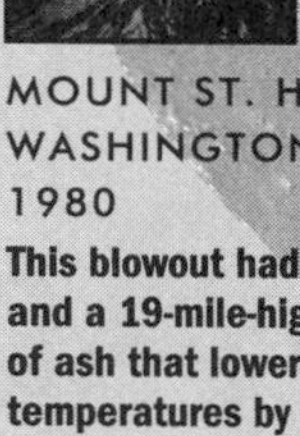
–USGS

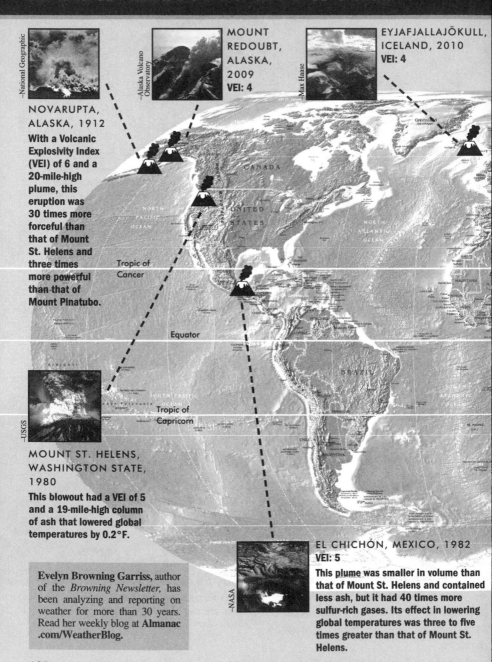

MOUNT ST. HELENS, WASHINGTON STATE, 1980

This blowout had a VEI of 5 and a 19-mile-high column of ash that lowered global temperatures by 0.2°F.

–NASA

EL CHICHÓN, MEXICO, 1982

VEI: 5

This plume was smaller in volume than that of Mount St. Helens and contained less ash, but it had 40 times more sulfur-rich gases. Its effect in lowering global temperatures was three to five times greater than that of Mount St. Helens.

Evelyn Browning Garriss, author of the *Browning Newsletter,* has been analyzing and reporting on weather for more than 30 years. Read her weekly blog at **Almanac.com/WeatherBlog.**

Here are some volcanic eruptions that have affected weather around the globe:

—USGS

MOUNT PINATUBO,
THE PHILIPPINES, 1991

With a VEI of 6, this was the second largest eruption in the 20th century. Ash from it cooled the globe 0.9°F.

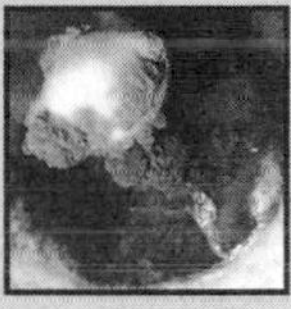

—NASA

SARYCHEV
PEAK,
RUSSIA,
2009

VEI: 4

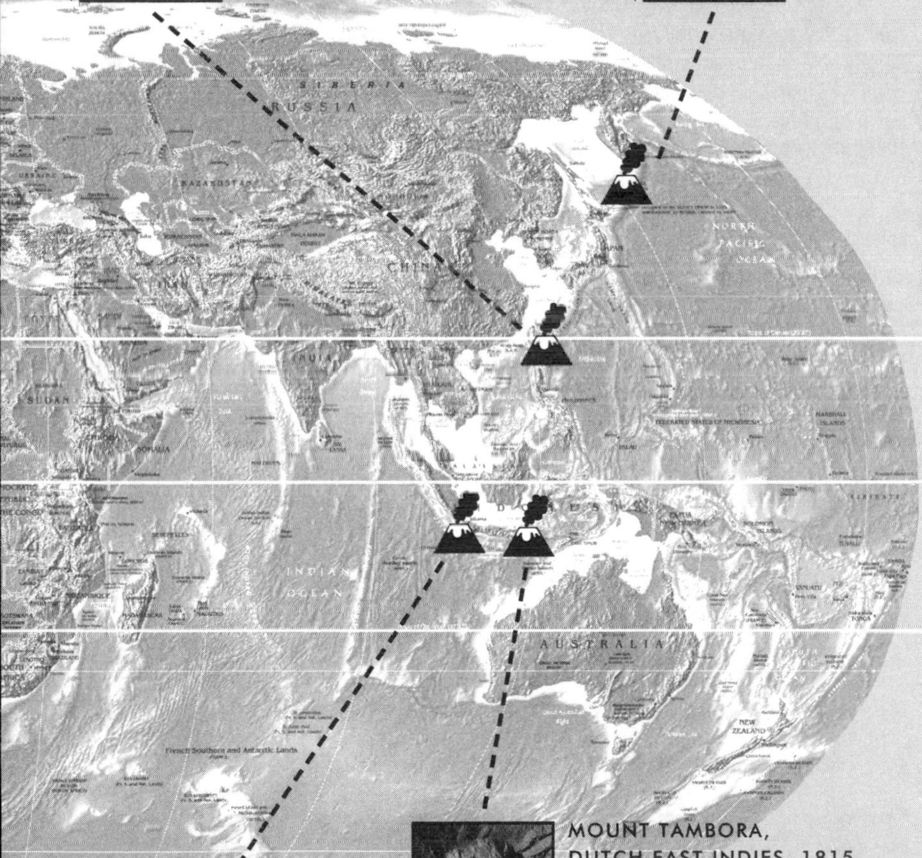

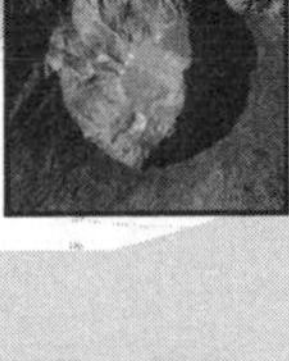

—NASA

MOUNT TAMBORA,
DUTCH EAST INDIES, 1815

This was the largest known eruption in more than 1,600 years, with a VEI of 7. Its dust and chemicals contributed to the infamous "year without a summer"—1816—when cold temperatures prevailed and summer frost occurred in the Northeast, causing crops to fail.

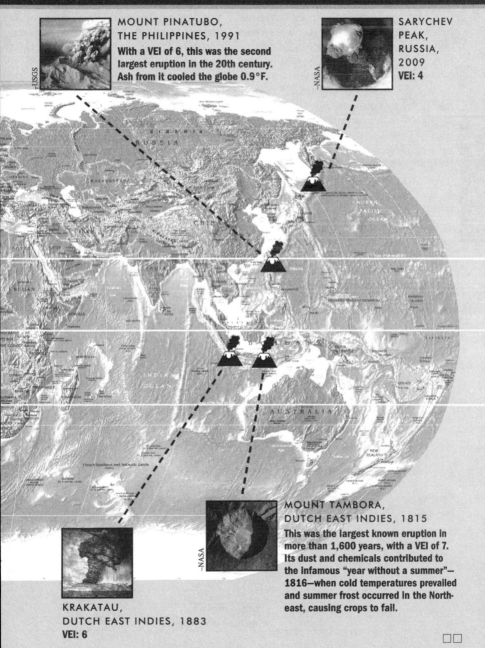

KRAKATAU,
DUTCH EAST INDIES, 1883

VEI: 6

How We Predict the Weather

We derive our weather forecasts from a secret formula that was devised by the founder of this Almanac, Robert B. Thomas, in 1792. Thomas believed that weather on Earth was influenced by sunspots, which are magnetic storms on the surface of the Sun.

Over the years, we have refined and enhanced that formula with state-of-the-art technology and modern scientific calculations. We employ three scientific disciplines to make our long-range predictions: solar science, the study of sunspots and other solar activity; climatology, the study of prevailing weather patterns; and meteorology, the study of the atmosphere. We predict weather trends and events by comparing solar patterns and historical weather conditions with current solar activity.

Our forecasts emphasize temperature and precipitation deviations from averages, or normals. These are based on 30-year statistical averages prepared by government meteorological agencies and updated every 10 years. The most-recent tabulations span the period 1971 through 2000.

We believe that nothing in the universe happens haphazardly, that there is a cause-and-effect pattern to all phenomena. However, although neither we nor any other forecasters have as yet gained sufficient insight into the mysteries of the universe to predict the weather with total accuracy, our results are almost always very close to our traditional claim of 80 percent.

WEATHER

How Accurate Was Our Forecast Last Winter?

■ We predicted that winter season temperatures would be below normal, on average, in regions 1 through 10, above normal in regions 11 through 15, and near normal in region 16. The accuracy of those forecasts is shown below, using a city selected from each region. We were correct in the direction of departure from normal in every region, our forecast was within 0.6 degrees F in every region, and our forecasts differed from actual conditions by less than 0.2 degree F, on average.

We were also correct in our forecasts of where snowfall would be above normal; however, the areas of above-normal snowfall were larger than we forecast. We expected above-normal snowfall in the Mid-Atlantic, but it extended north through most of the Northeast; in western New York, but it extended west through the Lower Lakes; and in northern Minnesota, but it extended south to North Texas and west through the northern High Plains.

The Northeast and Ohio Valley had more precipitation than we forecast, while Texas and Oklahoma had less. In the remaining 13 regions, we were correct in the direction of precipitation departure from normal in all or much of the region, or 81 percent accurate.

Thus, our winter temperature and precipitation forecast was 90.6 percent accurate.

Region/City	Dec.–Feb. Temp. Variations From Normal (degrees F) PREDICTED	ACTUAL
1/Burlington	–0.1	–0.1
2/Philadelphia	–0.8	–0.6
3/Harrisburg	–1.5	–1.4
4/Raleigh	–1.0	–0.8
5/Miami	–0.3	–0.1
6/Chicago	–0.7	–0.5
7/Charleston	–0.4	–0.8
8/Nashville	–0.6	–0.6
9/Minneapolis	–0.8	–0.9
10/Topeka	–0.2	–0.4
11/Oklahoma City	+0.2	+0.8
12/Denver	+0.2	+0.8
13/Boise	+1.2	+1.2
14/El Paso	+1.2	+1.2
15/Eugene	+0.6	+0.7
16/Los Angeles	–0.0	–0.1

Weather Regions

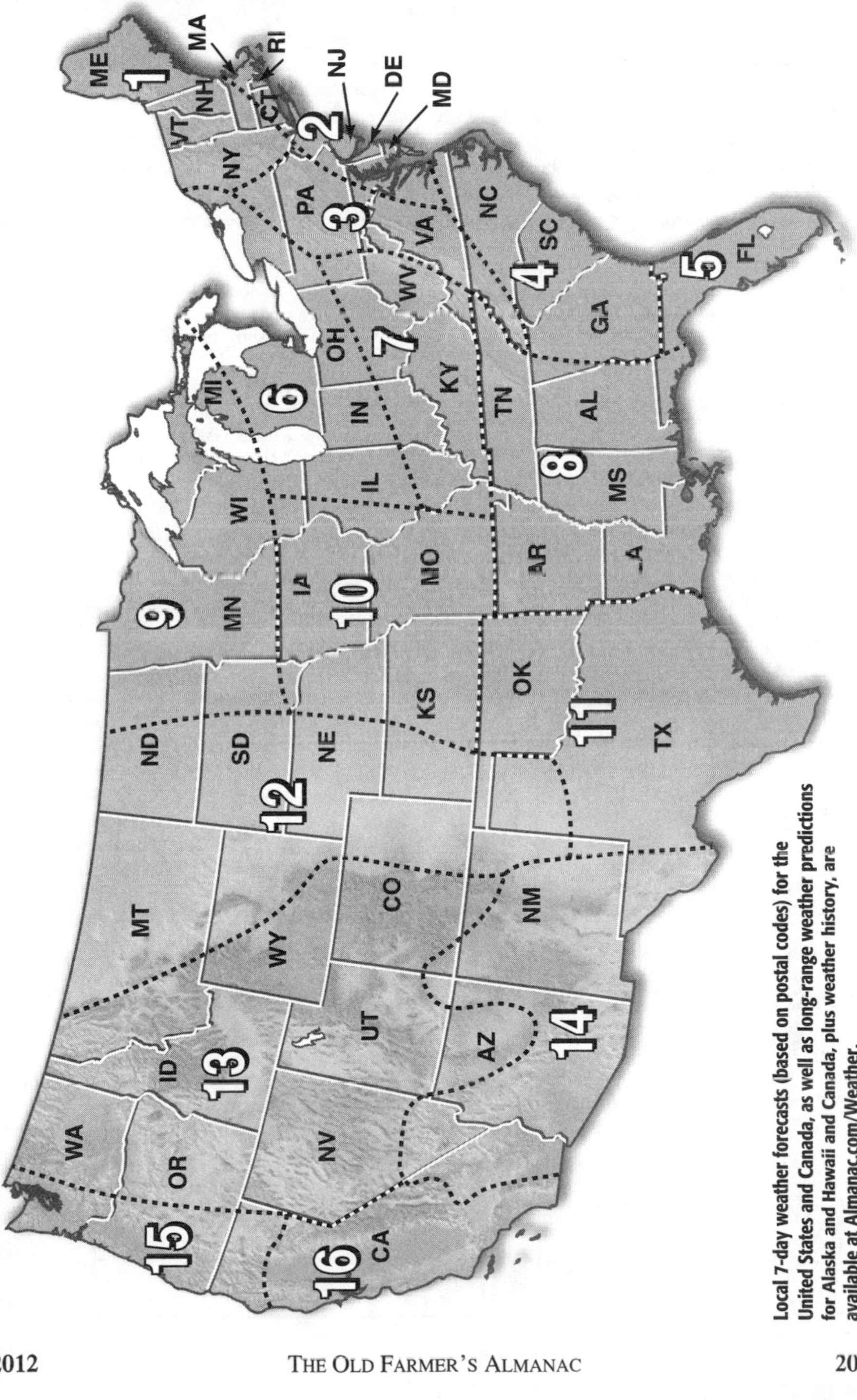

Local 7-day weather forecasts (based on postal codes) for the United States and Canada, as well as long-range weather predictions for Alaska and Hawaii and Canada, plus weather history, are available at Almanac.com/Weather.

Northeast

SUMMARY: Winter will be a bit colder than normal, on average, with below-normal precipitation and near-normal snowfall. The coldest periods will occur in late January, early to mid- and late February, and mid-March, with the snowiest periods in mid-December, mid- to late January, and mid- and late February.

April and May will be much cooler and drier than normal.

Summer temperatures will be near normal, on average, with near- to below-normal rainfall. The hottest periods will be in early to mid-June, late July, and early August.

September and October will be warmer than normal. Precipitation will be above normal in the north and below normal in the south.

NOV. 2011: Temp. 34° (1° above avg.); precip. 2" (1.5" below avg.). 1–5 Rainy periods, quite mild. 6–8 Flurries, cold. 9–16 Snow north, showers south, then sunny, chilly. 17–23 Rainy periods, mild. 24–27 Snow, then sunny, cold. 28–30 Snow north, rain south; milder.

DEC. 2011: Temp. 29° (5° above avg. north, 1° below south); precip. 3" (avg.). 1–4 Rainy periods, quite mild. 5–8 Flurries, seasonable. 9–16 Snow showers; mild, then cold. 17–21 Blizzard, then windy, cold. 22–23 Heavy snow, seasonable. 24–29 Snow showers, mild. 30–31 Sunny, cold.

JAN. 2012: Temp. 23° (3° above avg.); precip. 2" (1" below avg.). 1–8 Sunny, then snow showers, mild. 9–12 Sunny, cold. 13–19 Snow north, showers south, then sunny, mild. 20–26 Snowstorm, then snow showers, seasonable. 27–31 Snow showers, very cold.

FEB. 2012: Temp. 14° (7° below avg.); precip. 2" (0.5" below avg.). 1–3 Sunny, turning mild. 4–7 Snow showers, very cold. 8–12 Snow, then sunny, very cold. 13–16 Snowy periods, mild. 17–20 Snow showers, cold. 21–25 Snow, then sunny, cold. 26–29 Snowstorm.

MAR. 2012: Temp. 29° (4° below avg.); precip. 1.5" (1.5" below avg.). 1–2 Sunny, cold. 3–6 Snow north; sunny, mild south. 7–13 Snowy periods, then sunny, very cold. 14–19 Snow, then sunny, mild. 20–23 Showers, seasonable. 24–26 Sunny, warm. 27–31 Rain and snow, cold.

APR. 2012: Temp. 41° (4° below avg.); precip. 2.5" (2" below avg. north, 1" above south). 1–7 Showers, then sunny, cool. 8–12 Rainy periods, cool. 13–17 Rain and snow showers, cool. 18–24 Sunny, turning warm. 25–30 Showers, cool.

MAY 2012: Temp. 50° (6° below avg.); precip. 3" (0.5" above avg. north, 1.5" below south). 1–5 Snow north, rainy periods south; chilly. 6–12 Rainy periods, cool. 13–17 Sunny; chilly nights. 18–24 Showers, then sunny, cool. 25–31 Sunny, very warm.

JUNE 2012: Temp. 66° (avg. north, 2° above south); precip. 2.5" (2" below avg. north, avg. south). 1–5 Showers, warm. 6–9 Sunny, hot. 10–18 Showers; cool, then warm. 19–22 Sunny, nice. 23–30 Scattered t-storms; warm, then cool.

JULY 2012: Temp. 70° (2° above avg. north, 1° below south); precip. 5" (1" above avg.). 1–9 Scattered t-storms, seasonable. 10–14 Sunny, warm. 15–18 T-storms, humid. 19–28 Scattered t-storms, seasonable. 29–31 Sunny, warm.

AUG. 2012: Temp. 65.5° (1.5° below avg.); precip. 3.5" (1" above avg. north, 2" below south). 1–10 T-storms, then sunny, seasonable. 11–15 T-storms, warm. 16–20 Sunny, cool. 21–27 Rainy periods, cool. 28–31 Sunny, nice.

SEPT. 2012: Temp. 60.5° (1.5° above avg.); precip. 4" (2" above avg. north, 1" below south). 1–5 T-storms, then sunny, cool. 6–13 Sunny, warm. 14–18 Rainy, cool. 19–23 Sunny, then showers, warm. 24–26 Sunny, warm. 27–30 Showers, then sunny, cool.

OCT. 2012: Temp. 49.5° (1.5° above avg.); precip. 3.5" (avg.). 1–4 Rainy, mild. 5–8 Sunny, cool. 9–16 Showers, mild. 17–24 Rain, then sunny, chilly. 25–31 Rainy, mild, then sunny, cool.

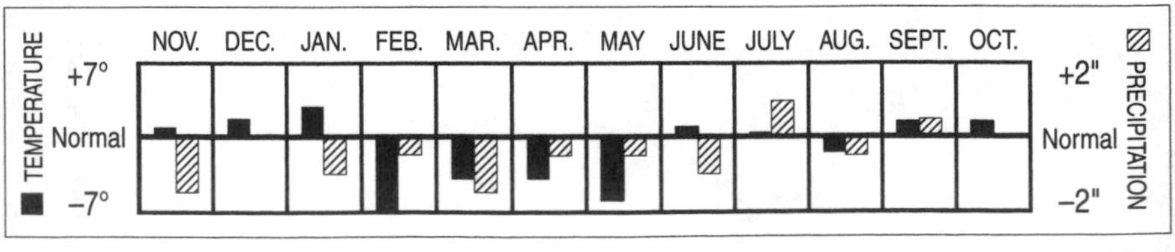

Atlantic Corridor

SUMMARY: Winter will be drier than normal, with near-normal temperatures but above-normal snowfall. The coldest periods will be in mid-December and early and mid-February. The snowiest periods will be in mid-December, mid- and late January, and late February.

April and May will be much cooler than normal. Rainfall will be above normal in the north and below normal in the south.

Summer will be cooler and rainier than normal, with the hottest periods in early and mid-July.

September and October will be cooler and drier than normal.

NOV. 2011: Temp. 46.5° (0.5° below avg.); precip. 1.5" (2" below avg.). 1–5 Rainy periods, warm. 6–9 Sunny, cool. 10–16 Showers, cool. 17–22 Rainy periods, mild. 23–27 Showers, then sunny, cold. 28–30 Sprinkles.

DEC. 2011: Temp. 38° (1° above avg. northeast, 1° below southeast); precip. 3" (avg.). 1–4 Showers, warm. 5–9 Rain and snow, then sunny, cool. 10–12 Sunny, warm. 13–16 Rain and snow, then sunny, cold. 17–20 Snowstorm, then sunny, cold. 21–27 Rain, then sunny, seasonable. 28–31 Rain and snow showers.

JAN. 2012: Temp. 38° (5° above avg.); precip. 2.5" (1" below avg.). 1–6 Rain, then sunny, mild. 7–11 Showers, then sunny, seasonable. 12–19 Snow, then sunny, warm. 20–24 Rain to snow, then sunny, cold. 25–29 Rain and snow north; sunny, mild south. 30–31 Blizzard.

FEB. 2012: Temp. 28° (5° below avg.); precip. 4" (1" above avg.). 1–2 Sunny, very cold. 3–4 Snow to rain. 5–9 Sunny; cold, then warm. 10–16 Snowy periods, cold. 17–19 Sunny, very cold. 20–23 Snow showers, cold. 24–26 Rain, mild. 27–29 Stormy; snow north, rain south.

MAR. 2012: Temp. 41.5° (4° below avg. north, 1° above south); precip. 2.5" (1.5" below avg.). 1–4 Sunny, warm. 5–12 Rain to snow, then sunny, cold. 13–19 Rain and snow, then sunny, cool. 20–26 Rain, then sunny, warm. 27–29 Showers, then sunny, cool. 30–31 Rain and snow north; sunny, warm south.

APR. 2012: Temp. 49° (5° below avg. north, 1° below south); precip. 4.5" (1" above avg.). 1–7 Showers, then sunny, cool. 8–12 Rainy, cool north; t-storms, warm south. 13–20 Showers, cool. 21–24 Sunny, nice. 25–30 Showers, cool.

MAY 2012: Temp. 56.5° (5.5° below avg.); precip. 3" (2" above avg. north, 2" below south). 1–8 Rainy periods, cool. 9–13 Sunny, turning warm. 14–17 Rain, then sunny, cool. 18–21 Rain, then sunny, seasonable. 22–24 Showers, cool. 25–31 Sunny, turning warm.

JUNE 2012: Temp. 70° (1° below avg.); precip. 4.5" (1" above avg.). 1–9 Showers north; sunny, warm south. 10–14 T-storms, then sunny, cool. 15–18 Heavy t-storms, warm and humid. 19–22 Sunny, cool. 23–30 Scattered t-storms, cool.

JULY 2012: Temp. 75° (1° below avg.); precip. 6" (2" above avg.). 1–9 Scattered t-storms; hot, then seasonable. 10–12 Sunny, warm. 13–20 T-storms, then sunny, hot. 21–31 Scattered t-storms, warm and humid.

AUG. 2012: Temp. 71.5° (2.5° below avg.); precip. 6" (2" above avg.). 1–7 Scattered t-storms, turning cooler. 8–11 Sunny, warm. 12–15 Scattered t-storms, seasonable. 16–19 Rainy, cool. 20–23 Sunny. 24–31 T-storms, then sunny, cool.

SEPT. 2012: Temp. 65.5° (1.5° below avg.); precip. 2" (1.5" below avg.). 1–7 T-storms, then sunny, cool. 8–13 Showers, then sunny, warm. 14–20 Showers, then sunny, cool. 21–25 T-storms, then sunny, cool. 26–28 Sunny, warm. 29–30 Showers, cool.

OCT. 2012: Temp. 54° (2° below avg.): precip. 3" (0.5" below avg.). 1–4 Showers, warm. 5–8 Sunny, cool. 9–11 Showers, warm. 12–17 Sunny, cool. 18–24 Rain, then sunny, cool. 25–27 Showers, warm. 28–31 Sunny, cold.

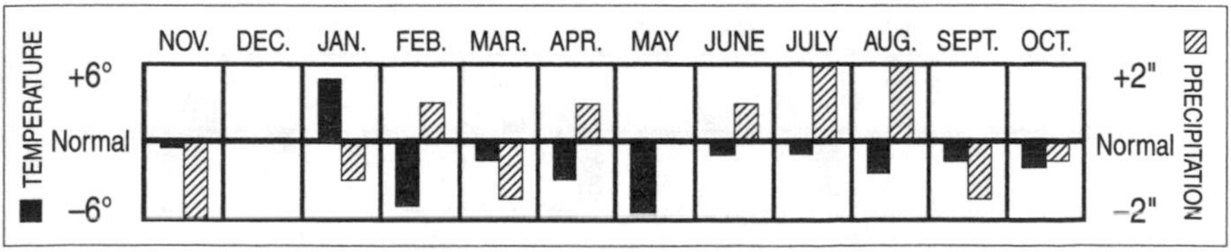

Appalachians

SUMMARY: Winter will be slightly milder and much drier than normal, although snowfall will be above normal. The coldest periods will be in mid-December and early and mid- to late February. The snowiest periods will be in early to mid-December, mid-January, and mid-February.

April and May will be cooler and drier than normal, with May especially chilly.

Summer will be a bit cooler than normal, with the hottest periods in early June and early July. Rainfall will be below normal in the north and above normal in the south.

September and October will be much cooler and drier than normal.

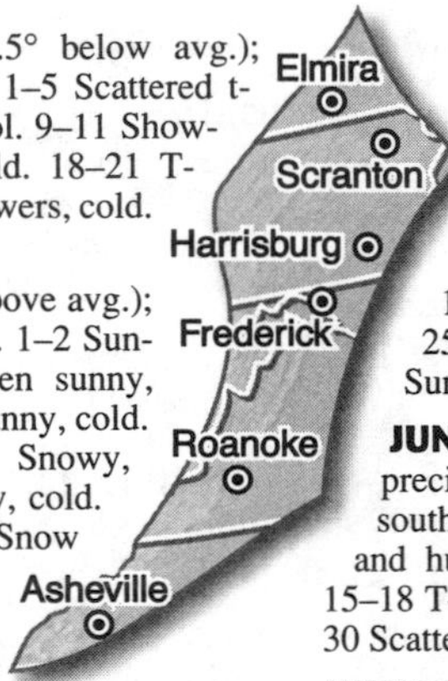

NOV. 2011: Temp. 42° (0.5° below avg.); precip. 2.5" (1" below avg.). 1–5 Scattered t-storms, warm. 6–8 Sunny, cool. 9–11 Showers, warm. 12–17 Sunny, cold. 18–21 T-storms, mild. 22–27 Snow showers, cold. 28–30 Showers, mild.

DEC. 2011: Temp. 33° (1° above avg.); precip. 2.5" (0.5" below avg.). 1–2 Sunny, warm. 3–5 T-storms, then sunny, cold. 6–9 Heavy snow, then sunny, cold. 10–12 Sunny, mild. 13–17 Snowy, cold. 18–22 Sunny, then snow, cold. 23–27 Sunny, mild. 28–31 Snow showers, cold.

JAN. 2012: Temp. 33.5° (5.5° above avg.); precip. 2" (1" below avg.). 1–7 A few rain and snow showers, mild. 8–11 Sunny, turning cold. 12–19 Snow, then sunny, unseasonably mild. 20–21 Rain to snow. 22–26 Snowy periods north; showers, mild south. 27–31 Snow showers, cold.

FEB. 2012: Temp. 23° (5° below avg.); precip. 3" (0.5" above avg.). 1–6 Snow showers, very cold. 7–9 Sunny, mild. 10–14 Snow, then flurries, cold. 15–22 Snow showers, very cold. 23–25 Sunny, mild. 26–29 Rain to snow.

MAR. 2012: Temp. 40.5° (avg. north, 3° above south); precip. 2.5" (0.5" below avg.). 1–4 Sunny, mild. 5–7 Showers, mild. 8–12 Rain to snow, then sunny, cold. 13–17 Rain and snow showers, chilly. 18–20 Sunny, mild. 21–27 Showers, then sunny, warm. 28–31 Showers, warm.

APR. 2012: Temp. 49° (1° below avg.); precip. 3.5" (avg.). 1–3 Showers, mild. 4–6 Sunny, cool. 7–13 Showers, warm, then sunny, cool. 14–16 Showers, warm. 17–18 Rain, mountain snow; cool. 19–23 Rain, then sunny, cool. 24–27 T-storms, then sunny, cool. 28–30 Rainy, raw.

MAY 2012: Temp. 54.5° (5.5° below avg.); precip. 3" (1" below avg.). 1–8 Showers, cool. 9–11 Sunny, cool. 12–19 T-storms, then sunny, cool. 20–25 Sunny, warm, then rainy, cool. 26–31 Sunny, warm.

JUNE 2012: Temp. 69° (1° above avg.); precip. 4" (1.5" below avg. north, 1" above south). 1–5 Sunny, hot. 6–10 T-storms, hot and humid. 11–14 Scattered t-storms, cool. 15–18 T-storms, warm. 19–22 Sunny, cool. 23–30 Scattered t-storms, seasonable.

JULY 2012: Temp. 72° (1° below avg.); precip. 4" (0.5" above avg.). 1–11 Scattered t-storms; hot, then cool. 12–15 Sunny, nice. 16–25 A few t-storms, seasonable. 26–31 Scattered t-storms, warm.

AUG. 2012: Temp. 68° (3° below avg.); precip. 4" (0.5" above avg.). 1–11 T-storms, then sunny, comfortable. 12–20 A few t-storms, cool. 21–31 Sunny, cool.

SEPT. 2012: Temp. 62.5° (avg. north, 3° below south); precip. 2" (1.5" below avg.). 1–8 T-storms, then sunny, cool. 9–14 Scattered t-storms, warm. 15–19 Showers, cool. 20–25 T-storms, then sunny, cool. 26–30 Sunny, warm, then showers.

OCT. 2012: Temp. 50° (3° below avg.); precip. 3" (avg.). 1–6 Showers, then sunny, cool. 7–11 Scattered showers, warm. 12–17 Sunny, pleasant. 18–23 Showers, then sunny, cold. 24–27 Showers, mild. 28–31 Sunny, cold.

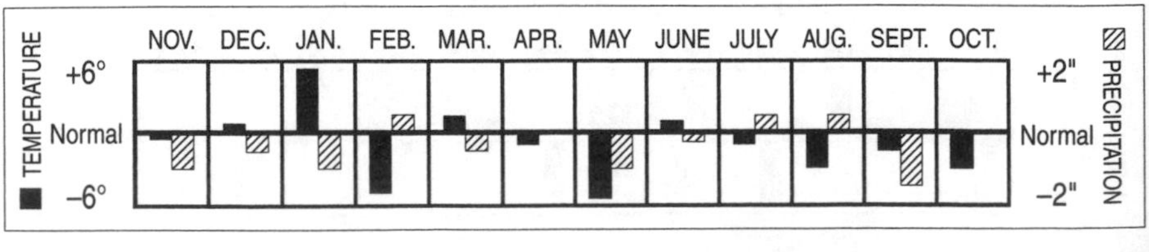

Southeast

SUMMARY: Winter temperatures will be near or slightly above normal, with below-normal precipitation and near-normal snowfall. The coldest periods will be in mid-December and early and mid-February. The snowiest periods will be in mid-December and early February.

April and May will be cooler than normal, especially in the west, with much-above-normal rainfall in the southeast and near-normal rainfall elsewhere.

Summer will be much cooler than normal, with above-normal rainfall. The hottest temperatures will be in mid- to late July and mid-August.

September and October will be much cooler and drier than normal, despite a hurricane threat in early to mid-September.

NOV. 2011: Temp. 54° (1° below avg.); precip. 2" (1" below avg.). 1–5 T-storms, warm. 6–17 Sunny, cool. 18–21 T-storms, warm. 22–30 A few showers; cool, then warm.

DEC. 2011: Temp. 46.5° (0.5° below avg.); precip. 5.5" (avg. north, 4" above south). 1–6 Rainy periods; mild, then cold. 7–10 Sunny, cool. 11–15 Rainy periods east, sunny west; seasonable. 16–20 Rain and snow north, rain south, then sunny, cold. 21–31 Rainy periods, varying temperatures.

JAN. 2012: Temp. 48° (3° above avg.); precip. 4" (0.5" below avg.). 1–3 Rainy, mild. 4–5 Heavy rain southeast, sunny elsewhere; cold. 6–9 Rainy periods, mild. 10–13 Sunny east, showers west; chilly. 14–20 Sunny, then rainy, warm. 21–24 Sunny, seasonable. 25–31 Showers, mild.

FEB. 2012: Temp. 43° (3° below avg.); precip. 3" (1" below avg.). 1–7 Periods of rain and wet snow, cold. 8–9 Sunny, mild. 10–22 Periods of rain and wet snow, turning cold. 23–29 Sunny, then rainy, mild.

MAR. 2012: Temp. 58.5° (3.5° above avg.); precip. 2.5" (2" below avg.). 1–7 Rainy periods, mild. 8–12 Sunny, chilly. 13–15 Rainy periods, chilly. 16–18 A shower or two, mild. 19–31 Showers, then sunny, warm.

APR. 2012: Temp. 64° (2° above avg. east, avg. west); precip. 2.5" (0.5" below avg.). 1–4 Sunny, then t-storms, warm. 5–7 Showers, cool. 8–11 Scattered t-storms, very warm. 12–20 Sunny, then t-storms, cool. 21–30 Sunny, then t-storms, cool.

MAY 2012: Temp. 68.5° (2.5° below avg.); precip. 6.5" (avg. northwest, 6" above southeast). 1–8 Scattered t-storms, warm. 9–13 A t-storm or two, cool. 14–17 Heavy rain, chilly. 18–21 Sunny, mild. 22–31 Rainy periods, cool.

JUNE 2012: Temp. 75° (2° below avg.); precip. 4.5" (avg.). 1–4 Sunny, cool. 5–9 A few t-storms, seasonable. 10–12 Heavy rain. 13–18 Isolated t-storms, warm. 19–20 Heavy t-storms. 21–30 A few t-storms, seasonable.

JULY 2012: Temp. 78° (3° below avg.); precip. 5.5" (1" above avg.). 1–9 Scattered t-storms, cool. 10–14 T-storms, mainly south; cool. 15–31 Scattered P.M. t-storms, seasonable.

AUG. 2012: Temp. 76° (3° below avg.); precip. 6" (1" above avg.). 1–6 Scattered t-storms, seasonable. 7–11 Isolated t-storms, cool. 12–20 Scattered t-storms, hot. 21–25 T-storms east, sunny west; seasonable. 26–31 Isolated t-storms, cooler.

SEPT. 2012: Temp. 70° (4° below avg.); precip. 1.5" (3" below avg.). 1–9 T-storms, then sunny, cool. 10–15 Hurricane threat. 16–22 Sunny, then t-storms, cool. 23–28 Sunny; cool, then warm. 29–30 T-storms.

OCT. 2012: Temp. 60° (4° below avg.); precip. 3" (1" below avg.). 1–8 Showers, then sunny, cool. 9–11 T-storms, seasonable. 12–16 Sunny, cool. 17–22 T-storms, then sunny, cool. 23–28 Showers, varying temperatures. 29–31 Sunny, cool.

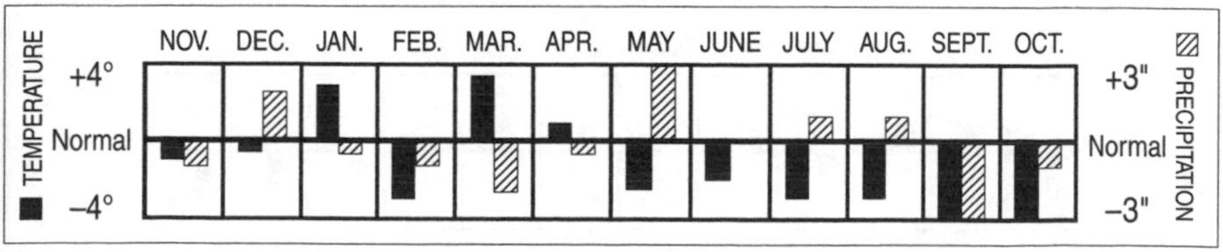

Florida

SUMMARY: Winter temperatures will be above normal in the north and below normal in the south, with below-normal rainfall. The coldest temperatures will be in early to mid-December, mid-January, and mid-February.

April and May will be warmer and drier than normal.

Summer will be slightly cooler and much rainier than normal, with the hottest periods in early and mid-July and mid-August.

September and October will be cooler than normal, with rainfall much below normal in the north and much above normal in the south. Expect a hurricane in early September, especially in South Florida.

NOV. 2011: Temp. 66.5° (1° below avg. north, 4° below south); precip. 0.5" (2" below avg.). 1–12 Sunny, warm north; a few t-storms south. 13–18 Scattered showers, cool. 19–20 Sunny, warm. 21–26 T-storms, then sunny, cool. 27–30 Scattered showers, warm.

DEC. 2011: Temp. 62° (avg. north, 2° below avg. south); precip. 1.5" (1" below avg.). 1–3 A few t-storms, warm. 4–8 Showers, then sunny, cool. 9–15 Showers, then sunny, cool. 16–22 Sunny, turning warm. 23–27 Showers, warm. 28–31 Sunny; cool, then warm.

JAN. 2012: Temp. 64° (3° above avg.); precip. 2" (2" below avg. north, 1" above south). 1–6 Showers, then sunny, warm. 7–8 Showers, warm. 9–16 Sunny north, rainy periods south; cool, then warm. 17–20 T-storms, warm. 21–26 Sunny; cool, then warm. 27–31 A few showers, warm.

FEB. 2012: Temp. 60° (1° below avg.); precip. 4.5" (2" above avg.). 1–6 Rainy periods; cool north, warm south. 7–13 Sunny, warm. 14–20 T-storms, then sunny, cold. 21–25 Sunny, turning warm. 26–29 Scattered t-storms, warm.

MAR. 2012: Temp. 68.5° (3.5° above avg. north, 0.5° below south); precip. 1" (2" below avg.). 1–8 Sunny, very warm. 9–13 T-storms, then sunny, cool. 14–19 Showers, then sunny, warm. 20–24 T-storms, seasonable. 25–31 Sunny, warm.

APR. 2012: Temp. 73° (5° above avg. north, 1° below south); precip. 0.5" (2" below avg.). 1–4 Sunny, warm. 5–19 Mainly sunny, a t-storm or two; very warm north, seasonable south. 20–26 Sunny, nice. 27–30 T-storms, warm.

MAY 2012: Temp. 78° (1° above avg.); precip. 3.5" (2" above avg. north, 3" below south). 1–8 Sunny, hot. 9–17 Scattered t-storms, turning cool. 18–24 Sunny, hot. 25–31 Daily t-storms, seasonable.

JUNE 2012: Temp. 80° (1° below avg.); precip. 10.5" (4" above avg.). 1–5 A few t-storms, cool. 6–11 Heavy t-storms, cool. 12–20 Scattered t-storms, seasonable. 21–30 Daily t-storms, warm and humid.

JULY 2012: Temp. 82° (avg.); precip. 7.5" (1" above avg.). 1–6 Sunny, hot. 7–17 Scattered t-storms, seasonable. 18–21 T-storms, hot. 22–26 Sunny, warm. 27–31 Daily t-storms, warm and humid.

AUG. 2012: Temp. 80° (1° below avg.); precip. 9.5" (2" above avg.). 1–6 Daily t-storms, warm. 7–12 Sunny, hot north; daily t-storms, warm south. 13–15 T-storms, warm. 16–20 Sunny, hot. 21–31 Scattered t-storms, seasonable.

SEPT. 2012: Temp. 78° (2° below avg.); precip. 8" (5" below avg. north, 7" above south). 1–2 Scattered t-storms, warm. 3–8 Hurricane threat. 9–14 Sunny, warm. 15–18 T-storms, then sunny, cool. 19–25 T-storms, then sunny, cool north; t-storms, cool south. 26–30 Sunny, warm north; t-storms south.

OCT. 2012: Temp. 73° (2° below avg.); precip. 3.5" (2" below avg. north, 1" above south). 1–7 Rain, then sunny, cool. 8–11 Showers, warm. 12–18 Sunny, cool, then warm north; t-storms south. 19–24 Sunny, nice. 25–31 T-storms, then sunny, chilly.

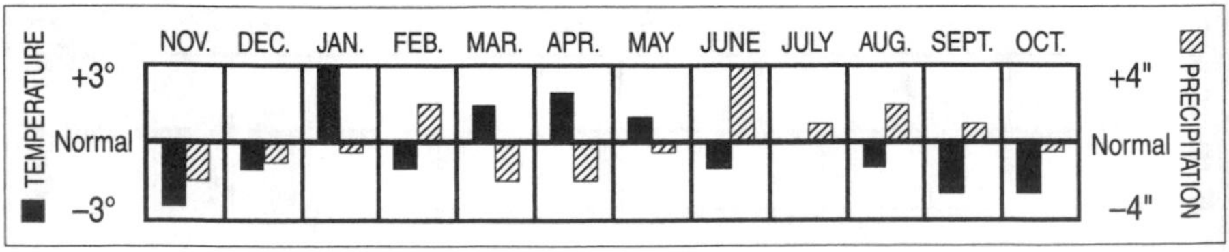

Region 6 Forecast

Lower Lakes

SUMMARY: Winter will be slightly milder than normal, on average, with the coldest periods in late November, mid-December, late January, and early and mid-February. Precipitation will be below normal, with near-normal snowfall. The snowiest periods will be in mid-December, mid- and late January, mid-February, and mid-March.

April and May will be cooler and drier than normal.

Summer temperatures will be below normal, on average, with below-normal rainfall. The hottest periods will be in early to mid-June and early and mid-July.

September and October will be cooler and rainier than normal.

NOV. 2011: Temp. 42° (2° above avg.); precip. 3.5" (avg. east, 2" above west). 1–8 Rain, then sunny, cool. 9–14 T-storms, warm, then sunny, cool. 15–20 Showers, warm. 21–23 Rain to snow. 24–27 Snow showers, very cold. 28–30 Ice to rain, warmer.

DEC. 2011: Temp. 31° (2° above avg.); precip. 2" (1" below avg.). 1–2 T-storms, warm. 3–10 Rain to snow, then sunny, turning mild. 11–19 Lake snows, cold. 20–26 Snow, then flurries, turning milder. 27–31 Periods of rain and snow, mild.

JAN. 2012: Temp. 28° (4° above avg.); precip. 1.5" (1" below avg.). 1–4 Snow showers, seasonable. 5–7 Sunny, mild. 8–12 Snow showers, cold. 13–17 Sunny, quite mild. 18–23 Snowstorm, then lake snows, cold. 24–31 Snowstorm, then lake snows, very cold.

FEB. 2012: Temp. 20° (4° below avg.); precip. 1" (1" below avg.). 1–3 Snow showers, turning milder. 4–6 Lake snows, very cold. 7–11 Sunny, mild, then snow showers, cold. 12–16 Snow showers, cold. 17–19 Lake snows, very cold. 20–22 Snow, then snow showers, cold. 23–29 Snow showers, seasonable.

MAR. 2012: Temp. 38° (2° above avg.); precip. 2.5" (0.5" below avg.). 1–4 Sunny, mild. 5–7 Showers, mild. 8–12 Snowy periods, cold. 13–17 Snow, then flurries, cold. 18–24 Showers, then sunny, warm. 25–28 Rain, then sunny, cool. 29–31 Rainy; mild, then cool.

APR. 2012: Temp. 46° (1° below avg.); precip. 3" (0.5" below avg.). 1–5 Showers, then sunny, cool. 6–10 A few t-storms, warm. 11–13 Sunny, cool. 14–22 Rain to snow, then sunny, cool. 23–31 A few showers; warm.

MAY 2012: Temp. 54° (4° below avg.); precip. 2.5" (1" below avg.). 1–4 Rainy periods, cool. 5–10 Showers, cool. 11–16 Sunny, warm, then showers, cool. 17–25 Sunny, cool. 26–31 Scattered t-storms, warm.

JUNE 2012: Temp. 68° (3° above avg. east, 1° below west); precip. 2.5" (1" below avg.). 1–9 Scattered t-storms, hot. 10–17 Scattered t-storms; hot east, cool west. 18–20 Sunny, cool. 21–24 Scattered t-storms, warm. 25–30 T-storms, then sunny, cool.

JULY 2012: Temp. 71° (1° below avg.); precip. 2.5" (1" below avg.). 1–4 Scattered t-storms, hot. 5–10 T-storms, then sunny, cool. 11–15 Scattered t-storms. 16–23 Sunny; hot, then cool. 24–31 Scattered t-storms; hot, then cool.

AUG. 2012: Temp. 66° (4° below avg.); precip. 3" (1" below avg.). 1–7 T-storms, then sunny, cool. 8–13 Sunny, then t-storms, warm. 14–18 Sunny, cool. 19–22 T-storms; warm east, cool west. 23–27 T-storms east, sunny west; cool. 28–31 Sunny, cool.

SEPT. 2012: Temp. 63° (avg.); precip. 3.5" (1.5" above avg. east, 1" below west). 1–5 Showers, then sunny, cool. 6–12 Sunny east, t-storms west; warm. 13–18 T-storms, then sunny, cool. 19–23 Rainy periods, very cool. 24–27 Sunny, warm. 28–30 Showers, cool.

OCT. 2012: Temp. 49.5° (1° below avg. east, 4° below west); precip. 4.5" (2" above avg.). 1–5 Rain, then sunny, cool. 6–11 Rainy periods, warm. 12–16 Sunny; cool, then warm. 17–18 T-storms. 19–22 Snow, then sunny, cool. 23–27 Rainy periods, mild. 28–31 Rain and snow showers, chilly.

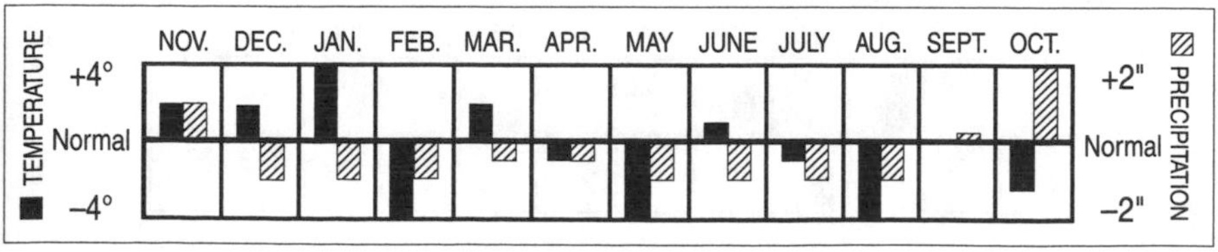

Ohio Valley

SUMMARY: Winter temperatures will be near or slightly above normal, on average, despite a cold February. Other cold periods will occur in late November, mid- and late December, and late January. Precipitation will be near or slightly above normal in the east and below normal in the west, with near-normal snowfall. The snowiest periods will occur in late November, late December, mid- and late January, and mid-February.

April and May will be cooler and rainier than normal, on average.

Summer will be cooler and drier than normal, with the hottest periods in early to mid-June and early July.

September and October will be cooler and drier than normal.

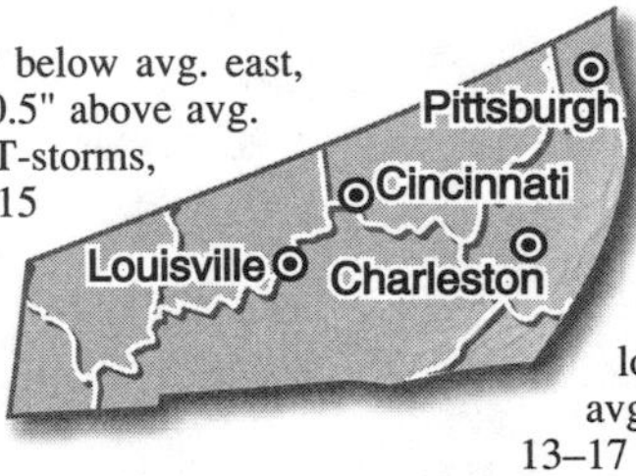

NOV. 2011: Temp. 45° (0.5° below avg. east, 1° above west); precip. 3.5" (0.5" above avg. east, 1" below west). 1–3 T-storms, warm. 4–8 Sunny, cool. 9–15 Showers, then sunny, cool. 16–20 Sunny, then rain, warm. 21–27 Snow, then snow showers, very cold. 28–30 Rainy, mild.

DEC. 2011: Temp. 36° (1° above avg.); precip. 2" (1" below avg.). 1–8 T-storms, then flurries, cold. 9–11 Sunny, mild. 12–20 Snow showers, turning cold. 21–24 Snow, then flurries, cold. 25–31 Showers, then flurries, cold.

JAN. 2012: Temp. 36° (5° above avg.); precip. 2" (1" below avg.). 1–4 Snow showers, cold. 5–7 Flurries, mild. 8–12 Snow, then snow showers, cold. 13–18 Sprinkles, very mild. 19–23 Rain to snow, then snow showers, cold. 24–28 Rain to snow, then flurries, cold. 29–31 Snowy, cold.

FEB. 2012: Temp. 26° (6° below avg.); precip. 3.5" (2" above avg. east, 1" below west). 1–5 Snow showers, cold. 6–9 Showers, mild. 10–16 Snow, then snow showers, cold. 17–20 Snow, very cold. 21–25 Sunny, turning mild. 26–29 Heavy rain to snow, turning cold.

MAR. 2012: Temp. 48° (4° above avg.); precip. 4" (0.5" above avg. east, 1" below west). 1–7 Sunny, then showers, turning warm. 8–12 Rain to snow, then snow showers, cold. 13–17 Rain and snow showers, cool. 18–20 Sunny, warm. 21–26 T-storms, then sunny, warm. 27–31 T-storms, warm.

APR. 2012: Temp. 53° (1° below avg.); precip. 5.5" (2" above avg.). 1–5 Showers, then sunny, cool. 6–10 Scattered t-storms, warm. 11–22 Sunny, then a few t-storms, cool. 23–25 T-storms, warm. 26–30 Sunny, then rain, cool.

MAY 2012: Temp. 59° (4° below avg.); precip. 4" (0.5" below avg.). 1–12 Scattered t-storms, cool. 13–17 Sunny, cool. 18–27 A few t-storms, cool. 28–31 Sunny, warm.

JUNE 2012: Temp. 74° (4° above avg. east, avg. west); precip. 2.5" (1.5" below avg.). 1–13 T-storms, then sunny, hot. 14–20 Scattered t-storms, cooler. 21–30 A few t-storms; warm, then cool.

JULY 2012: Temp. 75° (1° below avg.); precip. 4" (avg.). 1–5 Scattered t-storms, hot. 6–10 Sunny, cool. 11–22 Scattered t-storms, seasonable. 23–28 A few t-storms, warm. 29–31 Sunny, nice.

AUG. 2012: Temp. 70° (4° below avg.); precip. 2" (2" below avg.). 1–9 T-storms, then sunny, cool. 10–13 T-storms, warm. 14–16 Sunny, cool. 17–23 T-storms, seasonable. 24–31 Sunny; cool, then warm.

SEPT. 2012: Temp. 65.5° (2.5° below avg.); precip. 2" (1" below avg.). 1–6 T-storms, then sunny, cool. 7–12 Sunny, warm. 13–18 T-storms, then sunny, cool. 19–22 Rainy periods, cool. 23–27 Sunny, turning warm. 28–30 Showers, cool.

OCT. 2012: Temp. 53° (3° below avg.); precip. 3" (0.5" above avg.). 1–5 Rain, then sunny, cool. 6–9 Rain, then sunny, warm. 10–16 Rain, then sunny, cool. 17–22 A few showers, cool. 23–27 Rainy, mild. 28–31 Snow showers, cold.

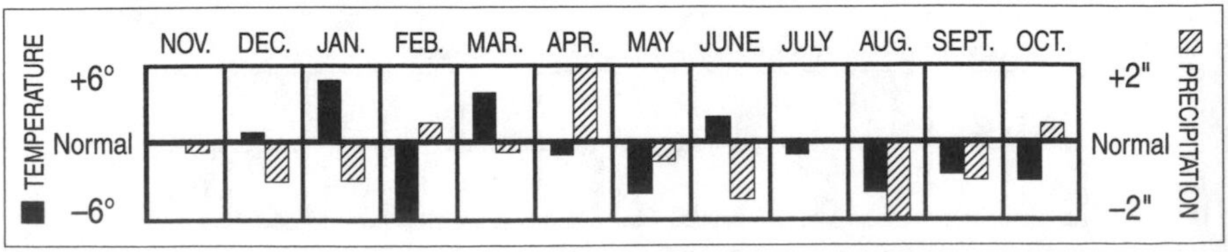

Deep South

SUMMARY: Winter will be much drier than normal, with temperatures above normal in the north and near normal in the south, on average. The coldest periods will be in the early and late parts of December, January, and February. Snowfall will be below normal and limited to the north, with the snowiest periods in mid-December, mid-January, and early to mid-February.

April and May will be slightly warmer and wetter than normal.

Summer will be cooler and rainier than normal, with the hottest periods in early and mid-June and mid-July.

September and October will be cooler and drier than normal.

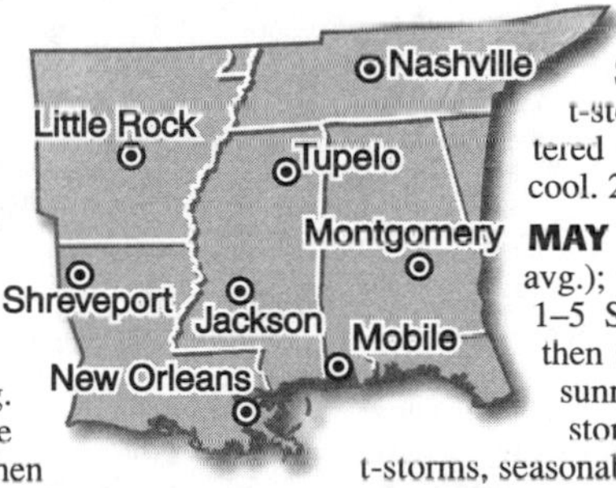

NOV. 2011: Temp. 57.5° (3° above avg.); precip. 2.5" (2.5" below avg.). 1–4 T-storms, warm. 5–18 Sunny; cool, then warm. 19–25 Showers, then sunny, chilly. 26–30 Showers, warm.

DEC. 2011: Temp. 46° (avg. north, 2° below avg. south); precip. 6" (1" above avg.). 1–8 Heavy rain, then sunny, cold. 9–14 Rain, then sunny, warm. 15–18 Snow north, rain south, then sunny, very cold. 19–25 Rainy periods, cool. 26–29 Sunny, cool. 30–31 Rain.

JAN. 2012: Temp. 46.5° (5° above avg. north, avg. south); precip. 5" (2" below avg. northeast, 2" above southwest). 1–5 Sunny north, rain south; cold. 6–11 Rain, then sunny, cool. 12–16 Rain and snow, then sunny, warm. 17–19 T-storms, warm. 20–24 Sunny; cold, then warm. 25–28 Rain, then sunny, cool. 29–31 T-storms, then sunny, cold.

FEB. 2012: Temp. 43° (3° below avg.); precip. 4" (1" above avg. north, 3" below south). 1–3 Sunny, cool. 4–8 Showers, then sunny, mild. 9–13 Rain and snow north; t-storms, warm south. 14–19 Sunny, cold. 20–25 Rain, then sunny, warm. 26–29 Rain, then cold.

MAR. 2012: Temp. 61° (8° above avg. north, 2° above south); precip. 2" (4" below avg.). 1–7 Sunny, turning warm. 8–12 T-storms, then sunny, cool. 13–17 Rain, then sunny, nice. 18–31 T-storms, then sunny, warm.

APR. 2012: Temp. 66° (3° above avg.); precip. 5.5" (1" above avg.). 1–2 Sunny, warm. 3–10 Scattered t-storms, very warm. 11–19 Scattered t-storms, warm. 20–22 Sunny, cool. 23–30 A few t-storms, cool.

MAY 2012: Temp. 70° (1° below avg.); precip. 4.5" (0.5" below avg.). 1–5 Sunny, warm. 6–11 T-storms, then sunny, cool. 12–21 Rain, then sunny, quite pleasant. 22–24 T-storms, warm. 25–31 Scattered t-storms, seasonable.

JUNE 2012: Temp. 78.5° (0.5° above avg.); precip. 6" (1" above avg.). 1–4 Sunny, hot. 5–10 Sunny, hot north; scattered t-storms south. 11–17 Scattered t-storms, hot. 18–25 T-storms, cool north; sunny, hot south. 26–30 T-storms, cool.

JULY 2012: Temp. 79° (3° below avg.); precip. 5.5" (1" above avg.). 1–11 T-storms, then sunny, cool. 12–17 Scattered t-storms, warm. 18–21 T-storms north, sunny south, seasonable. 22–25 Sunny, warm. 26–31 T-storms, then sunny, nice.

AUG. 2012: Temp. 75° (6° below avg.); precip. 5.5" (1" below avg. northeast, 3" above southwest). 1–7 T-storms, then sunny, cool. 8–21 A few t-storms, cool. 22–31 Sunny, then scattered t-storms, cool.

SEPT. 2012: Temp.73° (3° below avg.); precip. 2.5" (2" below avg.). 1–6 T-storms, then sunny, cool. 7–13 Sunny, warm. 14–19 T-storms, then sunny, nice. 20–24 T-storms, then sunny, cool. 25–30 Sunny, warm.

OCT. 2012: Temp. 59° (6° below avg.); precip. 4" (1" above avg.). 1–6 T-storms, then sunny, cool. 7–15 T-storms, then sunny, cool. 16–27 Scattered t-storms, cool. 28–31 Sunny, cold.

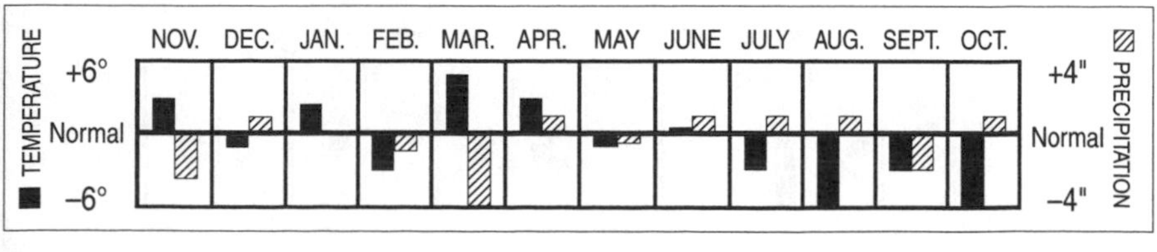

Upper Midwest

SUMMARY: Winter will be colder than normal, especially in February. Other cold periods will occur in mid- and late December and mid- and late January. Precipitation and snowfall will be below normal in the east and above normal in the west. The snowiest periods will be in early and mid-December, early to mid-February, and mid-March.

April and May will be much cooler and a bit drier than normal.

Summer will be cooler and drier than normal. The hottest periods will occur in mid-July and early August.

September and October will be cooler and drier than normal in most of the region.

NOV. 2011: Temp. 28° (avg.); precip. 1.5" (0.5" below avg.). 1–7 Snow, then sunny, cold. 8–10 Showers, mild. 11–17 Snow showers, then sunny, mild. 18–22 Rain, then snow, turning colder. 23–30 Snow showers; cold, then mild.

DEC. 2011: Temp. 15.5° (3° above avg. east, avg. west); precip. 2" (1" above avg.). 1–5 Snow, then sunny, cold. 6–12 A few rain and snow showers, mild. 13–16 Snow, then sunny, cold. 17–20 Snow, then sunny, cold. 21–24 Snow, then sunny, mild. 25–31 Snowy periods, cold.

JAN. 2012: Temp. 6.5° (2° above avg. east, 7° below west); precip. 1" (avg.). 1–5 Snow, then flurries, mild. 6–12 Snowy periods, turning very cold. 13–16 Sunny, mild. 17–20 Snow, then sunny, seasonable. 21–23 Snow, mild. 24–31 Snow showers, turning very cold.

FEB. 2012: Temp. 3° (8° below avg.); precip. 1" (1" below avg. east, 0.5" above west). 1–5 Snow showers, turning very cold. 6–11 Snowstorm, then sunny, bitter cold. 12–17 Flurries, milder, then bitter cold. 18–23 Sunny, turning mild. 24–29 Snow showers, cold.

MAR. 2012: Temp. 25° (2° above avg. east, 6° below west); precip. 1.5" (2" below avg. east, 2" above west). 1–11 Flurries; mild, then cold. 12–18 Snowstorm, then sunny, mild. 19–24 Showers, warm. 25–27 T-storms, then sunny, cool. 28–31 Rain and snow, cool.

APR. 2012: Temp. 39° (2° below avg.); precip. 2" (avg.). 1–4 Showers, then sunny, cool. 5–9 Scattered t-storms, warm. 10–11 Rain to snow, then sunny, cold. 12–17 Rain and snow showers, cool. 18–21 Sunny, turning milder. 22–30 T-storms, then sunny, cool.

MAY 2012: Temp. 51° (4° below avg.); precip. 2" (1" below avg.). 1–9 Rain and wet snow, then sunny, cool. 10–15 Showers, then sunny, cool. 16–24 Rain, then sunny, cool. 25–31 Sunny, then t-storms, warm.

JUNE 2012: Temp. 61° (3° below avg.); precip. 3.5" (0.5" below avg.). 1–5 A few t-storms, cool. 6–14 Scattered t-storms; warm, then cool. 15–18 T-storms, then sunny, cool. 19–23 Scattered t-storms, turning warm. 24–28 T-storms, then sunny, cool. 29–30 T-storms, seasonable.

JULY 2012: Temp. 67.5° (1.5° below avg.); precip. 2.5" (1" below avg.). 1–7 T-storms, then sunny, cool. 8–10 T-storms east, sunny west; cool. 11–14 Sunny, turning hot. 15–24 Scattered t-storms, seasonable. 25–28 T-storms, then sunny, cool. 29–31 T-storms, cool.

AUG. 2012: Temp. 65° (2° below avg.); precip. 1.5" (2" below avg.). 1–8 Sunny; cool, then hot. 9–15 T-storms, then sunny, cool. 16–20 T-storms; hot, then cool. 21–31 Sunny; cool, then very warm.

SEPT. 2012: Temp. 58° (avg.); precip. 1.5" (1.5" below avg.). 1–3 Sunny, cool. 4–6 Rain and heavy t-storms, cool. 7–13 Scattered t-storms, warm. 14–17 Sunny, cool. 18–22 Showers, then sunny, chilly. 23–27 Sunny, warm. 28–30 Rainy, cool.

OCT. 2012: Temp. 45° (1° below avg.); precip. 2.5" (2" above avg. east, 2" below west). 1–5 Rain to wet snow, then sunny, cool. 6–9 Rain, then sunny, cool. 10–14 Rain and snow showers east, sunny west; cool. 15–16 Sunny, warm. 17–22 Rain to snow, then flurries, cold. 23–25 Showers, mild. 26–31 Snow showers, cold.

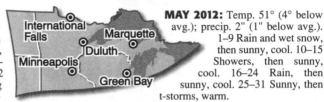

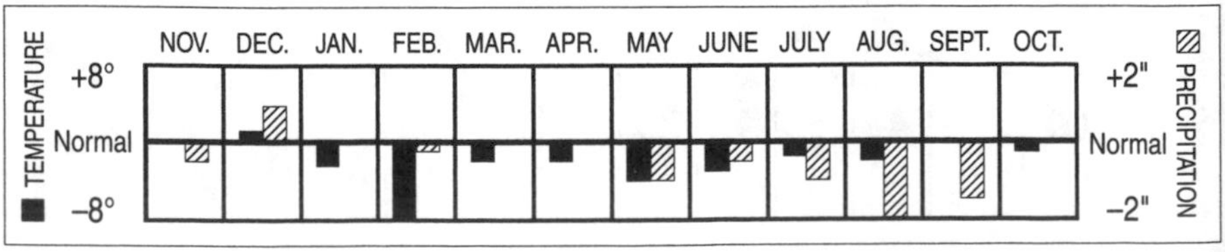

Heartland

SUMMARY: Winter temperatures will be above normal, on average, with below-normal precipitation and snowfall. The coldest periods will be in mid- and late December, mid-January, and mid-February. The snowiest periods will be in mid-December, late February, and early March.

April and May will be much cooler than normal, with near-normal precipitation.

Summer will be drier and cooler than normal, on average, despite hot spells in early and late July. If expected rains do not come in June, drought will be an issue.

September and October will be cooler and rainier than normal, with snow in late October.

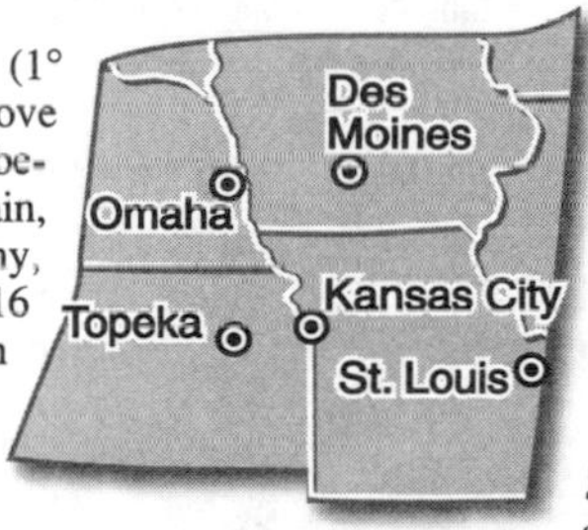

NOV. 2011: Temp. 52.5° (1° above avg. northeast, 8° above southwest); precip. 1.5" (1" below avg.). 1–7 Soaking rain, then sunny, chilly. 8–12 Sunny, warm, then t-storms, cool. 13–16 Sunny, warm. 17–23 Rain, then sunny, cool. 24–27 Flurries, cold. 28–30 Rainy, mild.

DEC. 2011: Temp. 31° (1° above avg.); precip. 1.5" (avg.). 1–5 T-storms, then flurries, cold. 6–14 Sunny, mild. 15–18 Snow, then sunny, cold. 19–23 Snowstorm, then sunny, cold. 24–31 Rain and snow showers; mild, then cold.

JAN. 2012: Temp. 30° (4° above avg.); precip. 1.5" (avg. north, 1" above avg. south). 1–3 Flurries, cold. 4–7 Sunny, mild. 8–12 Snow showers, very cold. 13–16 Sunny, warm. 17–21 Rain to snow, then sunny, cold. 22–25 Sunny, then rain, mild. 26–31 Snow showers, cold.

FEB. 2012: Temp. 27° (2° below avg.); precip. 0.5" (1" below avg.). 1–7 Sunny, mild. 8–18 Snow showers, cold. 19–24 Snow to rain, then sunny, mild. 25–29 Snow, then flurries, cold.

MAR. 2012: Temp. 49° (6° above avg.); precip. 0.5" (2" below avg.). 1–4 Snow, then sunny, warm. 5–11 Showers, then flurries, cold. 12–17 Rain and wet snow, then sunny, turning warm. 18–22 Rain, then sunny, warm. 23–31 Scattered t-storms, very warm.

APR. 2012: Temp. 52° (2° below avg.); precip. 4.5" (1" above avg.). 1–4 T-storms, then sunny, cool. 5–9 Scattered t-storms, very warm. 10–12 Sunny, cool. 13–19 Rainy periods; some snow north; chilly. 20–22 Sunny, nice. 23–30 Rainy periods, cool.

MAY 2012: Temp. 61° (3° below avg.); precip. 3.5" (1" below avg.). 1–4 Sunny, mild. 5–15 Scattered t-storms, cool. 16–19 Sunny, hot. 20–28 Rainy periods, then sunny, cool. 29–31 T-storms, warm.

JUNE 2012: Temp. 70° (3° below avg.); precip. 6.5" (2" above avg.). 1–9 Scattered t-storms, very warm. 10–14 Rainy periods, cool north; few t-storms, warm south. 15–22 Scattered t-storms; cool, then warm. 23–30 Sunny, cool.

JULY 2012: Temp. 76° (2° below avg.); precip. 2" (2" below avg.). 1–5 Scattered t-storms, hot. 6–10 Sunny, cool. 11–14 Sunny, seasonable. 15–22 Scattered t-storms; hot, then cool. 23–26 Sunny, hot. 27–31 Scattered t-storms, humid.

AUG. 2012: Temp. 71° (5° below avg.); precip. 1" (2.5" below avg.). 1–8 T-storms, then sunny, cool. 9–14 T-storms, then sunny, cool. 15–18 Sunny, warm. 19–27 Scattered t-storms, cool. 28–31 Sunny, nice.

SEPT. 2012: Temp. 67° (avg.); precip. 5.5" (2" above avg.). 1–4 Sunny, warm. 5–13 A few t-storms, warm. 14–18 Sunny, cool. 19–22 Rain, then sunny, cool. 23–27 Sunny, turning very warm. 28–30 T-storms, warm.

OCT. 2012: Temp. 52° (4° below avg.); precip. 4" (1" above avg.). 1–5 T-storms, then sunny, cool. 6–10 Rainy periods, seasonable. 11–16 Sunny, turning warm. 17–20 Rain to snow, turning chilly. 21–26 Rainy periods, cool. 27–31 Snow, then sunny, cold.

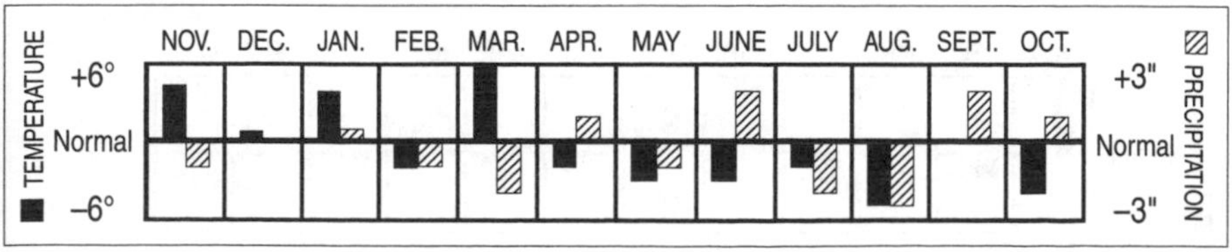

Texas–Oklahoma

SUMMARY: Winter temperatures will be milder than normal, on average, with much-below-normal rainfall. The coldest periods will occur in early and mid-December, early January, and early February. Snowfall will be below normal and limited to the north, with the snowiest periods in mid-December and early January.

April and May will continue warmer than normal, with rainfall above normal in the north and below normal in central and southern areas.

Summer will be a bit cooler than normal, on average, with the hottest periods in mid-June and early and late July. Rainfall will be slightly above normal in The Valley, but below normal elsewhere, with drought a threat.

September and October will be much cooler than normal, with rainfall below normal in the north and above in the south. Expect hurricanes in mid-September and early October, especially in The Valley.

NOV. 2011: Temp. 62° (6° above avg.); precip. 1.5" (1.5" below avg.). 1–4 Rainy periods, warm. 5–16 Sunny, warm. 17–25 T-storms, then sunny, cool. 26–30 T-storms, then sunny, warm.

DEC. 2011: Temp. 46° (2° below avg.); precip. 1" (1.5" below avg.). 1–7 T-storms, then very cold, freeze threat. 8–14 Rain, then sunny, warm. 15–18 Snow north, rain south, then sunny, cold. 19–25 Flurries north, rainy periods south; cool. 26–31 Sunny; cool, then warm.

JAN. 2012: Temp. 48° (5° above avg. north, 1° below south); precip. 1.5" (0.5" below avg.). 1–4 Rain and wet snow, then sunny, cold. 5–9 Rain, then sunny, warm. 10–17 Sunny north, showers south; cold, then warm. 18–24 Rain, then sunny, mild. 25–31 Rain, then sunny, cold north; rainy periods, mild, then cold south.

FEB. 2012: Temp. 47° (1° below avg.); precip. 1" (1" below avg.). 1–8 Sunny; cold, then warm. 9–13 Snow showers, then sunny, cold north; rainy periods, mild south. 14–19 Sunny, cool. 20–25 Rain, then sunny, warm. 26–29 Snow showers north, sprinkles south; cold.

MAR. 2012: Temp. 64° (6° above avg.); precip. 1.5" (1" below avg.). 1–5 Sunny, turning warm. 6–11 T-storms, then sunny, seasonable. 12–19 Scattered t-storms, warm. 20–22 Sunny, warm. 23–31 T-storms, then sunny, very warm.

APR. 2012: Temp. 70° (1° above avg. north, 7° above south); precip. 4" (4" above avg. north, 2" below south). 1–9 Scattered t-storms north and central, sunny south; very warm. 10–15 A few t-storms, warm. 16–21 A couple showers; cool north, warm south. 22–30 Scattered t-storms; warm, then cool north; turning hot south.

MAY 2012: Temp. 73° (avg.); precip. 3" (2" below avg.). 1–4 Sunny, very warm. 5–10 T-storms, then sunny, cool. 11–17 T-storms, then sunny, cool. 18–21 Sunny, warm. 22–27 T-storms, then sunny, cool. 28–31 Sunny, warm.

JUNE 2012: Temp. 81° (1° above avg.); precip. 2" (2" below avg.). 1–3 Sunny, hot. 4–12 T-storms, then sunny, hot. 13–18 Scattered t-storms, hot. 19–24 Sunny, warm. 25–30 T-storms, then sunny north; t-storms south.

JULY 2012: Temp. 83° (1° below avg. north, 1° above south); precip. 2" (1" below avg.). 1–5 Sunny, hot. 6–15 Scattered t-storms, cool. 16–19 Sunny, warm. 20–31 T-storms, then sunny, hot.

AUG. 2012: Temp. 78° (4° below avg.); precip. 4" (1" below avg. north, 4" above south). 1–6 T-storms, then sunny, cool. 7–12 Scattered t-storms, cool. 13–23 Sunny, seasonable north; t-storms, cool south. 24–31 Several t-storms, cool.

SEPT. 2012: Temp. 75° (1° below avg.); precip. 6" (1" below avg. north, 6" above south). 1–5 Sunny, cool. 6–9 T-storms. 10–14 Scattered t-storms north, hurricane threat south. 15–23 Scattered t-storms, cool. 24–30 Sunny, warm.

OCT. 2012: Temp. 63° (4° below avg.); precip. 3" (1" below avg.). 1–4 Sunny, cool north; hurricane threat south. 5–7 Sunny, warm. 8–13 T-storms, then sunny, cool. 14–21 Sunny, warm. 22–28 T-storms, then sunny, cool. 29–31 Sunny north, rain south; cool.

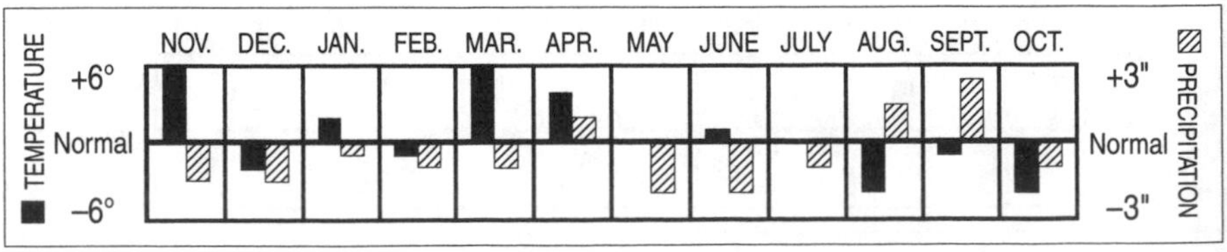

High Plains

SUMMARY: Winter will be drier than normal, with above-normal temperatures, on average. The coldest periods will occur in early and middle periods of December, January, and February. Snowfall will be above normal in the north and near to below normal elsewhere, with the snowiest periods in early November, early and mid-December, and early March.

April and May will be cooler and wetter than normal, with several periods of wet snow in mid-April.

Summer temperatures will be cooler than normal, with near-normal rainfall. The hottest periods will be in early and mid-July and mid-August.

September will be warmer and wetter than normal. October will be cooler and drier.

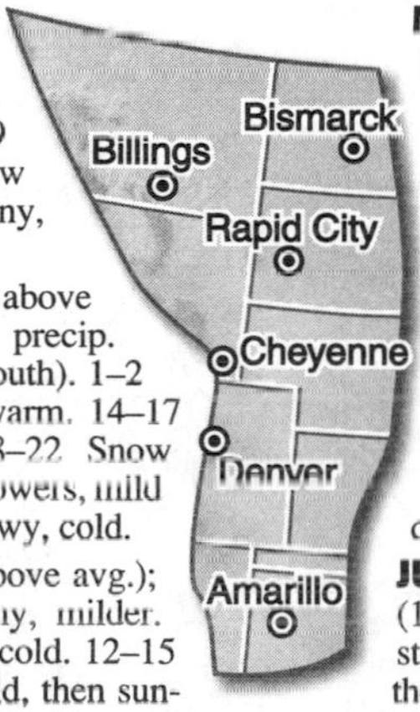

NOV. 2011: Temp. 37° (3° below avg. north, 5° above south); precip. 1" (avg.). 1–5 Snow, then sunny, cold. 6–19 Sunny, warm. 20–25 Snow showers, cold. 26–28 Sunny, mild. 29–30 Snow showers.

DEC. 2011: Temp. 28° (4° above avg. north, 2° below south); precip. 0.5" (avg. north, 0.5" below south). 1–2 Snow. 3–13 Sunny, turning warm. 14–17 Snow, then sunny, cold. 18–22 Snow showers, cold. 23–29 Snow showers, mild north; sunny south. 30–31 Snowy, cold.

JAN. 2012: Temp. 31° (6° above avg.); precip. 0.5" (avg.). 1–5 Sunny, milder. 6–11 Snow, then sunny, very cold. 12–15 Sunny, mild. 16–22 Snow, cold, then sunny, mild. 23–31 Snow showers, cold.

FEB. 2012: Temp. 26° (1° below avg.); precip. 0.5" (avg.). 1–6 Snow showers, then sunny, mild. 7–16 Snow showers, cold. 17–21 Sunny, mild. 22–26 Snow showers, turning cold north; sunny, mild south. 27–29 Snow showers, cold.

MAR. 2012: Temp. 41° (2° below avg. north, 8° above south); precip. 0.5" (0.5" below avg.). 1–2 Sunny, warm. 3–11 Snow, then flurries, cold. 12–16 Snow north, rain south, then sunny, warm. 17–21 T-storms, then sunny, warm. 22–31 Rain and snow showers, cool north; sunny, warm south.

APR. 2012: Temp. 44° (8° below avg. north, avg. south); precip. 3.5" (1.5" above avg.). 1–5 A few t-storms, warm. 6–10 Rain to snow, then sunny, cool. 11–19 Rain and snow showers, chilly north; sunny, warm, then t-storms south. 20–30 Heavy wet snow, then sunny north; sunny, then showers south; chilly.

MAY 2012: Temp. 55° (3° below avg.); precip. 3.5" (1" above avg.). 1–7 Rain to heavy snow, then sunny, cool north; sunny, warm, then showers south. 8–11 Sunny, turning warm. 12–16 Showers, then sunny, warm. 17–26 A few t-storms, cool. 27–31 T-storms; cool north, warm south.

JUNE 2012: Temp. 63° (4° below avg.); precip. 4" (1" above avg.). 1–7 T-storms, cool north; sunny, turning hot south. 8–14 Scattered t-storms, seasonable. 15–19 T-storms, then sunny, cool. 20–22 Sunny north, t-storms south; cool. 23–26 Sunny, cool north; t-storms south. 27–30 T-storms.

JULY 2012: Temp. 72° (avg.); precip. 1.5" (1" below avg. north, avg. south) 1–13 T-storms, then sunny, hot north; sunny, hot, then t-storms, cool south. 14–16 Sunny, warm. 17–23 T-storms, then sunny, hot. 24–31 A few t-storms; cool north, hot south.

AUG. 2012: Temp. 70.5° (2° above avg. north, 3° below south); precip. 1.5" (0.5" below avg.). 1–4 Sunny north, t-storms south; cool. 5–17 Sunny, hot north; scattered t-storms south. 18–23 Scattered t-storms, warm. 24–31 T-storms, then sunny, warm north; a few t-storms, cool south.

SEPT. 2012: Temp. 63° (2° above avg.); precip. 2" (0.5" above avg.). 1–3 Sunny, warm. 4–12 T-storms, cool. 13–18 Sunny, warm. 19–24 Sunny, hot, then t-storms north; t-storms, then sunny, warm south. 25–30 Scattered t-storms, cooler.

OCT. 2012: Temp. 47° (2° below avg.); precip. 0.5" (0.5" below avg.). 1–4 Sunny, nice. 5–9 Rain and wet snow, then sunny, cool. 10–15 Sunny, turning warm. 16–20 Showers and flurries, then sunny, cool. 21–24 Rain, then sunny, warm. 25–31 Rain to snow, then sunny, cold.

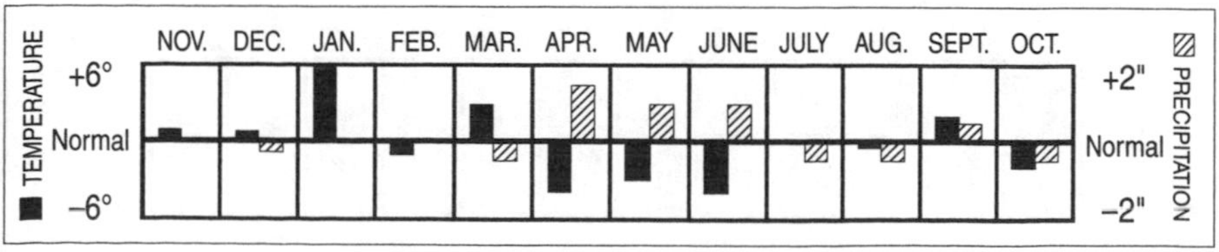

Intermountain

SUMMARY: Winter temperatures will be above normal, especially in the south, with the coldest periods in early and late December and mid- and late February. Precipitation and snowfall will be above normal in the north and below normal in the south. The snowiest periods will occur in early November, mid-December, mid-January, and early and late March.

April and May will be much cooler and snowier than normal.

Summer will be hotter and drier than normal in the north and cooler and wetter in the south. The hottest periods will be in early July and much of August.

September and October will be slightly warmer and drier than normal.

NOV. 2011: Temp. 43° (4° above avg.); precip. 2.5" (1" above avg.). 1–4 Rain and snow, heavy south; cold. 5–13 Rainy periods north, sunny south; quite mild. 14–17 Showers, then sunny, cool. 18–25 Rainy periods north, sunny south; mild. 26–30 Periods of rain and snow, turning cold.

DEC. 2011: Temp. 27° (4° below avg.); precip. 1" (0.5" below avg.). 1–2 Sunny, cold. 3–13 Snow, then rainy periods north; sunny south; turning mild. 14–16 Sunny. 17–21 Snow, then sunny, cold. 22–31 Periods of rain and snow, mild north; snow showers, cold south.

JAN. 2012: Temp. 35° (5° above avg.); precip. 1.5" (0.5" above avg. north, 1" below south). 1–12 Periods of rain and snow north, sunny south; turning mild. 13–18 Flurries and sprinkles north; rain, then heavy snow central and south. 19–24 Rainy periods north and central, sunny south; mild. 25–31 Showers, then sunny north; sunny south; mild.

FEB. 2012: Temp. 34° (1° above avg.); precip. 0.5" (1" below avg.). 1–11 Sunny, then periods of rain and snow north; sunny south; mild, then cold. 12–20 Sunny north, showers and flurries south; mild. 21–29 Occasional snow, turning cold.

MAR. 2012: Temp. 42.5° (2° below avg. northwest, 3° above southeast); precip. 1.5" (0.5" above avg. north, 0.5" below south). 1–7 Periods of rain and snow; mild, then cold. 8–17 Occasional rain, mild. 18–21 Sunny, mild. 22–25 Snow, heavy south, then sunny, cold. 26–31 Showers.

APR. 2012: Temp. 43° (6° below avg.); precip. 1.5" (0.5" above avg.). 1–3 Sunny, cool. 4–11 Rainy periods, cool north; rain to heavy snow, then sunny, cool south. 12–17 Snow, then sunny, cool. 18–21 Rain and wet snow north, sunny south; cool. 22–26 Heavy snow central, flurries and sprinkles elsewhere; cool. 27–30 Rain, then sunny, mild.

MAY 2012: Temp. 52° (2° below avg.); precip. 1" (avg.). 1–5 Rain and wet snow north; sunny, cool south. 6–15 Sunny, warmer. 16–23 Showers, cooler. 24–31 Rainy periods, cool.

JUNE 2012: Temp. 66° (3° above avg. north, 3° below south); precip. 0.8" (0.5" below avg. north, 1" above south). 1–10 Rain, then sunny, warm north; rainy periods, cool central; sunny, cool south. 11–18 T-storms, then sunny, warm. 19–25 Showers, then sunny, hot. 26–30 Scattered t-storms, cooler.

JULY 2012: Temp. 74° (1° above avg.); precip. 0.8" (0.5" below avg. north, 1" above south). 1–5 Isolated t-storms, hot. 6–15 Scattered t-storms, sunny, very warm. 16–23 Scattered t-storms, seasonable. 24–31 Sunny, north; t-storms, cool south.

AUG. 2012: Temp. 75° (6° above avg. north, avg. south); precip. 0.5" (0.5" below avg.). 1–16 Sunny, hot north; scattered t-storms, seasonable south. 17–25 T-storms, then sunny, hot north; scattered t-storms, seasonable south. 26–31 Scattered t-storms, hot periods.

SEPT. 2012: Temp. 64° (2° above avg.); precip. 1" (avg.). 1–4 Scattered t-storms, cool. 5–9 Sunny; warm north, cool south. 10–18 Sunny north, scattered showers south; warm. 19–21 Sunny, warm. 22–30 Rainy periods, turning cool.

OCT. 2012: Temp. 50° (1° below avg.); precip. 0.5" (0.5" below avg.). 1–2 Sunny, nice. 3–13 Rain, then sunny north; sunny south; seasonable. 14–22 Rainy periods, cool north; sunny, warm south. 23–31 Sunny; cool north, mild south.

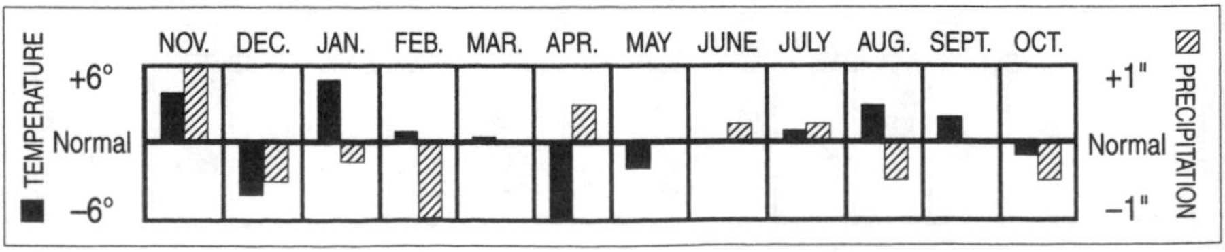

Desert Southwest

SUMMARY: Winter will be cooler and drier than normal, with below-normal snowfall. The coldest periods will occur in late December, mid-January, and late February. The snowiest periods will occur in mid- and late February.

April and May will be much cooler than normal, especially in the west, with near-normal rainfall.

Summer will be slightly cooler than normal, on average, with near-normal rainfall. The hottest periods will be in late June, mid-July, and early and mid-August.

September and October will be cooler and drier than normal.

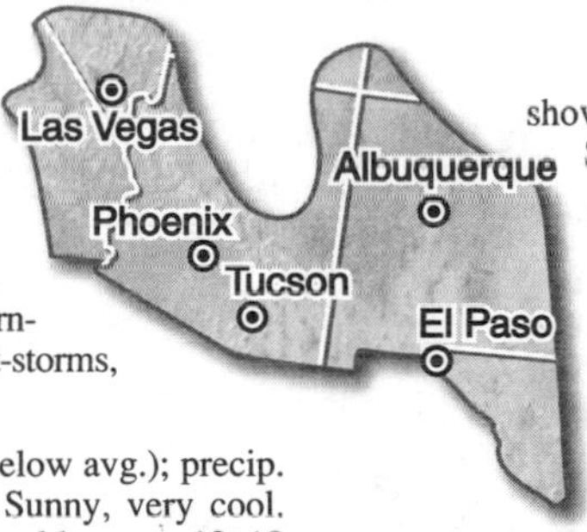

NOV. 2011: Temp. 57° (2° above avg.); precip. 0.5" (avg.). 1–5 Showers, then sunny, cool. 6–15 Sunny, warm. 16–20 Scattered showers, then sunny, cool. 21–25 Sunny, turning warm. 26–30 Scattered t-storms, very warm.

DEC. 2011: Temp. 41° (6° below avg.); precip. 0.2" (0.3" below avg.). 1–6 Sunny, very cool. 7–12 Sunny; cool east, seasonable west. 13–18 Sunny, very cool. 19–31 T-storms, then sunny, cold.

JAN. 2012: Temp. 46° (1° below avg.); precip. 0.2" (0.3" below avg.). 1–7 Sunny; cool, then mild. 8–12 Sunny, cool. 13–23 Sunny east, scattered showers west; cool. 24–31 Isolated showers; warm, then cool.

FEB. 2012: Temp. 48° (2° below avg.); precip. 0.2" (0.3" below avg.). 1–7 Sunny; cool, then mild. 8–11 Sunny, cool. 12–20 Rain and snow showers east, sunny west; cool. 21–24 Sunny, turning mild. 25–29 Rain and snow showers, then sunny, cold.

MAR. 2012: Temp. 58.5° (5° above avg. east, 2° below west); precip. 0.2" (0.3" below avg.). 1–3 Sunny, mild. 4–11 Scattered showers, then sunny, warm. 12–21 Scattered showers, then sunny, warm. 22–25 Showers, cool. 26–31 Scattered showers, warm east; sunny, cool west.

APR. 2012: Temp. 58° (2° below avg. east, 10° below west); precip. 0.4" (0.1" below avg.). 1–3 Sunny; warm east, cool west. 4–6 Showers, quite cool. 7–11 Scattered showers, warm east; sunny, cool west. 12–17 Sunny, cool east; scattered showers, quite cool west. 18–30 Sunny, cool.

MAY 2012: Temp. 71° (2° below avg.); precip. 0.7" (0.2" above avg.). 1–8 Sunny; warm, then cool. 9–16 Sunny; seasonable east, hot west. 17–25 Scattered t-storms, then sunny, cool. 26–31 Scattered t-storms, cool.

JUNE 2012: Temp. 80° (3° below avg.); precip. 1" (0.5" above avg.). 1–5 Sunny, cool. 6–13 Scattered t-storms, cool. 14–27 Scattered t-storms, cool east; sunny, hot west. 28–30 T-storms, humid.

JULY 2012: Temp. 87° (avg.); precip. 1" (0.5" below avg.). 1–15 Scattered t-storms, seasonable. 16–25 Isolated t-storms, hot. 26–31 A few t-storms, turning cooler.

AUG. 2012: Temp. 83.5° (4° below avg. east, 1° above west); precip. 1.5" (avg.). 1–16 A few t-storms, cool east; isolated t-storms, hot west. 17–23 Scattered t-storms, hot. 24–31 A few t-storms, cooler.

SEPT. 2012: Temp. 77° (1° below avg.); precip. 1" (avg.). 1–5 Isolated t-storms, warm. 6–13 Scattered t-storms, cool. 14–18 Scattered t-storms, warm. 19–21 Sunny, cool east; t-storms, warm west. 22–30 Isolated t-storms; very warm, then cool.

OCT. 2012: Temp. 65° (avg. east, 4° below west); precip. 0.5" (0.5" below avg.). 1–7 Scattered showers east, sunny west; cool, then warm. 8–12 Sunny, cool. 13–21 Sunny, warm. 22–31 Showers, then sunny, cool.

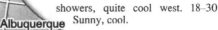

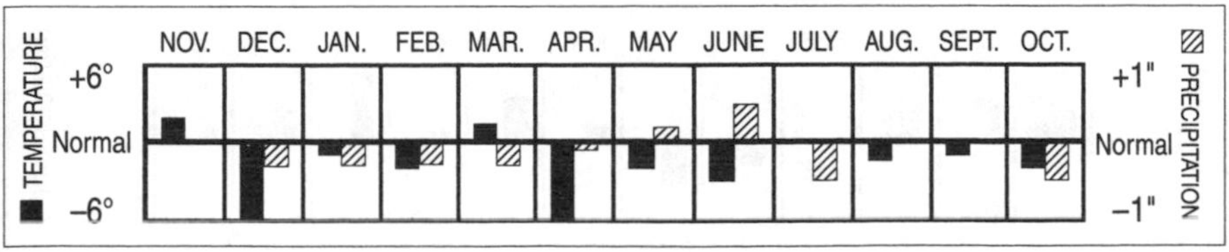

Pacific Northwest

SUMMARY: Winter temperatures will be above normal, on average, especially in the south. Precipitation will be above normal in the north and below in the south, with below-normal snowfall. The coldest and snowiest periods will occur in late December, early to mid-February, and early March.

April and May will be cooler and drier than normal.

Summer will be much warmer and slightly drier than normal. The hottest periods will occur in early and late July and early and mid-August.

September and October will be warmer than normal, with above-normal rainfall in Washington and Oregon and near-normal rainfall in California.

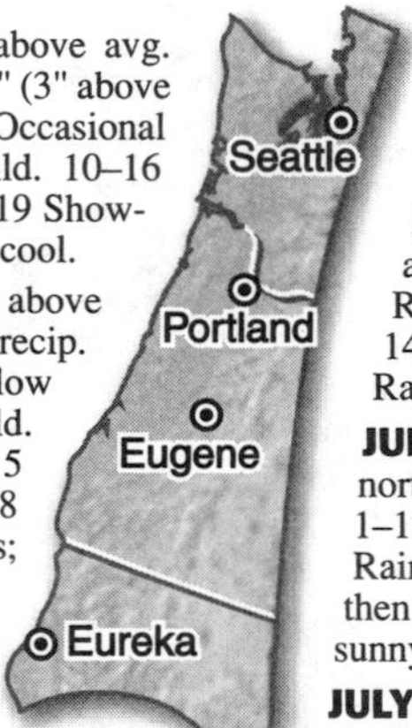

NOV. 2011: Temp. 49.5° (1° above avg. north, 4° above south); precip. 11" (3" above avg. north, 6" above south). 1–3 Occasional rain, cool. 4–9 Heavy rain, mild. 10–16 Rainy periods, turning cool. 17–19 Showers, chilly. 20–30 Rainy periods, cool.

DEC. 2011: Temp. 45.5° (2° above avg. north, 5° above south); precip. 5.5" (3" above avg. north, 5" below south). 1–6 Rainy periods, mild. 7–11 Occasional rain, mild. 12–15 Rain, then sunny, cool. 16–18 Rainy, mild. 19–23 Sprinkles; cool, then mild. 24–27 Rainy, mild. 28–31 Rain to snow, then showers, cool.

JAN. 2012: Temp. 45.5° (2° above avg. north, 5° above south); precip. 8" (2" above avg.). 1–2 Sunny, mild. 3–8 Rainy periods, mild. 9–10 Sunny, cool. 11–18 Stormy, mild, then occasional rain, cool. 19–22 Stormy, mild. 23–27 Sunny, cool, then rainy periods, mild. 28–31 Sunny, cool.

FEB. 2012: Temp. 43° (2° below avg. north, avg. south); precip. 2.5" (2.5" below avg.). 1–6 Rainy periods, seasonable. 7–11 Rain and wet snow, chilly. 12–16 Sunny, seasonable. 17–23 Occasional rain and drizzle, cool. 24–29 Sunny, cool.

MAR. 2012: Temp. 45° (2° below avg.); precip. 3" (1" above avg. north, 3" below south). 1–4 Rain and wet snow, cool. 5–11 Sunny, then rainy periods, mild. 12–23 Rainy periods, cool. 24–27 Sunny, nice. 28–31 Rain, then sunny, seasonable.

APR. 2012: Temp. 46.5° (3.5° below avg.); precip. 2.5" (0.5" below avg.). 1–4 Rain, then sunny, seasonable. 5–11 Rainy periods, cool. 12–16 Showers, seasonable. 17–21 Rainy, cool. 22–30 Sunny, turning warm.

MAY 2012: Temp. 56.5° (1.5° above avg.); precip. 1.5" (0.5" below avg.). 1–7 Rain, then sunny, cool. 8–13 Sunny, warm. 14–20 Showers, then sunny, cool. 21–26 Rainy periods, cool. 27–31 Sunny, warm.

JUNE 2012: Temp. 63.5° (2° above avg. north, 5° above south); precip. 1.5" (avg.). 1–12 Sunny; cool, then very warm. 13–18 Rain, then sunny, warm. 19–27 Showers, then sunny, turning hot. 28–30 Sprinkles, then sunny, cool.

JULY 2012: Temp. 65.5° (1° above avg.); precip. 0.1" (0.4" below avg.). 1–5 Sunny, turning hot. 6–11 Sunny, seasonable. 12–17 Showers, then sunny, warm. 18–27 Showers, then sunny, hot. 28–31 Sunny, cool.

AUG. 2012: Temp. 70.5° (5.5° above avg.); precip. 0.2" (0.8" below avg.). 1–12 Sunny, hot. 13–21 Scattered t-storms, then sunny, hot. 22–31 Isolated t-storms, warm.

SEPT. 2012: Temp. 64° (3° above avg.); precip. 2.5" (0.5"above avg. north, 2" above south). 1–4 Rainy periods, cool. 5–9 Sunny, turning hot. 10–16 Scattered showers, warm. 17–21 Sunny, very warm. 22–28 Rainy periods, cool, then warm. 29–30 Showers, mild.

OCT. 2012: Temp. 55° (1° above avg.); precip. 3" (1.5" above avg. north, 2" below south). 1–2 Sunny, warm. 3–6 Rainy periods, mild. 7–10 Sunny, nice. 11–18 Rainy periods, seasonable. 19–24 Stormy, then showers, warm. 25–30 Sunny, seasonable. 31 Rain, seasonable.

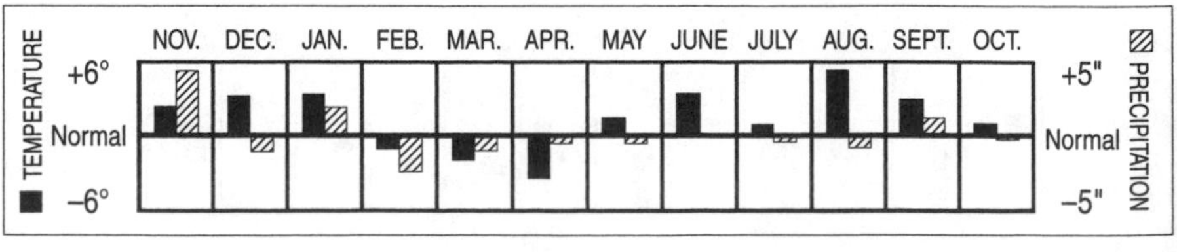

Region 16 Forecast

Pacific Southwest

SUMMARY: Winter temperatures will be below normal, on average, with the coldest periods in mid- and late December, mid-January, and early February. Precipitation will be much above normal in the north and below normal in the south. The stormiest periods will be in early to mid-November and December, with mid-January being the snowiest period in the mountains.

April and May will be cooler and rainier than normal.

Summer will be warmer than normal, with near-normal rainfall. The hottest periods will be in mid-July and much of August.

September and October will be warmer than normal, with slightly below-normal rainfall. Expect hot weather in early and mid-September.

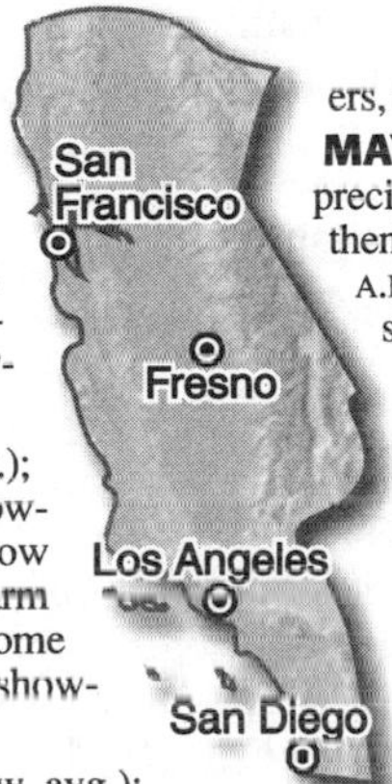

NOV. 2011: Temp. 59.5° (4° above avg. northeast, 1° below southwest); precip. 4.5" (3" above avg.). 1–6 Occasional rain and drizzle, cool. 7–9 T-storms north, sunny south; warm. 10–11 Sunny, mild. 12–19 Rain and t-storms, then sunny, cool. 20–24 Showers, mild. 25–30 Stormy, mild.

DEC. 2011: Temp. 51° (2° below avg.); precip. 0.5" (1.5" below avg.). 1–6 Showers, then sunny, seasonable. 7–14 Low clouds, misty, cool north; sunny, warm south. 15–19 Valley fog and drizzle, some sun elsewhere; cool. 20–31 Scattered showers, then sunny, cool.

JAN. 2012: Temp. 52.5° (0.5° below avg.); precip. 5.5" (5" above avg. north, 0.5" below south). 1–6 Sunny; cool, then warm. 7–12 Sunny, cool. 13–18 Stormy, cool. 19–24 Showers and t-storms, seasonable. 25–31 Sunny coast, clouds and drizzle inland; cool.

FEB. 2012: Temp. 54° (1° below avg.); precip. 0.5" (2.5" below avg.). 1–3 Sunny coast, clouds and fog inland; cool. 4–8 Scattered showers; warm, then cool. 9–16 Sunny, nice. 17–22 Rain, then sunny, warm. 23–29 Rain, then sunny, warm.

MAR. 2012: Temp. 56° (1° below avg.); precip. 4" (4" above avg. north, 0.5" below south). 1–9 Stormy periods; cool, then mild. 10–16 Showers north; A.M. clouds, P.M. sun south; mild. 17–20 Sunny, seasonable. 21–25 Stormy, cool. 26–31 Showers and t-storms, mainly north; cool.

APR. 2012: Temp. 56° (4° below avg.); precip. 3" (2" above avg.). 1–2 Sunny, cool. 3–5 Rainy, cool. 6–10 Rainy periods north; A.M. clouds, P.M. sun south; cool. 11–17 Rainy, cool. 18–26 Showers, then sunny, cool. 27–30 Showers.

MAY 2012: Temp. 63° (1° below avg.); precip. 1" (0.5" above avg.). 1–6 Showers, then sunny, cool. 7–9 Sunny, hot. 10–15 A.M. clouds, P.M. sun, seasonable coast; sunny, hot inland. 16–23 Cloudy, sprinkles coast; sunny, turning cool inland. 24–31 Showers, then sunny, cool.

JUNE 2012: Temp. 69° (3° above avg. northeast, 1° below southwest); precip. 0.1" (avg.). 1–7 Coastal fog and drizzle; sunny, cool inland. 8–20 A.M. fog, P.M. sun, cool coast; sunny, warm inland. 21–30 A.M. clouds, P.M. sun, coast; sunny, hot inland.

JULY 2012: Temp. 72° (1° above avg.); precip. 0" (avg.). 1–8 A.M. clouds, P.M. sun, seasonable coast; sunny, cool, then hot inland. 9–14 Sunny, nice. 15–18 A.M. fog and drizzle, P.M. sun coast; sunny inland; seasonable. 19–22 Sunny, hot. 23–31 Sunny, seasonable.

AUG. 2012: Temp. 74° (2° above avg.); precip. 0.1" (avg.). 1–3 A.M. clouds, P.M. sun coast; sunny inland; warm. 4–22 Sunny; warm coast, hot inland. 23–26 Scattered showers, hot. 27–31 Sunny.

SEPT. 2012: Temp. 72° (2° above avg.); precip. 0.4" (0.2" above avg.). 1–9 Sunny; hot, then seasonable. 10–14 Scattered showers, hot. 15–20 A.M. clouds coast; sunny, hot inland. 21–28 Scattered t-storms, turning cooler. 29–30 Sunny, nice.

OCT. 2012: Temp. 67° (2° above avg.); precip. 0.2" (0.3" below avg.). 1–7 Sunny; warm north, cool south. 8–11 Sunny, hot. 12–19 Scattered showers, then sunny, cool. 20–26 Scattered showers, then sunny, very warm. 27–31 Scattered showers north, sunny south; warm.

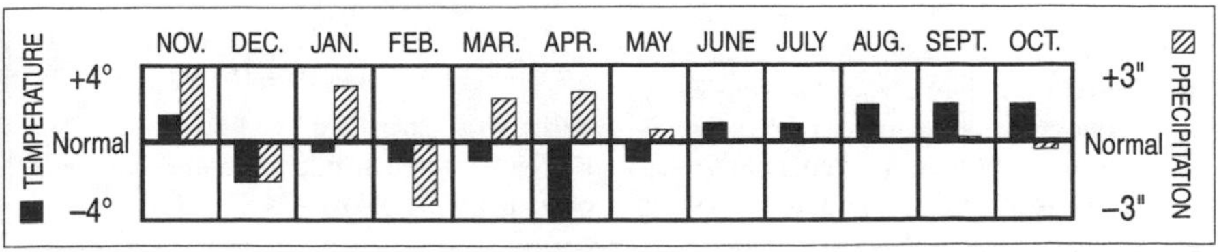

Winter Weather Terms

Winter Storm Outlook

■ Issued prior to a winter storm watch. An outlook is issued when forecasters believe that storm conditions are possible, usually 48 to 60 hours before the beginning of a storm.

Winter Storm Watch

■ Indicates the possibility of a winter storm and is issued to provide 12 to 36 hours' notice. A watch is announced when the specific timing, location, and path of a storm are undetermined. Be alert to changing weather conditions, and avoid unnecessary travel.

Winter Storm Warning

■ Indicates that a severe winter storm has started or is about to begin. A warning is issued when more than 6 inches of snow, a significant ice accumulation, a dangerous windchill, or a combination of the three is expected. Anticipated snow accumulation during a winter storm is 6 or more inches in 24 hours. You should stay indoors during the storm.

Heavy Snow Warning

■ Issued when snow accumulations are expected to approach or exceed 6 inches in 12 hours but will not be accompanied by significant wind. The warning could also be issued if 8 or more inches of snow accumulation is expected in a 24-hour period. During a heavy snow warning, freezing rain and sleet are not expected.

Blizzard Warning

■ Indicates that sustained winds or frequent gusts of 35 miles per hour or greater will occur in combination with considerable falling and/or blowing snow for at least 3 hours. Visibility will often be reduced to less than one-quarter mile.

Whiteout

■ Caused by falling and/or blowing snow that reduces visibility to zero miles—typically only a few feet. Whiteouts are most frequent during blizzards and can occur

rapidly, often blinding motorists and creating chain-reaction crashes involving multiple vehicles.

Northeaster

■ Usually produces heavy snow and rain and creates tremendous waves in Atlantic coastal regions, often causing beach erosion and structural damage. Wind gusts associated with these storms can exceed hurricane force in intensity. A northeaster gets its name from the strong, continuous, northeasterly ocean winds that blow in over coastal areas ahead of the storm.

Sleet

■ Frozen or partially frozen rain in the form of ice pellets that hit the ground so fast that they bounce and do not stick to it. However, the pellets can accumulate like snow and cause hazardous conditions for pedestrians and motorists.

Freezing Rain

■ Liquid precipitation that turns to ice on contact with a frozen surface to form a smooth ice coating called a glaze.

Ice Storm Warning

■ Issued when freezing rain results in ice accumulations measuring ½ inch thick or more. Ice this thick can cause trees and utility lines to fall down, creating power outages.

Windchill Advisory

■ Issued when windchill temperatures are expected to be between –20° and –34°F.

Windchill Warning

■ Issued when windchill temperatures are expected to be below –34°F.

Frosts and Growing Seasons

■ Dates given are normal averages for a light freeze; local weather and topography may cause considerable variations. The possibility of frost occurring after the spring dates and before the fall dates is 50 percent. The classification of freeze temperatures is usually based on their effect on plants. **Light freeze:** 29° to 32°F—tender plants killed. **Moderate freeze:** 25° to 28°F—widely destructive effect on most vegetation. **Severe freeze:** 24°F and colder—heavy damage to most plants.

–courtesy of National Climatic Data Center

State	City	Growing Season (days)	Last Spring Frost	First Fall Frost	State	City	Growing Season (days)	Last Spring Frost	First Fall Frost
AK	Juneau	148	May 8	Oct. 4	ND	Bismarck	129	May 14	Sept. 21
AL	Mobile	274	Feb. 28	Nov. 29	NE	Blair	167	Apr. 25	Oct. 10
AR	Pine Bluff	240	Mar. 16	Nov. 12	NE	North Platte	137	May 9	Sept. 24
AZ	Phoenix	*	*	*	NH	Concord	123	May 20	Sept. 21
AZ	Tucson	333	Jan. 19	Dec. 18	NJ	Newark	217	Apr. 3	Nov. 7
CA	Eureka	323	Jan. 27	Dec. 16	NM	Carlsbad	215	Mar. 31	Nov. 2
CA	Sacramento	297	Feb. 10	Dec. 4	NM	Los Alamos	149	May 11	Oct. 8
CA	San Francisco	*	*	*	NV	Las Vegas	284	Feb. 16	Nov. 27
CO	Denver	156	Apr. 30	Oct. 4	NY	Albany	153	May 2	Oct. 3
CT	Hartford	165	Apr. 26	Oct. 9	NY	Syracuse	167	Apr. 28	Oct. 13
DE	Wilmington	202	Apr. 10	Oct. 30	OH	Akron	192	Apr. 18	Oct. 28
FL	Miami	*	*	*	OH	Cincinnati	192	Apr. 13	Oct. 23
FL	Tallahassee	239	Mar. 22	Nov. 17	OK	Lawton	222	Mar. 29	Nov. 7
GA	Athens	227	Mar. 24	Nov. 7	OK	Tulsa	224	Mar. 27	Nov. 7
GA	Savannah	268	Mar. 1	Nov. 25	OR	Pendleton	187	Apr. 13	Oct. 18
IA	Atlantic	148	May 2	Sept. 28	OR	Portland	236	Mar. 23	Nov. 15
IA	Cedar Rapids	163	Apr. 25	Oct. 6	PA	Franklin	163	May 6	Oct. 17
ID	Boise	148	May 10	Oct. 6	PA	Williamsport	167	Apr. 30	Oct. 15
IL	Chicago	186	Apr. 20	Oct. 24	RI	Kingston	147	May 8	Oct. 3
IL	Springfield	182	Apr. 13	Oct. 13	SC	Charleston	260	Mar. 9	Nov. 25
IN	Indianapolis	181	Apr. 17	Oct. 16	SC	Columbia	213	Apr. 1	Nov. 1
IN	South Bend	175	Apr. 26	Oct. 19	SD	Rapid City	140	May 9	Sept. 27
KS	Topeka	174	Apr. 19	Oct. 11	TN	Memphis	235	Mar. 22	Nov. 13
KY	Lexington	192	Apr. 15	Oct. 25	TN	Nashville	204	Apr. 6	Oct. 28
LA	Monroe	256	Mar. 3	Nov. 15	TX	Amarillo	184	Apr. 18	Oct. 20
LA	New Orleans	302	Feb. 12	Dec. 11	TX	Denton	242	Mar. 18	Nov. 16
MA	Worcester	170	Apr. 26	Oct. 14	TX	San Antonio	270	Feb. 28	Nov. 25
MD	Baltimore	200	Apr. 11	Oct. 29	UT	Cedar City	132	May 21	Oct. 1
ME	Portland	156	May 2	Oct. 6	UT	Spanish Fork	167	May 1	Oct. 16
MI	Lansing	145	May 10	Oct. 3	VA	Norfolk	247	Mar. 20	Nov. 23
MI	Marquette	154	May 11	Oct. 13	VA	Richmond	206	Apr. 6	Oct. 30
MN	Duluth	124	May 21	Sept. 23	VT	Burlington	147	May 8	Oct. 3
MN	Willmar	153	Apr. 30	Oct. 1	WA	Seattle	251	Mar. 10	Nov. 17
MO	Jefferson City	187	Apr. 13	Oct. 18	WA	Spokane	153	May 2	Oct. 3
MS	Columbia	247	Mar. 13	Nov. 16	WI	Green Bay	150	May 6	Oct. 4
MS	Vicksburg	240	Mar. 20	Nov. 16	WI	Sparta	133	May 13	Sept. 24
MT	Fort Peck	140	May 8	Sept. 26	WV	Parkersburg	183	Apr. 21	Oct. 22
MT	Helena	121	May 19	Sept. 18	WY	Casper	119	May 22	Sept. 19
NC	Fayetteville	221	Mar. 28	Nov. 5					

**Frosts do not occur every year.*

QUELL THE SMELL

It's not necessary to buy expensive deodorants and sprays to keep you and your home smelling fresh. You can eliminate almost any offending odor by using items already in your household.

BLOW OFF BAD BREATH

Chew coffee beans, aniseed, carrots, citrus peels, or parsley.

On You

BANISH B.O.

Rub armpits with a slice of lemon or lime.

SWEETEN STINKY FEET

Soak feet daily in 2 cups of brewed black tea combined with 2 quarts of water.

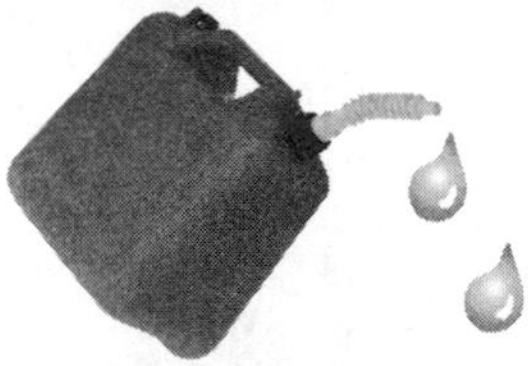

GET GASOLINE ODOR GONE

- Wash hands with lemon juice or vinegar.
- Put smelly clothes into a trash bag, sprinkle with baking soda, close, and let sit for a few days. Then wash as usual.

SPRUCE UP STINKY SHOES

- Sprinkle salt inside your shoes, enough to cover the soles. Let sit overnight, then shake out and discard.
- Stuff crumpled newspaper inside shoes when you're not wearing them.

Compiled by Mare-Anne Jarvela

There is nothing like an odor to stir memories.

–William McFee, English-born American writer (1881–1966)

In the Kitchen

FREE HANDS OF FISH SMELL

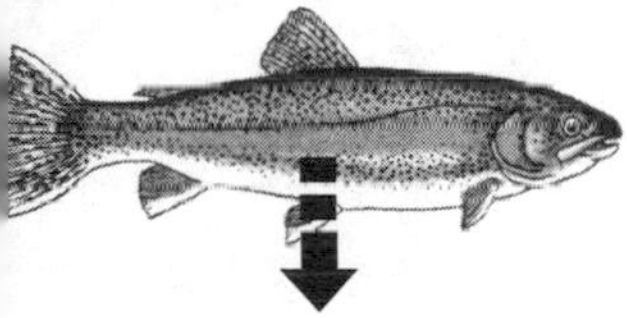

- **Rub hands with a piece of a lemon or with mustard powder.**
- **Rinse hands with white vinegar.**

CLEAR THE AIR OF FISH SMELL

- Soak fish in milk before cooking it.
- Hang a wet towel in the kitchen. The towel will absorb the smell.

EXPEL ONION OR GARLIC ODOR

- **Rub your fingers on anything made of stainless steel (pan, faucet, sink).**
- **Scrub hands with fresh coffee grounds.**

SNUFF OUT SKUNKY CABBAGE

Wrap a couple of thick chunks of bread in cheesecloth and add this to the cooking water.

Around the House

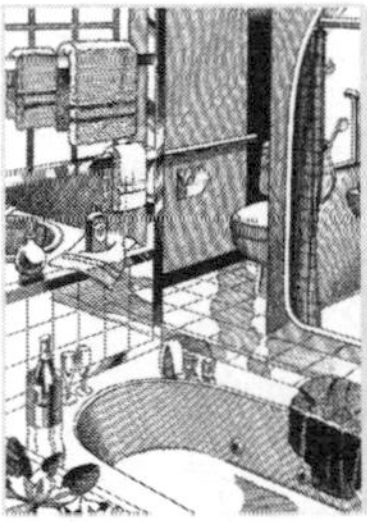

FRESHEN THE BATHROOM

Put pulverized charcoal or baking soda into an open container. Replace every week.

GIVE SMOKE THE SLIP

- ❖ Set out saucers of white vinegar near offending furniture and in stinky rooms.
- ❖ Scatter orange or lemon peels.

continued

They that smell least, smell best.

–Unknown

PERFUME PAINT

Mix 1 teaspoon of vanilla extract into 1 gallon of paint before painting.

TREAT A TRASH CAN

- Sprinkle 1 cup of baking soda or put crumpled newspaper in the bottom, under the liner/bag.
- Sprinkle pulverized charcoal in an empty trash can, cover tightly, and let sit overnight.

From or On Animals

DOG SMELL

- Sprinkle baking soda on the dog's coat and work it into the fur with your hands. Brush out the baking soda.
- Put 1 tablespoon of fresh ground coffee into a frying pan over low heat to "roast" the grounds. Place the warm pan in the room with the dog. (Be sure to keep it out of the dog's reach.)

PET URINE ON CARPET

Rinse with cool water. Mix 1 teaspoon of dishwashing detergent with 1 cup of warm water. Dip a clean dish towel into the liquid and dab the stain. Then dab with fresh water and blot dry. Next, mix ⅓ cup of white vinegar with ⅔ cup of water and dab the stain. Again, dab with fresh water and blot dry. Allow to dry totally (a minimum of 24 hours), then sprinkle with baking soda. Let that sit for a few hours. Vacuum.

SKUNK STINK

Shampoo only the area sprayed by the skunk. In a bucket, mix 1 quart of hydrogen peroxide, ¼ cup of baking soda, and 1 teaspoon of liquid soap. Wet the pet and work the solution into the fur with your hands (avoid the eyes). Rinse. (This remedy may dry out the dog's skin. If so, use a good-quality creme rinse to replenish moisture once the skunk smell is gone.)

The STRANGE CASE of Bobby Dunbar

A century ago, a couple in Louisiana were reunited with their missing son. Or were they?

by Jeff Baker

A Day at the Lake

On August 23, 1912, Percy and Lessie Dunbar of Opelousas, Louisiana, took their two young sons to nearby Swayze Lake for a fishing outing with friends. Just before noon, as the families prepared lunch, 4-year-old Bobby wandered away from the group. As soon as the Dunbars realized that he was missing, they and their friends searched the woods around the lake in a panic. Soon hundreds of volunteers and law-enforcement officers joined them.

Only a few footprints were ever found. Local officials dynamited parts of the lake and killed alligators in the grim hope of recovering the boy's body. When a resident reported having seen a "strange man" in the area, the searchers began to suspect that Bobby had been abducted.

Days turned into weeks, with no sign of Bobby. Percy Dunbar, unsatisfied with the efforts of police, hired a private detective, who printed postcards bearing the boy's photo and description and distributed them from Texas to Florida. *(continued)*

Captivated by a scrapbook and newspaper clippings about the case, Margaret Dunbar Cutright spent more than a decade poring over articles and legal files relating to her grandfather's disappearance.

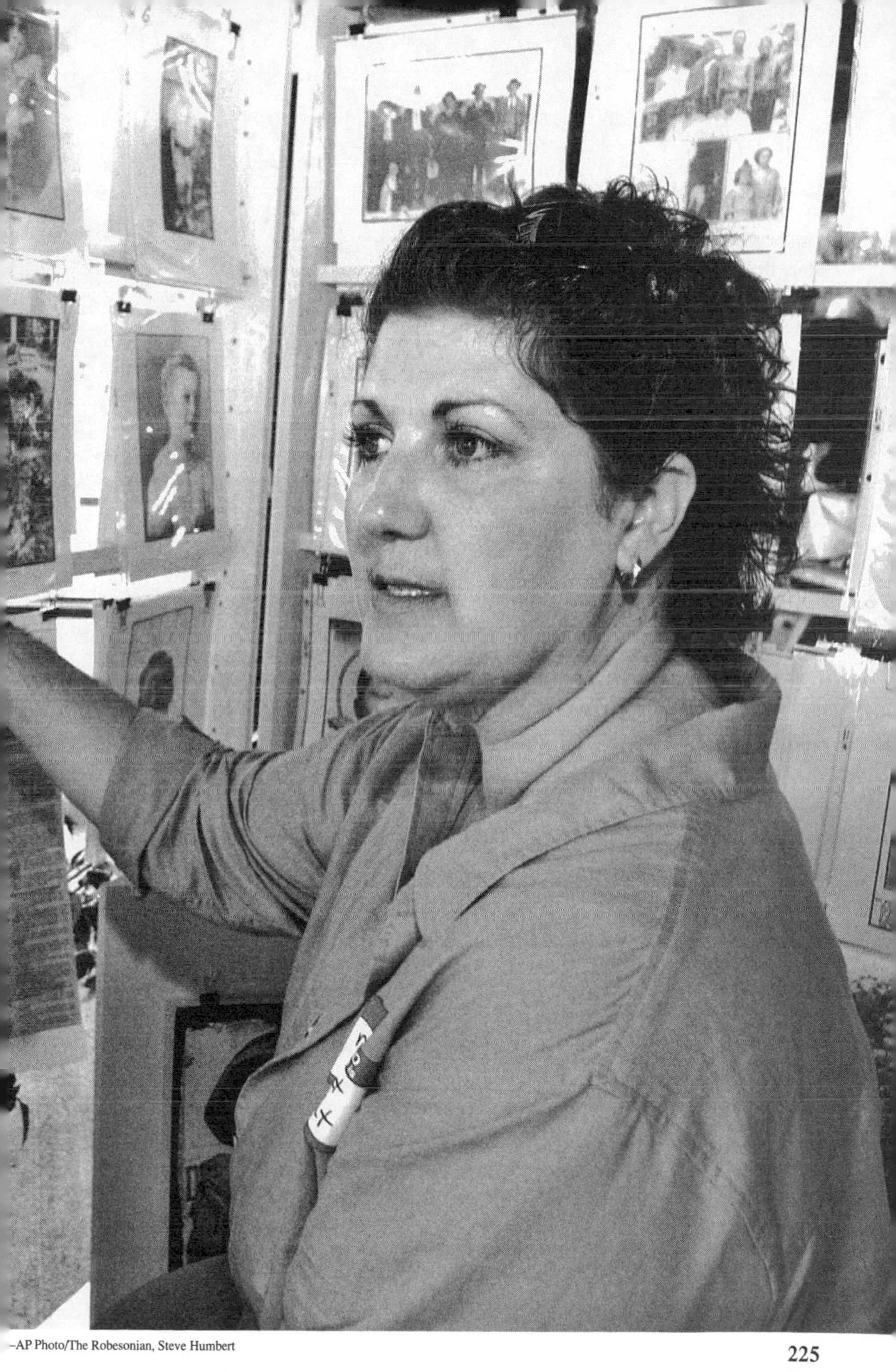

–AP Photo/The Robesonian, Steve Humbert

"It is my boy!"

The boy standing next to the car was believed to be Bobby Dunbar in this 1913 photo taken a few days after he was presumably found.

Police in Hub, Mississippi, announced 8 months later that a boy fitting Bobby Dunbar's description had been found in the company of a handyman who was traveling through in a tented wagon. The Dunbars rushed to Mississippi. On seeing the child, however, Lessie was not certain that the boy was Bobby. The child did not seem to recognize her or her other son; in fact, he shied away from them.

The next day, after noticing a scar on the boy's toe and a mole on his neck (similar to distinguishing marks on Bobby), Lessie shouted, "Thank God, it is my boy!" She then slumped in a faint.

Soon after, the boy rode atop a garlanded fire engine, the star attraction of a parade welcoming Bobby Dunbar back to Opelousas.

Bobby or Bruce?

The joyous reunion story might have ended there had William Cantwell Walters, the itinerant handyman, not claimed so vociferously that he had not kidnapped the boy and that the child was not Bobby Dunbar. According to Walters, the boy was Bruce Anderson, son of Julia Anderson, a family friend in North Carolina who had entrusted him to Walters while she traveled to visit a sick relative.

In an attempt to resolve the situation, a New Orleans newspaper paid to bring Ms. Anderson to Opelousas. She had not seen her son in 15 months and, like Lessie Dunbar, had trouble identifying the child. Finally, she said that her "mother's heart" was sure that he was her son, Bruce.

Amidst the uncertainty, a court-appointed arbiter was asked to choose with whom the boy would go. He decided in favor of the Dunbars.

Trying Times

Walters's sensational 2-week trial made front-page news across the country and became the subject of newsreels, songs, and souvenir postcards. Despite his defense—Julia Anderson's corroboration of Walters's story, plus witness testimony that Walters had been seen traveling with a boy months before the Dunbar disappearance and that he had not been anywhere near Swayze Lake at the time—he was convicted of kidnapping and sentenced to life in prison.

Walters served more than 2 years before his case was overturned on appeal. Prosecutors decided not to try him again, and he was set free. He left Mississippi and was thought to have drifted

The past is never dead. It's not even past.

–William Faulkner, American writer (1897–1961)

into Florida. He faded into obscurity, and Walters family reunions were abuzz for decades with speculation about their ancestor being a kidnapper.

Julia Anderson settled in Mississippi, married, and had eight more children, yet she never ceased believing that her son, Bruce, was being raised as Bobby Dunbar.

The boy called Bobby Dunbar went on to hold a good job, marry, and father four children. He died in 1966, but his story did not.

A Granddaughter's Doubts

Margaret Dunbar Cutright grew up hearing of her grandfather's disappearance and recovery. When she was an adult, her father gave her a scrapbook of newspaper clippings about the case. Captivated and curious, Cutright became an amateur genealogist, historian, and sleuth. She devoted a decade to poring over more than 1,000 newspaper articles and a 900-page legal file and traveled throughout Louisiana, Mississippi, and North Carolina to find relatives of the principals and ask for their recollections.

The more she learned, the more she doubted that William Walters had kidnapped Bobby Dunbar. Acting on her suspicions would call into question the identity of her grandfather and subsequent generations, including herself, but she had to know.

Cutright realized that only a DNA test would solve the mystery. However, her father, Robert Dunbar Jr., refused to participate in the test, saying that he didn't need it to know who he was. Even if his father weren't Bobby Dunbar, he argued, what would it prove? Only the truth, Cutright reasoned: that William Walters was not a kidnapper and that Julia Anderson's son, Bruce, had, in fact, been taken from her.

Ultimately, yet over the objections of his siblings, Robert Jr. agreed to the DNA test in 2004. His sample would be compared against that of his first cousin, David Dunbar, establishing their relationship and, thus, fraternity between Robert Jr.'s father (Bobby Dunbar) and David's father (Bobby's putative brother).

The Final Answer

Margaret Dunbar Cutright revealed the results of the DNA test at a Walters family reunion. "He was innocent," she told the gathered relatives. The crowd, silent with suspense while she spoke, broke into applause. Robert Jr.'s DNA and that of his cousin had not matched: They were not related and neither were their fathers. The boy who had been lost was not the boy who had been found—presumably, Bruce Anderson.

The fate of the "real" Bobby Dunbar is still unknown. It is assumed that he fell into Swayze Lake and drowned. □□

Planting by the Moon's Phase

This age-old practice suggests that the Moon in its cycles affects plant growth.

■ Plant flowers and vegetables that bear crops above ground during the light, or waxing, of the Moon: from the day the Moon is new to the day it is full.

■ Plant flowering bulbs and vegetables that bear crops below ground during the dark, or waning, of the Moon: from the day after it is full to the day before it is new again.

The Moon Favorable columns give the best planting days based on the Moon's phases for 2012. (See the **Left-Hand Calendar Pages, 108–134,** for the exact days of the new and full Moons.) The Planting Dates columns give the safe periods for planting in areas that receive frost. See **Frosts and Growing Seasons, page 219,** for first/last frost dates and the average length of the growing season in your area.

Get local seed-sowing dates at Almanac.com/PlantingTable.

- **Aboveground crops are marked *.**
- **(E) means early; (L) means late.**
- **Map shades correspond to shades of date columns.**

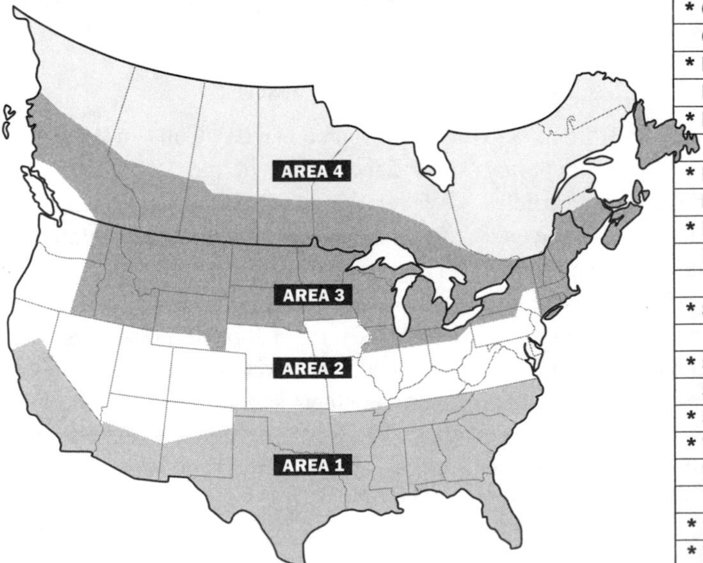

* Barley	
* Beans	(E)
	(L)
Beets	(E)
	(L)
* Broccoli plants	(E)
	(L)
* Brussels sprouts	
* Cabbage plants	
Carrots	(E)
	(L)
* Cauliflower plants	(E)
	(L)
* Celery plants	(E)
	(L)
* Collards	(E)
	(L)
* Corn, sweet	(E)
	(L)
* Cucumbers	
* Eggplant plants	
* Endive	(E)
	(L)
* Kale	(E)
	(L)
Leek plants	
* Lettuce	
* Muskmelons	
* Okra	
Onion sets	
* Parsley	
Parsnips	
* Peas	(E)
	(L)
* Pepper plants	
Potatoes	
* Pumpkins	
Radishes	(E)
	(L)
* Spinach	(E)
	(L)
* Squashes	
Sweet potatoes	
* Swiss chard	
* Tomato plants	
Turnips	(E)
	(L)
* Watermelons	
* Wheat, spring	
* Wheat, winter	

AREA 1		AREA 2		AREA 3		AREA 4	
anting tes	Moon Favorable	Planting Dates	Moon Favorable	Planting Dates	Moon Favorable	Planting Dates	Moon Favorable
.5–3/7	2/21–3/7	3/15–4/7	3/22–4/6	5/15–6/21	5/20–6/4, 6/19–21	6/1–30	6/1–4, 6/19–30
.5–4/7	3/22–4/6	4/15–30	4/21–30	5/7–6/21	5/20–6/4, 6/19–21	5/30–6/15	5/30–6/4
–31	8/17–31	7/1–21	7/1–3, 7/19–21	6/15–7/15	6/19–7/3	—	—
–29	2/8–20	3/15–4/3	3/15–21	5/1–15	5/6–15	5/25–6/10	6/5–10
–30	9/1–14, 9/30	8/15–31	8/15–16	7/15–8/15	7/15–18, 8/2–15	6/15–7/8	6/15–18, 7/4–8
5–3/15	2/21–3/8	3/7–31	3/7–8, 3/22–31	5/15–31	5/20–31	6/1–25	6/1–4, 6/19–25
–30	9/15–29	8/1–20	8/1, 8/17–20	6/15–7/7	6/19–7/3	—	—
1–3/20	2/21–3/8	3/7–4/15	3/7–8, 3/22–4/6	5/15–31	5/20–31	6/1–25	6/1–4, 6/19–25
1–3/20	2/21–3/8	3/7–4/15	3/7–8, 3/22–4/6	5/15–31	5/20–31	6/1–25	6/1–4, 6/19–25
5–3/7	2/15–20	3/7–31	3/9–21	5/15–31	5/15–19	5/25–6/10	6/5–10
–9/7	8/2–16, 9/1–7	7/7–31	7/7–18	6/15–7/21	6/15–18, 7/4–18	6/15–7/8	6/15–18, 7/4–8
5–3/7	2/21–3/7	3/15–4/7	3/22–4/6	5/15–31	5/20–31	6/1–25	6/1–4, 6/19–25
–31	8/17–31	7/1–8/7	7/1–3, 7/19–8/1	6/15–7/21	6/19–7/3, 7/19–21	—	—
5–29	2/21–29	3/7–31	3/7–8, 3/22–31	5/15–6/30	5/20–6/4, 6/19–30	6/1–30	6/1–4, 6/19–30
5–30	9/15–29	8/15–9/7	8/17–31	7/15–8/15	7/19–8/1	—	—
1–3/20	2/21–3/8	3/7–4/7	3/7–8, 3/22–4/6	5/15–31	5/20–31	6/1–25	6/1–4, 6/19–25
–30	9/15–29	8/15–31	8/17–31	7/1–8/7	7/1–3, 7/19–8/1	—	—
5–31	3/22–31	4/1–17	4/1–6	5/10–6/15	5/20–6/4	5/30–6/20	5/30–6/4, 6/19–20
–31	8/17–31	7/7–21	7/19–21	6/15–30	6/19–30	—	—
–4/15	3/7–8, 3/22–4/6	4/7–5/15	4/21–5/5	5/7–6/20	5/20–6/4, 6/19–20	5/30–6/15	5/30–6/4
–4/15	3/7–8, 3/22–4/6	4/7–5/15	4/21–5/5	6/1–30	6/1–4, 6/19–30	6/15–30	6/19–30
5–3/20	2/21–3/8	4/7–5/15	4/21–5/5	5/15–31	5/20–31	6/1–25	6/1–4, 6/19–25
5–9/7	8/17–31	7/15–8/15	7/19–8/1	6/7–30	6/19–30	—	—
1–3/20	2/21–3/8	3/7–4/7	3/7–8, 3/22–4/6	5/15–31	5/20–31	6/1–15	6/1–4
–30	9/15–29	8/15–31	8/17–31	7/1–8/7	7/1–3, 7/19–8/1	6/25–7/15	6/25–7/3
5–4/15	2/15–20, 3/9–21, 4/7–15	3/7–4/7	3/9–21, 4/7	5/15–31	5/15–19	6/1–25	6/5–18
5–3/7	2/21–3/7	3/1–31	3/1–8, 3/22–31	5/15–6/30	5/20–6/4, 6/19–30	6/1–30	6/1–4, 6/19–30
5–4/7	3/22–4/6	4/15–5/7	4/21–5/5	5/15–6/30	5/20–6/4, 6/19–30	6/1–30	6/1–4, 6/19–30
5–6/1	4/21–5/5, 5/20–6/1	5/25–6/15	5/25–6/4	6/15–7/10	6/19–7/3	6/25–7/7	6/25–7/3
–29	2/8–20	3/1–31	3/9–21	5/15–6/7	5/15–19, 6/5–7	6/1–25	6/5–18
0–3/15	2/21–3/8	3/1–31	3/1–8, 3/22–31	5/15–31	5/20–31	6/1–15	6/1–4
5–2/4	1/15–22	3/7–31	3/9–21	4/1–30	4/7–20	5/10–31	5/10–19
5–2/7	1/23–2/7	3/7–31	3/7–8, 3/22–31	4/15–5/7	4/21–5/5	5/15–31	5/20–31
5–30	9/15–29	8/7–31	8/17–31	7/15–31	7/19–31	7/10–25	7/19–25
–20	3/1–8	4/1–30	4/1–6, 4/21–30	5/15–6/30	5/20–6/4, 6/19–30	6/1–30	6/1–4, 6/19–30
0–29	2/10–20	4/1–30	4/7–20	5/1–31	5/6–19	6/1–25	6/5–18
–20	3/7–8	4/23–5/15	4/23–5/5	5/15–31	5/20–31	6/1–30	6/1–4, 6/19–30
–3/1	1/21–22, 2/8–20	3/7–31	3/9–21	4/15–30	4/15–20	5/15–6/5	5/15–19, 6/5
–21	10/1–14	9/7–30	9/7–14, 9/30	8/15–31	8/15–16	7/10–31	7/10–18
–3/15	2/7, 2/21–3/8	3/15–4/20	3/22–4/6	5/15–31	5/20–31	6/1–25	6/1–4, 6/19–25
–21	10/15–21	8/1–9/15	8/1, 8/17–31, 9/15	7/17–9/7	7/19–8/1, 8/17–31	7/20–8/5	7/20–8/1
–4/15	3/22–4/6	4/15–30	4/21–30	5/15–6/15	5/20–6/4	6/1–30	6/1–4, 6/19–30
–4/6	—	4/21–5/9	5/6–9	5/15–6/15	5/15–19, 6/5–15	6/1–30	6/5–18
–3/15	2/7, 2/21–3/8	3/15–4/15	3/22–4/6	5/1–31	5/1–5, 5/20–31	5/15–31	5/20–31
–20	3/7–8	4/7–30	4/21–30	5/15–31	5/20–31	6/1–15	6/1–4
–2/15	1/20–22, 2/8–15	3/15–31	3/15–21	4/7–30	4/7–20	5/10–31	5/10–19
–10/15	9/1–14, 9/30–10/14	8/1–20	8/2–16	7/1–8/15	7/4–18, 8/2–15	—	—
–4/7	3/22–4/6	4/15–5/7	4/21–5/5	5/15–6/30	5/20–6/4, 6/19–30	6/1–30	6/1–4, 6/19–30
–29	2/21–29	3/1–20	3/1–8	4/7–30	4/21–30	5/15–6/10	5/20–6/4
5–12/7	10/15–29, 11/13–28	9/15–10/20	9/15–29, 10/15–20	8/11–9/15	8/17–31, 9/15	8/5–30	8/17–30

Secrets of the Zodiac

The Man of the Signs

Ancient astrologers believed that each astrological sign influenced a specific part of the body. The first sign of the zodiac—Aries—was attributed to the head, with the rest of the signs moving down the body, ending with Pisces at the feet.

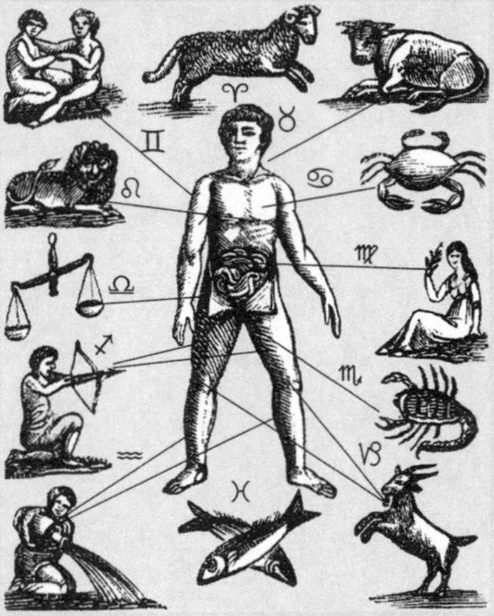

♈ Aries, head......	**ARI**	*Mar. 21–Apr. 20*
♉ Taurus, neck.....	**TAU**	*Apr. 21–May 20*
♊ Gemini, arms ...	**GEM**	*May 21–June 20*
♋ Cancer, breast....	**CAN**	*June 21–July 22*
♌ Leo, heart.......	**LEO**	*July 23–Aug. 22*
♍ Virgo, belly	**VIR**	*Aug. 23–Sept. 22*
♎ Libra, reins......	**LIB**	*Sept. 23–Oct. 22*
♏ Scorpio, secrets...	**SCO**	*Oct. 23–Nov. 22*
♐ Sagittarius, thighs	**SAG**	*Nov. 23–Dec. 21*
♑ Capricorn, knees	**CAP**	*Dec. 22–Jan. 19*
♒ Aquarius, legs ..	**AQU**	*Jan. 20–Feb. 19*
♓ Pisces, feet......	**PSC**	*Feb. 20–Mar. 20*

Astrology vs. Astronomy

■ **Astrology** is a tool we use to plan events according to the placements of the Sun, the Moon, and the planets in the 12 signs of the zodiac. In astrology, the planetary movements do not cause events; rather, they explain the path, or "flow," that events tend to follow. **Astronomy** is the study of the actual placement of the known planets and constellations. *(The placement of the planets in the signs of the zodiac is not the same astrologically and astronomically.)* The Moon's astrological place is given on **page 231;** its astronomical place is given in the **Left-Hand Calendar Pages, 108–134.**

The dates in the **Best Days table, page 232,** are based on the astrological passage of the Moon. However, consider all indicators before making any major decisions.

When Mercury Is Retrograde

■ Sometimes the other planets appear to be traveling backward through the zodiac; this is an illusion. We call this illusion *retrograde motion.*

Mercury's retrograde periods can cause our plans to go awry. However, this is an excellent time to reflect on the past. Intuition is high during these periods, and coincidences can be extraordinary.

When Mercury is retrograde, remain flexible, allow extra time for travel, and avoid signing contracts. Review projects and plans at these times, but wait until Mercury is direct again to make any final decisions.

In 2012, Mercury will be retrograde from March 12–April 10, July 15–August 8, and November 6–26.

–Celeste Longacre

Gardening by the Moon's Sign

Use the chart on the next page to find the best dates for the following garden tasks:

■ **Plant, transplant, and graft:** Cancer, Scorpio, or Pisces. Taurus, Virgo, and Capricorn are good second choices.

■ **Build/fix fences or garden beds:** Capricorn.

■ **Control insect pests, plow, and weed:** Aries, Gemini, Leo, Sagittarius, or Aquarius.

■ **Prune:** Aries, Leo, or Sagittarius. During a waxing Moon, pruning encourages growth; during a waning Moon, it discourages growth.

■ **Clean out the garden shed:** Virgo.

Setting Eggs by the Moon's Sign

■ Chicks take about 21 days to hatch. Those born under a waxing Moon, in the fruitful signs of Cancer, Scorpio, and Pisces, are healthier and mature faster. To ensure that chicks are born during these times, determine the best days to "set eggs" (to place eggs in an incubator or under a hen). To calculate, find the three fruitful birth signs on the chart below. **Use the Left-Hand Calendar Pages, 108–134,** to find the dates of the new and full Moons. Using only the fruitful dates between the new and full Moons, count back 21 days to find the best days to set eggs.

EXAMPLE:

The Moon is new on June 19 and full on July 3. Between these dates, on June 29 and 30, the Moon is in the sign of Scorpio. To have chicks born on June 29, count back 21 days; set eggs on June 8.

The Moon's Astrological Place, 2011–12

	Nov.	Dec.	Jan.	Feb.	Mar.	Apr.	May	June	July	Aug.	Sept.	Oct.	Nov.	Dec.
1	CAP	PSC	ARI	TAU	GEM	LEO	VIR	SCO	SAG	AQU	PSC	ARI	GEM	CAN
2	AQU	PSC	ARI	GEM	CAN	LEO	VIR	SCO	SAG	AQU	ARI	TAU	GEM	CAN
3	AQU	PSC	TAU	GEM	CAN	VIR	LIB	SAG	CAP	PSC	ARI	TAU	CAN	LEO
4	PSC	ARI	TAU	CAN	CAN	VIR	LIB	SAG	CAP	PSC	TAU	GEM	CAN	LEO
5	PSC	ARI	GEM	CAN	LEO	LIB	SCO	CAP	AQU	PSC	TAU	GEM	CAN	VIR
6	PSC	TAU	GEM	LEO	LEO	LIB	SCO	CAP	AQU	ARI	TAU	GEM	LEO	VIR
7	ARI	TAU	GEM	LEO	VIR	SCO	SAG	AQU	PSC	ARI	GEM	CAN	LEO	VIR
8	ARI	TAU	CAN	LEO	VIR	SCO	SAG	AQU	PSC	TAU	GEM	CAN	VIR	LIB
9	TAU	GEM	CAN	VIR	LIB	SAG	CAP	AQU	ARI	TAU	CAN	LEO	VIR	LIB
10	TAU	GEM	LEO	VIR	LIB	SAG	CAP	PSC	ARI	TAU	CAN	LEO	LIB	SCO
11	TAU	CAN	LEO	LIB	SCO	CAP	AQU	PSC	ARI	GEM	CAN	LEO	LIB	SCO
12	GEM	CAN	VIR	LIB	SCO	CAP	AQU	ARI	TAU	GEM	LEO	VIR	SCO	SAG
13	GEM	CAN	VIR	SCO	SAG	CAP	PSC	ARI	TAU	CAN	LEO	VIR	SCO	SAG
14	CAN	LEO	LIB	SCO	SAG	AQU	PSC	TAU	GEM	CAN	VIR	LIB	SAG	CAP
15	CAN	LEO	LIB	SAG	CAP	AQU	PSC	TAU	GEM	CAN	VIR	LIB	SAG	CAP
16	LEO	VIR	LIB	SAG	CAP	PSC	ARI	TAU	GEM	LEO	LIB	SCO	CAP	AQU
17	LEO	VIR	SCO	CAP	AQU	PSC	ARI	GEM	CAN	LEO	LIB	SCO	CAP	AQU
18	LEO	LIB	SCO	CAP	AQU	ARI	TAU	GEM	CAN	VIR	SCO	SAG	AQU	PSC
19	VIR	LIB	SAG	AQU	AQU	ARI	TAU	CAN	LEO	VIR	SCO	SAG	AQU	PSC
20	VIR	SCO	SAG	AQU	PSC	ARI	TAU	CAN	LEO	LIB	SAG	CAP	PSC	ARI
21	LIB	SCO	CAP	PSC	PSC	TAU	GEM	CAN	VIR	LIB	SAG	CAP	PSC	ARI
22	LIB	SAG	CAP	PSC	ARI	TAU	GEM	LEO	VIR	SCO	SAG	AQU	PSC	ARI
23	SCO	SAG	AQU	PSC	ARI	GEM	CAN	LEO	VIR	SCO	CAP	AQU	ARI	TAU
24	SCO	CAP	AQU	ARI	ARI	GEM	CAN	VIR	LIB	SAG	CAP	PSC	ARI	TAU
25	SAG	CAP	PSC	ARI	TAU	GEM	CAN	VIR	LIB	SAG	AQU	PSC	TAU	GEM
26	SAG	AQU	PSC	TAU	TAU	CAN	LEO	VIR	SCO	CAP	AQU	PSC	TAU	GEM
27	CAP	AQU	PSC	TAU	GEM	CAN	LEO	LIB	SCO	CAP	PSC	ARI	TAU	GEM
28	CAP	AQU	ARI	TAU	GEM	LEO	VIR	LIB	SAG	CAP	PSC	ARI	GEM	CAN
29	AQU	PSC	ARI	GEM	GEM	LEO	VIR	SCO	SAG	AQU	ARI	TAU	GEM	CAN
30	AQU	PSC	TAU	—	CAN	LEO	LIB	SCO	CAP	AQU	ARI	TAU	CAN	LEO
31	—	ARI	TAU	—	CAN	—	LIB	—	CAP	PSC	—	TAU	—	LEO

Best Days for 2012

This chart is based on the Moon's sign and shows the best days each month for certain activities.

–Celeste Longacre

	JAN.	FEB.	MAR.	APR.	MAY	JUNE	JULY	AUG.	SEPT.	OCT.	NOV.	DEC.
Quit smoking	13, 17	9, 13	11, 20	7, 16	14, 19	10, 15	7, 12	4, 8	5, 10	2, 7, 12	8, 12	6, 10
Begin diet to lose weight	13, 17	9, 13	11, 20	7, 16	14, 19	10, 15	7, 12	4, 8	5, 10	2, 7, 12	8, 12	6, 10
Begin diet to gain weight	26, 31	22, 27	7, 25	3, 22	1, 28	25, 29	22, 26	18, 22	19, 27	16, 24	21, 26	18, 23
Cut hair to encourage growth	3, 4, 25, 26	27, 28	6, 25, 26	5, 21, 22	3, 4, 30, 31	27, 28	24, 25	20, 21	17, 27	23, 24	26, 27	23, 24
Cut hair to discourage growth	14, 15	11, 12	9, 10	16, 17	18, 19	15, 16	12, 13	8, 9	10, 11	2, 3	10, 11	8, 9
Have dental care	12, 13	9, 10	7, 8	3, 4	1, 2, 28, 29	24, 25	22, 23	18, 19	14, 15	12, 13	8, 9	5, 6
Start projects	24	22	23	22	21	20	20	18	16	16	14	14
End projects	22	20	21	20	19	18	18	16	14	14	12	12
Go camping	19, 20	15, 16	13, 14	9, 10	7, 8	3, 4	28, 29	24, 25	21, 22	18, 19	14, 15	12, 13
Plant aboveground crops	25, 26	4, 5	3, 4, 30, 31	3, 4, 22	5, 23, 24	1, 2, 29, 30	26, 27	22, 23, 31	18, 19, 27	16, 17, 24, 25	21, 22	18, 19
Plant belowground crops	17, 18	9, 10	11, 12	12, 13	13, 14	10, 11	17, 18	3, 4, 13	1, 10, 11	7, 8	3, 4, 30	1, 2, 10, 11
Destroy pests and weeds	1, 2, 28, 29	24, 25	22, 23	19, 20	16, 17	12, 13	10, 11	6, 7	2, 3	1, 27, 28	23, 24	20, 21
Graft or pollinate	8, 9	4, 5	3, 4, 30, 31	26, 27	23, 24	20, 21	17, 18	13, 14	10, 11	7, 8	3, 4, 30	1, 2, 28, 29
Prune to encourage growth	1, 2, 28, 29	24, 25	5, 6, 23, 24	1, 2, 29, 30	26, 27	22, 23	1, 2, 28, 29	24, 25	21, 22	18, 19	14, 15	20, 21
Prune to discourage growth	10, 11	15, 16	13, 14	9, 10	7, 8, 16, 17	12, 13	9, 10	6, 7	2, 3	9, 10	6, 7	3, 4
Harvest above-ground crops	3, 4, 30, 31	27, 28	7, 25, 26	3, 4, 22	1, 2, 28, 29	24, 25	22, 23	18, 19	23, 24	20, 21	25, 26	23, 24
Harvest below-ground crops	12, 13	9, 10	15, 16	12, 13	18, 19	15, 16	12, 13	8, 9	5, 6	2, 3, 12	8, 9	5, 6
Can, pickle, or make sauerkraut	17, 18	13, 14	11, 12	8, 16	13, 14	10, 11	7, 8	3, 4, 13	1, 10, 11	7, 8	3, 4	1, 2, 10, 11
Cut hay	1, 2, 28, 29	24, 25	22, 23	19, 20	16, 17	12, 13	10, 11	6, 7	2, 3	1, 27, 28	23, 24	20, 21
Begin logging	21, 22	17, 18	15, 16	12, 13	9, 10	5, 6	3, 4, 30, 31	26, 27	23, 24	20, 21	16, 17	14, 15
Set posts or pour concrete	21, 22	17, 18	15, 16	12, 13	9, 10	5, 6	3, 4, 30, 31	26, 27	23, 24	20, 21	16, 17	14, 15
Breed animals	17, 18	13, 14	11, 12	7, 8	5, 6	1, 2, 29, 30	26, 27	22, 23	18, 19	16, 17	12, 13	10, 11
Wean animals or children	13, 17	9, 13	11, 20	7, 16	14, 19	10, 15	7, 12	4, 8	5, 10	2, 7, 12	8, 12	6, 10
Castrate animals	23, 24	19, 20	18, 19	14, 15	11, 12	8, 9	5, 6	1, 2, 29, 30	25, 26	22, 23	18, 19	16, 17
Slaughter livestock	17, 18	13, 14	11, 12	7, 8	5, 6	1, 2, 29, 30	26, 27	22, 23	18, 19	16, 17	12, 13	10, 11

See what to do when at Almanac.com/BestDays.

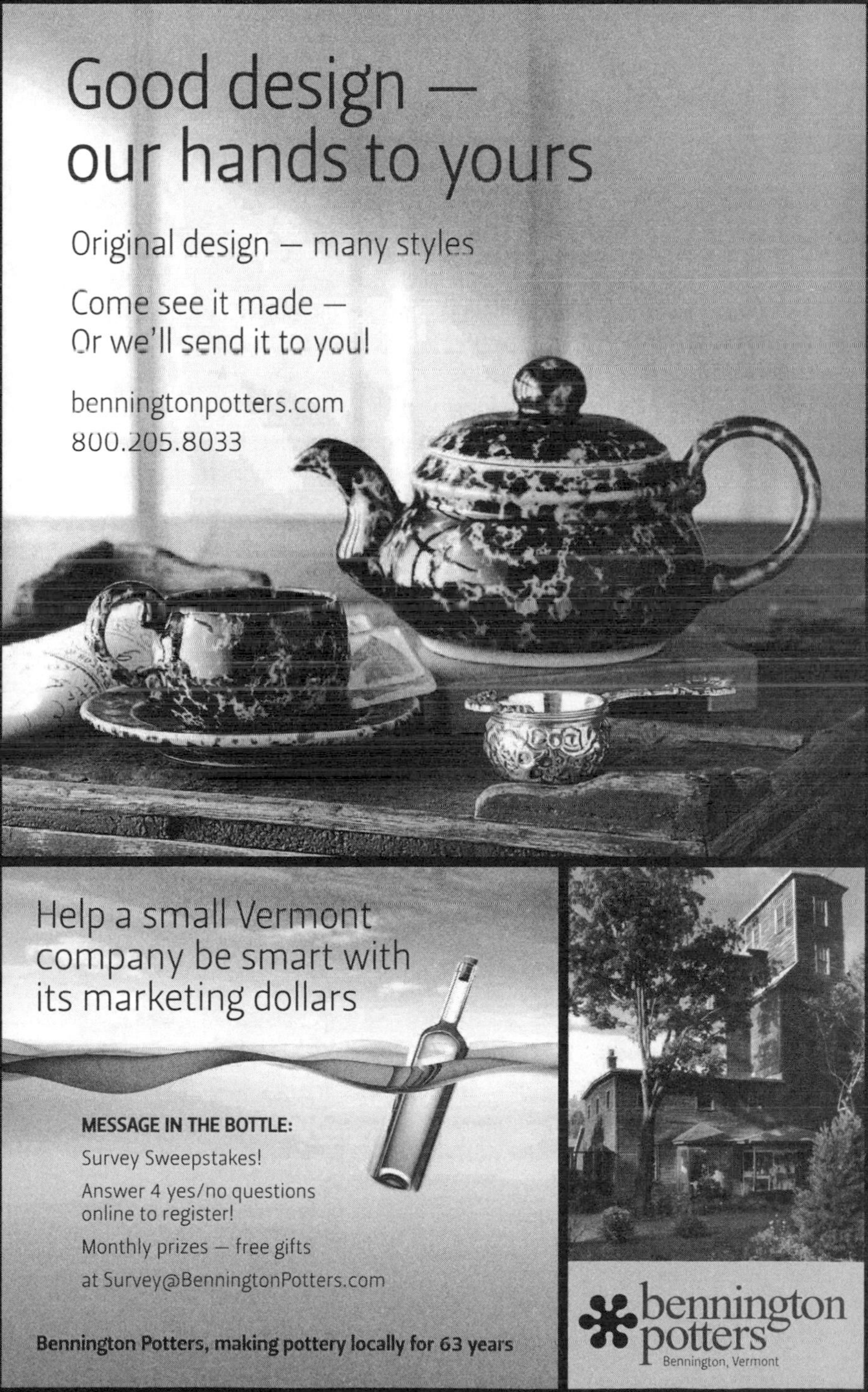
Good design —
our hands to yours
Original design — many styles
Come see it made —
Or we'll send it to you!
benningtonpotters.com
800.205.8033
Help a small Vermont
company be smart with
its marketing dollars
MESSAGE IN THE BOTTLE:
Survey Sweepstakes!
Answer 4 yes/no questions
online to register!
Monthly prizes — free gifts
at Survey@BenningtonPotters.com
Bennington Potters, making pottery locally for 63 years
bennington
potters
Bennington, Vermont

How Much Paint Do You Need?

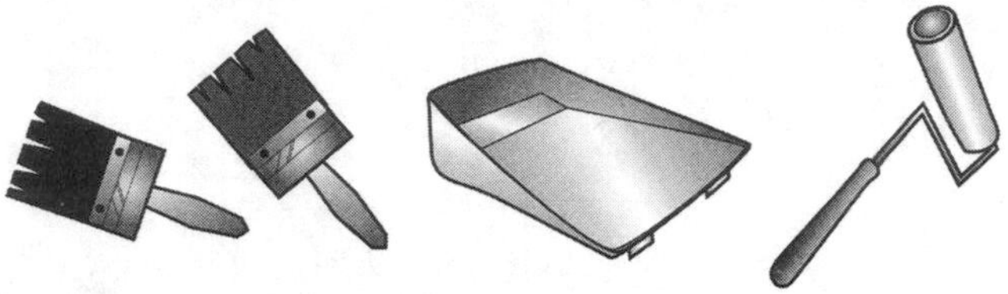

■ Estimate your room size and paint needs before you go to the store. Running out of a custom color halfway through the job could mean disaster. For the sake of the following exercise, assume that you have a 10x15-foot room with an 8-foot ceiling. The room has two doors and two windows.

For Walls

■ Measure the total distance (perimeter) around the room:

(10 ft. + 15 ft.) x 2 = 50 ft.

■ Multiply the perimeter by the ceiling height to get the total wall area:

50 ft. x 8 ft. = 400 sq. ft.

■ Doors are usually 21 square feet (there are two in this exercise):

21 sq. ft. x 2 = 42 sq. ft.

■ Windows average 15 square feet (there are two in this exercise):

15 sq. ft. x 2 = 30 sq. ft.

■ Take the total wall area and subtract the area for the doors and windows to get the wall surface to be painted:

400 sq. ft.	**(wall area)**
– 42 sq. ft.	**(doors)**
– 30 sq. ft.	**(windows)**
328 sq. ft.	

■ As a rule of thumb, one gallon of quality paint will usually cover 400 square feet. One quart will cover 100 square feet. Because you need to cover 328 square feet in this example, one gallon will be adequate to give one coat of paint to the walls. (Coverage will be affected by the porosity and texture of the surface. In addition, bright colors may require a minimum of two coats.)

For Ceilings

■ Using the rule of thumb for coverage above, you can calculate the quantity of paint needed for the ceiling by multiplying the width by the length:

10 ft. x 15 ft. = 150 sq. ft.

This ceiling will require approximately two quarts of paint. (A flat finish is recommended to minimize surface imperfections.)

For Doors, Windows, and Trim

■ The area for the doors and windows has been calculated above. (The windowpane area that does not get painted should allow for enough paint for any trim around doors and windows.) Determine the baseboard trim by taking the perimeter of the room, less 3 feet per door (3 ft. x 2 = 6 ft.), and multiplying this by the average trim width of your baseboard, which in this example is 6 inches (or 0.5 feet).

50 ft. (perimeter) – 6 ft. = 44 ft.
44 ft. x 0.5 ft. = 22 sq. ft.

■ Add the area for doors, windows, and baseboard trim.

42 sq. ft.	**(doors)**
+30 sq. ft.	**(windows)**
+22 sq. ft.	**(baseboard trim)**
94 sq. ft.	

One quart will be sufficient to cover the doors, windows, and trim in this example.

–courtesy M.A.B. Paints

Tide Corrections

■ Many factors affect the times and heights of the tides: the shoreline, the time of the Moon's southing (crossing the meridian), and the Moon's phase. The High Tide column on the **Left-Hand Calendar Pages, 108–134,** lists the times of high tide at Commonwealth Pier in Boston Harbor. The heights of some of these tides, reckoned from Mean Lower Low Water, are given on the **Right-Hand Calendar Pages, 109–135.** Use the table below to calculate the approximate times and heights of high tide at the places shown. Apply the time difference to the times of high tide at Boston and the height difference to the heights at Boston. A tide calculator can be found at **Almanac.com/Tides.**

EXAMPLE:

The conversion of the times and heights of the tides at Boston to those at Cape Fear, North Carolina, is given below:

High tide at Boston	**11:45 A.M.**
Correction for Cape Fear	**– 3 55**
High tide at Cape Fear	**7:50 A.M.**
Tide height at Boston	**11.6 ft.**
Correction for Cape Fear	**– 5.0 ft.**
Tide height at Cape Fear	**6.6 ft.**

Estimations derived from this table are *not* meant to be used for navigation. *The Old Farmer's Almanac* accepts no responsibility for errors or any consequences ensuing from the use of this table.

Tidal Site	Difference: Time (h. m.)	Height (ft.)
Canada		
Alberton, PE	*–5 45	–7.5
Charlottetown, PE	*–0 45	–3.5
Halifax, NS	–3 23	–4.5
North Sydney, NS	–3 15	–6.5
Saint John, NB	+0 30	+15.0
St. John's, NL	–4 00	–6.5
Yarmouth, NS	–0 40	+3.0
Maine		
Bar Harbor	–0 34	+0.9
Belfast	–0 20	+0.4
Boothbay Harbor	–0 18	–0.8
Chebeague Island	–0 16	–0.6
Eastport	–0 28	+8.4
Kennebunkport	+0 04	–1.0
Machias	–0 28	+2.8
Monhegan Island	–0 25	–0.8
Old Orchard	0 00	–0.8
Portland	–0 12	–0.6
Rockland	–0 28	+0.1
Stonington	–0 30	+0.1
York	–0 09	–1.0
New Hampshire		
Hampton	+0 02	–1.3
Portsmouth	+0 11	–1.5
Rye Beach	–0 09	–0.9
Massachusetts		
Annisquam	–0 02	–1.1
Beverly Farms	0 00	–0.5
Boston	0 00	0.0
Cape Cod Canal		
East Entrance	–0 01	–0.8
West Entrance	–2 16	–5.9
Chatham Outer Coast	+0 30	–2.8
Inside	+1 54	**0.4
Cohasset	+0 02	–0.07
Cotuit Highlands	+1 15	**0.3
Dennis Port	+1 01	**0.4
Duxbury–Gurnet Point	+0 02	–0.3
Fall River	–3 03	–5.0
Gloucester	–0 03	–0.8
Hingham	+0 07	0.0
Hull	+0 03	–0.2
Hyannis Port	+1 01	**0.3
Magnolia–Manchester	–0 02	–0.7
Marblehead	–0 02	–0.4
Marion	–3 22	–5.4
Monument Beach	–3 08	–5.4
Nahant	–0 01	–0.5
Nantasket	+0 04	–0.1
Nantucket	+0 56	**0.3
Nauset Beach	+0 30	**0.6
New Bedford	–3 24	–5.7
Newburyport	+0 19	–1.8
Oak Bluffs	+0 30	**0.2
Onset–R.R. Bridge	–2 16	–5.9
Plymouth	+0 05	0.0
Provincetown	+0 14	–0.4
Revere Beach	–0 01	–0.3
Rockport	–0 08	–1.0
Salem	0 00	–0.5
Scituate	–0 05	–0.7

(continued)

Tide Corrections

Tidal Site	Difference: Time (h. m.)	Height (ft.)
Wareham	–3 09	–5.3
Wellfleet	+0 12	+0.5
West Falmouth	–3 10	–5.4
Westport Harbor	–3 22	–6.4
Woods Hole		
Little Harbor	–2 50	**0.2
Oceanographic Institute	–3 07	**0.2
Rhode Island		
Bristol	–3 24	–5.3
Narragansett Pier	–3 42	–6.2
Newport	–3 34	–5.9
Point Judith	–3 41	–6.3
Providence	–3 20	–4.8
Sakonnet	–3 44	–5.6
Watch Hill	–2 50	–6.8
Connecticut		
Bridgeport	+0 01	–2.6
Madison	–0 22	–2.3
New Haven	–0 11	–3.2
New London	–1 54	–6.7
Norwalk	+0 01	–2.2
Old Lyme		
Highway Bridge	–0 30	–6.2
Stamford	+0 01	–2.2
Stonington	–2 27	–6.6
New York		
Coney Island	–3 33	–4.9
Fire Island Light	–2 43	**0.1
Long Beach	–3 11	–5.7
Montauk Harbor	–2 19	–7.4
New York City–Battery	–2 43	–5.0
Oyster Bay	+0 04	–1.8
Port Chester	–0 09	–2.2
Port Washington	–0 01	–2.1
Sag Harbor	–0 55	–6.8
Southampton		
Shinnecock Inlet	–4 20	**0.2
Willets Point	0 00	–2.3
New Jersey		
Asbury Park	–4 04	–5.3
Atlantic City	–3 56	–5.5
Bay Head–Sea Girt	–4 04	–5.3
Beach Haven	–1 43	**0.24
Cape May	–3 28	–5.3
Ocean City	–3 06	–5.9
Sandy Hook	–3 30	–5.0
Seaside Park	–4 03	–5.4
Pennsylvania		
Philadelphia	+2 40	–3.5
Delaware		
Cape Henlopen	–2 48	–5.3
Rehoboth Beach	–3 37	–5.7
Wilmington	+1 56	–3.8
Maryland		
Annapolis	+6 23	–8.5
Baltimore	+7 59	–8.3
Cambridge	+5 05	–7.8
Havre de Grace	+11 21	–7.7
Point No Point	+2 28	–8.1
Prince Frederick		
Plum Point	+4 25	–8.5
Virginia		
Cape Charles	–2 20	–7.0
Hampton Roads	–2 02	–6.9
Norfolk	–2 06	–6.6
Virginia Beach	–4 00	–6.0
Yorktown	–2 13	–7.0
North Carolina		
Cape Fear	–3 55	–5.0
Cape Lookout	–4 28	–5.7
Currituck	–4 10	–5.8
Hatteras		
Inlet	–4 03	–7.4
Kitty Hawk	–4 14	–6.2
Ocean	–4 26	–6.0
South Carolina		
Charleston	–3 22	–4.3
Georgetown	–1 48	**0.36
Hilton Head	–3 22	–2.9
Myrtle Beach	–3 49	–4.4
St. Helena		
Harbor Entrance	–3 15	–3.4
Georgia		
Jekyll Island	–3 46	–2.9
St. Simon's Island	–2 50	–2.9
Savannah Beach		
River Entrance	–3 14	–5.5
Tybee Light	–3 22	–2.7
Florida		
Cape Canaveral	–3 59	–6.0
Daytona Beach	–3 28	–5.3
Fort Lauderdale	–2 50	–7.2
Fort Pierce Inlet	–3 32	–6.9
Jacksonville		
Railroad Bridge	–6 55	**0.1
Miami Harbor Entrance	–3 18	–7.0
St. Augustine	–2 55	–4.9

**Varies widely; accurate within only 1½ hours. Consult local tide tables for precise times and heights.*

***Where the difference in the Height column is so marked, the height at Boston should be multiplied by this ratio.*

Time Corrections

■ Astronomical data for Boston is given on **pages 88, 92–93,** and **108–134.** Use the Key Letter shown to the right of each time on those pages with this table to find the number of minutes that you must add to or subtract from Boston time to get the correct time for your city. (Because of complex calculations for different locales, times are approximate.) For more information on the use of Key Letters and this table, **see How to Use This Almanac, page 104.**

Get times simply and specifically: Purchase astronomical times calculated for your zip code and presented like a Left-Hand Calendar Page at **MyLocalAlmanac.com.**

TIME ZONES: Codes represent *standard time.* Atlantic is −1, Eastern is 0, Central is 1, Mountain is 2, Pacific is 3, Alaska is 4, and Hawaii-Aleutian is 5.

State	City	North Latitude °	North Latitude '	West Longitude °	West Longitude '	Time Zone Code	Key Letters A (min.)	B (min.)	C (min.)	D (min.)	E (min.)
AK	Anchorage	61	10	149	59	4	–46	+27	+71	+122	+171
AK	Cordova	60	33	145	45	4	–55	+13	+55	+103	+149
AK	Fairbanks	64	48	147	51	4	–127	+2	+61	+131	+205
AK	Juneau	58	18	134	25	4	–76	–23	+10	+49	+86
AK	Ketchikan	55	21	131	39	4	–62	–25	0	+29	+56
AK	Kodiak	57	47	152	24	4	0	+49	+82	+120	+154
AL	Birmingham	33	31	86	49	1	+30	+15	+3	–10	–20
AL	Decatur	34	36	86	59	1	+27	+14	+4	–7	–17
AL	Mobile	30	42	88	3	1	+42	+23	+8	–8	–22
AL	Montgomery	32	23	86	19	1	+31	+14	+1	–13	–25
AR	Fort Smith	35	23	94	25	1	+55	+43	+33	+22	+14
AR	Little Rock	34	45	92	17	1	+48	+35	+25	+13	+4
AR	Texarkana	33	26	94	3	1	+59	+44	+32	+18	+8
AZ	Flagstaff	35	12	111	39	2	+64	+52	+42	+31	+22
AZ	Phoenix	33	27	112	4	2	+71	+56	+44	+30	+20
AZ	Tucson	32	13	110	58	2	+70	+53	+40	+24	+12
AZ	Yuma	32	43	114	37	2	+83	+67	+54	+40	+28
CA	Bakersfield	35	23	119	1	3	+33	+21	+12	+1	–7
CA	Barstow	34	54	117	1	3	+27	+14	+4	–7	–16
CA	Fresno	36	44	119	47	3	+32	+22	+15	+6	0
CA	Los Angeles–Pasadena–Santa Monica	34	3	118	14	3	+34	+20	+9	–3	–13
CA	Palm Springs	33	49	116	32	3	+28	+13	+1	–12	–22
CA	Redding	40	35	122	24	3	+31	+27	+25	+22	+19
CA	Sacramento	38	35	121	30	3	+34	+27	+21	+15	+10
CA	San Diego	32	43	117	9	3	+33	+17	+4	–9	–21
CA	San Francisco–Oakland–San Jose	37	47	122	25	3	+40	+31	+25	+18	+12
CO	Craig	40	31	107	33	2	+32	+28	+25	+22	+20
CO	Denver–Boulder	39	44	104	59	2	+24	+19	+15	+11	+7
CO	Grand Junction	39	4	108	33	2	+40	+34	+29	+24	+20
CO	Pueblo	38	16	104	37	2	+27	+20	+14	+7	+2
CO	Trinidad	37	10	104	31	2	+30	+21	+13	+5	0
CT	Bridgeport	41	11	73	11	0	+12	+10	+8	+6	+4
CT	Hartford–New Britain	41	46	72	41	0	+8	+7	+6	+5	+4
CT	New Haven	41	18	72	56	0	+11	+8	+7	+5	+4
CT	New London	41	22	72	6	0	+7	+5	+4	+2	+1
CT	Norwalk–Stamford	41	7	73	22	0	+13	+10	+9	+7	+5
CT	Waterbury–Meriden	41	33	73	3	0	+10	+9	+7	+6	+5
DC	Washington	38	54	77	1	0	+35	+28	+23	+18	+13
DE	Wilmington	39	45	75	33	0	+26	+21	+18	+13	+10

(continued)

Time Corrections

State	City	North Latitude °	North Latitude '	West Longitude °	West Longitude '	Time Zone Code	Key Letters A (min.)	B (min.)	C (min.)	D (min.)	E (min.)
FL	Fort Myers	26	38	81	52	0	+87	+63	+44	+21	+4
FL	Jacksonville	30	20	81	40	0	+77	+58	+43	+25	+11
FL	Miami	25	47	80	12	0	+88	+57	+37	+14	–3
FL	Orlando	28	32	81	22	0	+80	+59	+42	+22	+6
FL	Pensacola	30	25	87	13	1	+39	+20	+5	–12	–26
FL	St. Petersburg	27	46	82	39	0	+87	+65	+47	+26	+10
FL	Tallahassee	30	27	84	17	0	+87	+68	+53	+35	+22
FL	Tampa	27	57	82	27	0	+86	+64	+46	+25	+9
FL	West Palm Beach	26	43	80	3	0	+79	+55	+36	+14	–2
GA	Atlanta	33	45	84	24	0	+79	+65	+53	+40	+30
GA	Augusta	33	28	81	58	0	+70	+55	+44	+30	+19
GA	Macon	32	50	83	38	0	+79	+63	+50	+36	+24
GA	Savannah	32	5	81	6	0	+70	+54	+40	+25	+13
HI	Hilo	19	44	155	5	5	+94	+62	+37	+7	–15
HI	Honolulu	21	18	157	52	5	+102	+72	+48	+19	–1
HI	Lanai City	20	50	156	55	5	+99	+69	+44	+15	–6
HI	Lihue	21	59	159	23	5	+107	+77	+54	+26	+5
IA	Davenport	41	32	90	35	1	+20	+19	+17	+16	+15
IA	Des Moines	41	35	93	37	1	+32	+31	+30	+28	+27
IA	Dubuque	42	30	90	41	1	+17	+18	+18	+18	+18
IA	Waterloo	42	30	92	20	1	+24	+24	+24	+25	+25
ID	Boise	43	37	116	12	2	+55	+58	+60	+62	+64
ID	Lewiston	46	25	117	1	3	–12	–3	+2	+10	+17
ID	Pocatello	42	52	112	27	2	+43	+44	+45	+46	+46
IL	Cairo	37	0	89	11	1	+29	+20	+12	+4	–2
IL	Chicago–Oak Park	41	52	87	38	1	+7	+6	+6	+5	+4
IL	Danville	40	8	87	37	1	+13	+9	+6	+2	0
IL	Decatur	39	51	88	57	1	+19	+15	+11	+7	+4
IL	Peoria	40	42	89	36	1	+19	+16	+14	+11	+9
IL	Springfield	39	48	89	39	1	+22	+18	+14	+10	+6
IN	Fort Wayne	41	4	85	9	0	+60	+58	+56	+54	+52
IN	Gary	41	36	87	20	1	+7	+6	+4	+3	+2
IN	Indianapolis	39	46	86	10	0	+69	+64	+60	+56	+52
IN	Muncie	40	12	85	23	0	+64	+60	+57	+53	+50
IN	South Bend	41	41	86	15	0	+62	+61	+60	+59	+58
IN	Terre Haute	39	28	87	24	0	+74	+69	+65	+60	+56
KS	Fort Scott	37	50	94	42	1	+49	+41	+34	+27	+21
KS	Liberal	37	3	100	55	1	+76	+66	+59	+51	+44
KS	Oakley	39	8	100	51	1	+69	+63	+59	+53	+49
KS	Salina	38	50	97	37	1	+57	+51	+46	+40	+35
KS	Topeka	39	3	95	40	1	+49	+43	+38	+32	+28
KS	Wichita	37	42	97	20	1	+60	+51	+45	+37	+31
KY	Lexington–Frankfort	38	3	84	30	0	+67	+59	+53	+46	+41
KY	Louisville	38	15	85	46	0	+72	+64	+58	+52	+46
LA	Alexandria	31	18	92	27	1	+58	+40	+26	+9	–3
LA	Baton Rouge	30	27	91	11	1	+55	+36	+21	+3	–10
LA	Lake Charles	30	14	93	13	1	+64	+44	+29	+11	–2
LA	Monroe	32	30	92	7	1	+53	+37	+24	+9	–1
LA	New Orleans	29	57	90	4	1	+52	+32	+16	–1	–15
LA	Shreveport	32	31	93	45	1	+60	+44	+31	+16	+4
MA	Brockton	42	5	71	1	0	0	0	0	0	–1
MA	Fall River–New Bedford	41	42	71	9	0	+2	+1	0	0	–1
MA	Lawrence–Lowell	42	42	71	10	0	0	0	0	0	+1
MA	Pittsfield	42	27	73	15	0	+8	+8	+8	+8	+8
MA	Springfield–Holyoke	42	6	72	36	0	+6	+6	+6	+5	+5
MA	Worcester	42	16	71	48	0	+3	+2	+2	+2	+2

State	City	North Latitude °	North Latitude '	West Longitude °	West Longitude '	Time Zone Code	Key Letters A (min.)	Key Letters B (min.)	Key Letters C (min.)	Key Letters D (min.)	Key Letters E (min.)
MD	Baltimore	39	17	76	37	0	+32	+26	+22	+17	+13
MD	Hagerstown	39	39	77	43	0	+35	+30	+26	+22	+18
MD	Salisbury	38	22	75	36	0	+31	+23	+18	+11	+6
ME	Augusta	44	19	69	46	0	–12	–8	–5	–1	0
ME	Bangor	44	48	68	46	0	–18	–13	–9	–5	–1
ME	Eastport	44	54	67	0	0	–26	–20	–16	–11	–8
ME	Ellsworth	44	33	68	25	0	–18	–14	–10	–6	–3
ME	Portland	43	40	70	15	0	–8	–5	–3	–1	0
ME	Presque Isle	46	41	68	1	0	–29	–19	–12	–4	+2
MI	Cheboygan	45	39	84	29	0	+40	+47	+53	+59	+64
MI	Detroit–Dearborn	42	20	83	3	0	+47	+47	+47	+47	+47
MI	Flint	43	1	83	41	0	+47	+49	+50	+51	+52
MI	Ironwood	46	27	90	9	1	0	+9	+15	+23	+29
MI	Jackson	42	15	84	24	0	+53	+53	+53	+52	+52
MI	Kalamazoo	42	17	85	35	0	+58	+57	+57	+57	+57
MI	Lansing	42	44	84	33	0	+52	+53	+53	+54	+54
MI	St. Joseph	42	5	86	26	0	+61	+61	+60	+60	+59
MI	Traverse City	44	46	85	38	0	+49	+54	+57	+62	+65
MN	Albert Lea	43	39	93	22	1	+24	+26	+28	+31	+33
MN	Bemidji	47	28	94	53	1	+14	+26	+34	+44	+52
MN	Duluth	46	47	92	6	1	+6	+16	+23	+31	+38
MN	Minneapolis–St. Paul	44	59	93	16	1	+18	+24	+28	+33	+37
MN	Ortonville	45	19	96	27	1	+30	+36	+40	+46	+51
MO	Jefferson City	38	34	92	10	1	+36	+29	+24	+18	+13
MO	Joplin	37	6	94	30	1	+50	+41	+33	+25	+18
MO	Kansas City	39	1	94	20	1	+44	+37	+33	+27	+23
MO	Poplar Bluff	36	46	90	24	1	+35	+25	+17	+8	+1
MO	St. Joseph	39	46	94	50	1	+43	+38	+35	+30	+27
MO	St. Louis	38	37	90	12	1	+28	+21	+16	+10	+5
MO	Springfield	37	13	93	18	1	+45	+36	+29	+20	+14
MS	Biloxi	30	24	88	53	1	+46	+27	+11	–5	–19
MS	Jackson	32	18	90	11	1	+46	+30	+17	+1	–10
MS	Meridian	32	22	88	42	1	+40	+24	+11	–4	–15
MS	Tupelo	34	16	88	34	1	+35	+21	+10	–2	–11
MT	Billings	45	47	108	30	2	+16	+23	+29	+35	+40
MT	Butte	46	1	112	32	2	+31	+39	+45	+52	+57
MT	Glasgow	48	12	106	38	2	–1	+11	+21	+32	+42
MT	Great Falls	47	30	111	17	2	+20	+31	+39	+49	+58
MT	Helena	46	36	112	2	2	+27	+36	+43	+51	+57
MT	Miles City	46	25	105	51	2	+3	+11	+18	+26	+32
NC	Asheville	35	36	82	33	0	+67	+55	+46	+35	+27
NC	Charlotte	35	14	80	51	0	+61	+49	+39	+28	+19
NC	Durham	36	0	78	55	0	+51	+40	+31	+21	+13
NC	Greensboro	36	4	79	47	0	+54	+43	+35	+25	+17
NC	Raleigh	35	47	78	38	0	+51	+39	+30	+20	+12
NC	Wilmington	34	14	77	55	0	+52	+38	+27	+15	+5
ND	Bismarck	46	48	100	47	1	+41	+50	+58	+66	+73
ND	Fargo	46	53	96	47	1	+24	+34	+42	+50	+57
ND	Grand Forks	47	55	97	3	1	+21	+33	+43	+53	+62
ND	Minot	48	14	101	18	1	+36	+50	+59	+71	+81
ND	Williston	48	9	103	37	1	+46	+59	+69	+80	+90
NE	Grand Island	40	55	98	21	1	+53	+51	+49	+46	+44
NE	Lincoln	40	49	96	41	1	+47	+44	+42	+39	+37
NE	North Platte	41	8	100	46	1	+62	+60	+58	+56	+54
NE	Omaha	41	16	95	56	1	+43	+40	+39	+37	+36
NH	Berlin	44	28	71	11	0	–7	–3	0	+3	+7
NH	Keene	42	56	72	17	0	+2	+3	+4	+5	+6

(continued)

Time Corrections

State	City	North Latitude °	North Latitude '	West Longitude °	West Longitude '	Time Zone Code	Key Letters A (min.)	Key Letters B (min.)	Key Letters C (min.)	Key Letters D (min.)	Key Letters E (min.)
NH	Manchester–Concord	42	59	71	28	0	0	0	+1	+2	+3
NH	Portsmouth	43	5	70	45	0	–4	–2	–1	0	0
NJ	Atlantic City	39	22	74	26	0	+23	+17	+13	+8	+4
NJ	Camden	39	57	75	7	0	+24	+19	+16	+12	+9
NJ	Cape May	38	56	74	56	0	+26	+20	+15	+9	+5
NJ	Newark–East Orange	40	44	74	10	0	+17	+14	+12	+9	+7
NJ	Paterson	40	55	74	10	0	+17	+14	+12	+9	+7
NJ	Trenton	40	13	74	46	0	+21	+17	+14	+11	+8
NM	Albuquerque	35	5	106	39	2	+45	+32	+22	+11	+2
NM	Gallup	35	32	108	45	2	+52	+40	+31	+20	+11
NM	Las Cruces	32	19	106	47	2	+53	+36	+23	+8	–3
NM	Roswell	33	24	104	32	2	+41	+26	+14	0	–10
NM	Santa Fe	35	41	105	56	2	+40	+28	+19	+9	0
NV	Carson City–Reno	39	10	119	46	3	+25	+19	+14	+9	+5
NV	Elko	40	50	115	46	3	+3	0	–1	–3	–5
NV	Las Vegas	36	10	115	9	3	+16	+4	–3	–13	–20
NY	Albany	42	39	73	45	0	+9	+10	+10	+11	+11
NY	Binghamton	42	6	75	55	0	+20	+19	+19	+18	+18
NY	Buffalo	42	53	78	52	0	+29	+30	+30	+31	+32
NY	New York	40	45	74	0	0	+17	+14	+11	+9	+6
NY	Ogdensburg	44	42	75	30	0	+8	+13	+17	+21	+25
NY	Syracuse	43	3	76	9	0	+17	+19	+20	+21	+22
OH	Akron	41	5	81	31	0	+46	+43	+41	+39	+37
OH	Canton	40	48	81	23	0	+46	+43	+41	+38	+36
OH	Cincinnati–Hamilton	39	6	84	31	0	+64	+58	+53	+48	+44
OH	Cleveland–Lakewood	41	30	81	42	0	+45	+43	+42	+40	+39
OH	Columbus	39	57	83	1	0	+55	+51	+47	+43	+40
OH	Dayton	39	45	84	10	0	+61	+56	+52	+48	+44
OH	Toledo	41	39	83	33	0	+52	+50	+49	+48	+47
OH	Youngstown	41	6	80	39	0	+42	+40	+38	+36	+34
OK	Oklahoma City	35	28	97	31	1	+67	+55	+46	+35	+26
OK	Tulsa	36	9	95	60	1	+59	+48	+40	+30	+22
OR	Eugene	44	3	123	6	3	+21	+24	+27	+30	+33
OR	Pendleton	45	40	118	47	3	–1	+4	+10	+16	+21
OR	Portland	45	31	122	41	3	+14	+20	+25	+31	+36
OR	Salem	44	57	123	1	3	+17	+23	+27	+31	+35
PA	Allentown–Bethlehem	40	36	75	28	0	+23	+20	+17	+14	+12
PA	Erie	42	7	80	5	0	+36	+36	+35	+35	+35
PA	Harrisburg	40	16	76	53	0	+30	+26	+23	+19	+16
PA	Lancaster	40	2	76	18	0	+28	+24	+20	+17	+13
PA	Philadelphia–Chester	39	57	75	9	0	+24	+19	+16	+12	+9
PA	Pittsburgh–McKeesport	40	26	80	0	0	+42	+38	+35	+32	+29
PA	Reading	40	20	75	56	0	+26	+22	+19	+16	+13
PA	Scranton–Wilkes-Barre	41	25	75	40	0	+21	+19	+18	+16	+15
PA	York	39	58	76	43	0	+30	+26	+22	+18	+15
RI	Providence	41	50	71	25	0	+3	+2	+1	0	0
SC	Charleston	32	47	79	56	0	+64	+48	+36	+21	+10
SC	Columbia	34	0	81	2	0	+65	+51	+40	+27	+17
SC	Spartanburg	34	56	81	57	0	+66	+53	+43	+32	+23
SD	Aberdeen	45	28	98	29	1	+37	+44	+49	+54	+59
SD	Pierre	44	22	100	21	1	+49	+53	+56	+60	+63
SD	Rapid City	44	5	103	14	2	+2	+5	+8	+11	+13
SD	Sioux Falls	43	33	96	44	1	+38	+40	+42	+44	+46
TN	Chattanooga	35	3	85	19	0	+79	+67	+57	+45	+36
TN	Knoxville	35	58	83	55	0	+71	+60	+51	+41	+33
TN	Memphis	35	9	90	3	1	+38	+26	+16	+5	–3
TN	Nashville	36	10	86	47	1	+22	+11	+3	–6	–14

State/ Province	City	North Latitude °	North Latitude '	West Longitude °	West Longitude '	Time Zone Code	Key Letters A (min.)	Key Letters B (min.)	Key Letters C (min.)	Key Letters D (min.)	Key Letters E (min.)
TX	Amarillo	35	12	101	50	1	+85	+73	+63	+52	+43
TX	Austin	30	16	97	45	1	+82	+62	+47	+29	+15
TX	Beaumont	30	5	94	6	1	+67	+48	+32	+14	0
TX	Brownsville	25	54	97	30	1	+91	+66	+46	+23	+5
TX	Corpus Christi	27	48	97	24	1	+86	+64	+46	+25	+9
TX	Dallas–Fort Worth	32	47	96	48	1	+71	+55	+43	+28	+17
TX	El Paso	31	45	106	29	2	+53	+35	+22	+6	–6
TX	Galveston	29	18	94	48	1	+72	+52	+35	+16	+1
TX	Houston	29	45	95	22	1	+73	+53	+37	+19	+5
TX	McAllen	26	12	98	14	1	+93	+69	+49	+26	+9
TX	San Antonio	29	25	98	30	1	+87	+66	+50	+31	+16
UT	Kanab	37	3	112	32	2	+62	+53	+46	+37	+30
UT	Moab	38	35	109	33	2	+46	+39	+33	+27	+22
UT	Ogden	41	13	111	58	2	+47	+45	+43	+41	+40
UT	Salt Lake City	40	45	111	53	2	+48	+45	+43	+40	+38
UT	Vernal	40	27	109	32	2	+40	+36	+33	+30	+28
VA	Charlottesville	38	2	78	30	0	+43	+35	+29	+22	+17
VA	Danville	36	36	79	23	0	+51	+41	+33	+24	+17
VA	Norfolk	36	51	76	17	0	+38	+28	+21	+12	+5
VA	Richmond	37	32	77	26	0	+41	+32	+25	+17	+11
VA	Roanoke	37	16	79	57	0	+51	+42	+35	+27	+21
VA	Winchester	39	11	78	10	0	+38	+33	+28	+23	+19
VT	Brattleboro	42	51	72	34	0	+4	+5	+5	+6	+7
VT	Burlington	44	29	73	13	0	0	+4	+8	+12	+15
VT	Rutland	43	37	72	58	0	+2	+5	+7	+9	+11
VT	St. Johnsbury	44	25	72	1	0	–4	0	+3	+7	+10
WA	Bellingham	48	45	122	29	3	0	+13	+24	+37	+47
WA	Seattle–Tacoma–Olympia	47	37	122	20	3	+3	+15	+24	+34	+42
WA	Spokane	47	40	117	24	3	–16	–4	+4	+14	+23
WA	Walla Walla	46	4	118	20	3	–5	+2	+8	+15	+21
WI	Eau Claire	44	49	91	30	1	+12	+17	+21	+25	+29
WI	Green Bay	44	31	88	0	1	0	+3	+7	+11	+14
WI	La Crosse	43	48	91	15	1	+15	+18	+20	+22	+25
WI	Madison	43	4	89	23	1	+10	+11	+12	+14	+15
WI	Milwaukee	43	2	87	54	1	+4	+6	+7	+8	+9
WI	Oshkosh	44	1	88	33	1	+3	+6	+9	+12	+15
WI	Wausau	44	58	89	38	1	+4	+9	+13	+18	+22
WV	Charleston	38	21	81	38	0	+55	+48	+42	+35	+30
WV	Parkersburg	39	16	81	34	0	+52	+46	+42	+36	+32
WY	Casper	42	51	106	19	2	+19	+19	+20	+21	+22
WY	Cheyenne	41	8	104	49	2	+19	+16	+14	+12	+11
WY	Sheridan	44	48	106	58	2	+14	+19	+23	+27	+31
CANADA											
AB	Calgary	51	5	114	5	2	+13	+35	+50	+68	+84
AB	Edmonton	53	34	113	25	2	–3	+26	+47	+72	+93
BC	Vancouver	49	13	123	6	3	0	+15	+26	+40	+52
MB	Winnipeg	49	53	97	10	1	+12	+30	+43	+58	+71
NB	Saint John	45	16	66	3	–1	+28	+34	+39	+44	+49
NS	Halifax	44	38	63	35	–1	+21	+26	+29	+33	+37
NS	Sydney	46	10	60	10	–1	+1	+9	+15	+23	+28
ON	Ottawa	45	25	75	43	0	+6	+13	+18	+23	+28
ON	Peterborough	44	18	78	19	0	+21	+25	+28	+32	+35
ON	Thunder Bay	48	27	89	12	0	+47	+61	+71	+83	+93
ON	Toronto	43	39	79	23	0	+28	+30	+32	+35	+37
QC	Montreal	45	28	73	39	0	–1	+4	+9	+15	+20
SK	Saskatoon	52	10	106	40	1	+37	+63	+80	+101	+119

General Store

A special section featuring unique mail-order products for all our readers who shop by mail.

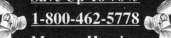

Lumber and Nails

■ The amount of lumber and nails you need will depend on your project, but these guidelines will help you determine quantities of each.

Lumber Width and Thickness (in inches)

Nominal Size	Actual Size DRY OR SEASONED	Nominal Size	Actual Size DRY OR SEASONED
1 x 3	¾ x 2½	2 x 3	1½ x 2½
1 x 4	¾ x 3½	2 x 4	1½ x 3½
1 x 6	¾ x 5½	2 x 6	1½ x 5½
1 x 8	¾ x 7¼	2 x 8	1½ x 7¼
1 x 10	¾ x 9¼	2 x 10	1½ x 9¼
1 x 12	¾ x 11¼	2 x 12	1½ x 11¼

Nail Sizes

The nail on the left is a 5d (five-penny) finish nail; on the right, 20d common. The numbers below the nail sizes indicate the approximate number of nails per pound.

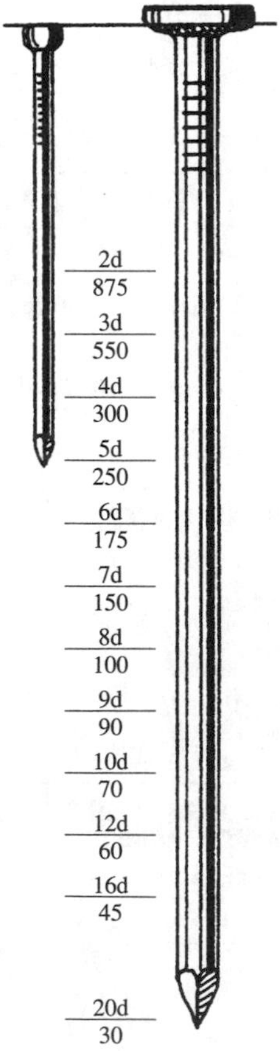

Lumber Measure in Board Feet

Size in inches	LENGTH 12 ft.	14 ft.	16 ft.	18 ft.	20 ft.
1 x 4	4	4⅔	5⅓	6	6⅔
1 x 6	6	7	8	9	10
1 x 8	8	9⅓	10⅔	12	13⅓
1 x 10	10	11⅔	13⅓	15	16⅔
1 x 12	12	14	16	18	20
2 x 3	6	7	8	9	10
2 x 4	8	9⅓	10⅔	12	13⅓
2 x 6	12	14	16	18	20
2 x 8	16	18⅔	21⅓	24	26⅔
2 x 10	20	23⅓	26⅔	30	33⅓
2 x 12	24	28	32	36	40
4 x 4	16	18⅔	21⅓	24	26⅔
6 x 6	36	42	48	54	60
8 x 8	64	74⅔	85⅓	96	106⅔
10 x 10	100	116⅔	133⅓	150	166⅔
12 x 12	144	168	192	216	240

General Store Classifieds

For advertising information, contact Bernie Gallagher, 203-263-7171.

AIRTIGHT STORAGE SOLUTIONS

THE GAMMA SEAL LID
for pest-proof air- and liquid-tight storage.
Easy on/off. Quick access to grain, pet food, fertilizer, seed, tools, food, and more.
www.freckleface.com

ART

OLD MOVIE POSTERS WANTED
Fair Market Prices paid for 1890s–1960s Movie Posters. Buying All Sizes, Any Condition.
Also buying Live Music Posters.
Will travel to buy collections.
Free Appraisals
Call Ralph, Toll-Free, 800-392-4050

ATLAS OF THE HEAVENS
Sky Map. Bring the starry nights indoors!
Beautiful poster displays constellations, galaxies, nebulas. Includes Hubble/NASA photos & meteor showers calendar. Size: 30"x24". $15.00.
www.HeavensAtlas.com

ASTROLOGY

GIFTED HEALER
Solves all problems, troubles, unusual sickness, bad luck, love, life. Removes evil influences & nature problems; brings back lovers to stay, good luck, money. Uncle Doc Shedrickrack, Hwy. 48, 7905 Bluff Rd., Gadsden SC 29052
803-353-0659

FREE LIVE PSYCHICS. 5-min. Free Reading. Powerful Guidance. Gifted Spiritual answers for Love, Destiny, Fortune, & Happiness. Call 888-970-3399.

MISS LISA. A gifted astrology reader and advisor with positive results. Will help you with all problems. Waycross, GA. 912-283-3206.

ALEXIS MORGAN. Makes your lover crazy about you! Reunites in 60 minutes! Phone: 415-691-5218. www.lovecenterbyalexismorgan.com

WWW.AZUREGREEN.NET. Pyramid-charged Magical Products. Jewelry, Incense, Bumper Stickers, Herbs, Candles. 7,000 items. 413-623-2155.

FREE SPIRITUAL CATALOG
Luck, Money, Love can be yours.
Over 5,000 items.
Church Goods Co., Dept. OFA, PO Box 718, Glenview IL 60025
www.LuckShop.com

FREE READING
Powerful love specialist.
Psychic Amelia Powers restores Love, Marriage, Business, Health. Reunites Lovers within days.
Troubled, need answers?
3618 Walnut Hill, Dallas TX 75229
Call 214-646-4865

MONICA, GOD-GIFTED PSYCHIC
Reunites lovers permanently. Guaranteed!
Helps: Business, Marriage, and Health.
Removes negative energy.
Restores peace of mind, happiness.
Don't wait! Call now! Free question!
800-253-0588 or **214-778-9332**

SPIRITUAL ADVICE. Help for all problems: relationships, nature, money, jobs. See results in 3 days. Call Mother Dewberry, 912-264-3259.

MRS. KING, spiritual reader, advisor, helps in matters of life where others have failed. Call now, 912-283-0635.

REV. EVETTE. Answers all questions, solves life's problems. Need help desperately? Does what others claim! Call immediately, 100% guaranteed! PO Box 80322, Chattanooga TN 37414. 423-894-6699.

PSYCHIC JOYCE. God-gifted. Solves all problems. Reunites lovers to stay! Guaranteed results! Call 972-313-5232.

ASHLEY LOVE SPELLS. Resolves all problems. Returns lovers. Restores happiness. Immediate results. Call 972-201-5576.

GUARANTEED. Ann Lee removes evil bad luck, enemies; restores nature relationships; spells for love, money, health protection. 540-449-2152.

SISTER ROGERS, psychic reader and advisor. Can help you with problems, love, business, marriage, and health. 912-285-2066.

FREE LIVE PSYCHIC READING! Powerful Guidance. Accurate answers for Love, Destiny, Money, Problems. Call 888-351-7811.

BEAUTY AND HEALTH

BEEKEEPING

DOCTOR ABRAHAM
Healer of the Heart.
Bring your lover back to stay!
Restores Health, Happiness,
Good Luck, & Money.
Call toll-free: 855-559-8080

HOLYLAND CRYSTALS
can change your life overnight. Help in love, health, and money, and remove evil. $25. They really work! PO Box 111852, Nashville TN 37222.
Toll-free: 877-506-4868

HURTING? WORRIED? CONFUSED? Are you searching for answers? Lost in Love? Superior Psychic Consultant. 407-709-6469.

MRS. RUTH, Southern-born spiritualist. Removes evil, bad luck. Helps all problems. Free sample reading. 3938 Hwy. 431 South, Eufaula AL 36027. 334-616-6363.

STEAM MODEL TOYS

WORKING STEAM ENGINES! Stationary Engines, Steam Tractors, Rollers, Trains, & Accessories. Great discounts! Catalog: $6.95, refundable. Yesteryear Toys & Books Inc., Box 537, Alexandria Bay NY 13607. 800-481-1353. www.yesteryeartoys.com

WANTED TO BUY

BUYING VINTAGE RADIOS, vacuum tubes, microphones, Western Electric items, audio amplifiers, turntables, old movie equipment. 203-272-6030. Larry2942@cox.net

CASH FOR 78-RPM RECORDS!
Send $2 (refundable) for illustrated booklet identifying collectible labels, numbers, with actual prices I pay.
Docks, Box 780218(FA),
San Antonio TX 78278-0218

WINE & BEER MAKING

FREE ILLUSTRATED CATALOG
Fast service. Since 1967.
Kraus, PO Box 7850-YB,
Independence MO 64054
www.eckraus.com/offers/fd.asp
800-841-7404

The Old Farmer's Almanac consistently reaches a proven, responsive audience and is known for delivering readers who are active buyers. The 2013 edition closes on May 4, 2012. Ad opportunities are available in the *All-Seasons Garden Guide,* which closes on January 6, 2012, and on our Web site, Almanac.com. For ad rates, Web classifieds, or ad information, please contact Bernie Gallagher by email at OFAads@aol.com, by phone at 203-263-7171, by fax at 203-263-7174, or by mail at The Old Farmer's Almanac, PO Box 959, Woodbury CT 06798.

Raise funds the "Old" way!

You can sell *The Old Farmer's Almanac* books, calendars, and cookbooks to raise money for your PTA, school, church, or club. Your organization keeps 50 percent (that's HALF) of all money earned through sales.

The Almanac is more satisfying than cookies and lasts longer than candles. This year, put the "fun" in fund-raising and make people in your community smile.

Call us today to learn how your organization can benefit from our easy fund-raising program.
Contact Publisher Sherin Pierce at 603-563-8111, ext. 137, or email OFAfundraising@yankeepub.com.

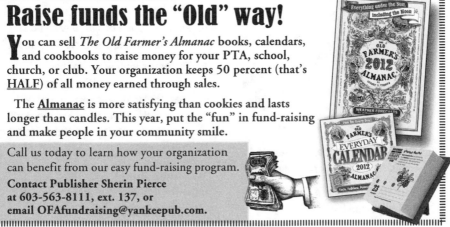

A sampling from the hundreds of letters, clippings, articles, and emails sent to us by Almanac readers from all over the United States and Canada during the past year.

How to Forecast RAIN with an ONION . . . and It Covers the Whole Year!

–courtesy of T.L.B., Dallas, Texas, who credits Tumbleweed Smith in the Midland *(Tex.)* Reporter-Telegram

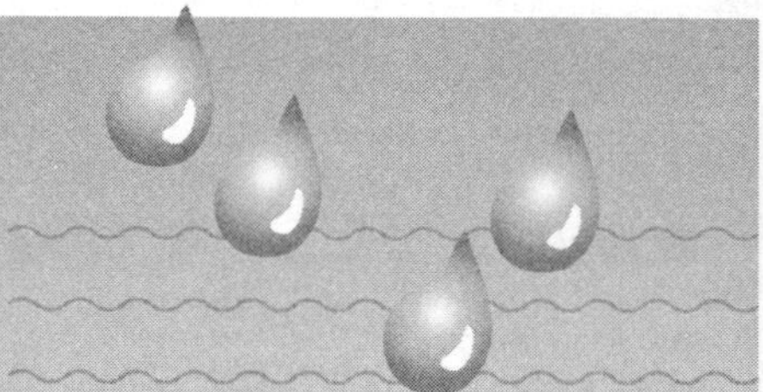

Butch Sohm, of Hamilton, Texas, uses an onion to prepare a rain forecast for the coming year. Most people in the area agree with him when he says, “It’s pretty accurate.”

Here’s how to do it:

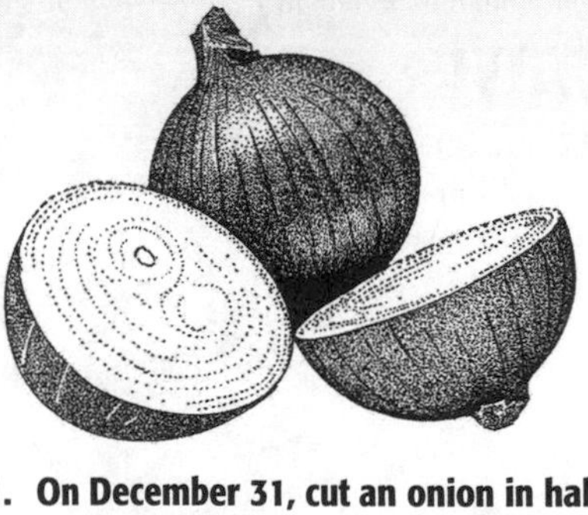

1. **On December 31, cut an onion in half about 15 minutes before midnight.**
2. **Peel off the layers so that you have 12 little onion bowls.**
3. **Arrange the bowls in two rows of six, with the biggest on the left. The top row represents January through June. The bottom row represents July through December.**
4. **Carefully remove the fine skin inside each bowl.**
5. **Put a teaspoon of salt in each bowl and then let the bowls sit for 1 hour.**
6. **The bowls with water in them will represent rainy months in the coming year; the dry bowls correspond with dry months. If the bowl has just a little water in it, expect just a little rain for that month.**

Two more things: You must use a white onion, and the process must take place in an unheated room.

Still Another Way to HYPNOTIZE A CHICKEN

–courtesy of A. S., Albany, New York

I've read articles in this Almanac about ways to hypnotize a chicken, and they were all methods with which I was unfamiliar. Here's a method I was taught many years ago: Gently restrain the chicken and place it on its back in your lap. Wave the flattened palm of your hand in a gentle circular motion about an inch or two from the chicken's beak. The chicken should go limp somewhere between five and ten circles.

Editor's note: Then what?

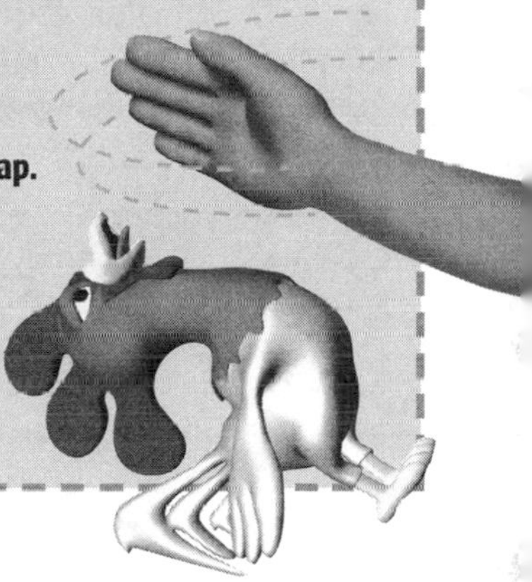

The Best INSULTS of ALL TIME

Years ago, insults meant something. Fortunately, they still do.

–courtesy of P. H., Evanston, Illinois

"He has no enemies but is intensely disliked by his friends."

–Oscar Wilde, Irish dramatist (1854–1900)

"He is not only dull himself, he is the cause of dullness in others."

–Samuel Johnson, British writer (1709–84)

"He loves nature in spite of what it did to him."

–Forrest Tucker, American actor (1919–86)

"He has van Gogh's ear for music."

–Billy Wilder, American film director (1906–2002)

"He is a self-made man and worships his creator."

–John Bright, British politician (1811–89)

"He had delusions of adequacy."

–Walter Kerr, American critic and writer (1913–96)

"He has all of the virtues I dislike and none of the vices I admire."

–Winston Churchill, British prime minister (1874–1965)

"He has never been known to use a word that might send a reader to the dictionary."

–William Faulkner, American writer (1897–1962)

"He is simply a shiver looking for a spine to run up."

–Paul Keating, Australian prime minister (b. 1944)

(continued)

FICTION OR FACT?

Check your knowledge of the origin of these common expressions. Answers follow.

–courtesy of F. P., West Caldwell, New Jersey

1. In Shakespeare's time, mattresses were secured on bed frames by ropes. When you pulled on the ropes, the mattress tightened, making the bed firmer to sleep on. Thus: **"good night, sleep tight."**

2. There was a time in England when the opening of a coffin that had been buried a long time might reveal scratch marks on the inside indicating that the person had been buried alive. Hence, they began tying a string on the wrist of a person about to be buried. The other end of the string would be tied to a bell located above ground. Thus: **"saved by the bell."**

3. In the old days, people took baths in a tub, with the men using the water first, followed by the women, the children, and, last of all, the baby. By then, of course, the water had become so dirty that you could lose someone in it. Thus: **"Don't throw out the baby with the bathwater."**

4. In some places, English houses had thatched roofs consisting of thick straw piled high with no wood underneath. In cold weather, cats and dogs (as well as other small animals) went up there to get warm. Sometimes, severe rainstorms caused some to slip through the straw and fall into the house. Thus: **"It's raining cats and dogs."**

ANSWERS

1. Fiction. The phrase "sleep tight" means to sleep soundly or well.

2. Fiction. It is boxing slang, dating from the second half of the 19th century and describes a pugilist who was spared defeat by the sound marking the end of the round.

3. Fact.

4. Fiction. The phrase alludes to the unsanitary conditions of 17th- and 18th-century England, where dead animal corpses in the filthy streets would be washed away in a heavy rain.

The CORNIEST JOKES of the Year

Well, these are among the corniest.

–courtesy of R. D., Barrie, Ontario

THE CORNIEST DOG JOKE

A man takes his Rottweiler to the vet and says, "My dog's cross-eyed. Is there anything you can do for him?"

"Well," says the vet, "let's have a look at him."

So he picks up the dog and examines his eyes, and then checks his teeth.

Finally, he says, "I'm going to have to put him down."

"What?! Because he's cross-eyed?"

"No," says the vet, "because he's really heavy."

• • • • • • • •

THE CORNIEST COW JOKE

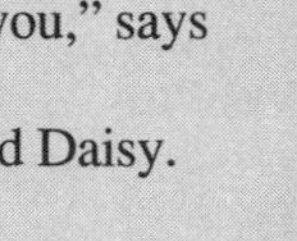

Two cows are standing next to each other in a field. Daisy says to Dolly, "I was artificially inseminated this morning."

"I don't believe you," says Dolly.

"It's true," replied Daisy. "No bull!"

• • • • • • • •

FINALLY, THE CORNIEST BAR JOKE

A man walks into a bar with a slab of asphalt under his arm and says, "A beer, please, and one for the road."

Remembering FIVE Best-Forgotten SCIENTIFIC STUDIES

Real? Yes. Important? Well, you decide . . .

–courtesy of B.J.W., Smithtown, New York, who credits Cynthia Fagen in the New York Post

Here are the recipients of five of the most memorable so-called Ig Nobel awards of recent times. These awards, administered by the *Annals of Improbable Research,* a science humor magazine that covers real experiments and studies, are celebrated annually at a ceremony at Harvard University in Cambridge, Massachusetts. Winning is considered by some, if not most, of the recipients to be "a dubious distinction."

1. A study describing a method for collecting whale snot by using a remote-control helicopter. *(Won by a team of British and Mexican scientists.)*

2. The discovery that roller-coaster riding can be a treatment for symptoms of asthma. *(Won by two psychologists from the Netherlands.)*

3. A study demonstrating that people slip and fall less often on ice when they wear their socks on the outside of their shoes. *(Won by three researchers from New Zealand.)*

4. A study showing that cows with names give more milk than nameless bovines. *(Won by two British researchers.)*

5. The invention of a brassiere that in an emergency can be quickly converted into two protective face masks—one for the wearer and one for a bystander. *(Won by three American public health scientists, who were also granted a patent for the device.)*

A FINAL THOUGHT

How is it that we put a man on the Moon before we figured out that it would be a good idea to put wheels on luggage?

Send your contribution for *The 2013 Old Farmer's Almanac* by January 27, 2012, to "A & P," The Old Farmer's Almanac, P.O. Box 520, Dublin, NH 03444, or email it to almanac@ypi.com (subject: A & P).

A Reference Compendium

CALENDAR

WEATHER

IN THE GARDEN

AROUND THE HOUSE

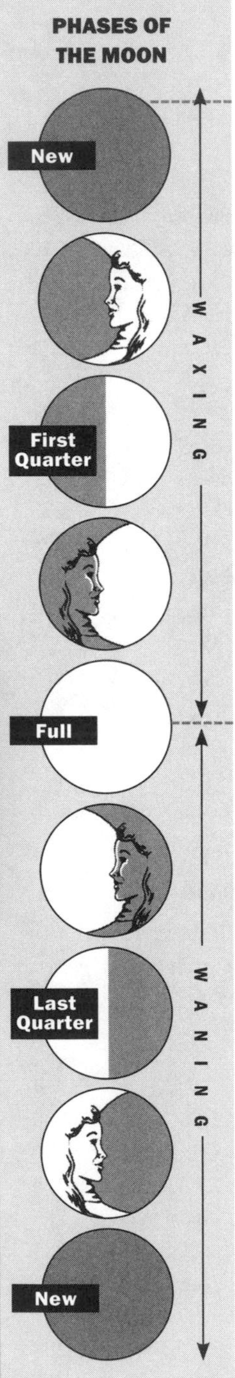

The Origin of Full-Moon Names

■ Historically, the Native Americans who lived in the area that is now the northern and eastern United States kept track of the seasons by giving a distinctive name to each recurring full Moon. This name was applied to the entire month in which it occurred. These names, and some variations, were used by the Algonquin tribes from New England to Lake Superior.

Name	Month	Variations
Full Wolf Moon	**January**	Full Old Moon
Full Snow Moon	**February**	Full Hunger Moon
Full Worm Moon	**March**	Full Crow Moon Full Crust Moon Full Sugar Moon Full Sap Moon
Full Pink Moon	**April**	Full Sprouting Grass Moon Full Egg Moon Full Fish Moon
Full Flower Moon	**May**	Full Corn Planting Moon Full Milk Moon
Full Strawberry Moon	**June**	Full Rose Moon Full Hot Moon
Full Buck Moon	**July**	Full Thunder Moon Full Hay Moon
Full Sturgeon Moon	**August**	Full Red Moon Full Green Corn Moon
Full Harvest Moon*	**September**	Full Corn Moon Full Barley Moon
Full Hunter's Moon	**October**	Full Travel Moon Full Dying Grass Moon
Full Beaver Moon	**November**	Full Frost Moon
Full Cold Moon	**December**	Full Long Nights Moon

**The Harvest Moon is always the full Moon closest to the autumnal equinox. If the Harvest Moon occurs in October, the September full Moon is usually called the Corn Moon.*

When Will the Moon Rise Today?

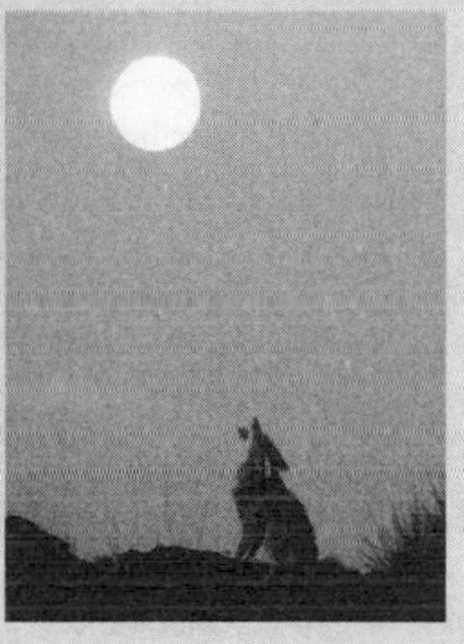

■ A lunar puzzle involves the timing of moonrise. If you enjoy the out-of-doors and the wonders of nature, you may wish to commit to memory the following gem:

The new Moon always rises near sunrise;

The first quarter near noon;

The full Moon always rises near sunset;

The last quarter near midnight.

Moonrise occurs about 50 minutes later each day.

Many Moons Ago

January's full Moon was called the **Wolf Moon** because it appeared when wolves howled in hunger outside the villages.

February's full Moon was called the **Snow Moon** because it was a time of heavy snow. It was also called the **Hunger Moon** because hunting was difficult and hunger often resulted.

March's full Moon was called the **Worm Moon** because, as the Sun increasingly warmed the soil, earthworms became active and their castings (excrement) began to appear.

April's full Moon was called the **Pink Moon** because it heralded the appearance of the moss pink, or wild ground phlox—one of the first spring flowers.

May's full Moon was called the **Flower Moon** because blossoms were abundant everywhere at this time.

June's full Moon was called the **Strawberry Moon** because it appeared when the strawberry harvest took place.

July's full Moon was called the **Buck Moon** because it arrived when male deer started growing new antlers.

August's full Moon was called the **Sturgeon Moon** because this large fish, which is found in the Great Lakes and Lake Champlain, was caught easily at this time.

September's full Moon was called the **Corn Moon** because this was the time to harvest corn.

The **Harvest Moon** is the full Moon that occurs closest to the autumnal equinox. It can occur in either **September** or **October.** At this time, crops such as corn, pumpkins, squash, and wild rice are ready for gathering.

October's full Moon was called the **Hunter's Moon** because this was the time to hunt in preparation for winter.

November's full Moon was called the **Beaver Moon** because it was the time to set beaver traps, before the waters froze over.

December's full Moon was called the **Cold Moon.** It was also called the **Long Nights Moon** because nights at this time of year were the longest.

The Origin of Month Names

January. For the Roman god Janus, protector of gates and doorways. Janus is depicted with two faces, one looking into the past, the other into the future.

February. From the Latin *februa,* "to cleanse." The Roman Februalia was a month of purification and atonement.

March. For the Roman god of war, Mars. This was the time of year to resume military campaigns that had been interrupted by winter.

April. From the Latin *aperio,* "to open (bud)," because plants begin to grow now.

May. For the Roman goddess Maia, who oversaw the growth of plants. Also from the Latin *maiores,* "elders," who were celebrated now.

June. For the Roman goddess Juno, patroness of marriage and the well-being of women. Also from the Latin *juvenis,* "young people."

July. To honor Roman dictator Julius Caesar (100 B.C.–44 B.C.). In 46 B.C., with the help of Sosigenes, he developed the Julian calendar, the precursor to the Gregorian calendar we use today.

August. To honor the first Roman emperor (and grandnephew of Julius Caesar), Augustus Caesar (63 B.C.–A.D. 14).

September. From the Latin *septem,* "seven," because this was the seventh month of the early Roman calendar.

October. From the Latin *octo,* "eight," because this was the eighth month of the early Roman calendar.

November. From the Latin *novem,* "nine," because this was the ninth month of the early Roman calendar.

December. From the Latin *decem,* "ten," because this was the tenth month of the early Roman calendar.

REFERENCE

Easter Dates (2012–16)

■ Christian churches that follow the Gregorian calendar celebrate Easter on the first Sunday after the paschal full Moon on or just after the vernal equinox.

YEAR	EASTER
2012	April 8
2013	March 31
2014	April 20
2015	April 5
2016	March 27

■ Eastern Orthodox churches follow the Julian calendar.

YEAR	EASTER
2012	April 15
2013	May 5
2014	April 20
2015	April 12
2016	May 1

Friggatriskaidekaphobia Trivia

Here are a few facts about Friday the 13th:

- In the 14 possible configurations for the annual calendar (see any perpetual calendar), the occurrence of Friday the 13th is this:

  6 of 14 years have one Friday the 13th.
  6 of 14 years have two Fridays the 13th.
  2 of 14 years have three Fridays the 13th.

- No year is without one Friday the 13th, and no year has more than three.
- 2012 has three Fridays the 13th.
- We say "Fridays the 13th" because it is hard to say "Friday the 13ths."
- Months that have a Friday the 13th begin on a Sunday.

The Origin of Day Names

■ The days of the week were named by ancient Romans with the Latin words for the Sun, the Moon, and the five known planets. These names have survived in European languages, but English names also reflect Anglo-Saxon and Norse influences.

English	Latin	French	Italian	Spanish	Anglo-Saxon and Norse
SUNDAY	dies Solis (Sol's day)	dimanche	domenica	domingo	Sunnandaeg (Sun's day)
		from the Latin for "Lord's day"			
MONDAY	dies Lunae (Luna's day)	lundi	lunedì	lunes	Monandaeg (Moon's day)
TUESDAY	dies Martis (Mars's day)	mardi	martedì	martes	Tiwesdaeg (Tiw's day)
WEDNESDAY	dies Mercurii (Mercury's day)	mercredi	mercoledì	miércoles	Wodnesdaeg (Woden's day)
THURSDAY	dies Jovis (Jupiter's day)	jeudi	giovedì	jueves	Thursdaeg (Thor's day)
FRIDAY	dies Veneris (Venus's day)	vendredi	venerdì	viernes	Frigedaeg (Frigga's day)
SATURDAY	dies Saturni (Saturn's day)	samedi	sabato	sábado	Saeterndaeg (Saturn's day)
		from the Latin for "Sabbath"			

How to Find the Day of the Week for Any Given Date

To compute the day of the week for any given date as far back as the mid-18th century, proceed as follows:

■ Add the last two digits of the year to one-quarter of the last two digits (discard any remainder), the day of the month, and the month key from the key box below. Divide the sum by 7; the remainder is the day of the week (1 is Sunday, 2 is Monday, and so on). If there is no remainder, the day is Saturday. If you're searching for a weekday prior to 1900, add 2 to the sum before dividing; prior to 1800, add 4. The formula doesn't work for days prior to 1753. From 2000 to 2099, subtract 1 from the sum before dividing.

Example:

The Dayton Flood was on March 25, 1913.

Last two digits of year:	13
One-quarter of these two digits:	3
Given day of month:	25
Key number for March:	4
Sum:	45

45 ÷ 7 = 6, with a remainder of 3. The flood took place on Tuesday, the third day of the week.

KEY	
January	1
leap year	0
February	4
leap year	3
March	4
April	0
May	2
June	5
July	0
August	3
September	6
October	1
November	4
December	6

REFERENCE

Animal Signs of the Chinese Zodiac

■ The animal designations of the Chinese zodiac follow a 12-year cycle and are always used in the same sequence. The Chinese year of 354 days begins 3 to 7 weeks into the western 365-day year, so the animal designation changes at that time, rather than on January 1. **See page 107** for the exact date of the start of the Chinese New Year.

Rat

Ambitious and sincere, you can be generous with your money. Compatible with the dragon and the monkey. Your opposite is the horse.

1900 1936 1984
1912 1948 1996
1924 1960 2008
1972

Ox or Buffalo

A leader, you are bright, patient, and cheerful. Compatible with the snake and the rooster. Your opposite is the sheep.

1901 1937 1985
1913 1949 1997
1925 1961 2009
1973

Tiger

Forthright and sensitive, you possess great courage. Compatible with the horse and the dog. Your opposite is the monkey.

1902 1938 1986
1914 1950 1998
1926 1962 2010
1974

Rabbit or Hare

Talented and affectionate, you are a seeker of tranquility. Compatible with the sheep and the pig. Your opposite is the rooster.

1903 1939 1987
1915 1951 1999
1927 1963 2011
1975

Dragon

Robust and passionate, your life is filled with complexity. Compatible with the monkey and the rat. Your opposite is the dog.

1904 1940 1988
1916 1952 2000
1928 1964 2012
1976

Snake

Strong-willed and intense, you display great wisdom. Compatible with the rooster and the ox. Your opposite is the pig.

1905 1941 1989
1917 1953 2001
1929 1965 2013
1977

Horse

Physically attractive and popular, you like the company of others. Compatible with the tiger and the dog. Your opposite is the rat.

1906 1942 1990
1918 1954 2002
1930 1966 2014
1978

Sheep or Goat

Aesthetic and stylish, you enjoy being a private person. Compatible with the pig and the rabbit. Your opposite is the ox.

1907 1943 1991
1919 1955 2003
1931 1967 2015
1979

Monkey

Persuasive, skillful, and intelligent, you strive to excel. Compatible with the dragon and the rat. Your opposite is the tiger.

1908 1944 1992
1920 1956 2004
1932 1968 2016
1980

Rooster or Cock

Seeking wisdom and truth, you have a pioneering spirit. Compatible with the snake and the ox. Your opposite is the rabbit.

1909 1945 1993
1921 1957 2005
1933 1969 2017
1981

Dog

Generous and loyal, you have the ability to work well with others. Compatible with the horse and the tiger. Your opposite is the dragon.

1910 1946 1994
1922 1958 2006
1934 1970 2018
1982

Pig or Boar

Gallant and noble, your friends will remain at your side. Compatible with the rabbit and the sheep. Your opposite is the snake.

1911 1947 1995
1923 1959 2007
1935 1971 2019
1983

A Table Foretelling the Weather Through All the Lunations of Each Year, or Forever

■ This table is the result of many years of actual observation and shows what sort of weather will probably follow the Moon's entrance into any of its quarters. For example, the table shows that the week following January 1, 2012, will have a hard frost, because the Moon enters the first quarter that day at 1:15 A.M. EST. (See the **Left-Hand Calendar Pages, 108–134,** for 2012 Moon phases.)

Editor's note: Although the data in this table is taken into consideration in the yearlong process of compiling the annual long-range weather forecasts for *The Old Farmer's Almanac,* we rely far more on our projections of solar activity.

Time of Change	Summer	Winter
Midnight to 2 A.M.	Fair	Hard frost, unless wind is south or west
2 A.M. to 4 A.M.	Cold, with frequent showers	Snow and stormy
4 A.M. to 6 A.M.	Rain	Rain
6 A.M. to 8 A.M.	Wind and rain	Stormy
8 A.M. to 10 A.M.	Changeable	Cold rain if wind is west; snow, if east
10 A.M. to noon	Frequent showers	Cold with high winds
Noon to 2 P.M.	Very rainy	Snow or rain
2 P.M. to 4 P.M.	Changeable	Fair and mild
4 P.M. to 6 P.M.	Fair	Fair
6 P.M. to 10 P.M.	Fair if wind is northwest; rain if wind is south or southwest	Fair and frosty if wind is north or northeast; rain or snow if wind is south or southwest
10 P.M. to midnight	Fair	Fair and frosty

This table was created more than 175 years ago by Dr. Herschell for the Boston Courier; *it first appeared in* The Old Farmer's Almanac *in 1834.*

REFERENCE

Safe Ice Thickness*

Ice Thickness	Permissible Load
3 inches	Single person on foot
4 inches	Group in single file
7½ inches	Passenger car (2-ton gross)
8 inches	Light truck (2½-ton gross)
10 inches	Medium truck (3½-ton gross)
12 inches	Heavy truck (8-ton gross)
15 inches	10 tons
20 inches	25 tons
30 inches	70 tons
36 inches	110 tons

***Solid, clear, blue/black pond and lake ice**

Slush ice has only half the strength of blue ice. The strength value of river ice is 15 percent less.

Heat Index °F (°C)

Temperature °F (°C)	Relative Humidity (%) 40	45	50	55	60	65	70	75	80
100 (38)	109 (43)	114 (46)	118 (48)	124 (51)	129 (54)	136 (58)			
98 (37)	105 (41)	109 (43)	113 (45)	117 (47)	123 (51)	128 (53)	134 (57)		
96 (36)	101 (38)	104 (40)	108 (42)	112 (44)	116 (47)	121 (49)	126 (52)	132 (56)	
94 (34)	97 (36)	100 (38)	103 (39)	106 (41)	110 (43)	114 (46)	119 (48)	124 (51)	129 (54)
92 (33)	94 (34)	96 (36)	99 (37)	101 (38)	105 (41)	108 (42)	112 (44)	116 (47)	121 (49)
90 (32)	91 (33)	93 (34)	95 (35)	97 (36)	100 (38)	103 (39)	106 (41)	109 (43)	113 (45)
88 (31)	88 (31)	89 (32)	91 (33)	93 (34)	95 (35)	98 (37)	100 (38)	103 (39)	106 (41)
86 (30)	85 (29)	87 (31)	88 (31)	89 (32)	91 (33)	93 (34)	95 (35)	97 (36)	100 (38)
84 (29)	83 (28)	84 (29)	85 (29)	86 (30)	88 (31)	89 (32)	90 (32)	92 (33)	94 (34)
82 (28)	81 (27)	82 (28)	83 (28)	84 (29)	84 (29)	85 (29)	86 (30)	88 (31)	89 (32)
80 (27)	80 (27)	80 (27)	81 (27)	81 (27)	82 (28)	82 (28)	83 (28)	84 (29)	84 (29)

EXAMPLE: *When the temperature is 88°F (31°C) and the relative humidity is 60 percent, the heat index,*

REFERENCE

The UV Index for Measuring Ultraviolet Radiation Risk

The U.S. National Weather Service's daily forecasts of ultraviolet levels use these numbers for various exposure levels:

UV Index Number	Exposure Level	Time to Burn	Actions to Take
0, 1, 2	Minimal	60 minutes	Apply SPF 15 sunscreen
3, 4	Low	45 minutes	Apply SPF 15 sunscreen; wear a hat
5, 6	Moderate	30 minutes	Apply SPF 15 sunscreen; wear a hat
7, 8, 9	High	15–25 minutes	Apply SPF 15 to 30 sunscreen; wear a hat and sunglasses
10 or higher	Very high	10 minutes	Apply SPF 30 sunscreen; wear a hat, sunglasses, and protective clothing

"Time to Burn" and "Actions to Take" apply to people with fair skin that sometimes tans but usually burns. People with lighter skin need to be more cautious. People with darker skin may be able to tolerate more exposure.

85	90	95	100
135 (57)			
126 (52)	131 (55)		
117 (47)	122 (50)	127 (53)	132 (56)
110 (43)	113 (45)	117 (47)	121 (49)
102 (39)	105 (41)	108 (42)	112 (44)
96 (36)	98 (37)	100 (38)	103 (39)
90 (32)	91 (33)	93 (34)	95 (35)
85 (29)	86 (30)	86 (30)	87 (31)

or how hot it feels, is 95°F (35°C).

What Are Cooling/ Heating Degree Days?

■ Each degree of a day's average temperature above 65°F is considered one cooling degree day, an attempt to measure the need for air-conditioning. If the average of the day's high and low temperatures is 75°, that's ten cooling degree days.

Similarly, each degree of a day's average temperature below 65° is considered one heating degree and is an attempt to measure the need for fuel consumption. For example, a day with temperatures ranging from 60° to 40° results in an average of 50°, or 15 degrees less than 65°. Hence, that day would be credited as 15 heating degree days.

How to Measure Hail

■ The **Torro Hailstorm Intensity Scale** was introduced by Jonathan Webb of Oxford, England, in 1986 as a means of categorizing hailstorms. The name derives from the private and mostly British research body named the TORnado and storm Research Organisation.

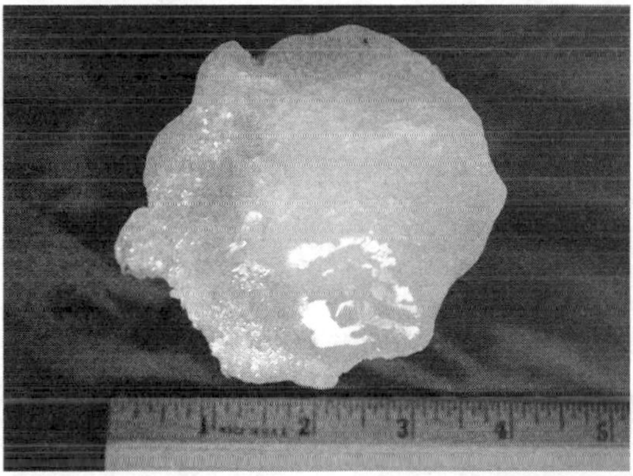

INTENSITY/DESCRIPTION OF HAIL DAMAGE

H0 True hail of pea size causes no damage

H1 Leaves and flower petals are punctured and torn

H2 Leaves are stripped from trees and plants

H3 Panes of glass are broken; auto bodies are dented

H4 Some house windows are broken; small tree branches are broken off; birds are killed

H5 Many windows are smashed; small animals are injured; large tree branches are broken off

H6 Shingle roofs are breached; metal roofs are scored; wooden window frames are broken away

H7 Roofs are shattered to expose rafters; autos are seriously damaged

H8 Shingle and tile roofs are destroyed; small tree trunks are split; people are seriously injured

H9 Concrete roofs are broken; large tree trunks are split and knocked down; people are at risk of fatal injuries

H10 Brick houses are damaged; people are at risk of fatal injuries

How to Measure Wind Speed

■ The **Beaufort Wind Force Scale** is a common way of estimating wind speed. It was developed in 1805 by Admiral Sir Francis Beaufort of the British Navy to measure wind at sea. We can also use it to measure wind on land.

Admiral Beaufort arranged the numbers 0 to 12 to indicate the strength of the wind from calm, force 0, to hurricane, force 12. Here's a scale adapted to land.

"Used Mostly at Sea but of Help to All Who Are Interested in the Weather"

Beaufort Force	Description	When You See or Feel This Effect	Wind Speed (mph)	Wind Speed (km/h)
0	Calm	Smoke goes straight up	less than 1	less than 2
1	Light air	Wind direction is shown by smoke drift but not by wind vane	1–3	2–5
2	Light breeze	Wind is felt on the face; leaves rustle; wind vanes move	4–7	6–11
3	Gentle breeze	Leaves and small twigs move steadily; wind extends small flags straight out	8–12	12–19
4	Moderate breeze	Wind raises dust and loose paper; small branches move	13–18	20–29
5	Fresh breeze	Small trees sway; waves form on lakes	19–24	30–39
6	Strong breeze	Large branches move; wires whistle; umbrellas are difficult to use	25–31	40–50
7	Moderate gale	Whole trees are in motion; walking against the wind is difficult	32–38	51–61
8	Fresh gale	Twigs break from trees; walking against the wind is very difficult	39–46	62–74
9	Strong gale	Buildings suffer minimal damage; roof shingles are removed	47–54	75–87
10	Whole gale	Trees are uprooted	55–63	88–101
11	Violent storm	Widespread damage	64–72	102–116
12	Hurricane	Widespread destruction	73+	117+

Retired Atlantic Hurricane Names

These storms have been some of the most destructive and costly.

NAME	YEAR
Jeanne	2004
Dennis	2005
Katrina	2005
Rita	2005
Stan	2005
Wilma	2005
Dean	2007
Felix	2007
Noel	2007
Gustav	2008
Ike	2008
Paloma	2008
Igor	2010
Tomas	2010

Atlantic Tropical (and Subtropical) Storm Names for 2012		
Alberto	Joyce	Tony
Beryl	Kirk	Valerie
Chris	Leslie	William
Debby	Michael	
Ernesto	Nadine	
Florence	Oscar	
Gordon	Patty	
Helene	Rafael	
Isaac	Sandy	

Eastern North-Pacific Tropical (and Subtropical) Storm Names for 2012		
Aletta	John	Tara
Bud	Kristy	Vicente
Carlotta	Lane	Willa
Daniel	Miriam	Xavier
Emilia	Norman	Yolanda
Fabio	Olivia	Zeke
Gilma	Paul	
Hector	Rosa	
Ileana	Sergio	

How to Measure Hurricane Strength

■ The **Saffir-Simpson Hurricane Scale** assigns a rating from 1 to 5 based on a hurricane's intensity. It is used to give an estimate of the potential property damage and flooding expected along the coast from a hurricane landfall. Wind speed is the determining factor in the scale, as storm surge values are highly dependent on the slope of the continental shelf in the landfall region. Wind speeds are measured using a 1-minute average.

Category One. Average wind: 74–95 mph. No real damage to building structures. Damage primarily to unanchored mobile homes, shrubbery, and trees. Also, some coastal road flooding and minor pier damage.

Category Two. Average wind: 96–110 mph. Some roofing material, door, and window damage to buildings. Considerable damage to vegetation, mobile homes, and piers. Coastal and low-lying escape routes flood 2 to 4 hours before arrival of center. Small craft in unprotected anchorages break moorings.

Category Three. Average wind: 111–130 mph. Some structural damage to small residences and utility buildings; minor amount of curtainwall failures. Mobile homes destroyed. Flooding near coast destroys smaller structures; larger structures damaged by floating debris.

Category Four. Average wind: 131–155 mph. More extensive curtainwall failures with some complete roof failures on small residences. Major beach erosion. Major damage to lower floors near the shore.

Category Five. Average wind: 156+ mph. Complete roof failures on many residences and industrial buildings. Some complete building failures; small buildings blown over or away. Major damage to lower floors located less than 15 feet above sea level (ASL) and within 500 yards of the shoreline.

REFERENCE

How to Measure a Tornado

■ The original **Fujita Scale** (or F Scale) was developed by Dr. Theodore Fujita to classify tornadoes based on wind damage. All tornadoes, and other severe local windstorms, were assigned a number according to the most intense damage caused by the storm. An enhanced F scale (EF) was implemented in the United States on February 1, 2007. The new EF scale uses three-second gust estimates based on a more detailed system for assessing damage, taking into account different building materials.

F SCALE		EF SCALE (U.S.)
F0 • 40–72 mph (64–116 km/h)	**light damage**	**EF0 • 65–85 mph (105–137 km/h)**
F1 • 73–112 mph (117–180 km/h)	**moderate damage**	**EF1 • 86–110 mph (138–178 km/h)**
F2 • 113–157 mph (181–253 km/h)	**considerable damage**	**EF2 • 111–135 mph (179–218 km/h)**
F3 • 158–207 mph (254–332 km/h)	**severe damage**	**EF3 • 136–165 mph (219–266 km/h)**
F4 • 208–260 mph (333–419 km/h)	**devastating damage**	**EF4 • 166–200 mph (267–322 km/h)**
F5 • 261–318 mph (420–512 km/h)	**incredible damage**	**EF5 • over 200 mph (over 322 km/h)**

Wind/Barometer Table

Barometer (Reduced to Sea Level)	Wind Direction	Character of Weather Indicated
30.00 to 30.20, and steady	westerly	Fair, with slight changes in temperature, for one to two days.
30.00 to 30.20, and rising rapidly	westerly	Fair, followed within two days by warmer and rain.
30.00 to 30.20, and falling rapidly	south to east	Warmer, and rain within 24 hours.
30.20 or above, and falling rapidly	south to east	Warmer, and rain within 36 hours.
30.20 or above, and falling rapidly	west to north	Cold and clear, quickly followed by warmer and rain.
30.20 or above, and steady	variable	No early change.
30.00 or below, and falling slowly	south to east	Rain within 18 hours that will continue a day or two.
30.00 or below, and falling rapidly	southeast to northeast	Rain, with high wind, followed within two days by clearing, colder.
30.00 or below, and rising	south to west	Clearing and colder within 12 hours.
29.80 or below, and falling rapidly	south to east	Severe storm of wind and rain imminent. In winter, snow or cold wave within 24 hours.
29.80 or below, and falling rapidly	east to north	Severe northeast gales and heavy rain or snow, followed in winter by cold wave.
29.80 or below, and rising rapidly	going to west	Clearing and colder.

Note: *A barometer should be adjusted to show equivalent sea-level pressure for the altitude at which it is to be used. A change of 100 feet in elevation will cause a decrease of 1/10 inch in the reading.*

REFERENCE

Windchill Table

■ As wind speed increases, your body loses heat more rapidly, making the air feel colder than it really is. The combination of cold temperature and high wind can create a cooling effect so severe that exposed flesh can freeze.

WIND SPEED (mph)	TEMPERATURE (°F)														
Calm	35	30	25	20	15	10	5	0	−5	−10	−15	−20	−25	−30	−35
5	31	25	19	13	7	1	−5	−11	−16	−22	−28	−34	−40	−46	−52
10	27	21	15	9	3	−4	−10	−16	−22	−28	−35	−41	−47	−53	−59
15	25	19	13	6	0	−7	−13	−19	−26	−32	−39	−45	−51	−58	−64
20	24	17	11	4	−2	−9	−15	−22	−29	−35	−42	−48	−55	−61	−68
25	23	16	9	3	−4	−11	−17	−24	−31	−37	−44	−51	−58	−64	−71
30	22	15	8	1	−5	−12	−19	−26	−33	−39	−46	−53	−60	−67	−73
35	21	14	7	0	−7	−14	−21	−27	−34	−41	−48	−55	−62	−69	−76
40	20	13	6	−1	−8	−15	−22	−29	−36	−43	−50	−57	−64	−71	−78
45	19	12	5	−2	−9	−16	−23	−30	−37	−44	−51	−58	−65	−72	−79
50	19	12	4	−3	−10	−17	−24	−31	−38	−45	−52	−60	−67	−74	−81
55	18	11	4	−3	−11	−18	−25	−32	−39	−46	−54	−61	−68	−75	−82
60	17	10	3	−4	−11	−19	−26	−33	−40	−48	55	62	69	76	84

Frostbite occurs in ░ **30 minutes** ▒ **10 minutes** ▓ **5 minutes**

EXAMPLE: When the temperature is 15°F and the wind speed is 30 miles per hour, the windchill, or how cold it feels, is −5°F. For a Celsius version of this table, visit Almanac.com/WindchillCelsius.

–courtesy National Weather Service

REFERENCE

How to Measure Earthquakes

■ Seismologists have developed a new measurement of earthquake size, called Moment Magnitude, that is more accurate than the previously used Richter scale, which is precise only for earthquakes of a certain size and at a certain distance from a seismometer. All earthquakes can now be compared on the same scale.

Magnitude	Effect
Less than 3	Micro
3–3.9	Minor
4–4.9	Light
5–5.9	Moderate
6–6.9	Strong
7–7.9	Major
8 or more	Great

A Gardener's Worst Phobias

Name of Fear	Object Feared
Alliumphobia	Garlic
Anthophobia	Flowers
Apiphobia	Bees
Arachnophobia	Spiders
Batonophobia	Plants
Bufonophobia	Toads
Dendrophobia	Trees
Entomophobia	Insects
Lachanophobia	Vegetables
Melissophobia	Bees
Mottephobia	Moths
Myrmecophobia	Ants
Ornithophobia	Birds
Ranidaphobia	Frogs
Rupophobia	Dirt
Scoleciphobia	Worms
Spheksophobia	Wasps

Herbs to Plant in Lawns

Choose plants that suit your soil and your climate. All these can withstand mowing and considerable foot traffic.

Ajuga or bugleweed *(Ajuga reptans)*
Corsican mint *(Mentha requienii)*
Dwarf cinquefoil *(Potentilla tabernaemontani)*
English pennyroyal *(Mentha pulegium)*
Green Irish moss *(Sagina subulata)*
Pearly everlasting *(Anaphalis margaritacea)*
Roman chamomile *(Chamaemelum nobile)*
Rupturewort *(Herniaria glabra)*
Speedwell *(Veronica officinalis)*
Stonecrop *(Sedum ternatum)*
Sweet violets (*Viola odorata* or *V. tricolor*)
Thyme *(Thymus serpyllum)*
White clover *(Trifolium repens)*
Wild strawberries *(Fragaria virginiana)*
Wintergreen or partridgeberry *(Mitchella repens)*

REFERENCE

Lawn-Growing Tips

■ Test your soil: The pH balance should be 7.0 or more; 6.2 to 6.7 puts your lawn at risk for fungal diseases. If the pH is too low, correct it with liming, best done in the fall.

■ The best time to apply fertilizer is just before it rains.

■ If you put lime and fertilizer on your lawn, spread half of it as you walk north to south, the other half as you walk east to west to cut down on missed areas.

■ Any feeding of lawns in the fall should be done with a low-nitrogen, slow-acting fertilizer.

■ In areas of your lawn where tree roots compete with the grass, apply some extra fertilizer to benefit both.

■ Moss and sorrel in lawns usually means poor soil, poor aeration or drainage, or excessive acidity.

■ Control weeds by promoting healthy lawn growth with natural fertilizers in spring and early fall.

■ Raise the level of your lawn-mower blades during the hot summer days. Taller grass resists drought better than short.

■ You can reduce mowing time by redesigning your lawn, reducing sharp corners and adding sweeping curves.

■ During a drought, let the grass grow longer between mowings, and reduce fertilizer.

■ Water your lawn early in the morning or in the evening.

Flowers and Herbs That Attract Butterflies

Allium	*Allium*
Aster	*Aster*
Bee balm	*Monarda*
Butterfly bush	*Buddleia*
Catmint	*Nepeta*
Clove pink	*Dianthus*
Cornflower	*Centaurea*
Creeping thyme	*Thymus serpyllum*
Daylily	*Hemerocallis*
Dill	*Anethum graveolens*
False indigo	*Baptisia*
Fleabane	*Erigeron*
Floss flower	*Ageratum*
Globe thistle	*Echinops*
Goldenrod	*Solidago*
Helen's flower	*Helenium*
Hollyhock	*Alcea*
Honeysuckle	*Lonicera*
Lavender	*Lavandula*
Lilac	*Syringa*
Lupine	*Lupinus*
Lychnis	*Lychnis*
Mallow	*Malva*
Mealycup sage	*Salvia farinacea*
Milkweed	*Asclepias*
Mint	*Mentha*
Oregano	*Origanum vulgare*
Pansy	*Viola*
Parsley	*Petroselinum crispum*
Phlox	*Phlox*
Privet	*Ligustrum*
Purple coneflower	*Echinacea purpurea*
Purple loosestrife	*Lythrum*
Rock cress	*Arabis*
Sea holly	*Eryngium*
Shasta daisy	*Chrysanthemum*
Snapdragon	*Antirrhinum*
Stonecrop	*Sedum*
Sweet alyssum	*Lobularia*
Sweet marjoram	*Origanum majorana*
Sweet rocket	*Hesperis*
Tickseed	*Coreopsis*
Zinnia	*Zinnia*

Flowers* That Attract Hummingbirds

Beard tongue	*Penstemon*
Bee balm	*Monarda*
Butterfly bush	*Buddleia*
Catmint	*Nepeta*
Clove pink	*Dianthus*
Columbine	*Aquilegia*
Coral bells	*Heuchera*
Daylily	*Hemerocallis*
Desert candle	*Yucca*
Flag iris	*Iris*
Flowering tobacco	*Nicotiana alata*
Foxglove	*Digitalis*
Larkspur	*Delphinium*
Lily	*Lilium*
Lupine	*Lupinus*
Petunia	*Petunia*
Pincushion flower	*Scabiosa*
Red-hot poker	*Kniphofia*
Scarlet sage	*Salvia splendens*
Soapwort	*Saponaria*
Summer phlox	*Phlox paniculata*
Trumpet honeysuckle	*Lonicera sempervirens*
Verbena	*Verbena*
Weigela	*Weigela*

***Note: Choose varieties in red and orange shades, if available.**

pH Preferences of Trees, Shrubs, Vegetables, and Flowers

■ An accurate soil test will indicate your soil pH and will specify the amount of lime or sulfur that is needed to bring it up or down to the appropriate level. A pH of 6.5 is just about right for most home gardens, since most plants thrive in the 6.0 to 7.0 (slightly acidic to neutral) range. Some plants (azaleas, blueberries) prefer more strongly acidic soil in the 4.0 to 6.0 range, while a few (asparagus, plums) do best in soil that is neutral to slightly alkaline. Acidic, or sour, soil (below 7.0) is counteracted by applying finely ground limestone, and alkaline, or sweet, soil (above 7.0) is treated with ground sulfur.

Common Name	Optimum pH Range
Trees and Shrubs	
Apple	5.0–6.5
Ash	6.0–7.5
Azalea	4.5–6.0
Basswood	6.0–7.5
Beautybush	6.0–7.5
Birch	5.0–6.5
Blackberry	5.0–6.0
Blueberry	4.0–5.0
Boxwood	6.0–7.5
Cherry, sour	6.0–7.0
Chestnut	5.0–6.5
Crab apple	6.0–7.5
Dogwood	5.0–7.0
Elder, box	6.0–8.0
Fir, balsam	5.0–6.0
Fir, Douglas	6.0–7.0
Hemlock	5.0–6.0
Hydrangea, blue-flowered	4.0–5.0
Hydrangea, pink-flowered	6.0–7.0
Juniper	5.0–6.0
Laurel, mountain	4.5–6.0
Lemon	6.0–7.5
Lilac	6.0–7.5
Maple, sugar	6.0–7.5
Oak, white	5.0–6.5
Orange	6.0–7.5
Peach	6.0–7.0
Pear	6.0–7.5
Pecan	6.4–8.0
Pine, red	5.0–6.0
Pine, white	4.5–6.0
Plum	6.0–8.0
Raspberry, red	5.5–7.0
Rhododendron	4.5–6.0
Spruce	5.0–6.0
Walnut, black	6.0–8.0
Willow	6.0–8.0
Vegetables	
Asparagus	6.0–8.0
Bean, pole	6.0–7.5
Beet	6.0–7.5
Broccoli	6.0–7.0
Brussels sprout	6.0–7.5
Carrot	5.5–7.0
Cauliflower	5.5–7.5
Celery	5.8–7.0
Chive	6.0–7.0
Cucumber	5.5–7.0
Garlic	5.5–8.0
Kale	6.0–7.5
Lettuce	6.0–7.0
Pea, sweet	6.0–7.5
Pepper, sweet	5.5–7.0
Potato	4.8–6.5
Pumpkin	5.5–7.5
Radish	6.0–7.0
Spinach	6.0–7.5
Squash, crookneck	6.0–7.5
Squash, Hubbard	5.5–7.0
Tomato	5.5–7.5
Flowers	
Alyssum	6.0–7.5
Aster, New England	6.0–8.0
Baby's breath	6.0–7.0
Bachelor's button	6.0–7.5
Bee balm	6.0–7.5
Begonia	5.5–7.0
Black-eyed Susan	5.5–7.0
Bleeding heart	6.0–7.5
Canna	6.0–8.0
Carnation	6.0–7.0
Chrysanthemum	6.0–7.5
Clematis	5.5–7.0
Coleus	6.0–7.0
Coneflower, purple	5.0–7.5
Cosmos	5.0–8.0
Crocus	6.0–8.0
Daffodil	6.0–6.5
Dahlia	6.0–7.5
Daisy, Shasta	6.0–8.0
Daylily	6.0–8.0
Delphinium	6.0–7.5
Foxglove	6.0–7.5
Geranium	6.0–8.0
Gladiolus	5.0–7.0
Hibiscus	6.0–8.0
Hollyhock	6.0–8.0
Hyacinth	6.5–7.5
Iris, blue flag	5.0–7.5
Lily-of-the-valley	4.5–6.0
Lupine	5.0–6.5
Marigold	5.5–7.5
Morning glory	6.0–7.5
Narcissus, trumpet	5.5–6.5
Nasturtium	5.5–7.5
Pansy	5.5–6.5
Peony	6.0–7.5
Petunia	6.0–7.5
Phlox, summer	6.0–8.0
Poppy, oriental	6.0–7.5
Rose, hybrid tea	5.5–7.0
Rose, rugosa	6.0–7.0
Snapdragon	5.5–7.0
Sunflower	6.0–7.5
Tulip	6.0–7.0
Zinnia	5.5–7.0

Produce Weights and Measures

Vegetables

Asparagus: 1 pound = 3 cups chopped

Beans (string): 1 pound = 4 cups chopped

Beets: 1 pound (5 medium) = 2½ cups chopped

Broccoli: ½ pound = 6 cups chopped

Cabbage: 1 pound = 4½ cups shredded

Carrots: 1 pound = 3½ cups sliced or grated

Celery: 1 pound = 4 cups chopped

Cucumbers: 1 pound (2 medium) = 4 cups sliced

Eggplant: 1 pound = 4 cups chopped = 2 cups cooked

Garlic: 1 clove = 1 teaspoon chopped

Leeks: 1 pound = 4 cups chopped = 2 cups cooked

Mushrooms: 1 pound = 5 to 6 cups sliced = 2 cups cooked

Onions: 1 pound = 4 cups sliced = 2 cups cooked

Parsnips: 1 pound = 1½ cups cooked, puréed

Peas: 1 pound whole = 1 to 1½ cups shelled

Potatoes: 1 pound (3 medium) sliced = 2 cups mashed

Pumpkin: 1 pound = 4 cups chopped = 2 cups cooked and drained

Spinach: 1 pound = ¾ to 1 cup cooked

Squashes (summer): 1 pound = 4 cups grated = 2 cups sliced and cooked

Squashes (winter): 2 pounds = 2½ cups cooked, puréed

Sweet potatoes: 1 pound = 4 cups grated = 1 cup cooked, puréed

Swiss chard: 1 pound = 5 to 6 cups packed leaves = 1 to 1½ cups cooked

Tomatoes: 1 pound (3 or 4 medium) = 1½ cups seeded pulp

Turnips: 1 pound = 4 cups chopped = 2 cups cooked, mashed

Fruit

Apples: 1 pound (3 or 4 medium) = 3 cups sliced

Bananas: 1 pound (3 or 4 medium) = 1¾ cups mashed

Berries: 1 quart = 3½ cups

Dates: 1 pound = 2½ cups pitted

Lemon: 1 whole = 1 to 3 tablespoons juice; 1 to 1½ teaspoons grated rind

Lime: 1 whole = 1½ to 2 tablespoons juice

Orange: 1 medium = 6 to 8 tablespoons juice; 2 to 3 tablespoons grated rind

Peaches: 1 pound (4 medium) = 3 cups sliced

Pears: 1 pound (4 medium) = 2 cups sliced

Rhubarb: 1 pound = 2 cups cooked

REFERENCE

Sowing Vegetable Seeds

Sow or plant in cool weather	Beets, broccoli, brussels sprouts, cabbage, lettuce, onions, parsley, peas, radishes, spinach, Swiss chard, turnips
Sow or plant in warm weather	Beans, carrots, corn, cucumbers, eggplant, melons, okra, peppers, squash, tomatoes
Sow or plant for one crop per season	Corn, eggplant, leeks, melons, peppers, potatoes, spinach (New Zealand), squash, tomatoes
Resow for additional crops	Beans, beets, cabbage, carrots, kohlrabi, lettuce, radishes, rutabagas, spinach, turnips

A Beginner's Vegetable Garden

■ A good size for a beginner's vegetable garden is 10x16 feet. It should have crops that are easy to grow. A plot this size, planted as suggested below, can feed a family of four for one summer, with a little extra for canning and freezing (or giving away).

Make 11 rows, 10 feet long, with 6 inches between them. Ideally, the rows should run north and south to take full advantage of the sunlight. Plant the following:

ROW

1 Zucchini (4 plants)
2 Tomatoes (5 plants, staked)
3 Peppers (6 plants)
4 Cabbage

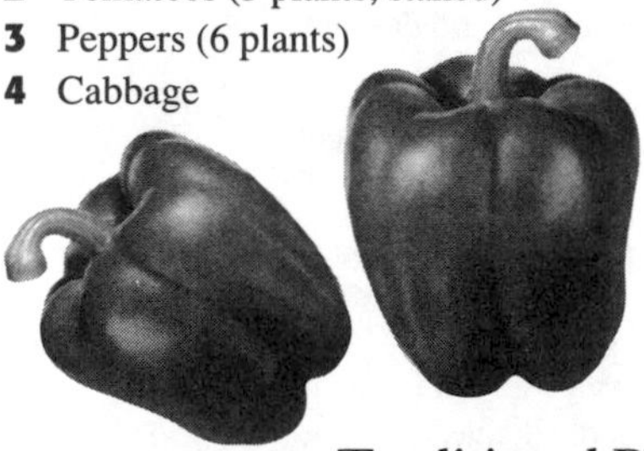

ROW

5 Bush beans
6 Lettuce
7 Beets
8 Carrots
9 Chard
10 Radishes
11 Marigolds (to discourage rabbits!)

Traditional Planting Times

■ Plant **corn** when elm leaves are the size of a squirrel's ear, when oak leaves are the size of a mouse's ear, when apple blossoms begin to fall, or when the dogwoods are in full bloom.

■ Plant **lettuce, spinach, peas,** and other cool-weather vegetables when the lilacs show their first leaves or when daffodils begin to bloom.

■ Plant **tomatoes, early corn,** and **peppers** when dogwoods are in peak bloom or when daylilies start to bloom.

■ Plant **cucumbers** and **squashes** when lilac flowers fade.

■ Plant **perennials** when maple leaves begin to unfurl.

■ Plant **morning glories** when maple trees have full-size leaves.

■ Plant **pansies, snapdragons,** and other hardy annuals after the aspen and chokecherry trees leaf out.

■ Plant **beets** and **carrots** when dandelions are blooming.

When to . . .

	. . . FERTILIZE	. . . WATER
Beans	After heavy bloom and set of pods	Regularly, from start of pod to set
Beets	At time of planting	Only during drought conditions
Broccoli	3 weeks after transplanting	Only during drought conditions
Brussels sprouts	3 weeks after transplanting	At transplanting
Cabbage	3 weeks after transplanting	2 to 3 weeks before harvest
Carrots	In the fall for the following spring	Only during drought conditions
Cauliflower	3 weeks after transplanting	Once, 3 weeks before harvest
Celery	At time of transplanting	Once a week
Corn	When 8 to 10 inches tall, and when first silk appears	When tassels appear and cobs start to swell
Cucumbers	1 week after bloom, and 3 weeks later	Frequently, especially when fruits form
Lettuce	2 to 3 weeks after transplanting	Once a week
Melons	1 week after bloom, and again 3 weeks later	Once a week
Onion sets	When bulbs begin to swell, and when plants are 1 foot tall	Only during drought conditions
Parsnips	1 year before planting	Only during drought conditions
Peas	After heavy bloom and set of pods	Regularly, from start of pod to set
Peppers	After first fruit-set	Once a week
Potato tubers	At bloom time or time of second hilling	Regularly, when tubers start to form
Pumpkins	Just before vines start to run, when plants are about 1 foot tall	Only during drought conditions
Radishes	Before spring planting	Once a week
Spinach	When plants are one-third grown	Once a week
Squashes, summer	Just before vines start to run, when plants are about 1 foot tall	Only during drought conditions
Squashes, winter	Just before vines start to run, when plants are about 1 foot tall	Only during drought conditions
Tomatoes	2 weeks before, and after first picking	Twice a week

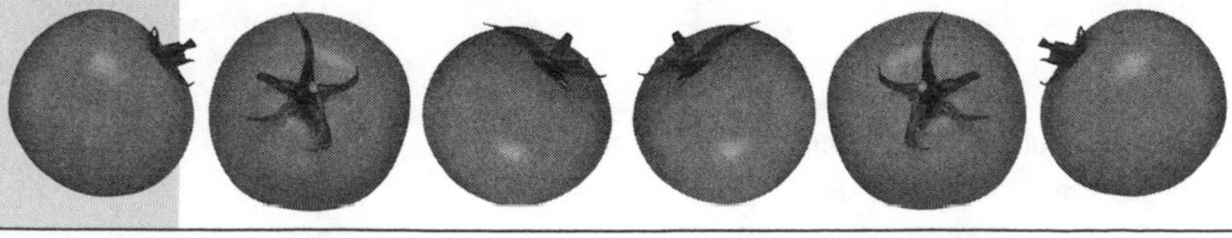

How to Grow Herbs

HERB	START SEEDS INDOORS	START SEEDS OUTDOORS* (weeks before last spring frost)	HEIGHT/SPREAD (inches)	SOIL	LIGHT**
Basil	6–8	Anytime after	12–24/12	Rich, moist	○
Borage	Not recommended	Anytime after	12–36/12	Rich, well-drained, dry	○
Chervil	Not recommended	3–4 before	12–24/8	Rich, moist	◑
Chives	8–10	3–4 before	12–18/18	Rich, moist	○
Cilantro/ coriander	Not recommended	Anytime after	12–36/6	Light	○◑
Dill	Not recommended	4–5 before	36–48/12	Rich	○
Fennel	4–6	Anytime after	48–80/18	Rich	○
Lavender, English	8–12	1–2 before	18–36/24	Moderately fertile, well-drained	○
Lavender, French	Not recommended	Not recommended	18–36/24	Moderately fertile, well-drained	○
Lemon balm	6–10	2–3 before	12–24/18	Rich, well-drained	○◑
Lovage	6–8	2–3 before	36–72/36	Fertile, sandy	○◑
Mint	Not recommended	Not recommended	12–24/18	Rich, moist	◑
Oregano	6–10	Anytime after	12–24/18	Poor	○
Parsley	10–12	3–4 before	18–24/6–8	Medium-rich	◑
Rosemary	8–10	Anytime after	48–72/48	Not too acid	○
Sage	6–10	1–2 before	12–48/30	Well-drained	○
Sorrel	6–10	2–3 after	20–48/12–14	Rich, organic	○
Summer savory	4–6	Anytime after	4–15/6	Medium rich	○
Sweet cicely	6–8	2–3 after	36–72/36	Moderately fertile, well-drained	○◑
Tarragon, French	Not recommended	Not recommended	24–36/12	Well-drained	○◑
Thyme, common	6–10	2–3 before	2–12/7–12	Fertile, well-drained	○◑

***Recommend minimum soil temperature of 70° to germinate**

** ○ **full sun** ◑ **partial shade**

REFERENCE

GROWTH TYPE
Annual
Annual, biennial
Annual, biennial
Perennial
Annual
Annual
Annual
Perennial
Tender perennial
Perennial
Perennial
Perennial
Tender perennial
Biennial
Tender perennial
Perennial
Perennial
Annual
Perennial
Perennial
Perennial

Drying Herbs

Before drying, remove any dead or diseased leaves or stems. Wash under cool water, shake off excess water, and put on a towel to dry completely. Air drying preserves an herb's essential oils; use for sturdy herbs. A microwave dries herbs more quickly, so mold is less likely to develop; use for moist, tender herbs.

- **Hanging Method:** Gather four to six stems of fresh herbs in a bunch and tie with string, leaving a loop for hanging. Or, use a rubber band with a paper clip attached to it. Hang the herbs in a warm, well-ventilated area, out of direct sunlight, until dry. For herbs that have full seed heads, such as dill or coriander, use a paper bag. Punch holes in the bag for ventilation, label it, and put the herb bunch into the bag before you tie a string around the top of the bag. The average drying time is 1 to 3 weeks.

- **Microwave Method:** This is better for small quantities, such as a cup or two at a time. Arrange a single layer of herbs between two paper towels and put them in the microwave for 1 to 2 minutes on high power. Let the leaves cool. If they are not dry, reheat for 30 seconds and check again. Repeat as needed. Let cool. Do not overcook, or the herbs will lose their flavor.

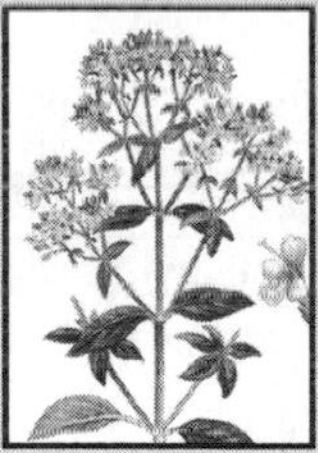

Storing Herbs and Spices

- **Fresh herbs:** Dill and parsley will keep for about 2 weeks with stems immersed in a glass of water tented with a plastic bag. Most other fresh herbs (and greens) will keep for short periods unwashed and refrigerated in tightly sealed plastic bags with just enough moisture to prevent wilting. For longer storage, use moisture- and gas-permeable paper and cellophane. Plastic cuts off oxygen to the plants and promotes spoilage.

- **Spices and dried herbs:** Store in a cool, dry place.

Cooking With Herbs

- **Bouquet garni** is usually made with bay leaves, thyme, and parsley tied with string or wrapped in cheesecloth. Use to flavor casseroles and soups. Remove after cooking.

- **Fines herbes** use equal amounts of fresh parsley, tarragon, chives, and chervil chopped fine. Commonly used in French cooking, they make a fine omelet or add zest to soups and sauces. Add to salads and butter sauces, or sprinkle on noodles, soups, and stews.

How to Grow Bulbs

	COMMON NAME	LATIN NAME	HARDINESS ZONE	SOIL	SUN/ SHADE*	SPACING (inches)
SPRING-PLANTED BULBS	Allium	*Allium*	3–10	Well-drained/moist	○	12
	Begonia, tuberous	*Begonia*	10–11	Well-drained/moist	◑●	12–15
	Blazing star/ gayfeather	*Liatris*	7–10	Well-drained	○	6
	Caladium	*Caladium*	10–11	Well-drained/moist	◑●	8–12
	Calla lily	*Zantedeschia*	8–10	Well-drained/moist	○◑	8–24
	Canna	*Canna*	8–11	Well-drained/moist	○	12–24
	Cyclamen	*Cyclamen*	7–9	Well-drained/moist	◑	4
	Dahlia	*Dahlia*	9–11	Well-drained/fertile	○	12–36
	Daylily	*Hemerocallis*	3–10	Adaptable to most soils	○◑	12–24
	Freesia	*Freesia*	9–11	Well-drained/moist/sandy	○◑	2–4
	Garden gloxinia	*Incarvillea*	4–8	Well-drained/moist	○	12
	Gladiolus	*Gladiolus*	4–11	Well-drained/fertile	○◑	4–9
	Iris	*Iris*	3–10	Well-drained/sandy	○	3–6
	Lily, Asiatic/Oriental	*Lilium*	3–8	Well-drained	○◑	8–12
	Peacock flower	*Tigridia*	8–10	Well-drained	○	5–6
	Shamrock/sorrel	*Oxalis*	5–9	Well-drained	○◑	4–6
	Windflower	*Anemone*	3–9	Well-drained/moist	○◑	3–6
FALL-PLANTED BULBS	Bluebell	*Hyacinthoides*	4–9	Well-drained/fertile	○◑	4
	Christmas rose/ hellebore	*Helleborus*	4–8	Neutral–alkaline	○◑	18
	Crocus	*Crocus*	3–8	Well-drained/moist/fertile	○◑	4
	Daffodil	*Narcissus*	3–10	Well-drained/moist/fertile	○◑	6
	Fritillary	*Fritillaria*	3–9	Well-drained/sandy	○◑	3
	Glory of the snow	*Chionodoxa*	3–9	Well-drained/moist	○◑	3
	Grape hyacinth	*Muscari*	4–10	Well-drained/moist/fertile	○◑	3–4
	Iris, bearded	*Iris*	3–9	Well-drained	○◑	4
	Iris, Siberian	*Iris*	4–9	Well-drained	○◑	4
	Ornamental onion	*Allium*	3–10	Well-drained/moist/fertile	○	12
	Snowdrop	*Galanthus*	3–9	Well-drained/moist/fertile	○◑	3
	Snowflake	*Leucojum*	5–9	Well-drained/moist/sandy	○◑	4
	Spring starflower	*Ipheion uniflorum*	6–9	Well-drained loam	○◑	3–6
	Star of Bethlehem	*Ornithogalum*	5–10	Well-drained/moist	○◑	2–5
	Striped squill	*Puschkinia scilloides*	3–9	Well-drained	○◑	6
	Tulip	*Tulipa*	4–8	Well-drained/fertile	○◑	3–6
	Winter aconite	*Eranthis*	4–9	Well-drained/moist/fertile	○◑	3

* ○ **full sun** ◑ **partial shade** ● **full shade**

DEPTH (inches)	BLOOMING SEASON	HEIGHT (inches)	NOTES
3–4	Spring to summer	6–60	Usually pest-free; a great cut flower
1–2	Summer to fall	8–18	North of Zone 10, lift in fall
4	Summer to fall	8–20	An excellent flower for drying; north of Zone 7, plant in spring, lift in fall
2	Summer	8–24	North of Zone 10, plant in spring, lift in fall
1–4	Summer	24–36	Fragrant; north of Zone 8, plant in spring, lift in fall
Level	Summer	18 60	North of Zone 8, plant in spring, lift in fall
1–2	Spring to fall	3–12	Naturalizes well in warm areas; north of Zone 7, lift in fall
4–6	Late summer	12–60	North of Zone 9, lift in fall
2	Summer	12–36	Mulch in winter in Zones 3 to 6
2	Summer	12–24	Fragrant; can be grown outdoors in warm climates
3–4	Summer	6–20	Does well in woodland settings
3 6	Early summer to early fall	12 80	North of Zone 10, lift in fall
4	Spring to late summer	3–72	Divide and replant rhizomes every two to five years
4 6	Early summer	36	Fragrant; self-sows; requires excellent drainage
4	Summer	18–24	North of Zone 8, lift in fall
2	Summer	2–12	Plant in confined area to control
2	Early summer	3–18	North of Zone 6, lift in fall
3–4	Spring	8–20	Excellent for borders, rock gardens and naturalizing
1–2	Spring	12	Hardy, but requires shelter from strong, cold winds
3	Early spring	5	Naturalizes well in grass
6	Early spring	14–24	Plant under shrubs or in a border
3	Midspring	6–30	Different species can be planted in rock gardens, woodland gardens, or borders
3	Spring	4–10	Self-sows easily; plant in rock gardens, raised beds, or under shrubs
2–3	Late winter to spring	6–12	Use as a border plant or in wildflower and rock gardens; self-sows easily
4	Early spring to early summer	3–48	Naturalizes well; good cut flower
4	Early spring to midsummer	18–48	An excellent cut flower
3–4	Late spring to early summer	6–60	Usually pest-free; a great cut flower
3	Spring	6–12	Best when clustered and planted in an area that will not dry out in summer
4	Spring	6–18	Naturalizes well
3	Spring	4–6	Fragrant; naturalizes easily
4	Spring to summer	6–24	North of Zone 5, plant in spring, lift in fall
3	Spring	4–6	Naturalizes easily; makes an attractive edging
4–6	Early to late spring	8–30	Excellent for borders, rock gardens, and naturalizing
2–3	Late winter to spring	2–4	Self-sows and naturalizes easily

Substitutions for Common Ingredients

ITEM	QUANTITY	SUBSTITUTION
Baking powder	1 teaspoon	¼ teaspoon baking soda plus ¼ teaspoon cornstarch plus ½ teaspoon cream of tartar
Buttermilk	1 cup	1 tablespoon lemon juice or vinegar plus milk to equal 1 cup; or 1 cup plain yogurt
Chocolate, unsweetened	1 ounce	3 tablespoons cocoa plus 1 tablespoon butter, shortening, or vegetable oil (dissolve the cocoa in the recipe's liquid)
Cracker crumbs	¾ cup	1 cup dry bread crumbs; or 1 tablespoon quick-cooking oats (for thickening)
Cream, heavy	1 cup	¾ cup milk plus ⅓ cup melted butter (this will not whip)
Cream, light	1 cup	⅞ cup milk plus 3 tablespoons melted, unsalted butter
Cream, sour	1 cup	⅞ cup buttermilk or plain yogurt plus 3 tablespoons melted, unsalted butter
Cream, whipping	1 cup	⅔ cup well-chilled evaporated milk, whipped; or 1 cup nonfat dry milk powder whipped with 1 cup ice water
Egg	1 whole	2 yolks plus 1 tablespoon cold water; or 3 tablespoons vegetable oil plus 1 tablespoon water (for baking); or 2 to 3 tablespoons mayonnaise (for cakes)
Egg white	1 white	2 teaspoons meringue powder plus 3 tablespoons water, combined
Flour, all-purpose	1 cup	1 cup plus 3 tablespoons cake flour (not advised for cookies or quick breads); or 1 cup self-rising flour (omit baking powder and salt from recipe); or 1¼ cups rye or coarsely ground whole grain flour; or 1 cup cornmeal
Flour, cake	1 cup	1 cup minus 3 tablespoons sifted all-purpose flour plus 3 tablespoons cornstarch
Flour, self-rising	1 cup	1 cup all-purpose flour plus 1½ teaspoons baking powder plus ½ teaspoon salt
Herbs, dried	1 teaspoon	1 tablespoon fresh, minced and packed
Honey	1 cup	1¼ cups sugar plus ½ cup liquid called for in recipe (such as water or oil)
Ketchup	1 cup	1 cup tomato sauce plus ¼ cup sugar plus 3 tablespoons apple-cider vinegar plus ½ teaspoon salt plus pinch of ground cloves combined; or 1 cup chili sauce
Lemon juice	1 teaspoon	½ teaspoon vinegar
Mayonnaise	1 cup	1 cup sour cream or plain yogurt; or 1 cup cottage cheese (puréed)
Milk, skim	1 cup	⅓ cup instant nonfat dry milk plus ¾ cup water

ITEM	QUANTITY	SUBSTITUTION
Milk, to sour	1 cup	1 tablespoon vinegar or lemon juice plus milk to equal 1 cup. Stir and let stand 5 minutes.
Milk, whole	1 cup	½ cup evaporated whole milk plus ½ cup water; or ¾ cup 2 percent milk plus ¼ cup half-and-half
Molasses	1 cup	1 cup honey or dark corn syrup
Mustard, dry	1 teaspoon	1 tablespoon prepared mustard less 1 teaspoon liquid from recipe
Oat bran	1 cup	1 cup wheat bran or rice bran or wheat germ
Oats, old-fashioned (rolled)	1 cup	1 cup steel-cut Irish or Scotch oats
Quinoa	1 cup	1 cup millet or couscous (whole wheat cooks faster) or bulgur
Sugar, dark-brown	1 cup	1 cup light-brown sugar, packed; or 1 cup granulated sugar plus 2 to 3 tablespoons molasses
Sugar, granulated	1 cup	1 cup firmly packed brown sugar; or 1¾ cups confectioners' sugar (makes baked goods less crisp); or 1 cup superfine sugar
Sugar, light-brown	1 cup	1 cup granulated sugar plus 1 to 2 tablespoons molasses; or ½ cup dark-brown sugar plus ½ cup granulated sugar
Sweetened condensed milk	1 can (14 oz.)	1 cup evaporated milk plus 1¼ cups granulated sugar. Combine and heat until sugar dissolves.
Vanilla bean	1-inch bean	1 teaspoon vanilla extract
Vinegar, apple-cider	—	malt, white-wine, or rice vinegar
Vinegar, balsamic	1 tablespoon	1 tablespoon red- or white-wine vinegar plus ½ teaspoon sugar
Vinegar, red-wine	—	white-wine, sherry, champagne, or balsamic vinegar
Vinegar, rice	—	apple-cider, champagne, or white-wine vinegar
Vinegar, white-wine	—	champagne, fruit (raspberry), rice, or red-wine vinegar
Yeast	1 cake (⅗ oz.)	1 package or 1 scant tablespoon active dried yeast
Yogurt, plain	1 cup	1 cup sour cream (thicker; less tart) or buttermilk (thinner; use in baking, dressings, sauces)

Types of Fat

■ One way to minimize your total blood cholesterol is to manage the amount and types of fat in your diet. Aim for monounsaturated and polyunsaturated fats; avoid saturated and trans fats.

■ **Monounsaturated fat** lowers LDL (bad cholesterol) and may raise HDL (good cholesterol) or leave it unchanged. Found in almonds, avocados, canola oil, cashews, olive oil, peanut oil, and peanuts.

■ **Polyunsaturated fat** lowers LDL and may lower HDL. Includes omega-3 and omega-6 fatty acids. Found in corn oil, cottonseed oil, fish such as salmon and tuna, safflower oil, sesame seeds, soybeans, and sunflower oil.

■ **Saturated fat** raises both LDL and HDL. Found in chocolate, cocoa butter, coconut oil, dairy products (milk, butter, cheese, ice cream), egg yolks, palm oil, and red meat.

■ **Trans fat** raises LDL and lowers HDL. A type of fat common in many processed foods, such as most margarines (especially stick), vegetable shortening, partially hydrogenated vegetable oil, many commercial fried foods (doughnuts, french fries), and commercial baked goods (cookies, crackers, cakes).

Calorie-Burning Comparisons

■ If you hustle through your chores to get to the fitness center, relax. You're getting a great workout already. The left-hand column lists "chore" exercises, the middle column shows the number of calories burned per minute per pound of body weight, and the right-hand column lists comparable "recreational" exercises. For example, a 150-pound person forking straw bales burns 9.45 calories per minute, the same workout he or she would get playing basketball.

Chopping with an ax, fast	**0.135**	Skiing, cross country, uphill
Climbing hills, with 44-pound load	**0.066**	Swimming, crawl, fast
Digging trenches	**0.065**	Skiing, cross country, steady walk
Forking straw bales	**0.063**	Basketball
Chopping down trees	**0.060**	Football
Climbing hills, with 9-pound load	**0.058**	Swimming, crawl, slow
Sawing by hand	**0.055**	Skiing, cross country, moderate
Mowing lawns	**0.051**	Horseback riding, trotting
Scrubbing floors	**0.049**	Tennis
Shoveling coal	**0.049**	Aerobic dance, medium
Hoeing	**0.041**	Weight training, circuit training
Stacking firewood	**0.040**	Weight lifting, free weights
Shoveling grain	**0.038**	Golf
Painting houses	**0.035**	Walking, normal pace, asphalt road
Weeding	**0.033**	Table tennis
Shopping for food	**0.028**	Cycling, 5.5 mph
Mopping floors	**0.028**	Fishing
Washing windows	**0.026**	Croquet
Raking	**0.025**	Dancing, ballroom
Driving a tractor	**0.016**	Drawing, standing position

Freezer Storage Time

(freezer temperature 0°F or colder)

Product	Months in Freezer
Fresh meat	
Beef	6 to 12
Lamb	6 to 9
Veal	6 to 9
Pork	4 to 6
Ground beef, veal, lamb, pork	3 to 4
Frankfurters	1 to 2
Sausage, fresh pork	1 to 2
Ready-to-serve luncheon meats	Not recommended
Poultry	
Chicken or turkey (whole)	12
Chicken or turkey (parts), Rock Cornish game hens, game birds	6 to 9
Duck, cooked poultry (in gravy), chicken, turkey	4
Goose, squab	4 to 6
Cooked poultry (breaded, fried)	4
Giblets	3 to 4
Cooked poultry (plain meat)	4
Fresh fruits (prepared for freezing)	
All fruits except those listed below	10 to 12
Avocados, bananas	3
Lemons, limes, plantains	4 to 6
Fresh vegetables (prepared for freezing)	
Beans, beets, bok choy, broccoli, Brussels sprouts, cabbage, carrots, cauliflower, celery, corn, greens, kohlrabi, leeks, mushrooms, okra, onions, peas, peppers, soybeans, spinach, summer squashes	10 to 12
Asparagus, rutabagas, turnips	8 to 10
Artichokes, eggplant	6 to 8
Tomatoes (overripe or sliced)	2
Bamboo shoots, cucumbers, endive, lettuce, radishes, watercress	Not recommended
Cheese (except those listed below)	6
Cottage cheese, cream cheese, feta, goat, fresh mozzarella, Neufchâtel, Parmesan, processed cheese (opened)	Not recommended

Product	Months in Freezer
Dairy products	
Margarine (not diet)	12
Butter	6 to 9
Cream, half-and-half	4
Milk	3
Ice cream	1 to 2
Yogurt	1 to 2

Freezing Hints

For meals, remember that a quart container holds four servings, and a pint container holds two servings.

To prevent sticking, spread the food to be frozen (berries, hamburgers, cookies, etc.) on a cookie sheet and freeze until solid. Then place in plastic bags and freeze.

Label foods for easy identification. Write the name of the food, number of servings, and date of freezing on containers or bags.

Freeze foods as quickly as possible by placing them directly against the sides of the freezer.

Arrange freezer into sections for each food category.

If power is interrupted, or if the freezer is not operating normally, do not open the freezer door. Food in a loaded freezer will usually stay frozen for 2 days if the freezer door remains closed during that time period.

Plastics

■ In your quest to go green, use this guide to use and sort plastic. The number, usually found with a triangle symbol on a container, indicates the type of resin used to produce the plastic. Call **1-800-CLEANUP** for recycling information in your state.

1 PETE

Number 1 • *PETE or PET (polyethylene terephthalate)*

IS USED IN .... microwavable food trays; salad dressing, soft drink, water, and beer bottles

STATUS .... hard to clean; absorbs bacteria and flavors; avoid reusing

IS RECYCLED TO MAKE .. carpet, furniture, new containers, Polar fleece

2 HDPE

Number 2 • *HDPE (high-density polyethylene)*

IS USED IN .... household cleaner and shampoo bottles, milk jugs, yogurt tubs

STATUS .... transmits no known chemicals into food

IS RECYCLED TO MAKE .. detergent bottles, fencing, floor tiles, pens

3 V

Number 3 • *V or PVC (vinyl)*

IS USED IN .... cooking oil bottles, clear food packaging, mouthwash bottles

STATUS .... is believed to contain phalates that interfere with hormonal development; avoid

IS RECYCLED TO MAKE .. cables, mudflaps, paneling, roadway gutters

4 LDPE

Number 4 • *LDPE (low-density polyethylene)*

IS USED IN .... bread and shopping bags, carpet, clothing, furniture

STATUS .... transmits no known chemicals into food

IS RECYCLED TO MAKE .. envelopes, floor tiles, lumber, trash-can liners

5 PP

Number 5 • *PP (polypropylene)*

IS USED IN .... ketchup bottles, medicine and syrup bottles, drinking straws

STATUS .... transmits no known chemicals into food

IS RECYCLED TO MAKE .. battery cables, brooms, ice scrapers, rakes

6 PS

Number 6 • *PS (polystyrene)*

IS USED IN .... disposable cups and plates, egg cartons, take-out containers

STATUS .... is believed to leach styrene, a possible human carcinogen, into food; avoid

IS RECYCLED TO MAKE .. foam packaging, insulation, light switchplates, rulers

7 OTHER

Number 7 • *Other (miscellaneous)*

IS USED IN .... 3- and 5-gallon water jugs, nylon, some food containers

STATUS .... contains bisphenol A, which has been linked to heart disease and obesity; avoid

IS RECYCLED TO MAKE .. custom-made products

Heat Values

Firewood

High Heat Value

1 cord = 200–250 gallons of fuel oil

- American beech
- Apple
- Ironwood
- Red oak
- Shagbark hickory
- Sugar maple
- White ash
- White oak
- Yellow birch

Medium Heat Value

1 cord = 150–200 gallons of fuel oil

- American elm
- Black cherry
- Douglas fir
- Red maple
- Silver maple
- Tamarack
- White birch

Low Heat Value

1 cord = 100–150 gallons of fuel oil

- Aspen
- Cottonwood
- Hemlock
- Lodgepole pine
- Red alder
- Redwood
- Sitka spruce
- Western red cedar
- White pine

Fuels

Fuel	**BTU** (approx.)	**Unit of Measure**
Oil	141,000	Gallon
Coal	31,000	Pound
Natural gas	1,000	Cubic foot
Steam	1,000	Cubic foot
Electricity	3,413	Kilowatt-hour
Gasoline	124,000	Gallon

How Many Trees in a Cord of Wood?

DIAMETER OF TREE (4½' ABOVE GROUND)	NUMBER OF TREES (PER CORD)
4"	50
6"	20
8"	10
10"	6
12"	4
14"	3

A Few Clues About Cords of Wood

- A cord of wood is a pile of logs 4 feet wide by 4 feet high by 8 feet long.
- A cord of wood may contain from 77 to 96 cubic feet of wood.
- The larger the unsplit logs, the larger the gaps, with fewer cubic feet of wood actually in the cord.
- A cord of air-dried, dense hardwood weighs about 2 tons (4,000 pounds).
- From one cord of firewood, you could make 7,500,000 toothpicks, 460,000 personal checks, 30 Boston rockers, or 12 dining room tables with each table seating eight.

REFERENCE

Metric Conversion

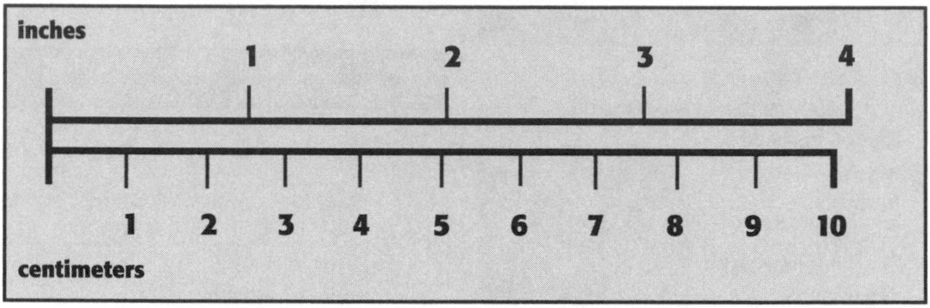

U.S. measure	x this number	= metric equivalent / metric measure	x this number	= U.S. equivalent
inch	2.54	centimeter	0.39	inch
foot	30.48	centimeter	0.033	foot
yard	0.91	meter	1.09	yard
mile	1.61	kilometer	0.62	mile
square inch	6.45	square centimeter	0.15	square inch
square foot	0.09	square meter	10.76	square foot
square yard	0.8	square meter	1.2	square yard
square mile	0.84	square kilometer	0.39	square mile
acre	0.4	hectare	2.47	acre
ounce	28.0	gram	0.035	ounce
pound	0.45	kilogram	2.2	pound
short ton (2,000 pounds)	0.91	metric ton	1.10	short ton
ounce	30.0	milliliter	0.034	ounce
pint	0.47	liter	2.1	pint
quart	0.95	liter	1.06	quart
gallon	3.8	liter	0.26	gallon

■ If you know the U.S. measurement and want to convert it to metric, multiply it by the number in the left shaded column (example: 1 inch equals 2.54 centimeters). If you know the metric measurement, multiply it by the number in the right shaded column (example: 2 meters equals 2.18 yards).

Where Do You Fit in Your Family Tree?

■ Technically it's known as consanguinity; that is, the quality or state of being related by blood or descended from a common ancestor. These relationships are shown below for the genealogy of five generations of one family.

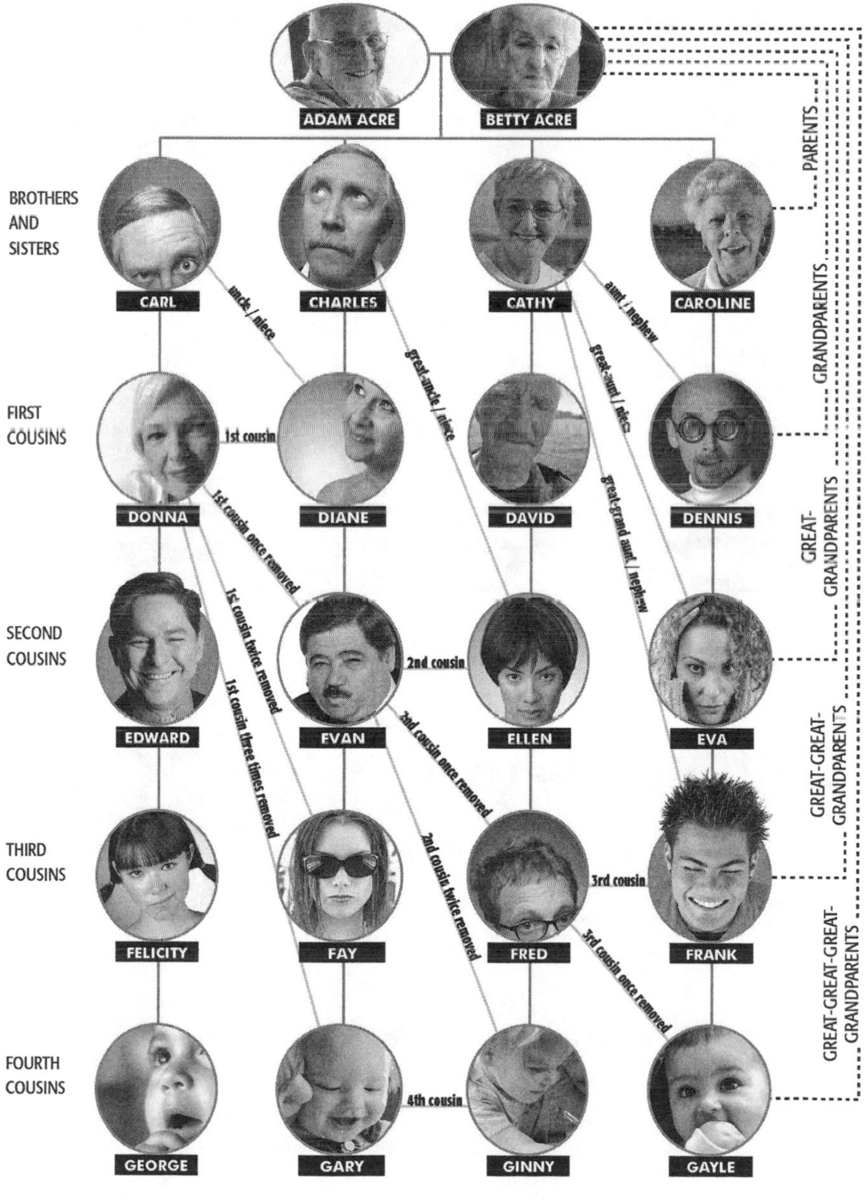

Knots

overhand knot

figure-eight knot

granny knot

square knot

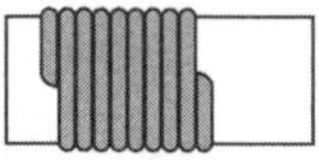

common whipping

fisherman's knot

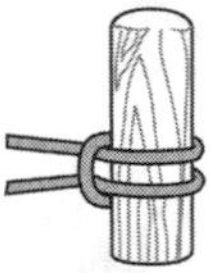

cow hitch

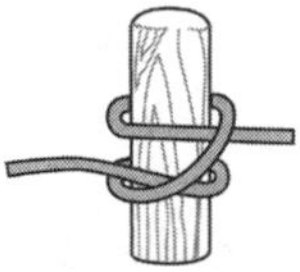

clove hitch

heaving line knot

sheet bend

double sheet bend

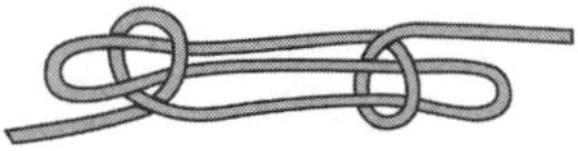

sheepshank

bowline

running bowline

bowline on a bight

When you come to the end of your rope, tie a knot and hang on.

–Franklin Delano Roosevelt, 32nd U.S. president (1882–1945)